The Debate on Money
in Europe

The Debate on Money in Europe

Alberto Giovannini

The MIT Press
Cambridge, Massachusetts
London, England

This book was set in Palatino by Asco Trade Typesetting Ltd., Hong Kong and was printed and bound in the United States of America.

Library of Congress Cataloging-in-Publication Data

Giovannini, Alberto.
  The debate on money in Europe / Alberto Giovannini.
    p.   cm.
  Includes bibliographical references and index.
  ISBN 0-262-07168-1 (hc : alk. paper)
  1. Monetary policy—Europe. 2. Foreign exchange rates—Europe.
3. Monetary unions—Europe. I. Title.
HG925.G56   1995
332.4'94—dc20
                                                    95-15934
                                                       CIP

To Patrizia, Camilla, and Tommaso

Contents

Preface

An economist who can claim to have been an active participant in a debate that has inflamed technicians, politicians and public opinion should consider himself lucky. Having had a chance to work intensely on the issues of monetary integration in Europe, I had the good fortune to appreciate fully the power of ideas and to watch monetary economics come alive. This book contains my own work on these issues: far from being conclusive, it illustrates the sort of ideas that have characterized what I consider one of the most important debates in economics in this century.

Many friends and colleagues have helped me, directly or indirectly, in this work. First of all my teachers, Giorgio Basevi and Rudiger Dornbusch; they both made me understand how important institutions are in monetary theory. In addition Rudi taught me, by his own example, how to do research and write papers. Francesco Giavazzi, co-author of much of the work in this field, spurred my interest on these issues and helped me stay in touch with Europe. Richard Portes, through his Centre for Economic Policy Research, has been the earliest and probably most enthusiastic supporter of my research in this field. Luigi Spaventa, Martin Feldstein, Paul Krugman, Ronald McKinnon, and Franco Modigliani always enjoyed discussing my ideas and provided stimulating criticism. Among government officials, I owe special gratitude to Mario Sarcinelli who, serving as president of the Monetary Committee of the European Community, has engaged me in the most stimulating discussions on the European currency question that I recall. Tommaso Padoa Schioppa and Massimo Russo have read and provided important comments on much of the work in this book. The people at The MIT Press were patient in waiting for the manuscript, and Veronica de Romanis was patient in serving as a research assistant to a researcher who was never available. Finally, I should thank my co-authors for working with me and for allowing me to include our joint papers in this volume: without Marcello De Cecco, Zhaohui Chen, Francesco Giavazzi, and Luigi Spaventa, this book would be much shorter.

Acknowledgments

Most of the essays in this book have appeared in other forms and are reprinted here with permission. Chapter 2 was originally published in *Blueprints for Exchange Rate Management*, Marcus Miller (ed.), Academic Press, 1989. Chapter 3 is reprinted from *A Retrospective on the Bretton Woods System*, University of Chicago Press, 1993. (© 1993 by the National Bureau of Economic Research. All rights reserved.)

Chapter 4 will appear in a forthcoming issue of *European Economic Review*; chapter 13 was printed in *European Economic Review* 36 (June 1992). Elsevier Science provided permission to reprint these essays, as well as chapter 14, which was previously published in the *Carnegie-Rochester Conference Series on Public Policy*, 1992.

Chapters 5 and 6 originally appeared in *A European Central Bank? Perspectives on Monetary Unification after Ten Years of the EMS*, Marcello De Cecco and Alberto Giovannini (eds.), Cambridge University Press, 1989. Chapter 7 was published in *Essays in International Finance* 178 (November 1990). Chapter 8 is reprinted from the Brookings Institution's *Brookings Papers on Economic Activity* 2 (August 1990). Chapter 9 is drawn from *Economics for the New Europe*, Anthony R. Atkinson and Renato Brunetta (eds.), Macmillan/New York University Press, 1992. Chapter 10 is taken from *European Economy 1990*, Commission of the European Communities, Brussels; Chapter 11 is reprinted from *International Economic Outlook* 1 (June 1991), published by the Centre for Economic Forecasting at London Business School.

"I'M HOPING FOR A PIECE OF THE BUNDESBANK TO GO WITH MY PIECE OF THE BERLIN WALL."

Cartoon appeared in the *Financial Times* on September 16, 1992, in the immediate aftermath of the crisis of the European Monetary System. Reprinted with permission of Jeremy Banx and the *Financial Times*.

1   Introduction

1.1   The European Currency Question

In recent years Europeans have been questioning with increasing keenness whether to do away with their national moneys and replace them with a currency that would be acceptable in the whole of Europe. The debate on the ideal monetary arrangement in Europe has involved public opinion as well as academic and policy circles. Questions that the economics profession finds difficult to tackle have dominated the media and everyday political discourse.

This phenomenon, although certainly of extreme interest to social scientists, is not new. Indeed, at key junctures in the last 100 years of European history concerns about individual countries' monetary policies and their effects on their neighboring European countries have been publicly voiced. The novelty of the recent years is the dimension that the debate has taken and the progress that the project for currency unification has achieved. The debate on money in Europe has become important not only from the perspective of monetary economics, but also as a social and political phenomenon.

1.2   Perspectives on the Debate

All of the key questions in monetary economics have been raised in the debate on money in Europe. For example, the question of whether having a single currency would be a superior arrangement than the current regime—one of many, largely independent, national currencies—is of course a very interesting version of the central question in monetary theory, that is, the neutrality of money. Much of the impetus for monetary reform has come from a view taken on another key question in monetary economics: that of the effectiveness of monetary policy in the presence of high international capital mobility. Finally, another pillar of monetary economics, the theory of money demand, as been furthered by the numerous analyses and valuable empirical research on the stability of monetary aggregates in different countries, and the comparative stability of a theoretical European monetary aggregate.

From the perspective of international relations, the debate underscores the effects of increased economic integration on the relations among countries and the existing economic institutions. In Europe, more than elsewhere, a view has developed that existing institutions, created at a time of separation of national goods and financial markets, are inadequate when goods and financial markets become integrated. The question thus is whether trade liberalization, technological progress in communications and their effects on goods and financial assets trade are forcing a change on existing institutions. Broadly speaking, the question is whether the traditional concept of the nation-state becomes obsolete in modern-day integrated markets.

Finally, the debate on money in Europe is also interesting from the political science perspective. The key issue is the identification of constituencies in favor or against monetary union: it is quite difficult to associate the proponents of the creation of a single European currency with a given political view. A good illustration of this phenomenon is the case involving two illustrious critics of the project of monetary integration: Robert Barro of Harvard University and Paul Krugman of Stanford University. Being on opposite political poles, they have labelled the project of monetary union as belonging to the political side they respectively oppose: Barro (1992) has labelled monetary union a leftist idea, while Krugman (1994) has labelled it a conservative one.

1.3   Evolution of the Debate

How has the debate evolved over the years? A useful starting point is the Werner Report of 1971 (and its precursor, the Barre Report, 1969). There the desirability of a move toward a single currency was justified because of the problems raised by excessive exchange-rate volatility. The intellectual heritage of this position was that of the critics of the interwar demise of the gold standard, who feared that governments' discretionary control on exchange rates raises the risk of competitive devaluations. The turmoil in the foreign exchange markets, occurring only months after the endorsement of the Werner Report by EC member states, seems to have all but eliminated the drive to monetary union inspired by the fear of the effects of currency instability.

The European Monetary System (EMS), started in 1979, and the Single European Act of 1986 have revived the movement for a single currency: the Delors Report, published in 1989, attempted to address the need to move to a single currency by claiming that perfectly integrated markets were going to make the management of less-than-perfectly integrated monetary policies too difficult to pursue.

In the economics profession these ideas quickly gained many supporters. Opponents of these theories and their policy implications were either silent or few. Yet, the ideas put forward by the opponents of the project of monetary union deserve more study than they have attracted so far. Two types of opposition have been expressed. The first, inspired by free-market liberalism, claimed that a reform of this significance should be the outcome of spontaneous market developments; the single currency should be freely chosen by the market, not imposed by governments. This was a criticism of the project of monetary union sponsored by the European Commission, not of the idea of monetary union per se. It advocated a sort of experiment in currency substitution: let the people use all European currencies in their transactions by abolishing all prohibitions to the use of other European currencies in all EC member states. And then see which of the currencies is chosen.

The second more fundamental opposition to the project of monetary union was supported by those who believe that a monetary union has little justification if it involves countries that are different. Differences in economic performance require convergence before monetary union (this is the so-called convergence or economists' view on monetary union). More radically, differences in institutions cannot efficiently support a monetary union. According to this more radical view, the only meaningful currency area is the nation-state.

Where is the debate now? The foreign exchange crisis of 1992 and 1993, not surprisingly, has strengthened the opposition to EMU. The project has been regarded as the cause of the problems faced by countries that were attempting to avoid exchange-rate realignments. Those countries that have realigned (also called "policy-flexible" countries) have had a relatively better economic performance, and this has prompted some observers to draw the conclusion that lack of exchange-rate flexibility would imply the loss of an all-too-important, and very effective policy instrument.

The foreign exchange crises have, in part, given more credence to the gradualist, convergence-based approach to monetary union that characterizes the Maastricht Treaty. The fact that exchange-rate realignments

have not brought about an interruption of the process of inflation convergence means that now many countries have reached low inflation
without having to sustain an overly appreciated real exchange rate. In
some ways, the economics of convergence have never looked as good as
after the foreign exchange crises. On the other hand, most European
countries have experienced, in the period of high interest rates leading up
the currency crises, a significant worsening of their public finances.

The concern that several countries might be forced in the future to engineer monetary expansions to ease the burden of government debt is
now the most serious hurdle to further progress of monetary union. To
this should be added the worsening of the phenomenon of unemployment
in many countries. Although the economic recovery currently underway
in Europe will certainly alleviate both problems, the path to monetary
union in Europe still remains uncertain, despite very considerable recent
progress.

1.4   The Chapters in this Book

The chapters in this book are organized in four parts. The chapters in part
I discuss fixed-exchange-rate regimes. They are samples of the literature
on international monetary arrangements that boomed in the late 1980s.
This literature emphasizes expectations, credibility, and strategic interactions between policymakers and the "rest of the world," along with the
work on monetary policy in the Simons-Friedman-Barro tradition of the
University of Chicago. Interestingly, the literature also has a strong link
to Koichi Hamada's pioneering work on international policy interactions,
which initially received limited attention outside the international economics field, perhaps because of its great originality. Part I closes with a
chapter that attempts to provide an empirical content to the concept of
the credibility of an exchange-rate target and explore the determinants of
such credibility.

The chapters in part II illustrate the early ideas of the desirability of
monetary union and a European central bank that stemmed from the EMS
experience. The first chapter, written in 1985 and so far unpublished,
builds an argument for monetary union that sees the elimination of losses
from uncoordinated monetary policies and the complete integration of financial markets as benefits and the losses from region-specific shocks or
imbalances that may not be efficiently absorbed by existing fiscal systems
as necessary costs. The second chapter illustrates further the argument for
integrating monetary policies by creating a European central bank: this

institution would be required by financial markets' liberalization and the elimination of capital controls, which would make even marginally independent monetary policies difficult to manage. This argument was later taken up in the Delors Report and represents the main motivation for monetary union in the Delors project.

The chapters in part III, the core of this volume, deal with several aspects of the project for monetary union pursued by the European Community. The first two chapters criticize the gradualist approach adopted by the Community, suggesting that gradualism, in the absence of a fully credible commitment to monetary union at a foreseeable end of the transition period, is the greatest source of the project's fragility. The chapter on fiscal rules in the monetary union proposes the adoption of a criterion of non-entry to the monetary union, to encourage certain European countries to accelerate fiscal stabilization. A criterion of this sort was indeed adopted in the Maastricht Treaty in an article on excessive deficits. Although that provision of the Treaty has been at times severely criticized by academics, its implications are still to be fully understood: the application of that article gives Community bodies substantial latitude.

The chapter on money demand in an integrated European economy discusses modern aspects of currency competition. The following chapter, written in the spring of 1991, forecasts the collapse of the ERM and EMU. The reasoning here is that convergence in many countries has meant that the process of bringing down inflation has brought about substantial losses in competitiveness. Although the forecast on the collapse of the ERM proved to be correct, the forecast on the collapse of EMU, while it may prove correct, is based on a theory proved wrong by recent events. I claim that currency devaluations, while called for if the accumulated losses in competitiveness are large, will also stop the process of inflation convergence. The experience of the period after the foreign exchange crises has shown that devaluations have not stopped inflation convergence, perhaps because these devaluations have been accompanied, at least in some countries, by important policy reforms.

The last chapter in part III contains a discussion of the politics of international monetary reforms. I argue that, unlike in the case of international trade reforms, one cannot find stable constituencies for or against monetary reforms, because the economic gains and losses are hard to identify and the groups who gain or loose are even more difficult to identify. This theory is applied to interpret the recent political fortunes of the project of monetary integration in Europe.

The chapters in part IV tackle the issues that Europe would face if the project of monetary union were to proceed further. The first chapter discusses the practical issues of the currency reform, that is, the substitution of national moneys with a single, Europe-wide currency. I analyze the problem of adopting round conversion rates, as well as the problems of managing "last minute" currency realignments. The last chapter deals with the European central bank, as designed in the Maastricht Treaty. Two requirements are of paramount importance in the building of an efficient institution to manage monetary policy for the whole of Europe: a set of safeguards that can ensure the independence of the institution (that is, its ability to withstand pressures from individual groups or countries and to interpret autonomously the best interests of Europe as a whole) and a regulatory system that does not make the central bank hostage to national regulatory authorities. In the chapter I try to assess to what extent these requirements are met in the statutes of the European central bank that are codified in the Maastricht Treaty.

Ravenna, August 1993

References

Barro, R. J. 1992. "Europe's Road to Serfdom." *Wall Street Journal*, August 8.

Krugman, P. R. 1994. *Peddling Prosperity: Economic Sense and Nonsense in the Age of Diminished Expectations.* New York: W. W. Norton.

I

Background: Fixed Exchange Rates and Their Evolution

2

How Do Fixed-Exchange-Rate Regimes Work? Evidence from the Gold Standard, Bretton Woods, and the EMS

(August 1988)

2.1 Introduction

Few countries freely float their currencies: the *International Financial Statistics Supplement on Exchange Rates* (1985) lists only 12 out of 147 members of the IMF as "independently floating." While this list includes large countries like the United States, Japan and the United Kingdom, as many as 34 countries, for example, peg their currencies to the US dollar. Even so, in the current open-economy macroeconomics literature most theoretical and empirical papers deal with properly of flexible-exchange-rate regimes.

There exist two competing hypotheses on the working of fixed exchange rates. The "symmetry" hypothesis states that every country is concerned with the good functioning of the system, and cannot afford to deviate from world averages. Every country is just left to follow the "rules of the game," that is to avoid sterilizing balance of payments flows. This hypothesis is masterfully described by McCloskey and Zecher (1976).

If every country is just concerned with accommodating reserve flows in order to maintain its exchange-rate parities, however, the international monetary system as a whole suffers from an indeterminacy: there is no system-wide nominal anchor. According to the proponents of the symmetry hypothesis, this nominal anchor is provided by an external numeraire like gold, or is agreed upon by member countries through a process of international cooperation. Hence Helpman's (1981) labeling of this regime as a "cooperative peg."

The competing hypothesis states that fixed-exchange-rate regimes are inherently asymmetric: they are characterized by a "centre country" which provides the nominal anchor for the others, either by managing the gold parity in a centralized fashion, or by arbitrarily setting some other nominal anchor. This hypothesis has been proposed by Keynes (1930), and has been labeled by Helpman (1981) a "one-sided peg."[1] This chapter organizes and discusses the empirical evidence on the two hypotheses, by studying the institutional features and the data on three experiences with fixed rates: the international gold standard (from 1870 to 1913), the Bretton Woods regime (which lasted from 1958 to 1971) and the European Monetary System (EMS, started in March 1979, still in place).

Section 2.2 describes the institutional features of the three systems, with the objective of determining whether the institutions, *per se*, induce asymmetry. Section 2.3 describes another significant institutional aspect: the use of capital controls to limit the effectiveness of external constraints on monetary policy. Section 2.4 illustrates the two competing hypotheses with a simple theoretical model. Section 2.5 discusses the empirical evidence. Section 2.6 offers a few concluding observations.

2.2   Common Features of Fixed Exchange Rates: Institutional Setup

All the international monetary systems I study in this chapter are characterized by codified sets of rules, which bind countries adhering to them. These rules have increased in coverage and complexity in more recent years, but conserve a number of common features that it is useful to highlight. I divide the institutional arrangements of the three exchange regimes into three categories: a numeraire to set target exchange rates; "bands" for exchange rates, setting limits within which exchange rates could fluctuate without implying any actions by central banks to maintain the central parities; and provisions for central bank financing of balance-of-payments discrepancies and for correcting external imbalances.

2.2.1   Numeraire

Both the gold standard and the Bretton Woods regime were characterized by the use of gold as external numeraire. Under the gold standard, each currency had a specified official value in terms of gold—the mint par. At this value the central bank was ready to exchange domestic banknotes for gold coins.[2]

Under the Bretton Woods system, the IMF Articles of Agreement[3] stipulated that each member country declare its par value in terms of gold.[4] The dollar price of gold was $35 an ounce, and it was never changed, until the Smithsonian conference of December 1971. The main

difference between the gold standard and the Bretton Woods system is
that in the former regime monetary authorities—at least in those countries on a full gold standard (Britain, Germany and the US)[5]—were required by law to exchange domestic banknotes with gold coins at the par
value (plus or minus transactions costs), whereas after World War II central banks used gold in transactions among themselves, and intervened in
the private bullion market at their own discretion. Since the private sector
had no rights of official conversion of national currencies into gold,[6] gold
was much less of a direct constraint on national monetary policies than in
the gold standard era.[7]

With gold as an external numeraire, the gold standard and the Bretton
Woods system provide, in different degrees, an official nominal anchor for
all member countries. In the EMS, by contrast, this official nominal anchor
is altogether absent. Each EMS currency, and each currency in the European Community, has a central rate determined in terms of the European
Currency Unit (ECU), a basket unit of account that comprises a specified
quantity of every currency in the European Community. The ratio of any
two ECU central rates is used to obtain bilateral central rates, which are
the target rates for monetary authorities. Given that the ECU is just a
weighted average of the member countries' currencies, if n is the number
of currencies in the ECU, there are only $n - 1$ bilateral exchange rates to
be pegged: for this reason a nominal anchor is absent from the rules governing the EMS.[8]

2.2.2 Bands

In the gold standard regime, individual currencies' gold parities, and the
costs of shipping gold internationally, jointly implied bilateral bands
within which exchange rates could fluctuate without requiring any action
by monetary authorities. Whenever bilateral exchange rates reached the
limits of the bands, arbitrage opportunities would be available, involving
trades of gold with the central banks, and of foreign exchange in the market. Examples of these bilateral fluctuation bands are reported in table 2.1.
As the table shows, when the price of dollars in terms of francs in the foreign exchange market rose above 5.215, it was profitable to obtain gold
at the mint par from the Bank of France, ship it to the US, sell it to US
banks at the mint par, and simultaneously sell dollars for francs in the foreign exchange markets, thus profiting from the arbitrage. The width of
the gold standard band was determined by the cost of transporting gold
to different national markets: thus it varied over time and across different

Table 2.1
Bilateral fluctuation bands

Currency (x-rate)	Parity	Lower limit	Upper limit
	Gold standard		
Sterling ($/pound)	4.866	4.827	4.890
Franc (FF/$)	5.183	5.148	5.215
Mark (DM/$)	4.198	4.168	4.218
	Bretton woods		
Sterling ($/pound)	2.8	2.772	2.828
Franc (FF/$)	4.937	4.887	4.986
Mark (DM/$)	4.2	4.158	4.242
	European monetary system		
Franc (FF/DM)	2.310	2.258	2.362

Sources: Gold Standard: Morgenstern (1959). Sterling points are computed for gold trade from Britain to the US (in 1879). Franc and mark points are computed for trade from Paris and Berlin (respectively) to New York (in 1901). Bretion Woods: *International Financial Statistics*. Data refer to the year 1960. EMS: *European Economy*. Data refer to March 1979.

markets. The estimates by Morgenstern reported in table 2.1 have been recently reassessed by Clark (1984), Officer (1986) and Spiller and Wood (1988). The authors' results suggest that the volatility of the gold points was considerable, making it difficult to determine whether international gold arbitrage was indeed an effective constraint on domestic monetary policies.

In the Bretton Woods regime, in the absence of an obligation for central banks to trade in the gold market with the public—which implies fluctuation bands whose size is determined by the available arbitrage technology—bilateral fluctuation bands were set by fiat: central banks were required to keep their respective currencies within ± 1 percent of their stated parities. Although par rates were set in terms of gold, bilateral fluctuation bands were around dollar parities. As a result, all cross rates (not involving the dollar) had 2 percent fluctuation margins on each side.[9]

The bilateral fluctuation bands involving the EMS currencies are, for all currencies except the lira, 2.25 percent on each side of bilateral central rates. The lira can fluctuate up to 6 percent on each side of bilateral central rates. Thus, the fluctuation bands for all European bilateral rates excluding the lira rates are only slightly larger than those prevailing during the Bretton Woods years: 4.5 percent in the EMS, 4 percent during Bretton Woods. The EMS regime is further complicated by an "indicator of divergence," measuring the weighted average deviation of each currency from the other currencies in the ECU. When the indicator of divergence reaches a certain threshold, a country is supposed to take corrective actions.[10] These corrective actions, however, are not compulsory.[11]

2.2.3 Adjustment and Financing

During the gold standard central banks were compelled to take corrective actions by a combination of two mechanisms: the convertibility of banknotes into gold coin, which encouraged arbitrage by the private sector whenever exchange rates exceeded bilateral fluctuation limits, and the coverage of banknotes by gold, which forced central banks to maintain a certain ratio of gold reserves to circulating banknotes, thus reacting to fluctuations of their gold reserve.[12] Changes in the discount rate and open market operations (Bloomfield, 1959) were the standard corrective actions. Various central banks also resorted to the so called "manipulation of gold points" which I discuss below in section 2.3.

No central-bank financing arrangement was part of the institutional setup of the gold standard. However, a number of instances are recorded when central banks granted bilateral credit to each other. Ford (1962) notes that the Bank of France discounted sterling bills to ease the strain on London in the Autumn of 1906, 1907, 1909 and 1910. Kindleberger (1984) describes the cooperation between European central banks in the crisis of 1890, when the Bank of England asked the Russian State Bank not to draw on its deposits in London and obtained from the State Bank an 800,000 sterling gold loan, and from the Bank of France a loan of 3,000,000 sterling in gold.[13]

The Bretton Woods system and the EMS, by contrast, are characterized by a complex structure of loans available to finance balance-of-payments needs. These financial resources support the foreign exchange market intervention required to keep currencies within their fluctuation bands. Neither the IMF Articles of Agreement, nor the rules governing the EMS, spell out the actions that central banks have to take when exchange rates reach bilateral fluctuation margins. In both systems the modality of adjustment to external disequilibria is only specified through the rules governing the financing of central banks' external imbalances, though there are some concessions to the principle of symmetry (in the Bretton Woods regime through the clauses on "scarce" currencies, see Argy 1981, in the EMS with the divergence indicator, and the Very Short Term Financing Facility, described below).

Under the Bretton Woods regime member countries could draw on various tranches of their IMF "quota." These tranches are characterized by different degrees of "conditionality," that impose progressively tighter constraints on monetary and fiscal policies: resources are made available to the borrowers subject to their meeting certain prespecified performance criteria.[14]

The EMS rules for balance-of-payments financing appear to be designed to avoid crises: the central banks of the currencies reaching bilateral intervention margins are supposed to grant each other automatic credit (not subject to authorization) in unlimited amounts under the Very Short Term Financing Facility (VSTFF).[15] The Very Short Term Financing Facility can also be used to support foreign exchange market intervention within the marginal fluctuation bands, subject to the authorization of the central bank whose currency is being drawn. The Short Term Monetary Support, another form of financial assistance available to EMS central banks experiencing temporary balance-of-payments difficulties, is instead governed by a "quota" system similar to that used by the IMF.

2.2.4   Is Asymmetry Induced by the Institutions?

The very brief survey of institutional features of the three fixed-exchange-rate regimes suggests two observations. First, the basic structure of international monetary systems has not changed dramatically in the last century. In particular, despite the efforts of policymakers to improve upon the IMF Articles of Agreement, the features of the Bretton Woods system and the EMS are noticeably similar. Both systems are characterized essentially by a lack of an external nominal anchor (given the minor role played by gold during the Bretton Woods regime), and by elaborate structures of balance-of-payments financing arrangements, which stand in contrast to the absence of any explicit rules for central banks to follow when bilateral fluctuation margins are reached. The added complications of the EMS, regarding the divergence indicator, have proved impractical.[16] In the gold standard, instead, adjustment rules were provided by the market mechanism, and by each country's coverage system.

The second observation suggested by my survey is that the rules of the gold standard, Bretton Woods and the EMS do not seem *per se* to induce an asymmetric working of international adjustment. Except in the case of Bretton Woods—where the bilateral fluctuation bands of the dollar are narrower than those of the other currencies—none of the basic institutional features of the three fixed-exchange-rate regimes seems asymmetric.

At the same time, all the provisions of the EMS explicitly designed to avoid asymmetries, like the indicator of divergence and the Very Short Term Financing Facility, were never seriously binding. The indicator of divergence does not force any country to take specific actions, while the automatic and symmetric foreign exchange intervention that takes place under the VSTFF appears to be a small fraction of the total volume of foreign exchange market intervention by member countries.[17]

2.3 Capital Controls

It is often argued by international economists that "capital controls" are more frequently resorted to by countries belonging to fixed-exchange-rates arrangements (see, for example, Stockman, 1987). In this chapter I use the term "capital controls" to denote various regulatory manipulations of the market mechanism which underlies the adjustment to external imbalances. These regulations were directed at different markets in different periods. Hence, for example, international bond and money markets were relatively free from regulation during the gold standard (a time where the gold market was subjected to various controls), but not in the more recent fixed-rate regimes, Bretton Woods and the EMS. In all three cases central banks resorted to capital controls as an additional instrument of monetary management. Controlling international financial transactions allows a country to gain limited freedom from the "rules of the game" imposed by the domestic and international monetary system, by preventing or slowing down the adjustment that would occur if financial transactions were free.

Controls were frequently imposed in emergencies. The Bank of England suspended the convertibility of notes into gold, thereby freeing itself to issue fiat money, in 1847, 1857 and 1866 (Kindleberger, 1984). While some of these crises were domestic in origin, the suspension of convertibility was also a response to external gold drains: see, for example the discussion in Dornbusch and Frenkel (1984). Following Keynes (1930), they argue that the suspension of gold standard rules during crises suggests they were effective only in periods of quiet.[18] Another popular regulatory measure affecting financial and gold flows was the so-called manipulation of gold points, that is the change in the bid-ask spread on bullion charged by the central bank. The Bank of England increased its buying price for bar gold in the crisis year of 1890, and according to Scammell (1965) followed the same practice on several other occasions in the following years. Similar devices were used by the Bank of France and the Reichsbank (Bloomfield, 1959).

The use of regulatory controls as emergency measures is common also in the Bretton Woods and EMS years. Article VI of the IMF Articles of Agreement even allows the Fund to request countries with balance-of-payments problems to impose capital controls for a limited time, in order to prevent the use of Fund resources. In response to capital account deficits, the Kennedy Administration proposed an investment tax credit in 1961, and passed the Interest Equalization Tax in 1963—a tax on US residents' purchases of foreign securities—followed by the Foreign Credit Restraint Program and the Foreign Direct Investment Program—aimed at limiting foreign investments by commercial banks, other financial institutions, and industrial companies. French and Italian authorities tightened various measures to prevent capital outflows after the Summer of 1968 and the Fall of 1969.

The practice of using capital controls as a fine-tuning device to stem speculative flows has survived in the EMS. Countries like France and Italy which until recently have prohibited the non-firm private sector from trading in financial assets with the rest of the world, have used restrictions on international trade credits to slow down or speed up the response of short-term capital flows.[19]

Giavazzi and Giovannini (1986) argue that in the EMS France and Italy rely crucially on capital controls, witness the large divergences between domestic offshore interest rates on franc and lira assets. They see asymmetries of capital controls as a reflection of the central role played by the Bundesbank, and capital controls as instrumental for countries other than Germany to maintain their exchange rate targets in the EMS, without having to surrender completely their monetary sovereignty. This observation raises two related questions. Are all fixed-exchange-rate regimes characterized by asymmetries in the degree to which capital controls are used? Is the presence of these asymmetries an indication of the existence of a central country?

A broad overview of the use of capital controls suggests a positive answer to the first question. There is ample qualitative evidence and opinion (see for example, Bloomfield, 1959; Ford, 1962; Scammell, 1965) that the Bank of England tended to use administrative devices less frequently than its counterparts on the Continent. It is well known that the convertibility of banknotes into gold was not guaranteed by law in France, but was left to the central bank's discretion. The much less frequent changes of the discount rate by the Bank of France, relative to the Bank of England and the Reichsbank, tends to imply the effectiveness of the threat of inconvertibility, which was accompanied by numerous changes of the gold points. In Germany international shipments of gold were apparently discouraged by moral suasion. As Bloomfield (1959) reported, Reichsbank officials questioned by the United States National Monetary Commission denied that the central bank discouraged commercial banks from obtaining gold for export when the gold export point was reached, but admitted that at certain times German banks refrained from shipping gold when it was profitable to do so. This phenomenon is independently confirmed by Birch (1887), in his presidential address to the London Institute of Bankers:

I was raising the question, only a few days since, with some of the leading bankers in Berlin, whether the Bank of Germany would give large amounts of gold in exchange for its notes, and they explained to me that, if gold was required to use as currency, they had no difficulty in getting what they wanted, but that they were too Patriotic to think of going to the bank for gold with a view to making a profit on the export. (Birch, 1887, p. 510)

The evidence on asymmetric use of capital controls during the Bretton Woods years is, to some extent, less clearcut. While in the second postwar period as a whole the United States has regulated international capital flows less than its European conterparts, episodes like the Interest Equalization Tax were clearly motivated by concern for the external influence on domestic monetary management.

The imposition of capital controls was resorted to not only by deficit countries. In the months preceding the revaluation of the Deutsche mark in March 1961, the Bundesbank struggled with capital inflows by imposing a series of discriminatory measures meant to discourage foreign residents' purchases of German assets.[20] These measures included higher reserve requirements on foreign-owned deposits at German commercial banks, prohibition of the payment of interest on foreign-owned sight and time deposits, and prohibition of the sale of money-market paper to nonresidents.

In summary, the evidence on both the gold standard and the EMS suggest that countries other than Britain (during the gold standard) and Germany (in the EMS) imposed regulations in order to avoid compliance with the "rules of the game:" in an asymmetric system the rules of the game consist of accommodating fully the centre country's monetary policies.[21] Hence these regulations might have been suggested by a desire to maintain some degree of monetary sovereignty. The evidence on Bretton Woods seems to indicate that capital controls were resorted to more often outside of the US, although even the US experimented with them in a number of cases.

2.4   Symmetric and Asymmetric Fixed-Exchange-Rate Regimes: A Definition

The alternative hypotheses about the working of fixed exchange rates can be illustrated using the canonical model of the gold standard.[22] This model concentrates on the external influences on domestic monetary policy and on domestic aggregate variables. It relies on the assumption that monetary policy is powerless in affecting real variables, so that real and nominal variables are determined independently. This assumption, which is probably not accurate in practice, is not essential for the conclusions I will draw here, but is quite helpful to sharpen the distinction between the alternative hypotheses on the working of the international monetary system.

There are two countries, a domestic and a foreign country—whose variables are identified by an asterisk. The rate of inflation in each country is determined by the rate of money growth and a velocity shock, that is independent of monetary factors:

$$p = m + v \qquad p^* = m^* + v^* \tag{1}$$

where m is the rate of growth of money, and p the rate of inflation. v represents the rate of growth of velocity. The law of one price holds in the goods market.[23] Hence the rates of inflation at home and abroad are the same in equilibrium. Real rates of return on domestic and foreign securities are equalized except for a variable, x representing international portfolio shifts. x is independent of monetary policies:[24]

$$p = p^* \tag{2}$$

$$r^* = r + x \tag{3}$$

The balance sheets of the two central banks imply:

$$m = d - f \qquad m^* = d^* - f^* \tag{4}$$

In a fiat currency system, d could be interpreted as the change in domestic credit relative to the initial stock of nominal money. f is the outflow of foreign exchange reserves, also measured in terms of the initial stock of money. Under the gold standard, d and f are the rate of growth of the fiduciary issue and the outflow of gold, respectively. Since there are only two countries in the model, one country's gold or reserve outflows are the other country's inflows. Assuming that the two countries are of equal size, we have:

$$f = -f^* \tag{5}$$

Equations (1) to (5) imply the following expression for the world rate of inflation, and the flow of international reserves:

$$p = 0.5[(d + d^*) + (v + v^*)] \tag{6}$$

$$f = 0.5[(d - d^*) + (v - v^*)] \tag{7}$$

As equations (6) and (7) show, the world rate of inflation is a weighted average of the domestic and foreign rates of growth of domestic credit (adjusted for velocity shocks), while reserve flows are determined by the deviations of the domestic and foreign monetary policies and money demand shocks. Nominal interest rates are determined by the Fisher equation:

$$i = r + p \qquad i^* = r^* + p^* \tag{8}$$

I define the symmetric fixed-exchange-rate regime as follows. Under a symmetric fixed-exchange-rate regime each central bank attempts to control a domestic target and a foreign target, represented by the nominal interest rate, and the rate of change of foreign exchange reserves: the two target variables have the same weights and desired values in central banks' objectives. I borrow the assumption that central bankers' objectives can be determined by a domestic target and a foreign target from Gio vannini (1986), Eichengreen (1987), Giavazzi and Giovannini (1989) and Barsky et al. (1988). The specification of the domestic target in terms of the nominal rate of interest is due to Barro (1988) and Barsky et al. (1988). In a symmetric system, the objective (loss) functions are:

$$W = (i - \bar{i})^2 + bf^2 \tag{9}$$

$$W^* = (i^* - \bar{i})^2 + bf^{*2} \tag{10}$$

In a commodity-based system like the gold standard, the similarity of the two objective functions would arise from the common rules governing the convertibility of banknotes into gold coins, and from the similarity of the rules about specie coverage of banknote circulation. In a fiat system like the EMS, the similarity of the two objective functions would arise as a result of systematic international consultations among member countries, whose objective is to define common guidelines for monetary policy.

When central banks maximize (9) and (10) world interest rates and reserve flow are as follows:

$$i = \bar{i} - 0.5x \qquad i^* = \bar{i} + 0.5x \tag{11}$$

$$f = (0.5/b)x \tag{12}$$

International disturbances are equally shared by the two countries, and international reserve flows are inversely proportional to the importance of the external target in the two countries' objectives.

By contrast, I define the asymmetric system as follows: the centre country targets the domestic interest rate, while the other country minimizes fluctuation of international reserves. Hence countries' objective functions differ:

$$W = (i - \bar{i})^2 \tag{9'}$$

$$W^* = f^{*2} \tag{10'}$$

The reaction functions implied by (9') and (10') are:

$$d = 2(\bar{i} - r) - d^* - (v + v^*) \tag{13}$$

$$d^* = d + (v - v^*) \tag{14}$$

Equations (13) and (14) show that the centre country accommodates world money demand shocks, but—given the real rate of interest and money demand—it offsets any changes of domestic credit policy in the periphery. The country at the periphery accommodates the centre country's policy, and offsets differences in money demand shocks, which tend to give rise to international reserve flows. The equilibrium interest rates and reserve flows are:

$$i = \bar{i} \qquad i^* = \bar{i} + x \tag{15}$$

$$f = 0 \tag{16}$$

Equations (15) and (16) reveal most clearly the fundamental difference between symmetric and asymmetric fixed-exchange-rate systems: in an asymmetric system countries at the periphery give up control of their domestic target to achieve stability of foreign reserve flows. In equilibrium all international portfolio shifts are fully reflected in changes in the interest rates at the periphery, but do not change the interest rate of the centre country.

The illustration of the symmetric and asymmetric regimes adopted in this section—based on postulated asymmetries in the objectives of central bankers—was preferred to an alternative specification, based on the hypothesis that the centre country is a "Stackelberg leader." That model relies on the assumption that changes in monetary policies by countries other than the leader cannot elicit the leader's reaction. By contrast, the model I use has in my opinion the virtue of being based on a symmetric game structure, but is silent on what gives rise to the asymmetries in the objective functions. The asymmetries could be generated by four different phenomena, which I briefly review below. They include Mundell's (1968) "proper division of the burden of international adjustment," the presence of a "reserve currency" country, liquidity constraints affecting differently surplus and deficit countries, and the issue of "imported reputation."

Robert Mundell (1968) demonstrates that the adjustment to country-specific disturbances should be divided in inverse proportion to the sizes of the countries involved. In our problem, the adjustment to relative interest-rate shocks is carried out by the small country; the interest rate in the large country is unaffected. This result can be illustrated considering a world made up by two equally-sized regions: one occupied by a single large country (the "domestic country"), and the other by a large number of small countries (denoted by an asterisk, *), indexed by $j = 1, \ldots, N$.[25] In this world, the rate of inflation is:[26]

$$p_j^* = p = 0.5[(d_j + (1/N)\Sigma d_j^*) + (v + (1/N)\Sigma v_j^*)]. \tag{17}$$

Each small country's domestic credit policy has a negligible effect on its own rate of inflation. By contrast, the small countries' reserve flows are:

$$f_j^* = d_j^* + v_j^* - 0.5[(d_j + (1/N)\Sigma d_j^*) + (v + (1/N)\Sigma v_j^*)] \tag{18}$$

In equilibrium, deviations of the two target variables from their desired values are inversely related to the relative effectiveness of the instrument: hence the small countries end up nearly pegging their foreign exchange reserves, while the task of pegging the world interest rate is left to the centre country. This corresponds to the asymmetric regime postulated above.

A similar result would obtain if one of the two countries issues a "reserve" currency: this case is discussed by Swoboda (1978) and Genberg, Saidi and Swoboda (1982). An increase in high-powered money by the reserve-currency country has a larger effect on world inflation than the same increase from a non-reserve-currency country. The foreign exchange reserves of the other country increase by a multiple of the original monetary expansion, equal to the money multiplier of the reserve currency. Hence the non-reserve-currency central bank would be relatively ineffective at targeting the rate of interest, and, as above, would end up targeting foreign exchange reserves.

A third reason for the endogenous establishment of an asymmetric regime is the presence of constraints on the size of balance-of-payments deficits, justified, for example, by liquidity constraints. With identical objective functions, the equilibrium reserve outflow from the domestic country is given by equation (12). If the domestic country faces systematically positive realizations of x, i.e. it is a "deficit country," and if the costs of financing reserve outflows are large, the domestic country would find it advantageous to forego interest rate stability by accommodating fully the monetary policy of the centre country.

Finally, asymmetric exchange rate regimes could arise in the "imported credibility" models of Giavazzi and Giovannini (1987) and Giavazzi and Pagano (1988). These authors show that, when exchange-rate targets are fully credible, inflation-prone central banks might find it advantageous to accommodate fully to a central bank which has an "inflation fighter" reputation.[27]

2.5   Empirical Evidence

In this section I discuss the empirical evidence on the hypothesis that the three fixed-exchange-rates regimes worked asymmetrically. I first review the evidence on the timing of discount rate changes during the gold standard. Then I study the behaviour of interest rates around parity realignments, both during the Bretton Woods and the EMS. And finally I derive and test some stochastic implications of the model of section 2.4.

2.5.1   The Timing of Discount-Rate Changes during the Gold Standard

During the gold standard, changes in the Bank rate were considered the main policy instruments used by central banks to affect their gold reserves and international capital flows. Bloomfield (1959) and Eichengreen (1987) argue that British rate changes followed immediately by changes on the Continent are evidence suggestive of the central role of the Bank of England in the gold standard. To verify this hypothesis, I have looked at the data published by the US National Monetary Commission (1910), reporting dates and amounts of discount rate changes for Britain, France and Germany in the period from January 1889 to December 1907.

First, I have computed the number of occurrences when a change in the British discount rate was followed (within 1 week) by a change in the discount rate in France or Germany. During the period, the Bank of England changed the discount rate 104 times, increasing it 59 times, and decreasing it 45 times. The Reichsbank followed increases in the British discount rate 11 times, and followed rate decreases 14 times. There are also 14 cases when the Reichsbank discount rate changes preceded those of the

Table 2.2
The timing of discount-rate changes under the gold standard

	Dependent variables		
	GB	GER	FRA
R^2	0.434	0.956	0.982
DW	2.000	2.000	2.001
F-tests			
GB	0.000	0.432	0.780
GER	0.000	0.000	0.038
FRA	0.117	0.574	0.000

Sample: Weekly from January 1890 to December 1907. The entries denoted by F-test are the marginal significance levels of the null hypothesis that the coefficients of the lagged discount rates of the country of the corresponding row are not signficant in the regressions whose dependent variable is the country of the corresponding column.

Bank of England.[28] France, by contrast, followed changes of Bank rate much less frequently (a reflection of less intensive use of discount rate policy by the Bank of France). Only three British rate changes were followed by France within a week (2 negative and 1 positive), while France's discount rate adjustments were also followed by the Bank of England on three occasions (2 negative changes, 1 positive). In the case of France, there are also three instances of discount rate changes occuring the same day.[29]

Table 2.2 contains statistical tests of the timing of discount rate changes, using 992 weekly observations for the period mentioned above. I estimate a vector autoregression including 8 lags of the British, French and German rates, and test the joint significance of the coefficients of each set of lagged rates in each regression. The table shows no evidence of temporal precedence in the changes in the British rate. Instead, lagged values of the German discount rate are significantly correlated with Bank rate and the French discount rate.[30] In summary, there is very little evidence in support of the hypothesis that Bank rate changes preceded changes in discount rates on the continent. As I argue in Giovannini (1986), at least in the monthly data, there is a strong contemporaneous correlation between the British and the German rates.[31] This correlation, however, is almost entirely due to the common seasonal component in discount rate policies, and therefore cannot be interpreted as supporting the hypothesis of the leadership of the Bank of England.[32]

How should we interpret these results? The temporal pattern of discount-rate changes being tested in this section is consistent with a leader-follower structure, where the centre country's central bank always moves first, independently of the other central banks' actions, and taking their reactions into account. The empirical evidence presented here rejects this hypothesis.[33] This evidence, however, has no conclusive implications for the asymmetric model of the gold standard in section 2.4.[34]

2.5.2 The Asymmetric Behaviour of Interest Rates

A rather general implication of the model in Section 2.4 regards the behaviour of interest rates. While in a symmetric regime international portfolio shifts are reflected in both countries' interest rates, in an asymmetric regime the centre country's rate is unaffected, and international portfolio disturbances perturb only the other countries' rates.[35]

This result suggests a simple test of the asymmetry hypothesis, based on the observation of countries' interest rates in response to observable international portfolio shifts. The most natural choice of episodes of shifts between countries' assets is the periods preceding devaluations. Both under the Bretton Woods regime and in the EMS there have been several realignments of central parities, which have been prompted by countries' inability to withstand balance-of-payments difficulties, and have been anticipated—though to different degrees—by financial markets. In this section I analyze the behaviour of interest rates around the Bretton Woods realignments of March 1961 (Deutsche mark revalued), November 1967 (devaluation of sterling), August 1969 (French franc devalued), and October 1969 (Deutsche mark revalued).

Figures 2.1, 2.2 and 2.3 report monthly observations of 1-month Eurodollar deposit rates, and of the differential between the Eurodollar rate and a domestic money market in the US, during an interval of two years around the realignments of 1961, 1967 and 1969.[36] Figures 2.4, 2.5, 2.6 and 2.7 report weekly data (taken on Fridays) on the US Treasury Bills rate and the forward premium. The sources are the *Wall Street Journal* for the US interest rate, and the *Economist* for the forward premium. The forward premium is calculated using bilateral rates against sterling: it is the ratio of the 1-month forward rate (expressed in units of the currency per dollar) and the spot exchange rate, less 1 (the result is multiplied by 1200 to express the implied interest rate differential in percent per annum).

Figures 2.1 and 2.4 illustrate the behaviour of dollar interest rates and the DM/dollar forward premium corresponding to the revaluation of the mark on March 6, 1961. Figure 2.4 shows that the volatility of the interest rate differential implied by the forward market much exceeds the vol-

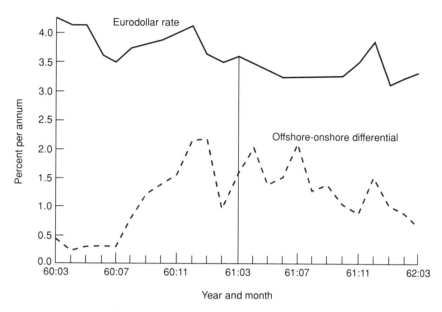

Figure 2.1
Dollar interest rates around the 1961 realignment

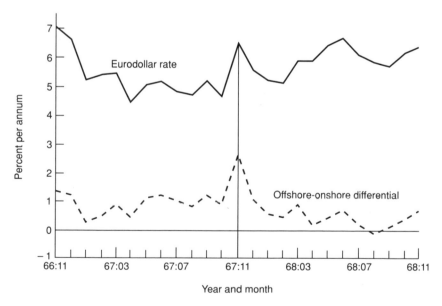

Figure 2.2
Dollar interest rates around the 1967 realignment

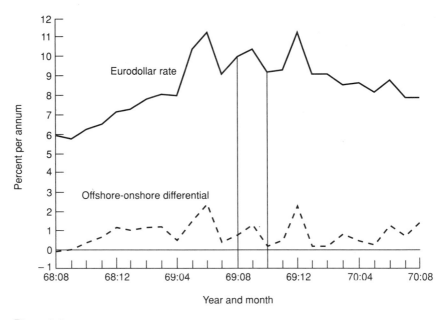

Figure 2.3
Dollar interest rates around the 1969 realignment

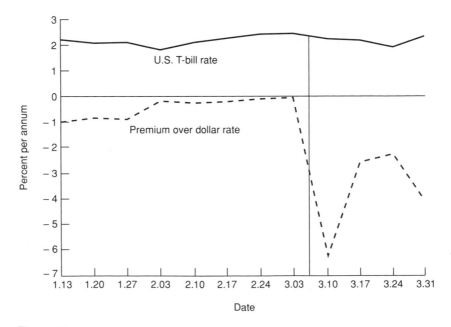

Figure 2.4
Forward premia around the 1961 realignment

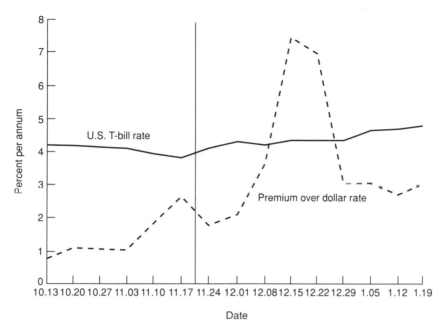

Figure 2.5
Forward premia around the 1967 realignment

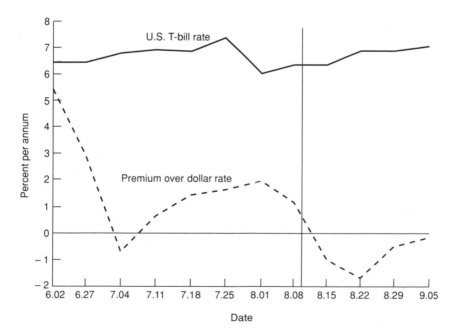

Figure 2.6
Forward premia around the August 1969 realignment

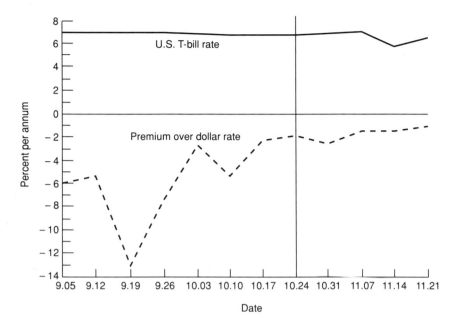

Figure 2.7
Forward premia around the October 1969 realignment

atility of the US Treasury bill rate. On January 13 the foreign exchange market implies a negative DM-dollar differential of about 1 percent. That differential decreases to −6 percent and −2.5 percent the weeks following the realignment. These large fluctuations of the interest-rate differential implied by the forward rate are accompanied by a much smaller increase of the Eurodollar rate (shown in Figure 2.1), which reached 4.14 percent in December 1960, but fell to about 3.5 percent the February before the revaluation of the DM.

Figures 2.2 and 2.5 report US rates and forward premia around the devaluation of sterling on November 20, 1967. Figure 2.2 shows a large peak in the Eurodollar interest rate and the offshore-domestic differential for the dollar in the month of November—suggesting that the sterling crisis had some repercussion on the dollar (evidence against the asymmetry hypothesis). Figure 2.5 shows wide swings in the forward discount on sterling, especially after the date of the devaluation, and a slight increase in the US TBill rate in the weeks preceding the devaluation.

Finally, figures 2.3, 2.6 and 2.7 illustrate the data for the August 11, 1969 devaluation of the franc, and the October 24 revaluation of the DM. As figure 2.3 shows, 1969 was a year of high and volatile Eurodollar in-

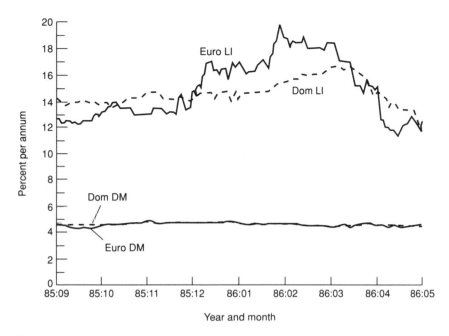

Figure 2.8
Onshore and offshore interest rates: Lira and DM (three month deposits)

terest rates. Figure 2.6 presents the data for the French devaluation. It shows that the forward market implied a very high differential between French and US interest rates at the end of June, without any large swings in the US TBill rate. The TBill rate, however, fell from 7.4 to 6.05 percent in the week preceding the devaluation. Figure 2.7 contrasts the relative stability of the US TBill rate with a sharp increase of the dollar-DM interest rate differential implied by the forward premium, which reached 13 percent on September 19.

Figures 2.8 and 2.9 report domestic and offshore interest rates for the lira, the French franc and the Deutsche mark, in the weeks preceding and immediately following the EMS realignment of April 7, 1986, when both the lira and the French franc were devalued relative to the Deutsche mark. This episode was first studied by Giavazzi and Giovannini (1987). The large swings of the offshore interest rates on the franc and the lira occur despite a strikingly stable pattern of domestic and offshore DM rates.

In summary, the behaviour of interest rates around devaluations strongly suggests the presence of asymmetry in the two EMS episodes. The sharp movements of dollar rates around the sterling devaluation in

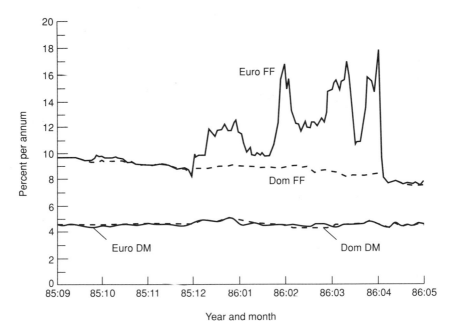

Figure 2.9
Onshore and offshore interest rates: French franc and DM (one-month deposits)

1967 are in contrast to the hypothesis that the US was the centre country
during the Bretton Woods years. The Bretton Woods data, however,
should be interpreted with caution, since this analysis cannot identify and
control for portfolio shifts that did not involve dollar assets: the maintained assumption is that the observed international interest rate differentials reflect incipient portfolio reallocations between dollar assets and
the assets denominated in the depreciating or appreciating currency.

2.5.3   Exploring the Stochastic Implications of the Asymmetric Model of Fixed Exchange Rates

Following the analysis of section 2.4, I assume that central banks minimize
the following objective functions:

$$W_t = -E_t[(y_{1t+j} - \bar{y}_{1t+j})^2 + b(y_{2t+j} - \bar{y}_{2t+j})^2] \tag{19}$$

$$W_t^* = -E_t[(y_{1t+j}^* - \bar{y}_{1t+j}^*)^2 + b(y_{2t+j}^* - \bar{y}_{2t+j}^*)^2] \tag{19'}$$

where y_1 and y_2 are the home and external target variables in both
countries (foreign-country variables denoted by a *). This maximization is

performed subject to equations describing the dynamics of the target variables:

$$Y_t = A(L)Y_{t-1} + B(L)Y_{t-1}^* + C(L)Z_t \qquad (20)$$

$$Y_t^* = A^*(L)Y_{t-1} + B^*(L)Y_{t-1}^* + C^*(L)Z_t \qquad (21)$$

where $A(L)$, $B(L)$ and $C(L)$ and the corresponding starred variables are polynomials in the lag operator. Y and Y^* are the vectors of targets for the domestic and the foreign country, and Z is a vector which includes exogenous variables, stochastic disturbances, and the instruments available to the two central bankers.

The first-order condition for the domestic central bank is

$$E_t(y_{1t} - \bar{y}_{1t}) = -bE_t(y_{2t} - \bar{y}_{2t}) \qquad (22)$$

A similar condition holds for the foreign central bank.

Equation (22) implies that, if b equals zero, deviations of the domestic target variable from its desired value should be uncorrelated with information at time t, and in particular with past realizations of the external target variable. Under the alternative hypothesis, lagged realizations of the external target variable—presumably correlated with the right hand side of equation (22)—are correlated with the term on the left-hand side. Intuitively, in the centre country the deviations of the domestic target from its desired value are white-noise errors.[37]

In order to derive testable implications, I need identifying assumptions about the unobservable term $\bar{y}_{1t}$. It is plausible to assume that it is uncorrelated with lagged values of the external target, thus allowing the domestic and the external targets to be more clearly isolated. In this case, when a country's monetary authority targets a domestic variable exclusively, lagged values of the external target should be uncorrelated with the domestic target. These tests are apparently similar to those performed by Pippinger (1984) and Dutton (1984), who analyzed central bank policies under the gold standard. As I stress in Giovannini (1986), however, the interpretation of my test is dramatically different. While I concentrate on the reduced-form properties of the data, implied by the alternative structures of the international monetary system, Pippinger and Dutton intend to estimate the parameters of central banks' reaction functions. These specifications, however, are not linked to an underlying optimization problem of central banks: hence the tests of the significance of individual parameters proposed by these authors are difficult to interpret.

Table 2.3
Test results: Gold standard

	Country		
	Britain	Germany	France
Sample	1889:12–1907:12	1892:12–1907:12	1900:10–1907:12
R^2	0.480	0.915	0.515
F-tests	0.271	0.004	0.029

Note: The entries denoted by F-test are the marginal significance levels of the null hypothesis that the coefficients of the lagged net imports of gold are not significant. The statistic is computed using the White (1980) correction of the variance-covariance matrix of disturbances.

Tables 2.3, 2.4 and 2.5 report the results of some exploratory tests of the asymmetry hypothesis. Table 2.3 contains the results for the gold standard data (monthly). I assume that the domestic target variable for each central bank is an index of coverage of the central bank's liabilities: the proportion of the gold reserve to total deposit liabilities in the Banking Department of the Bank of England, the proportion of cash to total demand liabilities in the Reichsbank,[38] and the ratio of the gold reserve to circulation in the Bank of France. In addition, I assume that the desired value of the target variable is constant (plausibly determined by national regulations on coverage, and by banking practice). For all three countries, I test whether lagged values of net imports of gold are significantly correlated with the target variable (in first difference), beyond a set of seasonal dummies.[39] The table shows that the null hypothesis of correlation is rejected at the 5 percent level in the case of Germany and France (the marginal significance level, the probability that the test statistic exceeds the reported value when the null hypothesis is true, is actually less than 1 percent in the case of Germany), but it is not rejected for Britain.

Table 2.4 contains the results for the Bretton Woods data (quarterly). The domestic target variable is assumed to be the domestic money-market interest rate, while the foreign target variable is the change in foreign exchange reserves relative to high-powered money.[40] As before, I include seasonal dummies in the regression. I find that past balance-of-payments flows are highly significantly correlated with the domestic money-market rate in the United States and in the United Kingdom. This correlation is insignificant in France and West Germany.

Table 2.5 contains the results for the EMS data. The specification of the regression equations is identical to that for the Bretton Woods data. The

Table 2.4
Test results: Bretton Woods

	Country			
	U.S.	U.K.	Germany	France
Sample	62:2–71:4	64:2–71:4	62:2–71:4	62:2–71:4
R^2	0.516	0.594	0.185	0.163
F-tests	0.000	0.000	0.518	0.400

Note: The entries denoted by F-test are the marginal significance levels of the null hypothesis that the coefficients of the lagged ratio of reserve flows relative to high powered money are not significant. The statistic is computed using the White (1980) correction of the variance-covariance matrix of disturbances.

Table 2.5
Test results: EMS

	Country		
	Germany	France	Italy
Sample	80:3–88:1	80:3–88:1	80:3–87:4
R^2	0.079	0.345	0.350
F-tests	0.690	0.009	0.003

Note: As Table 2.4.

hypothesis that lagged values of foreign reserve flows are orthogonal to the domestic target (nominal interest rate) is rejected at the 1 percent level in the case of France and Italy, but not in the case of West Germany. In summary, the test results agree with the "centre country" hypothesis in the case of the gold standard and the EMS, but not in the case of Bretton Woods.

2.6 Concluding Observations

The data seem to support the hypothesis of asymmetry, at least in the case of the gold standard and the EMS. Although the institutional setup in both regimes is clearly not inducing asymmetry, there are striking similarities in the use of capital controls. Furthermore, the evidence on interest rate behaviour and the statistical tests both support the asymmetric model.

In the case of Bretton Woods, the statistical model rejects the asymmetry hypothesis, and the evidence on interest rates is—at least in some cases—not as clearcut as in the case of the EMS.

In this chapter I have followed the strategy of trying to uncover evidence of asymmetry without exploiting the implications of specific models of asymmetric international monetary systems, like those mentioned in section 2.5. None of the factors giving rise to asymmetries described above, in my opinion, can alone fully explain all three historical experiences studied in this chapter. I do believe, though, that further empirical work should help to identify which of the alternative models of an asymmetric international monetary system best fit the individual historical experiences.

Notes

1. Recent supporters of the "asymmetry" hypothesis include Eichengreen (1987) on the gold standard, and Giavazzi and Giovannini (1989) on the European Monetary System.

2. In fact, each central bank quoted buying and selling prices for gold coins, which presumably represented the costs of minting and of administration of the bank. These buying and selling prices are also referred to as the gold points.

3. See Tew (1977) for an analysis of the IMF Articles of Agreement.

4. Countries could also declare their exchange rates "in terms of the US dollar of the weight and fineness in effect on July 1, 1944," that is, the gold parity could be defined in terms of the US dollar. Even with this method, however, the ultimate numeraire is gold.

5. In France the conversion of banknotes into coins was at the authorities' discretion.

6. Tew (1977) page 120.

7. The constraint operated through the influence on speculators' confidence exercised by deviations between the official and free-market prices of gold.

8. Since some currencies like the pound and the drachma are not part of the EMS exchange-rate arrangements, the missing external numeraire is in practice provided by these currencies.

9. The fluctuation bands of all cross exchange rates, including dollar rates, would have been 2 percent on each side, had they been set in terms of gold. Hence the Bretton Woods regime provided for narrower fluctuations of the dollar, relative to the other currencies.

10. "Diversified intervention, measures of domestic monetary policy, changes in central parities, or other measures of economic policy." (Monetary Committee, 1986).

11. See Spaventa (1982) for an illustration of the properties of the indicator of divergence. Spaventa observes that the indicator crosses the threshold less frequently for those currencies with a smaller weight in the ECU, and therefore it is not really a means of achieving symmetry in the system.

12. Few countries specified a constant ratio of circulation to reserves. As Eichengreen (1985) notes, England, among others, was on a fiduciary system, requiring full backing of note issue after a certain limit (the fiduciary issue) was reached. In Germany the Bank Act required that note circulation could not exceed a limit above three times the value of gold reserves, and if it did, the Reichsbank had to pay a 5 percent tax on the excess circulation. See US National Monetary Commission (1911).

13. See also Bloomfield (1959).

14. In the 1960s even the lowest conditionality resources, however, were not obtainable quickly enough to be usable to fend off balance-of-payments crises.

15. See Alesina and Grilli (1987) for an illustration of the effectiveness of these arrangements in avoiding speculative attacks. Credit lines for marginal intervention mature 75 days after the end of the month following the one in which the intervention has taken place.

16. See Giavazzi and Giovannini (1989) for a discussion.

17. Giavazzi and Giovannini (1989).

18. "… experience shows that, when severe stress comes, the gold standard is usually suspended. There is little evidence to support the view that authorities who cannot be trusted to run a nationally managed standard, can be trusted to run an international gold standard." (Keynes, 1930, p. 267).

19. In Giavazzi and Giovannini (1989) we show that the tightening and release of controls on international trade credits by France and Italy can be explained by the occurrence of balance-of payments difficulties, and are used very frequently by central banks. We also model the effects of controls on trade credits on the differentials between onshore and offshore rates.

20. Yeager (1966).

21. This point is shown explicitly in the next section.

22. See Dornbusch and Giovannini (1988), for example. Here I adopt the version of the model used by Barsky et al. (1988), who analyzed the international implications of the creation of the Federal Reserve System.

23. See Calomiris and Hubbard (1987) for a careful evaluation of the law of one price in goods and assets markets during the gold standard.

24. It can be shown that in this model a variable real exchange rate, not affected by monetary policy, is equivalent to x. Hence x can be interpreted as a general idiosyncratic shock in goods and assets markets.

25. This subdivision of the world economy, suggested to me by David Backus, facilitates the comparison with the symmetric case reported above.

26. From goods markets equilibrium, $d - f + v = i_i^* - f_i^* + v_i^*$, for all i. Summing these conditions over all i and using the condition that world reserve flows are zero, one can solve for f. To compute the world rate of inflation, substitute the expression for f into (4) and (1).

27. As Giavazzi and Giovannini (1989) stress, however, these models do not provide a justification as to why the centre-country would prefer such an arrangement over, for example, a flexible-exchange rate regime.

28. 7 times upwards, 7 downwards.

29. January 10 and January 24, 1889.

30. This evidence contrasts with the findings of Eichengreen (1987). He estimated monthly bivariate VARs which included the British discount rate and the German and French rate, respectively. He found that lagged values of the British rate were significantly correlated with both the French and the German rates. I was unable to reproduce these results by recon-

structing Eichengreen's sample. While my coefficient estimates are virtually identical to his, I found in the monthly data that lagged values of the British rate were not significantly correlated with the German rate, while lagged values of the French rate were significant in the Bank Rate regression.

31. Since the French rate changed few times in this period, I left it out of my analysis.

32. See Andreades (1909), Keynes (1930) and Ford (1962) for descriptions of the "autumnal drains" that prompted these reactions by central bankers.

33. Evidence on the timing structure of discount rates during the EMS is provided by Roubini (1988). Using quarterly data, he finds that lagged values of the German discount rate are correlated with Italian, Belgian and Danish rates, which he interprets as evidence of German leadership. Genberg, Saidi and Swoboda (1982) test the temporal precedence of US monetary policies during the Bretton Woods years: their evidence does not consistently support the hypothesis that US monetary policy changes preceded those in the rest of the world.

34. The limited use of Granger causality tests is argued in detail by Cooley and Leroy (1985).

35. Giavazzi and Giovannini (1987) show that the asymmetric behaviour of interest rates is also an implication of models where prices are sticky.

36. These data are obtained from *International Financial Statistics*.

37. See Sargent and Wallace (1976) for derivations of similar tests in the context of linear-quadratic control models.

38. Which equals the ratio of the sum of coin and Imperial treasury notes, divided by the sum of notes in circulation and other demand liabilities.

39. Since the theory does not predict that the disturbances should be i.i.d. under the null hypothesis, the test statistics are computed using the White (1980) correction for heteroskedasticity.

40. All the data are from *International Financial Statistics*. Valuation effects on foreign exchange reserves are calculated by subtracting the "other items" line from net foreign reserves at the central bank.

References

Alesina, A. and V. Grilli. 1987. "Avoiding Speculative Attacks on EMS Currencies: A Proposal," Economic Growth Center Discussion Paper No. 547, Yale University.

Andreades, A. 1909. *History of the Bank of England*, London: P. S. King & Son.

Argy, V. 1981. *The Postwar International Money Crisis*, London: George Allen and Unwin.

Barro, R. 1988. "Interest-Rate Smoothing," mimeo, Harvard University, March.

Barsky, R. B., N. G. Mankiw, J. A. Miron, and D. N. Weil. 1988. "The Worldwide Change in the Behaviour of Interest Rates and Prices in 1914." *European Economic Review* 32, 1123–54.

Birch, W. J. 1887. "Presidential Address," *Journal of the Institute of Bankers*, 503–36.

Bloomfield, A. 1959. *Monetary Policy Under the International Gold Standard: 1880–1914*, New York: Federal Reserve Bank of New York.

Calomiris, C. W. and R. G. Hubbard. 1987. "International Adjustment Under the Classical Gold Standard: Evidence for the U.S. and Britain, 1879–1914," mimeo, Northwestern University, May.

Clark, T. A. 1984. "Violations of the Gold Points, 1890–1908." *Journal of Political Economy* 92, 791–823.

Cooley, T. F. and S. F. Leroy. 1985 "Atheoretical Macroeconomics: A Critique," *Journal of Monetary Economics* 16, 283–308.

Dornbusch, R. and J. Frenkel. 1984. "The Gold Standard Crisis of 1847," *Journal of International Economics* 16, 1–27.

Dornbusch, R. and A. Giovannini. 1988. "Monetary Policy in the Open Economy" manuscript for the *Handbook of Monetary Theory*, ed. by F. Hahn and B. Friedman, February.

Dutton, J. 1984. "The Bank of England and the Rules of the Game Under the International Gold Standard: New Evidence," in M. D. Bordo and A. Schwartz, eds., *A Retrospective on the Classical Gold Standard 1821–1931*, Chicago: University of Chicago Press.

Eichengreen, B. 1985. "Editor's Introduction" in B. Eichengreen (ed.), *The Gold Standard in Theory and History*, New York: Methuen.

Eichengreen, B. 1987. "Conducting the International Orchestra: Bank of England Leadership Under the Classical Gold Standard," *Journal of International Money and Finance* 6, 5–29.

Ford, A. G. 1962. *The Gold Standard 1880–1914, Britain and Argentina*, Oxford: Oxford University Press.

Genberg, H., N. Saidi and A. K. Swoboda. 1982. "American and European Interest Rates and Exchange Rates: US Hegemony or Interdependence?" mimeo, International Center for Monetary and Banking Studies.

Giavazzi, F. and A. Giovannini. 1986. "The EMS and the Dollar," *Economic Policy* 2, 455–78.

Giavazzi, F. and A. Giovannini. 1987. "Models of the EMS: Is Europe a Greater Deutsche-Mark Area?" in R. C. Bryant and R. Portes (eds.), *Global Macroeconomics: Policy Conflict and Cooperation*, London: Macmillan.

Giavazzi, F. and A. Giovannini. 1989. *Limiting Exchange Rate Flexibility: The European Monetary System*, Cambridge, MA: MIT Press, forthcoming.

Giavazzi, F. and M. Pagano. 1988. "The Advantage of Tying One's Hands: EMS Discipline and Central Bank Credibility," *European Economic Review* 32, 1055–82.

Giovannini, A. 1986. "'Rules of the Game' During the International Gold Standard: England and Germany," *Journal of International Money and Finance* 5, 467–83.

Helpman, E. 1981. "An Exploration in the Theory of Exchange Rate Regimes," *Journal of Political Economy* 89, 865–90.

Keynes, J. M. 1930. *A Treatise on Money*, London: Macmillan.

Kindleberger, C. P. 1984. *A Financial History of Western Europe*, London: George Allen and Unwin.

McCloskey, D. N. and J. R. Zecher. 1976. "How the Gold Standard Worked, 1880–1913," in J. A. Frenkel and H. G. Johnson (eds.) *The Monetary Approach to the Balance of Payments*, London: Allen & Unwin.

Monetary Committee. 1986. *Compendium of Community Monetary Texts*, Brussels: European Community.

Morgenstern, O. 1959. *International Financial Transactions and Business Cycles*, Princeton: Princeton University Press.

Mundell, R. A. 1968. *International Economics*, New York: Macmillan.

Officer, L. H. 1986. "The Efficiency of the Dollar-Sterling Gold Standard, 1890–1908," *Journal of Political Economy* 94, 1038–73.

Pippinger, J. 1984. "Bank of England Operations 1893–1913," in M. D. Bordo and A. Schwartz, (eds.) *A Retrospective on the Classical Gold Standard 1821–1931*, Chicago: University of Chicago Press.

Roubini, N. 1988. "Sterilization Policies, Offsetting Capital Movements and Exchange Rate Intervention Policies in the EMS," mimeo, Harvard University.

Sargent, T. J. and N. Wallace. 1976. "Rational Expectations and the Theory of Economic Policy," *Journal of Monetary Economics* 2, 169–83.

Scammell, W. M. 1965. "The Working of the Gold Standard," *Yorkshire Bulletin of Economic and Social Research*, 32–45. Reprinted in B. Eichengreen, (eds.) *The Gold Standard in Theory and History*, New York: Methuen, 1985.

Spaventa, L. 1982. "Algebraic Properties and Economic Improprieties of the 'Indicator of Divergence' in the European Monetary System," in R. Cooper *et al.* (eds.) *The International Monetary System Under Flexible Exchange Rates—Essays in Honor of Robert Triffin*, Cambridge, MA: Ballinger.

Spiller, P. T. and R. O. Wood. 1988. "Arbitrage During the Dollar-Sterling Gold Standard, 1899–1908: An Econometric Approach," *Journal of Political Economy* 96, 882–92.

Stockman, A. C. 1987. "Real Exchange Rate Variability under Pegged and Floating Nominal Exchange Rate Systems: An Equilibrium Theory," mimeo, University of Rochester, October.

Swoboda, A. K. 1978. "Gold, Dollars, Euro-Dollars, and the World Money Stock under Fixed Exchange Rates," *American Economic Review* 68, 625–42.

Tew, B. 1977. *The Evolution of the International Monetary System 1945–77*, New York: John Wiley & Sons.

US National Monetary Commission. 1910. *Statistics for Great Britain, Germany and France*, Washington, DC: Government Printing Office.

US National Monetary Commission. 1911. *The Reichsbank 1876–1900*, Doc. 507, Washington, DC: Government Printing Office.

White, H. 1980. "A Heteroskedasticity-Consistent Covariance Matrix Estimator and Direct Test for Heteroskedasticity," *Econometrica* 48, 817–38.

Yeager, L. B. 1966. *International Monetary Relations*, New York: Harper & Row.

3

Bretton Woods and Its Precursors: Rules versus Discretion in the History of International Monetary Regimes

(August 1991)

3.1 Introduction

Are there predictable cycles in exchange-rate regimes? Can these cycles be predicted in terms of the rules-versus-discretion theory of monetary policy? Historical experience of the last 100 years provides a fascinating testing ground for this hypothesis. The classical gold standard was disrupted by World War I. After that, the majority of countries in the world returned to gold. The subsequent abandonment of gold occurred at a time of unprecedented economic and financial instability, and was followed by beggar-thy-neighbor trade policies and further political and economic instability. In the second postwar period, fixed exchange rates were reestablished. They broke down with the Viet-Nam era and the oil shock. They are being pursued again by European countries, both within and outside the European Community.

These events seem to suggest that floating rates are temporary arrangements that are resorted to whenever large enough shocks hit the world economy, but that, in the absence of shocks, countries go back to fixed rates. The rules-versus-discretion theory says that fixed exchange rates provide valuable commitments to national monetary authorities. Governments abandon these commitments only when exogenous shocks make it too onerous to "tie the hands" of monetary authorities.

In recent years, the theory of rules and discretion in monetary policy has fascinated scores of academic economists and policymakers alike. This chapter asks whether it can be applied to understand the history of the world monetary system, by focusing on the setup and the experience of the Bretton Woods regime, and comparing it with its predecessors, in particular the classical gold standard. Section 3.2 discusses the underpinnings, and some of the problems, of a theory of the evolution of the international monetary regime based on alternating rules and discretion.

Section 3.3 describes the rules that characterized the classical gold standard, and the motivations to return to gold in the interwar period. Section 3.4 evaluates—in light of the theories discussed in section 3.2—the British and US plan for world monetary reform published in 1943, and discusses the IMF Articles of Agreement. Section 3.5 contains an empirical analysis of the stabilizing properties of the gold standard and Bretton Woods rules. Section 3.6 offers a few concluding remarks.

3.2   Elements of a Theory of Exchange-Rate Regimes as Rules and Discretion

In the debate on monetary policy, the idea that fixed rules might improve the performance of monetary institutions has been a recurrent one. The earliest proponents of the superiority of rules were the members of the so-called currency school, opposing the banking school in the debate on the statute of the Bank of England. In the first half of the 20th century, the superiority of rules was most prominently claimed by the Cunliffe Committee (1918) and Simons (1936).[1]

The same idea has spurred a large amount of academic research on monetary policy in the last fifteen years, after the work of Kydland and Prescott (1977) Calvo (1978), Fischer (1980) and Barro and Gordon (1983) and has been exploited in the very recent discussions on the European Monetary System and exchange-rate policies of European countries outside the European Community. Several European policymakers, both within and outside the European Monetary System, have claimed that the "discipline" associated with a fixed exchange rate system, rather than making the job of monetary authorities harder, could actually help them fighting inflation more effectively.

In this section I explore an application to the rules-versus-discretion theory of monetary policy to the history of international monetary regimes. The basic hypothesis is that, if monetary policy rules are, under some conditions, preferred over discretion, countries would have a tendency to use them to constrain monetary authorities.

I do not present a formal model of the advantages of monetary policy rules for two reasons. First, a model of monetary policy rules, to add significantly to the existing literature,[2] needs some detail on the monetary transmission mechanism, which in the past 100 years has arguably adapted to technical progress and regulatory changes in financial markets, and to changes of wage contracting and pricing practices. Studying the effects of monetary policy and the adjustment mechanism during the gold standard and Bretton Woods is beyond the scope of this paper.[3] I will not refer to a specific model of the monetary transmission mechanism also to highlight the generality of the central results of the rules-versus-discretion literature.

The basic assumptions are three:

1. That monetary authorities' objectives do not coincide with the equilibrium the economy tends to settle at;

2. That monetary policies' effects on the economy depend on the extent to which they surprise the public;

3. That the public forms expectations rationally.

Two typical illustrations of assumption 1 are (i) the case of imperfectly competitive trade unions and/or price setters and (ii) the case of inflationary financing of budget deficits. In case (i) monetary authorities want to manipulate prices and exchange rates so as to affect the level of output (with monopolistic price and wage setters the level of output is "too low"). In case (ii) monetary authorities want to finance budget deficits at a minimum cost in terms of distortions. A third illustration, close to the second one, is that of monetary authorities attempting to lower the real interest rate to ease the cost of financing budget deficits.

Assumption 2 means that if the public can correctly anticipate policy actions, it will try to minimize any undesirable effects of them (see assumption 1 on the conflict between the monetary authority and the public), by taking actions so as to neutralize them. Assumption 3 means that monetary authorities cannot manipulate private expectations.

The implication of assumptions 1–3 is that in economies where monetary authorities are not subject to rules explicitly designed to prevent them from creating inflation, the equilibrium is one where the attempts of the authorities to surprise the public are frustrated by the public's anticipation of such behavior: inflation is higher and expansionary monetary policies are neutralized. What is the value of monetary rules? If such rules are credible, in the sense that the government cannot renege on them, the public forms expectations assuming that the rules are followed. To the extent that monetary rules are sufficiently restraining, the public's inflationary expectations will be stemmed, and therefore equilibrium inflation will be lower than under a discretionary regime. Since under discretion the government expansionary intentions are neutralized, equilibrium under rules is preferred to equilibrium under discretion as long as inflation is perceived to be costly. Thus, credible monetary rules are effective because they stabilize expectations.

Having established the desirability of rules as means of stabilizing expectations, we need to determine how the idea can be applied to the interpretation of the history of exchange-rate regimes, and in particular of the periodic abandonment of and return to fixed exchange rates. Assume, for a moment, that a regime of fixed exchange rates is a monetary rule, while a regime of floating rates is discretion (we go back to these assumptions below). How can a sequence of rules and discretion be endogenously chosen by monetary authorities, and hence be the equilibrium outcome of the interaction between monetary authorities and the public? We know that monetary authorities always have an incentive to abandon rules. This incentive can be stronger in situations where sticking to the rules is very costly (because, for example, of a negative supply shock, or because of unanticipated jumps in budget deficits). Indeed, one can find states of the world—which we can call "exceptional circumstances"—where the abandonment of rules would be desirable both by the monetary authorities and by the public. A sequence of rules and discretion would hence be possible if rules are abandoned only under exceptional circumstances, which can be unambiguously identified both by monetary authorities and the public, and are reinstated whenever the reasons for the suspension are gone away, or at any rate after a reasonably predictable length of time.

A model of contingent monetary rules is presented in Flood and Isard (1989a,b, 1990).[4] The basic idea of this model is that combining a rule with discretion makes the discretionary policy more effective when it is used. A rule with an escape clause might be preferred to a simple rule whenever the costs of sticking to the rule are large: as Persson and Tabellini (1991) show, this happens, for example, when the exogenous shocks to which the monetary authority has an incentive to react are highly volatile.

Application of escape clauses models to exchange-rate regimes are provided by de Kock and Grilli (1989) and Bordo and Kydland (1990). The model by de Kock and Grilli is the first formal application of the escape clauses idea to the history of exchange-rate regimes. These authors consider a small economy's choice between a fixed exchange rate (the rule), an adjustment of the fixed exchange rate (the escape), and a floating exchange rate. They explore the conditions under which a combination of rules and discretion (which requires a known value of the exogenous shock beyond which the authority exercises discretion) is an equilibrium: the monetary authority has no incentives to renege on it and the public believes the monetary authority.[5] Bordo and Kydland (1990) discuss the experience with the gold standard in terms of a model of rules with contingencies or escape clauses. They consider two kinds of contingencies: wars and financial crises.

The attempt to use an escape-clause model to explain the evolution of international monetary regimes raises a number of questions, which are not fully answered by the authors cited above, who concentrate on issues that only partially overlap with the one addressed in this chapter. First of all, can a fixed-exchange-rate system that does not rely on any explicit nominal anchor be likened to a monetary rule? The obvious difference between a commodity standard (that is a fixed-exchange-rate system with a nominal anchor) like the gold standard and a fixed-exchange-rate regime under a fiat currency system is that in the latter regime there is nothing preventing participating monetary authorities to generate inflation arbitrarily, as long as they do so in a coordinated fashion, to preserve the fixed parities. This is just an illustration of the well known "$n - 1$" problem: given n currencies, there are $n - 1$ independent bilateral exchange rates. Maintaining these $n - 1$ bilateral exchange rates fixed ties down as many national money stocks. Hence, there is one degree of freedom left. In the absence of exogenous rules the price level is arbitrarily determined by the remaining Nth country.

It could be claimed that, in practice, it is difficult to generate inflation through internationally coordinated monetary surprises, and therefore that a fixed rate regime is in general a powerful enough rule even in the absence of a commodity standard. Even accepting this claim, one would have to prove that a fixed exchange rate regime has built-in features that discourage worldwide inflation. For example, it can been argued that a fixed exchange rate system has a deflationary bias caused by liquidity constraints facing central bankers who try to finance balance-of-payments deficits. This view could provide a base for the hypothesis that even in a fiat currency system a fixed exchange rate regime is a satisfactory rule for monetary authorities. Thus, a candidate model of fixed exchange rates as monetary rules (a model of international monetary rules) relies on the proposition that fixed exchange rates have built in incentives towards monetary restraint, arising from the difficulties of financing balance-of-payments deficits.

An alternative candidate is the model of imported credibility. Under a fiat monetary system an independent central bank managed by a "conservative" governor (Rogoff, 1985) achieves outcomes similar to those of a commodity standard because an independent and conservative central banker is "exogenous," like the convertibility rule of a commodity standard.

The tenure and the behavior of the conservative central banker cannot be affected by the preferences of either the public or the fiscal authorities. The imported credibility model relies on the proposition that, by pegging the value of the national money to a currency managed by a conservative central banker, a country will import that banker's credibility, and reap the benefits highlighted by the "rules versus discretion" literature.[6]

The crucial logical link in both arguments presented above is of course that the fixed exchange rate is more credible than other policies. Why should a policy of pegging the currency to a low-inflation country be more believable than a policy of maintaining a low growth rate for the domestic money stock under a regime of floating exchange rates? To my knowledge, no general answers to this question have been offered so far. One notable feature of fixed exchange rates is that the price of a reference foreign currency is a highly visible, and unambiguous, target. Canzoneri (1985) shows that if the monetary authority has private information about, say, velocity shocks, it can lead the public to believe that it acts conservatively even when it does not. The strategies described by Canzoneri would not be possible under fixed exchange rates, because under that regime the monetary authority automatically accommodates velocity shocks. In general, it is easy to monitor compliance to a fixed-exchange-rate rule, and for that reason, the losses from suspending the rule might be larger (since the public knows exactly when the rule is suspended).

In sum, the answer to the first question—is a fixed exchange rate system under a fiat currency regime a monetary rule?—is "yes" only under two rather strong conditions: that the exchange rate is a more credible target than any other monetary target, and that the international system has built-in features that discourage global inflation (penalties for deficit countries, or independent and conservative central bankers).

We can ask a second question on the application of the escape clause model to the history of the international monetary system: can floating rates be regarded as a temporary suspension of the rules? It could be argued, for example, that exceptional circumstances only call for an adjustment of the exchange-rate peg, as in de Kock and Grilli, but not for a reversal to floating exchange rates. Alternatively, as Bordo and Kydland suggest, suspensions of convertibility at the time of financial crises are consistent with the escape clauses model. While this may well be true, its verification is beyond the objective of this chapter, which seeks to determine whether the more important and longer term regime shifts can be explained by the model of rules with escape clauses.

Analytically it should be possible to build a model where discretion is exercised over a known period of time. Bordo and Kydland stress, however, that the length of this period should be known. In a more complicated setting, the time of return to fixed rates could be a non-stochastic function of available information. Hence the answer to the second question—can floating rates be regarded as temporary suspension of rules?—is again a "yes," if the public can form reasonable expectations that fixed rates will be reinstated when a set of objective and known conditions are met. Thus, while in theory it is possible to accommodate temporary reversals to floating rates, an historical assessment of this model requires a careful analysis of returns to fixed rates. To be consistent with the model, returns to fixed rates have to be easily forecastable, and have to be motivated by the desire to reinstate monetary rules.

In conclusion there are elements in the rules-cum-escape-clauses model that could be used to interpret the historical evolution of exchange-rate regimes. However, as I stressed in this section, there are also conceptual problems with this exercise. The international gold standard system was one where national convertibility rules were automatically made consistent by the working of international financial markets. Under a fiat currency system, by contrast, it is not immediately apparent that a regime of fixed exchange rates can qualify as a monetary rule. If it does, under the conditions spelled out above, it is a very special kind of rule, purely international.

In the sections that follow I will try to provide evidence useful to verify the model. The exercise combines a discussion of the historical record with statistical work. Using the historical record, I will ask whether convertibility rules that characterize the gold standard were visible enough—a necessary condition to be credible—and whether the return to gold in the interwar years was regarded as a return to normalcy. I next examine in detail the setup of the Bretton Woods system, to determine whether in the minds of its builders such a system had to commit monetary authorities to price stability. The statistical analysis will discuss some evidence on the credibility of the gold points and of the fluctuation bands under the gold standard and Bretton Woods, respectively.

3.3 The Importance of Rules in the Experience of the Classical Gold Standard and the Return to Gold in the Interwar Period

In the classical gold standard, international monetary rules were not codified by an international government agency, but were the implication of convertibility rules embedded in national regulations, like central bank statutes.

While gold provided the external numeraire (or nominal anchor) to both the gold standard and the Bretton Woods regime, under the former regime central banks were obliged to intervene in the gold market to support the parity: they were ready to exchange domestic banknotes for gold coins at a specified official value—the mint par. By contrast, under Bretton Woods central banks were not obliged to intervene in the gold market. In addition, under the gold standard central bank statutes fixed or regulated the ratio between gold reserves and note circulation.

The ease of official gold convertibility in different countries is the subject of historical debate. The general agreement is that convertibility was easiest at the Bank of England, while certain continental central banks, like the Reichsbank and the Banque de France, in several instances discouraged "internal" and "external" drains of gold reserves.[7]

Another noticeable difference between the classical gold standard and the Bretton Woods system is the existence of a network of financial facilities for balance-of-payments financing. No official arrangements were in place under the gold standard, and yet, Ford (1962) and Kindleberger (1984) report a number of instances were informal loans between the Bank of England and other European central banks helped stem speculative pressures.[8] By contrast, the IMF Articles of Agreement (discussed in more detail in section 3.4.3) provide a complex system of facilities for the purpose of balance-of-payments financing.

Despite the absence of international monetary institutions, the gold standard rule was extremely visible: a necessary condition to be credible. The visibility of the gold standard rule was accompanied by public awareness on the value of commitment, especially in Britain. As Scammel's (1965) authoritative description of the classical gold standard succinctly puts it:

The Bank (of England) regarded the maintenance of the convertibility of sterling to gold as paramount and any sustained gold movement always led to action sooner or later.

The extent to which policymakers and their advisers valued commitment can be gauged from an analysis of the debates preceding the reestablishment of the gold standard in the interwar years. The Cunliffe Committee strongly advocated the return to the gold standard rule to induce stability in financial markets:

Nothing can contribute more to a speedy recovery from the effects of the war, and to the rehabilitation of the foreign exchanges, than the re-establishment of the currency upon a sound basis. [Cunliffe Committee, 1918]

The return to the gold standard was discussed in the 1920 Brussels conference and in the Genoa conference in 1922.[9] The Committee on Currency and Exchange of the Brussels conference did not mention gold explicitly. However, it advocated the elimination of exchange controls, the restoration of central bank independence, and the establishment of a common standard of value on which to base the new monetary system.

At the Genoa conference it was acknowledged that a return to gold at a parity different from the prewar would undermine the credibility of monetary authorities, by reminding investors of the authorities' control on gold parities. The delegates from France, Belgium and Italy were the strongest endorsers of the principle of the return to the prewar parity, and yet, as Eichengreen (1992) notes, the very same countries did not follow that principle a few years later.

Britain's resumption of the prewar parity, announced by Churchill in April 1925, is traditionally regarded as the best evidence of that country's commitment to the gold standard rule. Soon afterwards, that decision was widely regarded as an error, which cost much to Britain and other countries. Whether the economic disruptions of the 1930's were caused by Britain's decision alone, or by the policies that followed it but were not necessarily caused by it, remains an open question.[10]

As Bordo and Kydland (1990) suggest, the experience of the gold standard and of its return after World War I is *prima facie* evidence in favor of the model of rules with escape clauses. There is, however, disagreement also with this interpretation of the facts. For example, Temin (1991, p. 8) maintains that industrial countries resumed the gold standard because they considered it the "normal" way to run the world monetary system, and not necessarily because of their esteem of the discipline that characterizes a commodity standard. I do not attempt to resolve this controversy here, but concentrate instead of the second resumption of fixed rates, the Bretton Woods regime.

3.4   The Importance of Rules in the Design of Bretton Woods Institutions

The international monetary institutions of the second postwar are the outcome of the negotiations between the United States and Britain.[11] The objective of this section is to determine whether the builders of the Bretton Woods regime believed that a credible commitment of monetary authorities to price stability should be a crucial feature of the new monetary system.[12]

In 1943 the British and the U.S. Treasuries published two plans for international monetary reform, whose principal drafters were, respectively, John Maynard Keynes and Harry D. White. Both plans were characterized by an institution—the International Clearing Union in the British document and the International Stabilization Fund in the U.S. document—whose purposes were to help multilateral balance-of-payments financing, to economize in international means of payments, and to ensure a degree of exchange-rate stability. In the discussion below I leave aside the (substantial) parts of the two plans describing the mechanics of the international monetary institution except insofar as they relate to the question of the international monetary rule.

3.4.1   The British Plan

The objectives of the British plan, some of which are reported below, highlight the concerns of British policymakers:

• We need an instrument of international currency having general acceptability between nations [...]

• We need an orderly and agreed method of determining the relative exchange values of national currency units, so that unilateral action and competitive exchange depreciations are prevented.

• We need a *quantum* of international currency, which is neither determined in an unpredictable and irrelevant manner as, for example, by the technical progress in the gold industry, nor subject to large variations depending on the gold reserve policies of individual countries [...]

• We need a system [...] whereby pressure is exercised on any country whose balance of payments with the rest of the world is departing from equilibrium in either direction [...]

• More generally, we need a means of reassurance to a troubled world, by which any country whose own affairs are conducted with due prudence is relieved of anxiety, for causes which are not due of its own making, concerning its ability to meet its international liabilities; and which will, therefore, make unnecessary those methods of restriction and discrimination which countries have adopted hitherto [...] [British Information Services (1943a, p. 5).]

It seems clear that the establishment of a monetary rule whose aim is to discourage inflationary policies was not a declared intention of the British proposal. Indeed, the British document states plainly:

The plan aims at the substitution of expansionist, in place of contractionist, pressure on world trade. [British Information Services (1943a, p. 12).]

implying a belief that monetary policy can be consistently employed to stimulate international trade and economic expansion.

In the views of the British Treasury gold remains a standard of monetary value because

Gold still possesses great psychological value which is not being diminished by current events; and the desire to possess a gold reserve against unforeseen contingencies is likely to remain. Gold also has the merit of providing in point of form (whatever the underlying realities might be) an uncontroversial standard of value for international purposes, for which it would not yet be easy to find a serviceable substitute.

The British government suggested the introduction of an international currency for inter-governmental transactions, the *bancor*, to be defined in terms of a weight of gold. The value of *bancor* in terms of gold is however not unalterably fixed. Furthermore:

What, in the long run, the world may decide to do with gold is another matter. [British Information Services (1943a, p. 16).]

The above quotations summarize well the position of the British government. Gold is regarded as a necessary element of the new world monetary order because of its heritage, but not because any value is attached to it as a rule for conduct of monetary policy. The reference to the "great psychological value" of gold suggests awareness of the importance of credibility in a monetary system, but the rest of the document seems to imply that gold should not be sought as a mechanism to insure such credibility. Indeed, both the possibility to change the dollar value of the *bancor*, without any explicitly stated formal constraint, as well as the implicit allowance of a complete phasing out of gold, indicate that the British government was not at all concerned with the question of providing a worldwide anchor for monetary policy. Rather, the British proposal's central concern was adjustment and symmetry: see in particular its position on capital controls,[13] and the provision of charging interest on the negative clearing positions while at the same time taxing the creditor balances.

More importantly, changes in parities (defined in terms of *bancor*) did not require consultations, and were allowed whenever a criterion for unsustainability of external imbalances was met. The lack of concern with nominal anchors is confirmed by the following statement of the Chancellor of the Exchequer, Sir Kingsley Wood: "On the face of it, the (U.S. Treasury's) scheme appears to relate exchanges and balances more closely to gold than does the clearing union."[14]

In sum, the British proposal is based on the view that the international monetary system should not constitute a hindrance to expansionist monetary policies, and that monetary policies should not be used by individual countries to gain advantage from their neighbors (hence the call for exchange-rate stability): all of this seems quite far from the rule-based view of international monetary systems. The British position was probably motivated by two major concerns: avoiding the troubles of the interwar years, and providing a world environment that would help Britain ease out of its war debts.

The records circulated by the British Information Services (1943b) do not contain any criticism of the Keynes plan from the House of Commons and the House of Lords. Perhaps because of the powerful intellectual influence of Keynes, the British government and the parliament not only were not advocating the imposition of rules in the world monetary order, but openly declared their aversion to them. Their mistrust of the equilibrating forces of the international monetary system[15] implied the belief that interventionist monetary policies were necessary to ensure the proper support to economic activity. These interventionist policies, as Meltzer (1988) stresses, were in Keynes's view to be subject to rules, which however were not simple and were not designed with the sole purpose of limiting incentives to inflate.

3.4.2   The U.S. Plan

Similarly to Britain, the objectives of the U.S. plan do not mention the importance of rules in the new international monetary system. They are:

• To help stabilize the foreign exchange rates of the currencies of the United Nations [...]

• To shorten the periods and lessen the degree of disequilibrium in the international balance of payments of member countries.

• To help create conditions under which the smooth flow of foreign trade and of productive capital among member countries will be fostered.

• To facilitate the effective utilization of blocked foreign balances accumulating in some countries as a consequence of the war situation.

• To reduce the use of foreign exchange restrictions [...] (U.S. Treasury 1943).

The first two items grow from an interpretation of the interwar experience similar to the British: countries should not use exchange rates as beggar-thy-neighbor devices, and the international adjustment mechanism needs the intervention of governments. The last three, loosely inspired by the postwar U.S. philosophy based on multilateralism and non-discrimination, mainly regard the postwar reconstruction.

Despite the lack of mention of monetary restraint in its objectives, the U.S. Treasury proposal had strict rules on the linkage of the international currency, the *unitas*, with gold. According to the White plan, the *unitas* value was fixed in gold (137 and 1/7 grains of fine gold). Furthermore:

No change in the gold value of the *unitas* shall be made except with the approval of 85 percent of the member votes [...]

The value of the currency of each member country shall be established in terms of *unitas* and may not be altered except [...] with the approval of three fourths of the member votes including the representative of the country concerned. (U.S. Treasury 1943)

These changes would not be considered, unless when essential to the correction of fundamental disequilibrium in the balance of payments of the country in question.[16]

The British parliament was critical of the White plan, whose stress on fixing the gold content of currencies, and liberalizing world financial markets[17] they regarded as "the very things that smashed the world economic system which prevailed before the war" (British Information Services, 1943b, p. 40).[18]

Surprisingly, there is no evidence that the two plans faced significant opposition at home. The best known critic of the plans is John Williams.[19] Williams's strong prior is that the success of the international gold standard was due to the stability of its center country, Britain. Hence his suggestion that the post–WWII system also rely on center countries (which, in his view, should be more than one). However these center countries can guarantee a smooth functioning of the world system only if they cooperate in monetary affairs much more tightly than envisaged by the Bretton Woods charter.

The most interesting critique I was able to find comes from Benjamin Anderson, a professor of economics at the University of California at Los Angeles. Anderson's position appears to be very close to the "rules" theory of international monetary regimes:

Fixed rates in the foreign exchanges are eminently desirable. A temperature of 98.6 in the human body is eminently desirable, but a rigging of the thermometer so that it will always record 98.6 regardless of the fluctuations in the temperature of a sick patient is a rather futile performance. And a rigging of the foreign exchange markets so that they will record fixed rates among sound and unsound countries, regardless of a deterioration of the fundamentals governing the values of the moneys of the unsound countries, merely masks the facts of financial disease and disorder, and defers the time when these fundamentals must be dealt with. [Anderson (1944, p. 10)]

Yet, the reason why professor Anderson values international monetary restrain is, together with a general aversion to inflation—as in the models discussed in section 3.2—a very concrete concern that the new monetary system would allow debtor countries, and in particular Britain, to surreptitiously default on their war debts. Anderson envisaged Britain exploiting the multilateral clearing system it proposed by paying for its imports and servicing its debt from the United States not in "good dollars" or "still pretty good sterling," but in the currencies of the countries of its exports: "the bad francs, lire, marks, Greek drachmae, etc." The implicit assumption in this reasoning is, of course, that the real purchasing power of the "bad" currencies could not be ensured by the system of *bancor* or *unitas* parities, and by the linkage of these latter units of account with gold. In other words, Anderson viewed the fixed-rates regime transform itself into a regime of competitive inflation, caused by institutions that he regarded the most suitable to export the inflation tax.

3.4.3   The IMF Articles of Agreement

The Articles of Agreement of the International Monetary Fund contain elements of both the British and the U.S. proposals. In many ways, the Articles of Agreement further departed from the attempts to restore free capital movements and rules of conduct for monetary policy that appeared in the U.S. proposal.

The objectives of the IMF, spelled out in Article I, include international cooperation in monetary matters, high employment (through the expansion and balanced growth of international trade), exchange-rate stability, a multilateral payments system, balance-of-payments financing and adjustment. As in the case of the two proposals, no direct mention is made of either price stability or free trade in financial assets.

The provision regarding the nominal anchor are contained in Article IV. All member countries are required to express a central parity of their currencies, either in terms of gold, or in terms of dollars "of the weight and fineness in effect on July 1, 1944." Maximum fluctuations bands are also established to be 1 percent in either direction.[20] The article also discusses changes in par values. Countries can change exchange parities after consultations with the Fund, given the need to correct a "fundamental disequilibrium."[21] The Fund concurs with the proposed change if it is satisfied that it can correct the fundamental disequilibrium. If the Fund does not concur, and the parity is changed nevertheless, the country becomes ineligible to the Fund resources, unless the Fund otherwise determines.

Article IV represents a significant deviation from the White plan, which required a majority of the board in order to grant a change in the parity of any member currency. The mechanism of approval from the IMF is meant to safeguard the international monetary system from competitive exchange-rate changes, but is substantially less restrictive than the original U.S. proposal.

Article VI deals with capital flight. It says that a country facing sustained capital outflows does not have access to Fund resources to finance the resulting balance-of-payments problems. The Fund may require that country to impose capital controls, in order to avoid reserve losses. The article explicitly allows controls on capital movements that are not linked with the financing of international trade.

Finally Article VII, on scarce currencies, describes measures to replenish the Fund's holdings, as well as emergency measures to ration the scarce currency. No mention is made in the article of the fundamental problem that might give rise to the phenomenon of a scarce currency, divergent monetary policies, and of ways to correct the origins of the problem. In other words, monetary policy coordination (which under fixed rates amounts to the coordination of domestic credit policies) is induced indirectly, through the various alarm bells set up by the Fund. However, it is never mentioned or encouraged explicitly. The Articles of Agreement attempt to substitute the fixed, exogenous gold standard rules with a novel concept, monetary policy coordination. However, its official status is far below that of the convertibility rules of the gold standard: for this reason, this substitution seems to be incomplete, and not sufficiently effective.

Further light on the question of the importance of rules in the minds of the builders of the Bretton Woods system can be obtained from the replies of U.S. officials to various critics. Edwin Kemmerer (1945) echoed several of the concerns of Benjamin Anderson. He pointed to the ineffectiveness of the safeguards against changes in currency parities, noting that any country is free to generate "fundamental disequilibria" on its own, by pursuing expansionary monetary policies in support of budget laxity. To this and other similar criticism, Harry White responded:

Englishmen have not forgotten that in the sterling crisis of 1931 social services were cut in the attempt to maintain the fixed sterling parity. To use international monetary arrangements as a cloak for the enforcement of unpopular policies whose merits or demerits rest not on international monetary considerations as such but on the whole economic program and philosophy of the country concerned, would poison the atmosphere of international financial stability. [White (1945, p. 8)]

White's thinking, which well represents the opinion of experts and policymakers responsible for the Bretton Woods system, is clearly very far from the Cunliffe Report philosophy. His response to the Bretton Woods critics is that international monetary rules cannot be used as scapegoats for unpopular domestic policies. For this reason, monetary rules have been studiously minimized in the IMF charter.

In conclusion, the analysis of the IMF charter and what went into it suggests that the establishment of the Bretton Woods regime of fixed exchange rates cannot be viewed as the return to a monetary rule in the sense specified in section 3.2. The discussion in section 3.2 stressed that a fixed-rates regime can be considered a monetary rule under one of two conditions:

• it is based on a convertibility rule which implies a set of bilateral exchange rates and provides a nominal anchor;

• it is centered around an independent and conservative monetary authority, or has some other feature discouraging any country from pursuing expansionist monetary policies. In this setup, however, exchange rate parities need to be credible, that is costly to change.

The concept of an independent conservative monetary authority is absent from the Articles of Agreement, and so are "private" convertibility rules. While the price of gold maintained an important role of reference, countries were not heavily constrained in changing their own gold parities through changes in dollar parities. Such constraints, as historical experience demonstrated (see, in particular, Houthakker 1978) appeared more binding in the case of the U.S., although—as Giavazzi and Giovannini

(1989) stress—this could simply be a reflection of the asymmetry of the Bretton Woods regime.

3.5   Empirical Evidence on the Credibility of the Gold Standard and Bretton Woods Rules

In section 3.2 I have argued that the main implication of the models proving the superiority of monetary rules over discretion is that such rules help stabilize expectations. In this section I complement the discussion of the theory and of the historical record with empirical evidence. This evidence is meant to illustrate the behavior of expectations during the gold standard and Bretton Woods.

The strategy is to study prices in those markets where monetary authorities should have followed the rules; to derive estimates of private expectations, and to determine whether, and in what direction, such expectations were significantly affected by the monetary rules. The literature on the "rules of the game" discussing central bank policies under the gold standard—sometimes extended to fixed exchange rates in general—often mentions "rules" of behavior for central banks that are supposedly required to make the gold standard work. The "rules of the game" should not be confused with the rules studied here. The rules of the game are policies meant to assure that the central banks will not generate too large gold outflows or inflows, thus permitting gold convertibility both at home and abroad. They are arbitrary, in the sense that they rely on assumptions about the effects of central-bank operations on financial markets and gold flows.[22] By contrast, the monetary rules discussed here are specific actions that central banks were required to take (like convertibility of banknotes into gold at a given official price), which were often codified by laws and well known to all market participants.

The markets where authorities should have followed monetary rules are the financial markets, the gold market during the gold standard and the foreign exchange market during the Bretton Woods regime. In addition to being more focused, an analysis of financial markets has two other advantages over an analysis based on the study of inflation and output performances: it does not require assumptions about the transmission of monetary policy to the rest of the economy and can rely on better quality data.

The basic exercise carried out below is as follows. The gold standard and Bretton Woods rules imply a range within which exchange rates are supposed to fluctuate. From interest rates and forward exchange rates it is possible to derive estimates of expectations of exchange-rate changes. Below, I will try to determine whether exchange rate expectations were:

- consistent with the parities implied by the international rules;
- affected by those rules, and in what direction.

I consider samples from the classical gold standard period and the Bretton Woods years. The interwar gold standard is not included because the extreme political instability and economic fluctuations in the interwar years have likely added substantial volatility in financial markets, thus complicating the interpretation of the evidence.

3.5.1 The Data

3.5.1.1 Foreign Exchange Markets and Fluctuation Bands during the Gold Standard
Foreign exchange rates during the gold standard were stabilized by gold. Private citizens could convert national currencies into gold, and *vice versa* in transactions with national monetary authorities. Gold parities of individual national currencies implied bilateral exchange rates.

However, since arbitrage between the gold market and the foreign exchange market was costly, the bilateral exchange rates implied by the gold parities were not enough to tie down foreign exchanges in the financial markets. Exchange rates could fluctuate within a band whose size was determined by the costs of arbitrage between financial markets and the gold market. This band well exceeded the buying and selling points for gold used by central banks.

How did such arbitrage take place? Suppose, for example, that the dollar price of sterling in financial markets is less than the dollar price of sterling implied by the gold parity. The arbitrage consists in buying sterling for dollars in the financial market, and selling sterling for dollars through the monetary authorities. Hence, sterling should be brought to the Bank of England for conversion into gold, gold should be shipped to the U.S., and dollars should be bought from the U.S. Treasury in exchange for gold.

Since however these operations take time, a proper account of the costs of the transactions should reflect the interest cost represented by the shipment of gold. Figures 3.1 and 3.2 show a diagram of the transactions involved in the arbitrage. Figure 3.1 describes the case of export of gold from England to the U.S. At time 0, dollars are borrowed to purchase

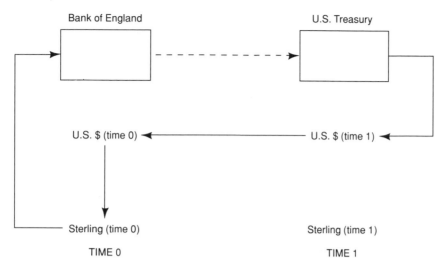

Figure 3.1
Scheme of arbitrage transactions: Export of gold from Britain to the United States

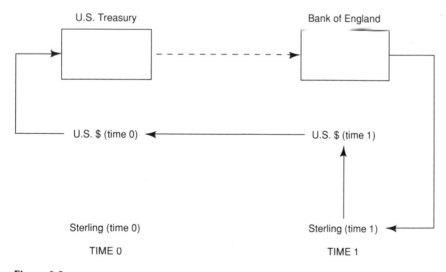

Figure 3.2
Scheme of arbitrage transactions: Export of gold from the United States to Britain

sterling in the spot foreign exchange market. Gold is bought from the Bank of England and is shipped to the U.S. When gold arrives at time 1 it is sold to the U.S. Treasury, and the proceeds are used, in part, to repay the dollar loan. Figure 3.2 describes arbitrage involving imports of gold into England. The sterling proceeds of the gold sale are sold in the forward exchange market, at a price fixed at time 0. Hence the transactions in the two figures all occur at prices known to the arbitrageur at time 0. The purchases of sterling and dollars necessary to start the operations could be financed with an alternative set of transactions, which are easy to figure out using the diagrams. To the extent that covered interest parity holds, the cost of these alternative transactions is approximately equal to the cost of the transactions reported in the figures.

In the case of the dollar-sterling exchange, monthly gold points are computed following Clark (1984) and Officer (1986), over the period January 1889 to December 1908. The cost of shipping gold is broken down into the interest cost (borrowing money to buy gold) or the opportunity cost (foregone interest during the voyage) and the direct costs (freight, insurance, packing, minting and abrasion). Whenever the spot exchange rate (dollar per pound) is lower than the official exchange rate discounted by the cost, it is profitable to import from Britain to the U.S.:

$$S_t < \frac{X}{Y}\left(\frac{1}{(1+i_{us})^{k/365}+c}\right) \tag{1}$$

X is the official dollar price of one ounce of "fine" gold as paid or received by the U.S. Treasury, i.e. \$20.67183.[23] Y is the official pound sterling price of one ounce of fine gold as paid or received by the Bank of England, i.e. £4.2409–4.2477.[24] X/Y is the official exchange rate or "mint parity," i.e. \$4.8666–4.8744 per pound sterling. S_t is the cable currency spot exchange rate (expressed in dollars per pound sterling) at time t, reported in London at the end of the first week of each month. The interest rate in the U.S., i_{us}, is the monthly average of the weekly average call money rates in New York during the period of shipping. The interest cost is calculated during the period of voyage between London and New York. Following Clark (1984), I assume that the arbitrageur finances his gold shipments in his country of residence. The direct shipping costs, c, consist of freight and insurance costs, packing, loading and unloading, abrasion, charges for assay and minting and finally incidental expenses. The costs are expressed as a percentage of the initial dollar investment. k is the transatlantic shipping time from London to New York.

An import gold point (import to the U.S. from Britain) is therefore expressed as:

$$G_t^I = \frac{X}{Y}\left(\frac{1}{(1+i_{us})^{k/365} + c}\right) \tag{2}$$

In order to determine whether it is profitable to export gold from the U.S., one has to take into account the exchange risk involved in receiving the proceeds of the gold shipment in foreign currencies at the end of the voyage. For a given length of the voyage, such risk can be eliminated by taking a forward exchange contract whereby pounds are converted into dollars at the rate F_t (dollars per pounds) at the date of reception of the gold. Whenever the forward rate is greater than the official exchange rate discounted by the shipping cost it is profitable to export gold from the U.S.:

$$F_t > \frac{X}{Y}\left((1+i_{us})^{k/365} + c\right) \tag{3}$$

Assuming that covered interest parity holds I compute the forward rate F_t for conversion of pounds into dollars at the date $t + k$ as.

$$F_t = S_t\left(\frac{1+i_{us}}{1+i_{uk}}\right)^{k/365} \tag{4}$$

Thus the gold export point becomes:

$$G_t^X = \frac{X}{Y}\left((1+i_{us})^{k/365} + c\right)\left(\frac{1+i_{uk}}{1+i_{us}}\right)^{k/365} \tag{5}$$

The British interest rate used, i_{uk}, is the weekly average of call money rate in London taken the first Friday of each month.

I calculate the gold points using the average direct costs of Officer (1889–1904: 0.65%–1905–1908: 0.5%). Clark and Officer differ in their calculations because the former does not include the cost of abrasion, minting and assay. The duration of the voyage between New York and London was estimated to range between 7 and 14 days. Following Goodhart (1969) I assume a fixed length of 10 days, i.e. $k = 10$. I ignore commissions costs in the financial markets for lack of accurate data.

To compute the gold points between Berlin and London and Paris and London I use the same formulas as above but change both the time and the costs of shipping gold between the respective cities. Following Einzig's (1931) estimation of shipping time and costs, I take $k = 3$ days between London and Berlin, and $k = 1$ day between London and Paris. I estimate the cost of shipping from London to Berlin to be $c = 0.02\%$ and the cost of shipping from London to Paris to be $c = 0.025\%$.

I study the joint behavior of interest rates, exchange rates and the gold points. The criteria adopted in the choice of interest rates are matching maturity, international tradeability and comparable default-risk characteristics. Given the data I was able to access, the securities that most closely approximate the above criteria are:

• For Britain, the prime bill rate, of 90 day maturity. It is the rate at which British banks discount "first class" bills. Once banks have "accepted" such bills, they become tradeable in a secondary market in London, where actors include discount houses and commercial banks. The prime bills rates were almost identical to the Treasury bills rate, which were not traded heavily until World War I. See Capie and Webber (1985).

• For the U.S., the commercial paper rate, of 60 to 90 day maturity. Issued in standard form by large distributors and manufacturers, eligible for rediscount, and with an active secondary market. See Macaulay (1938).

• For Germany, the market discount rate, of about 90 day maturity. This is the secondary market rate for bills accepted by the large incorporated banks and private banking houses. See Madden and Nadler (1935) and Bopp (1953).

• For France, the market rate of discount, of maturities ranging from 30 days to 6 months. The rates I used, taken from the U.S. National Monetary Commission (1910b) (which does not specify maturity), were very similar to the annual series of three-month rates reported by White (1933). This is a rate at which the large commercial banks bought in the market trade bills of the better quality. This secondary market was not as important as the London, New York or Berlin bills markets, because it lacked a strong group of intermediaries. Although most bills were discounted at the bank rate (which did not move for long periods of time), the market rate was much more sensitive to international financial news. (See White (1933, p. 201).)

3.5.1.2   *Foreign Exchange Markets and Fluctuation Bands during Bretton Woods*

For the Bretton Woods years, I assembled spot exchange rates, bilateral fluctuations bands, and forward rates for the period July 1955 to May 1971 (the time when the DM was floated), for the U.K., Germany and France relative to the U.S. While official convertibility of the pound, the

DM and the franc started only in December 1958, a well-developed foreign exchange market was allowed to operate since May 1953, when the authorities of eight European Payments Union members, including the three European countries mentioned above, agreed to standardize bilateral fluctuation margins to 75 percent on either side of their respective parities, and permitted commercial banks to trade their currencies freely within those bounds (Yaeger, 1966). My sample begins in July 1955 since that is the date when the forward rates published by Grubel (1966) start.

As I mentioned in section 3.4.3, the cornerstone of the IMF rules was the system of dollar or gold parities, around which spot exchange rates were permitted to fluctuate as far as 1 percent in either direction. Unlike the gold standard, under Bretton Woods bilateral fluctuation bands are fixed by law.

A major difference between the Bretton Woods regime and the classical gold standard is the widespread use of capital controls in the more recent regime. In many countries, international asset trade was encouraged only to the extent that it was needed to finance international goods trade. The IMF did not oppose these restrictive practices. As shown by Giovannini and Park (1992), if international trading firms cannot instantaneously shift their import and export flows by unlimited amounts to adapt to changes in interest rates, this form of restriction of capital account transactions induces wedges between interest rates in different countries. The implication is that domestic financial assets like treasury bills and interbank deposits cannot be considered internationally tradeable, and differentials between domestic and foreign interest rates include the tariff-equivalent of the quantitative capital restrictions mentioned above. For this reason, rather than studying interest-rate differentials I concentrate on forward premia. Forward premia are accurate measures of exchange-rate expectations to the extent that the required risk premia from foreign exchange speculation are small. Indeed, in the presence of capital controls deviations from covered interest-rate parity can be used as a tariff-equivalent measure of capital controls.[25]

3.5.2 The Evidence

3.5.2.1 Gold Standard

The gold points represent valid bounds for the fluctuations of exchange rates if all the transactions that are implied by them can take place at the given prices. A crucial link are the transactions with monetary authorities, exchanging gold for national currencies. The basic monetary rule of the gold standard is that monetary authorities should stand ready to exchange gold at the stated parity.

Figures 3.3, 3.4 and 3.5 report logs of the spot exchange rates of the pound relative to the dollar, the Reichsmark and the franc, respectively, together with my estimates of the gold points. I use logs to highlight the size of the fluctuation bands, which were less than 2 percent wide in the case of the dollar, and less than 1 percent wide in the case of the franc and the Reichsmark. Note also that the export (upper bound) and import (lower bound) points of gold fluctuate, especially in the case of the dollar. The estimates of the gold points for the U.S. dollar (figure 3.3) broadly match those of Officer (1986). The spot exchange rate touches the gold export point only on one occasion, in August 1895, most likely in correspondence of the collapse of the Morgan-Belmont syndicate.[26]

The Reichsmark rate (figure 3.4) crosses the import points on a few occasions in the three years after the Baring crisis of November 1890. The export point is touched in 1900, a year when stock prices collapsed, and many banks failed. A minor panic followed in December of that year. In March 1907, when another violation of the gold point is observed in figure 3.4 stock prices declined in Berlin and triggered a chain of bankruptcies. The franc crosses the gold point more often, but never by large amounts. Notice in particular the instance of the beginning of 1889, at the time of the collapse of the *Bourse* caused by the Panama Canal failure (January) and the breakdown of the copper corner (March).

Are the crossings of the gold points to be interpreted as unexploited arbitrage profit opportunities? I am reluctant to take that position, especially because my calculations do not account for commission in financial markets. It is conceivable that in periods of great uncertainty these commissions widen considerably, thus widening the gold points.

Figures 3.6, 3.7 and 3.8 plot the U.S., German and French interest rates together with bounds implied by the gold points. The two bounds are derived as follows. If the gold export point observed on any month is regarded by investors as the maximum value that the exchange rate can take over the maturity of short-term financial instruments, and if risk premia and other ex-ante rate-of-return differentials are second-order, then the interest rate on dollar, mark and franc assets can never exceed the following value:

$$\bar{R}_t = \left[(1 + R_t^*) \frac{\bar{S}}{S_t} - 1 \right],$$
(6)

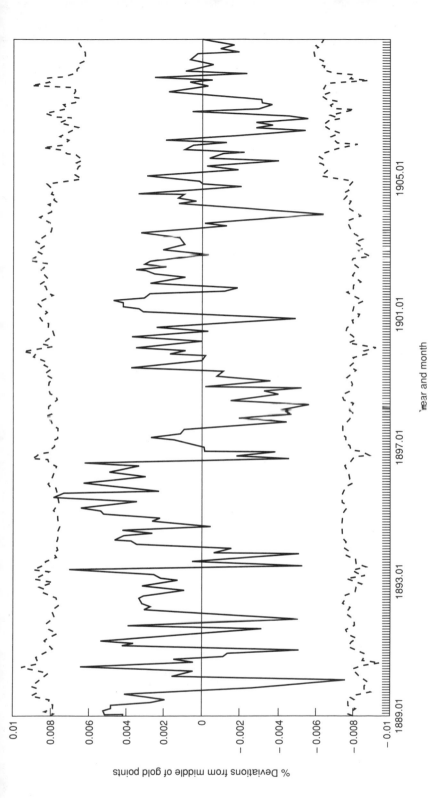

Figure 3.3
Dollar spot rate and gold points

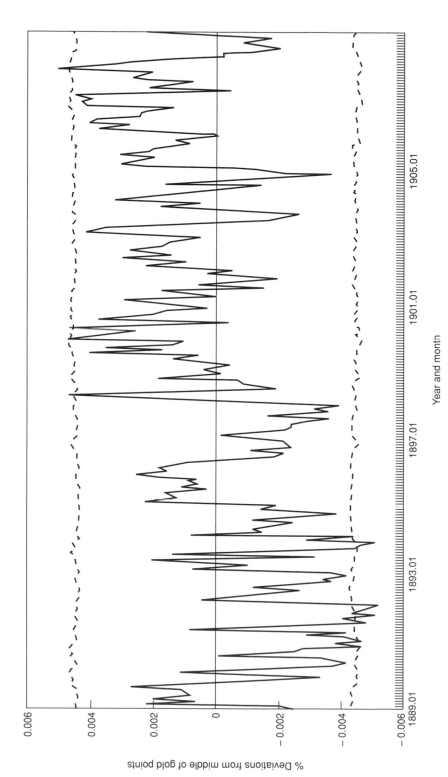

Figure 3.4
Reichsmark spot rate and gold points

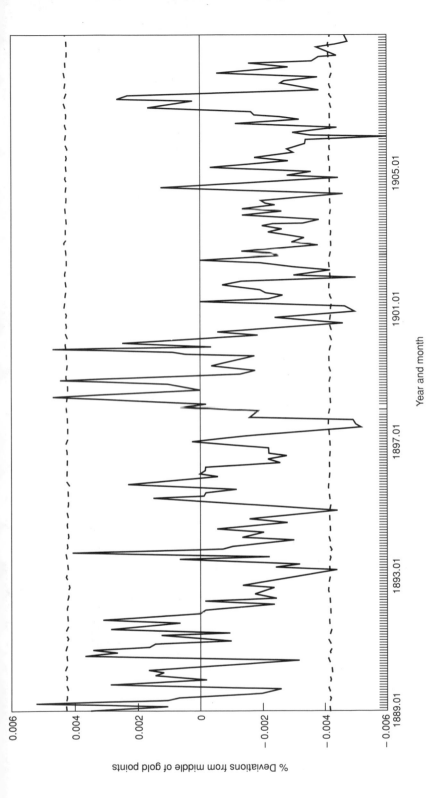

Figure 3.5
Franc spot rate and gold points

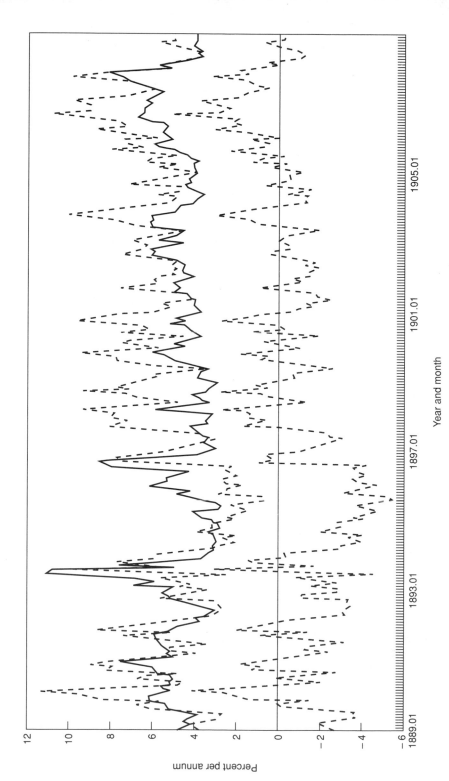

Figure 3.6
Dollar interest rate and credibility bounds

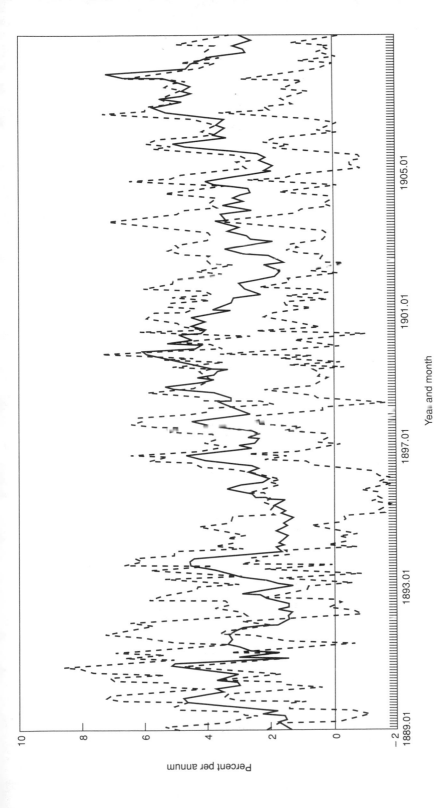

Figure 3.7
Reichsmark interest rate and credibility bounds

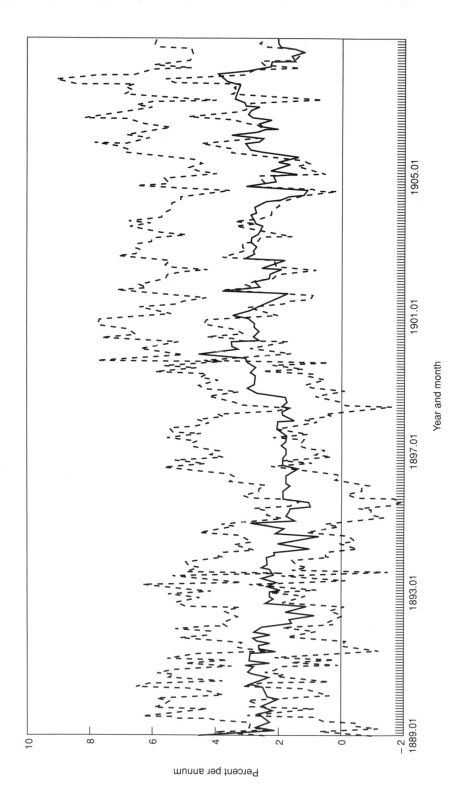

Figure 3.8
Franc interest rate and credibility bounds

where $\bar{S}$ denotes the gold export point, R^*_t is the rate of return on sterling financial assets in the money market, while S_t is the spot sterling exchange rate at time t. Similarly, the dollar, mark and franc money-market interest rates can never be lower than:

$$\underline{R}_t = \left[(1 + R^*_t) \frac{\underline{S}}{S_t} - 1 \right],$$ (7)

where $\underline{S}$ is the gold import point.

$\bar{R}_t$ and $\underline{R}_t$ are observable at every time t. If the actual interest rates denominated in dollars, marcs and francs at t are outside of these two bounds, either the margins are not credible—that is, agents expect that, *over the maturity of the interest rates considered*, the exchange rate can cross the margins—or required (ex-ante) rate-of-return differentials are non-zero (we assumed them to be zero to derive the upper and lower bounds for the interest rates).

The maintained assumption in these calculations is that investors do not require, ex ante, significantly different returns on assets denominated in different currencies. In other words, I assume that foreign exchange risk premia are insignificant. This assumption is corroborated by the lack of ability of asset pricing models to deliver sizable risk premia, given realistic processes for the variables driving risk and return in international financial markets.[27] Indeed, the observation that rate-of-return differentials in foreign exchange markets often seem to be highly persistent and therefore predictable might well be due to the phenomena discussed here, as for example in the famous case of the Mexican peso in 1976.

A complication of these calculations is that, as noted above, the gold points fluctuate stochastically. Therefore the appropriate thresholds for the calculations of the credibility bounds for interest rates are represented by the expectation of the gold points prevailing at the end of the maturity of the financial assets under consideration, under the assumption that gold parities are not changed. In practice, the fluctuation of bounds reported in figures 3.6 to 3.8 accounted for by the fluctuation of gold points is not recognizable with the naked eye. To verify this, I reproduced the three figures assuming constant gold points, equal to the average of the numbers computed above. The figures thus obtained were indistinguishable from figures 3.6 to 3.8.

Figure 3.6 shows that the dollar rate of interest is almost always within its credibility bounds. The big exceptions are the May–August 1893 financial panic and the 1895–96 period. In May–August 1893 convertibility was suspended and later a number of large non-financial business went bankrupt and stock prices declined. In the second half of 1895 the Belmont-Morgan syndicate collapsed (see above), in 1896 there was a bank panic with a decline in stock prices. In general, U.S. interest rates maintain consistently close to the upper bound. In the case of the Reichsmark, reported in figure 3.7, the upper credibility bound is surpassed clearly in 1907, at a time of the U.S. financial crisis, which was accompanied by stock price declines and business failures in Berlin. In the case of the franc (figure 3.8) the crossing of the bounds occur mostly—but not by large amounts—at the lower level, except for the January 1889 stock exchange collapse due to the Panama canal crisis mentioned above.

In general, figures 3.6, 3.7 and 3.8 suggest that the international co-movement of interest rates was substantial, and could very well be due to the credibility of the gold standard, which induced the belief that exchange rates could not cross the gold points.

Figures 3.9, 3.10 and 3.11 contain scatter plots, relating the percent deviation of the spot exchange rate from the middle of the gold points to the interest-rate differential. Under the hypothesis that the gold-standard rules stabilize expectations, such relation should be negative: the expected exchange-rate change decreases whenever the spot exchange rate reaches the upper fluctuation limit, and vice versa. The figures show that the relation is positive for the U.S. dollar, and negative for the Reichsmark and the franc. For all three currencies such relation is, however, not significant.

The absence of a negative relation between interest-rate differentials and the position of the exchange rate within the band raises a question about the credibility of the bands. Indeed, one would expect this relation not to be negative whenever agents forecast either suspensions of convertibility or changes in gold parities. Expectations of parity adjustments would interfere with the expectation of mean reversion of the exchange rates induced by the presence of the band. In this specific sense the rules of convertibility under the gold standard would not have much stabilizing power.

To obtain more precise estimates of expectations of parity adjustments, I rely on the method originally developed by Rose and Svensson (1991) and Svensson (1991), and modified by Chen and Giovannini (1991). The time-varying conditional expectation of devaluations is obtained by subtracting from the interest-rate differential 95 percent confidence bounds for the conditional expectation of exchange rate depreciation within the fluctuation band. The latter is computed, as in Chen and Giovannini (1991), from the projection of a nonlinear transformation of the exchange rate within the band into variables in agents' information sets.[28] The non-

Interest-rate differential

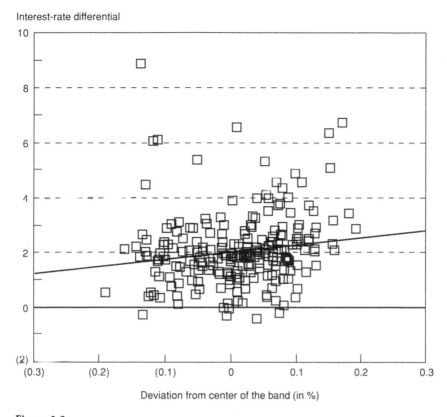

Deviation from center of the band (in %)

Figure 3.9
Relation between the interest rate differential and the position of the exchange rate in the band (dollar)

linear transformation is a way of making sure that agents actively exploit the information about the existence of the gold points.

The results for these calculations are a band for the null hypothesis of no changes in convertibility rules or gold parities expected for month τ. The null hypothesis is not rejected whenever zero is included in the bands' interval at month τ. These bands are reported in figures 3.12, 3.13 and 3.14. Only in the case of the U.S. dollar the 95 percent confidence intervals can be seen to move away from zero by sizable amounts, in the two years noted above, 1893 and 1895. This is not the case of the Reichsmark and the franc, despite the fact that for these two currencies fluctuation bands are roughly half the size of the dollar fluctuation bands. Thus, figures 3.12, 3.13 and 3.14 are consistent with the evidence from the scatter plots: figure 3.9 shows that the relation between the interest-rate differential and the position of the dollar/sterling rate in the band is

Interest-rate differential

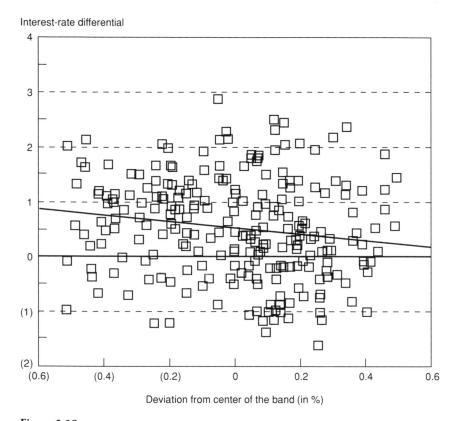

Deviation from center of the band (in %)

Figure 3.10
Relation between the interest rate differential and the position of the exchange rate in the band (Reichsmark)

positive (but insignificant), unlike the case of the franc and the Reichsmark. The absence of a stabilizing feature of the dollar/sterling gold points is most likely caused by the sizable fluctuations in expected gold parity changes.

3.5.2.2 Bretton Woods
Figures 3.15, 3.16 and 3.17 report the 3-month forward rates—Deutsche marks per dollar, sterling per dollar, French franc per dollar—together with the Bretton Woods fluctuation bands for the three currencies. These figures are equivalent to the plots of interest rates and credibility bounds reported for the gold standard. If the forward rate is a good proxy for the expected future spot exchange rate, a movement of the forward rate beyond the Bretton Woods limit indicates lack of credibility of the fixed-exchange-rate system.

Interest-rate differential

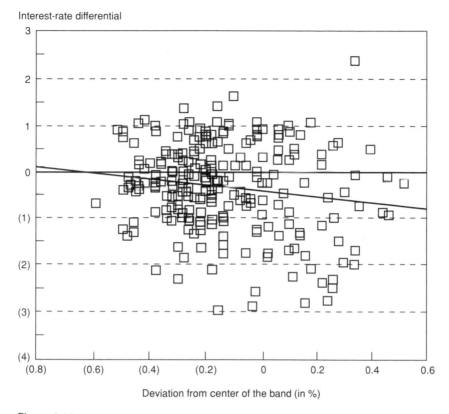

Deviation from center of the band (in %)

Figure 3.11
Relation between the interest rate differential and the position of the exchange rate in the band (franc)

In the case of the DM (Figure 3.15), the forward rate goes out of the bounds immediately after the 1961 realignment and, more noticeably, before the October 1969 revaluation. The 1969 episode was noted (Argy, 1981) as a franc-mark crisis, characterized by heavy speculative activity involving these two currencies. Figure 3.17 shows that, before the franc devaluation of August 1969, the forward rate reaches the upper fluctuation band for that currency. Figure 3.17 also shows that the largest deviation of the forward rate from the Bretton Woods bounds for the French franc occurs in September, November and December 1956 at the time of the Algeria and Suez crises. The experience of sterling is reported in figure 3.16. The forward rate exceeds the upper fluctuation limit at the time of the Suez crisis, and, significantly, after the November 1967 devaluation of sterling. As Tew (1977) notes, however, the Bank of England intervened in the forward market for sterling from the last quarter of 1964

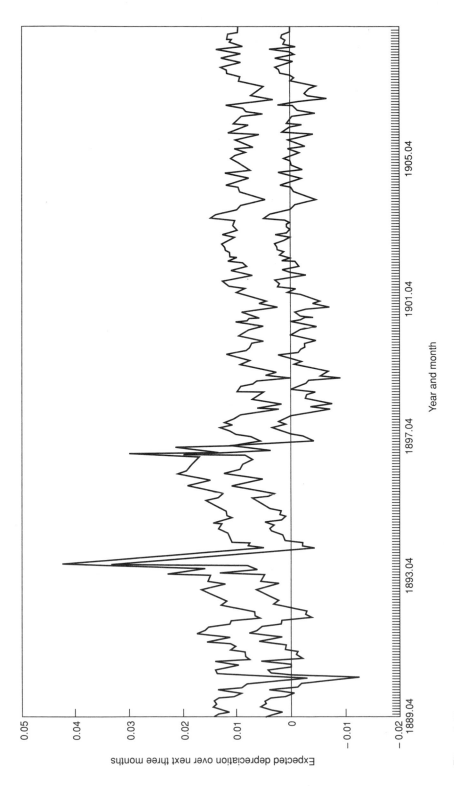

Figure 3.12
95 percent confidence intervals for the expected depreciation of the dollar

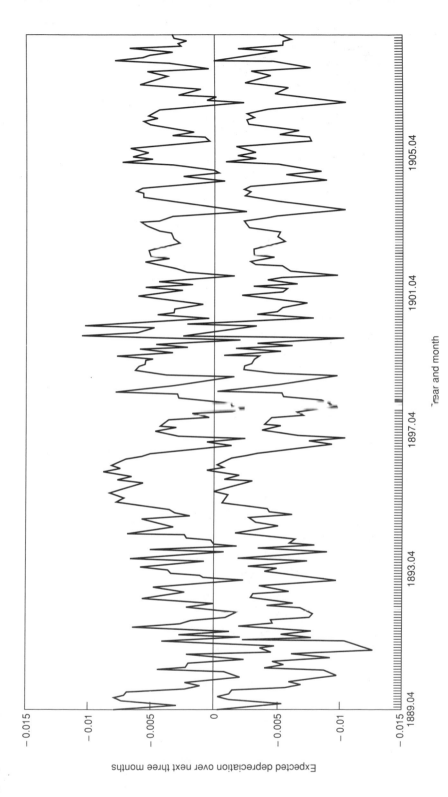

Figure 3.13
95 percent confidence intervals for the expected depreciation of the Reichsmark

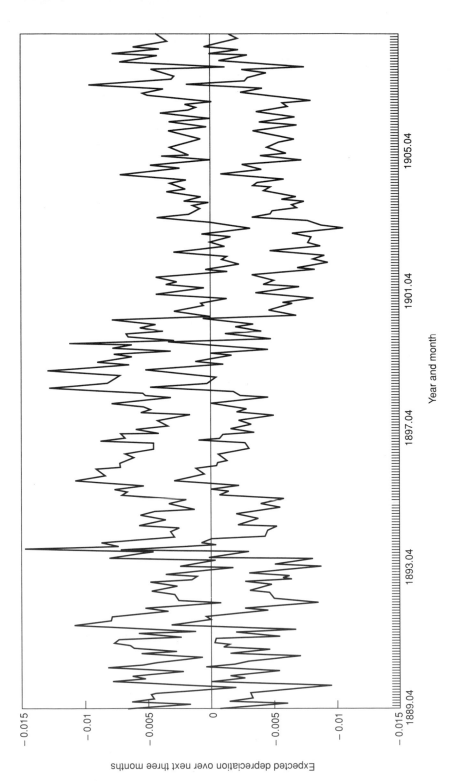

Figure 3.14
95 percent confidence intervals for the expected depreciation of the franc

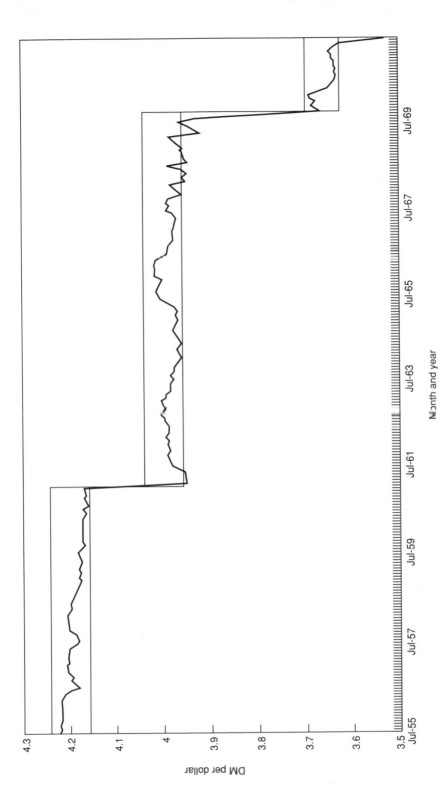

Figure 3.15
Deutsche mark/dollar three-month forward rate and parity bounds

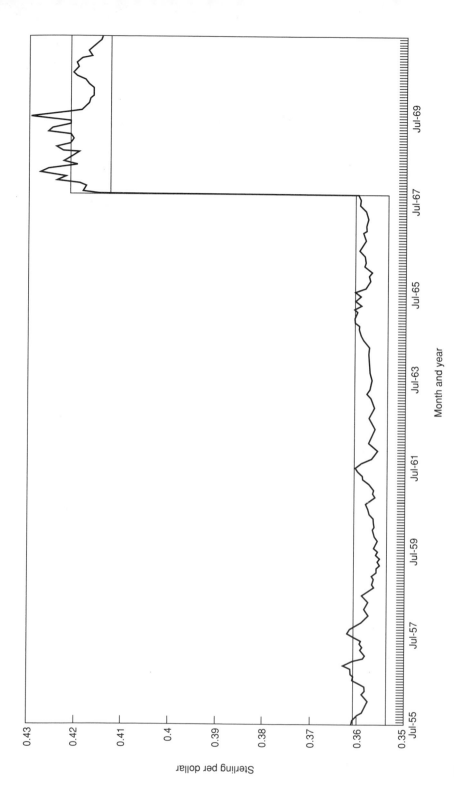

Figure 3.16
Sterling/dollar three-month forward rate and parity bounds

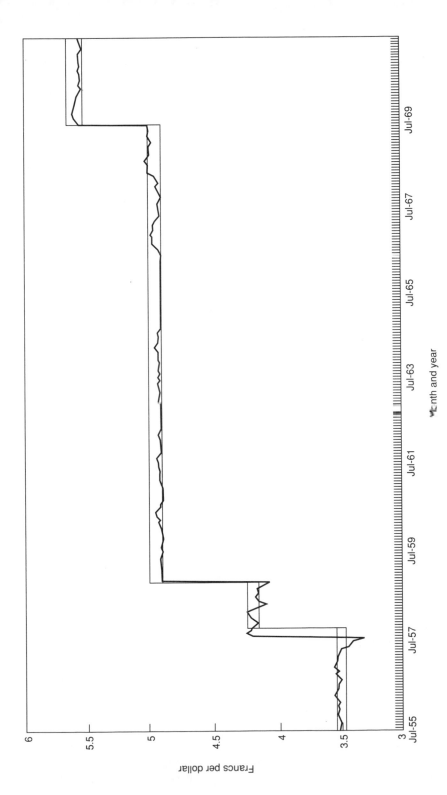

Figure 3.17
French franc/dollar three-month forward rate and parity bounds

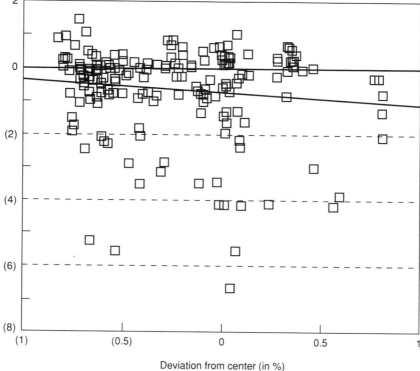

Figure 3.18
Relation between the forward premium and the position of the exchange rate in the band
(Deutsche mark)

to the devaluation of 1967. Whether these interventions were successful at keeping the forward premium below the level that reflected expectations of devaluation of sterling remains an open question.

Figures 3.18 and 3.19 show the scatter relations between the percent deviations of spot exchange rates from central parities and forward premia for the Deutsche mark and sterling. An equivalent figure for the French franc is missing, because of data problems with the market spot exchange rate for that country. For both currencies the diagrams do not show any systematic relation. Once again, this result might be due to the substantial fluctuations of the expected changes in the central parities of both the Deutsche mark and sterling, reported in figures 3.20 and 3.21. The figures reproduce calculations from Chen and Giovannini (1991), along the lines described above.[29] In the case of both currencies there are significant and sizable expectations of parity realignments towards the end

Forward premium (in % per annum)

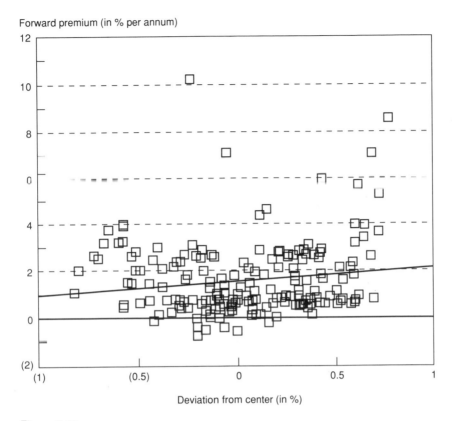

Deviation from center (in %)

Figure 3.19
Relation between the forward premium and the position of the exchange rate in the band (sterling)

of the sample. In the case of the Deutsche mark, expectations of revaluation are also observed in correspondence to the March 1961 realignment.

3.5.3   Discussion of the Evidence

The evidence presented above can be summarized as follows. For the gold standard period, we find that fluctuation bands are particularly narrow in the case of European currencies (Reichsmark and franc), while the dollar/ sterling band is of comparable magnitude to those of Bretton Woods. The narrow European bands appeared to be quite effective in linking sterling, franc and mark interest rates. There is some evidence of stability of expectations induced by the bands, measured by a negative correlation between interest rate differential and the position of exchange rates in the bands. This negative correlation, however, is not very strong in the

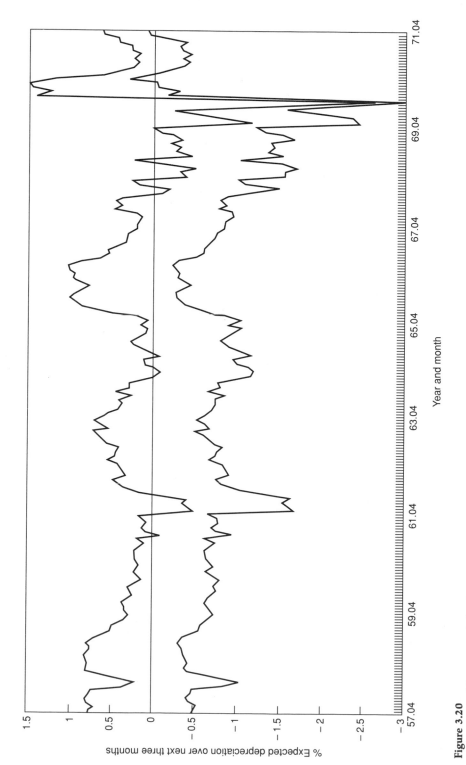

Figure 3.20
95 percent confidence intervals for the expected depreciation of the Deutsche mark

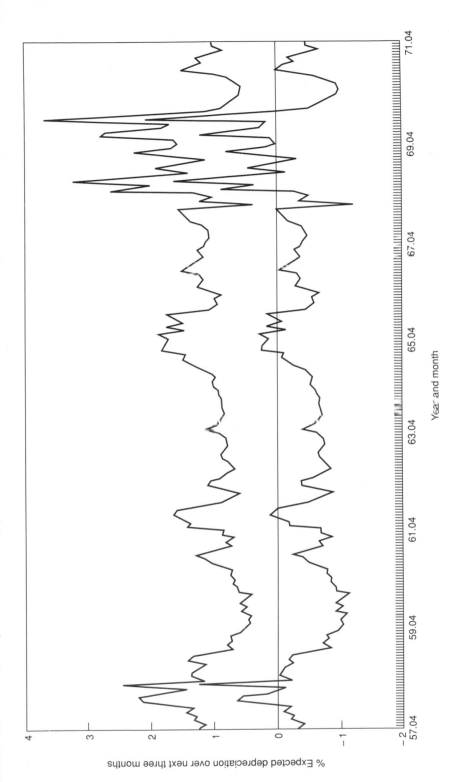

Figure 3.21
95 percent confidence intervals for the expected depreciation of sterling

% Expected depreciation over next three months

Year and month

sample. Tests of credibility of the convertibility rules do not seem to indicate that sizable violations of convertibility rules were expected to occur in the case of the franc and Reichsmark.

In the case of Bretton Woods the stabilizing properties of fluctuation bands appear to be even weaker than in the case of the gold standard, witness the less systematic relations between forward premia and the position of the sterling and Deutsche mark exchange rates in the bands. Estimates of expected exchange rate realignments appear sizable and significant towards the end of the Bretton Woods period, and surely explain, at least in part, the absence of systematic evidence on the stabilizing properties of the bands.

The natural question raised by this evidence is, was the gold standard a more credible regime than Bretton Woods? The discussion of the historical record suggests a positive reply, but the statistical evidence presented above is inconclusive. The evidence is inconclusive because it is a comparison of the two regimes which does not explicitly account for the exogenous shocks hitting the countries included in the samples. Hence the evidence cannot tell whether a world economy that functions under a gold standard can withstand turbulence better than a world economy functioning under a Bretton-Woods-type regime.

Despite the fact that the evidence presented above cannot be exploited to make statements about the relative credibility of the two regimes, the covariation of national interest rates during the gold standard seems particularly striking. It is striking because of the size of the fluctuation bands implied by the gold points. On average, the gold points fluctuation bands for European currencies were about half those prevailing during the Bretton Woods years for the same European currencies relative to the dollar. Despite these narrow bands, interest-rate differentials very rarely reflected expectations of exchange-rate changes outside the band. While the maturity of the interest rates somewhat decreases the power of the credibility tests of the previous section, it should be recalled that, for example, in the case of the European Monetary System fluctuation bands are as wide as 4.5 percent, and yet 3-month interest rates have violated them in several instances.[30]

3.6 Concluding Remarks

This chapter has looked at the Bretton Woods system from the perspective of a theory of the history of international monetary systems based on rules and discretion in monetary policy.

An application of the rules-cum-escape-clauses view of the history of the world monetary system runs into a number of problems. First, it is not clear that the model can be applied as is to fixed exchange-rate regimes under a fiat currency system. The difficulty of associating fixed exchange rates with monetary rules is a crucial one, given that the Bretton Woods regime cannot be likened to a commodity standard: banknotes were not convertible into gold, monetary authorities were not required to intervene in the gold market. Hence, even conceptually, it is not clear whether the return to fixed exchange rates after WWII is to be considered a reinstatement of a monetary rule.

The second, and probably most serious, problem of this theory of the world monetary system comes from an analysis of the historical record on the setup of the Bretton Woods institutions. In the second postwar period policymakers brushed aside the concept that credible monetary commitments are valuable—a concept used to justify the return to gold in the interwar years—and attempted to substitute the fixed convertibility rules of the gold standard with some form of monetary policy coordination. This compromise solution was probably caused by the keen resistance of the British delegation against any codification in the IMF Articles of Agreement of rules which would have forced a degree of monetary discipline on individual member countries' monetary authorities. Hence this compromise solution is the best evidence that the return to fixed exchange rates in the second postwar was not considered to be the reestablishment of monetary rules over discretion.

Analysis of the behavior of interest rates and exchange rates under the gold standard and Bretton Woods indicates that at times of large shocks official parities were not credible. In general, however, the statistical evidence is ambiguous on whether monetary rules have been credible under the gold standard and the Bretton Woods regime, or on whether one regime was more credible than the other. Yet, the data show that the very narrow gold standard bands contributed to keep European interest rates within narrow margin for many years. However, the emergence of significant realignments expectations in a number of cases is evidence not inconsistent with the rules-cum-escape clauses view of the world.

In sum, this chapter has shown that there might be value in credible monetary rules, witnessed by the stability of interest rates in a number of different periods, but that the return to fixed rates after WWII was not inspired by the desire to reinstate credible international monetary rules. This was probably because the interwar experience made the return to gold anachronistic and, as reiterated by the 1982 Gold Commission, impractical. The alternative sought out by the builders of the IMF was however little credible.

The rejection of the rules-cum-escape-clauses model raises the question of alternative interpretation of the evolution of the world monetary system. How then do we interpret the periodic returns to fixed exchange rates? Several authors do not seem to subscribe to the theory of rules and discretion explaining the abandoning and return to the gold standard. For example, Dornbusch and Frenkel (1984), following Keynes (1930), have argued that gold convertibility was always suspended if there was a need to. Dornbusch and Frenkel, like Keynes, do not claim that the resumption of convertibility was motivated by the value of the gold standard as a rule: while concentrating on the ease with which rules were abandoned, they are silent on the reasons to readopt them. They probably would subscribe to Temin's (1991) view that the gold standard was just regarded as the "normal" way of operating the world monetary system.

One alternative to the simple escape-clauses model probably inspired the officials who amended Article IV of the IMF Articles of Agreement (French and U.S. delegations in Rambouillet in November 1975, Williamson (1977)), which allowed countries to choose the exchange-rate regime they please. This theory is based on a Poole-like analysis of output fluctuations under alternative exchange-rate regimes,[31] and stresses the role of different shocks and their transmission under fixed and flexible rates as the main determinants of the choice of fixing or floating a country's currency. In a nutshell, this theory states that when LM shocks prevail, fixed exchange rates are superior, while floating rates are more desirable when IS shocks are more frequent. I do not know of attempts at applying this theory to the historical record, and I suspect that such attempts could be arduous, given the difficulty in identifying IS versus LM shocks.

I would propose a second alternative, inspired by several observations by Milton Friedman (see, for example, Friedman, 1968). According to this view, fixed rates, as well as floating rates, are abandoned because governments "try to do too much" with monetary policy instruments, necessarily lead monetary regimes to strains or breakdown, and are then drawn to experiment with alternative arrangements. In other words, this view maintains that in modern economies the pressures on monetary authorities to affect the allocation of resources probably far exceed the actual ability of monetary authorities to affect the real economy, given by the instruments at their disposal. This tension is what generates cycles in monetary regimes.

An exploration of these alternative models is called for to help refine the theory of monetary institutions, and improve our understanding of the history of the international monetary system.

Appendix A: Data Sources

A.1   Gold Standard

The period covered is January 1889 to December 1908. The National Monetary Commission (1910b) volumes have been used for the following data:

• Britain weekly average call money rate reported the first Friday of every month: Table 18, pp. 43–62.

• France market rates of discount reported the first Thursday of each month from weekly averages. Table 4, pp. 315–316.

• London spot exchange rates for dollar/pound, Mark/pound and franc/pound reported the end of the first week of each month. The monthly data between 1889 and 1898 are in Table 3, pp. 67–69 and the weekly data from 1899 to 1908 are in Table 4, pp. 70–74.

The U.S. call money rate and the U.S. commercial paper rate are reported in Macaulay (1938). The original source is the *Commercial and Financial Chronicle and its Financial Review*. The data I use are in the Macaulay's appendix, pp. A150–A154. Both the call money rates and the commercial paper rates are given monthly and represent averages of weekly data. The commercial paper rates have maturities of 60 to 90 days.

The British Prime Bank Bill rate is reported in Capie and Weber (1985, Table III.(10), column V, pp. 509–512). The original source is *The Economist*. The data are end-of-month and have a maturity of three months.

The German market rates of discount are reported in Bopp (1953, Appendix pp. 79–87). They are monthly averages of market discount rates. The original source is *Die Reichsbank, 1876–1910*.

The estimation of the costs and duration of shipping between London, Paris and Berlin is based on the calculations of Einzig (1931, Appendix pp. 148–154). For the costs and duration of the voyage between London and New York I follow the estimations of Clark and Officer.

A.2   Bretton Woods

The data for the spot exchange rates and the 3-month forward exchange rates for the United Kingdom, Germany and France from January 1957 to December 1960 are reported in Grubel (1966). All rates are end-of-month figures for weekly averages of daily observations. The original sources of the data are the Dresdner Bank, the Samuel Montagu's Review of Foreign Exchanges and the Morgan Guaranty Trust Company.

British, German and French spot and forward exchange rates from January 1961 to May 1971 were obtained from the International Financial Statistics of the International Monetary Fund. All rates are end-of-month figures. The spot rates are market rates and the 3-month forward rates are reported as annual discounts or premiums on the spot rates.

Notes

1. The latter claimed that a set of rules for monetary policy are the hallmark of a liberal system, while discretion, that is active management of the currency, "along with protectionism, is the prototype of all current 'planning' schemes." (1936, p. 3).

2. See, in particular, the surveys in Persson and Tabellini (1991) and Canzoneri and Henderson (1991).

3. On adjustment during Bretton Woods, see the paper by Maurice Obstfeld in this volume.

4. See also Persson and Tabellini (1991) for an illustration and a discussion of these models, as well as Lohmann (1990) and Flood and Isard (1990). Grossman and Van Huick (1988) exploit the same idea in an analysis of government debt repudiation.

5. In the paper by de Kock and Grilli (1989) the public punishes the authority which adopts a discretionary strategy even under "normal" realizations of the exogenous shock by reverting to floating exchange rates forever.

6. See Giavazzi and Pagano (1988).

7. See Bloomfield (1959).

8. Eichengreen (1992) also emphasizes the importance of these swap facilities. However, these swap facilities were informal, not codified in any official agreement.

9. See Eichengreen (1992).

10. See Eichengreen (1992) for a discussion.

11. Despite the fact that the countries participating to the Bretton Woods conference—the so-called United Nations—were 44.

12. For a discussion of the U.S.-British negotiations preceding the 1943 proposals, see in particular Gardner (1969). The relevant episode is the Atlantic conference of 1941 during which the general U.S. stance, multilateralism and nondiscrimination, was adopted by the Britain. At the same time the Lend-Lease program became law, and allowed the U.S. president discretion in assisting any country, but especially Britain, whose defense was considered vital for the U.S..

13. "It is widely held that control of capital movement, both inward and outward, should be a permanent feature of the postwar system." p. 17, para 33.

14. British Information Services (1943b, p.13)

15. Keynes writes to Richard Kahn in August 1941:

In the past five hundred years there have been only two periods of about fifty years each (the ages of Elizabeth and Victoria in English chronology) when the use of money for the conduct of international trade can be said to have 'worked',—first whilst the prodigious augmentation of the supply of silver from the new world was substituting the features of inflation for those of deflation (bringing a different sort of evil with it), and again in the second half of the nineteenth century when (for reasons to be developed below) the system of international investment pivoting on London transferred the *onus* of adjustment from the debtor to the creditor position.

To suppose that there exists some smoothly functioning automatic mechanism of adjustment which preserves equilibrium if only we trust to methods of *laissez-faire* is a doctrinaire delusion which disregards the lessons of historical experience without having behind it the support of sound theory. Keynes (1980, p. 21–22.).

16. The plan adds two transitional provisions for the immediate postwar period. The planadds two transitional provisions, for the immediate postwar period, meant to make the procedure of exchange-rate adjustments less restrictive, with a view that equilibrium rates might be harder to determine immediately at the end of World War II.

17. J. M. Keynes, in his presentation in the House of Lords, suggested that this is in fact a misreading of the White plan, which advocated liberalization of only current transactions.

18. Bob Boothby, in his statement at the House of Commons "We can never go back to the gold standard [...] we can never tolerate any outside interference with our inalienable right to impose such restrictions on the export of capital from this country as we wish."

19. See Williams (1943).

20. The article does not explicitly say whether these bands apply only to the dollar exchange rates or to all possible bilateral exchange rates.

21. Exchange-rate realignments below 10 percent do not need the Fund's approval.

22. For a discussion, see Giovannini (1986).

23. The official buying and selling prices of gold at the U.S. Treasury were identical. By contrast, the Bank of England charged a bid-ask spread.

24. These numbers are obtained from Einzig (1931). The appropriate side of the spread is taken for each calculation of the gold points.

25. See the Appendix for a description of the data sources.

26. See Friedman and Schwartz (1963). Garber and Grilli (1986) also provide a discussion of this period.

27. A discussion of the evidence on risk premia in foreign exchange markets appears in Dornbusch and Giovannini (1990).

28. Specifically, let x_t be the percent deviation of the exchange rate from the center of the band at month t, let L is the half-width of the band, and let $y_{t+3} = \ln[(L + x_{t+3})/(L - x_{t+3})]$. I project y_{t+3} on information available at month t, (including x_t, the 3-month interest-rate differential, y_t^2 and y_t^3), since the interest rates I use have a maturity of 3 months. I then obtain conditional expectations for the left-hand side variable, and 95 percent confidence intervals for the conditional expectation. These are transformed to obtain 95 percent confidence intervals for x_{t+3}. The confidence intervals for the of future exchange rates within the fluctuation bands are then subtracted from the interest rate differentials (adjusted by the current position of the exchange rate in the band) to obtain 95 percent confidence intervals for the expected

devaluation. The procedure is complicated in the case of the gold standard because gold points have not been fixed over the years, and some violations of the gold points are observed. This complication is bypassed by taking the average gold points to compute the dependent variable in the projection equation described above, and taking the very few violations of the gold points to be almost of the edge of the newly computed band. Such manipulations of the data are, in a sense, consistent with the observation above: the observed "violations" of the gold points might actually not be such, since the computed gold points do not account for financial commissions, and these might have been particularly high at times of crises.

29. In this case the variables included in the projection equations were various dummies corresponding to the subperiods when given parities were prevailing, y_t, y_t^2, y_t^3, the interest-rate differential and the log of relative money supplies.

30. For a discussion of the credibility of EMS bands, see Giovannini (1990).

31. For an illustration, see Obstfeld (1988).

References

Anderson, B. M. 1944. *Postwar Stabilization of Foreign Exchange—The Keynes-Morgenthau Plan Condemned—Outline of a Fundamental Solution*, New York: Economists' National Committee on Monetary Policy.

Argy, V. 1981. *The Postwar International Money Crisis: An Analysis*, London: George Allen & Unwin

Barro, R. J. and D. Gordon 1983. "A Positive Theory of Monetary Policy in a Natural Rate Model," *Journal of Political Economy*, 91: 589–610.

Bloomfield, A. 1959. *Monetary Policy under the International Gold Standard: 1880–1914* New York: Federal Reserve Bank of New York.

Bopp, K. R. 1953. "Reichsbank Operations, 1876–1914," mimeo, Federal Reserve Bank of Philadelphia.

Bordo, M. D. and F. E. Kydland. 1990. "The Gold Standard as a 'Rule,'" NBER Working Paper 3367, (May).

British Information Services. 1943a. *International Clearing Union*, New York: British Information Services, (April 8).

British Information Services. 1943b. *Parliamentary Debates on an International Clearing Union*, New York: British Information Services, (July).

Calvo, G. 1978. "On the Time Consistency of Optimal Policy in a Monetary Economy," *Econometrica* 46, (November): 1411–1428.

Canzoneri, M. B. 1985. "Monetary Policy Games and the Role of Private Information," *American Economic Review*, 75, no. 5, (December): 1056–1070.

Canzoneri, M. B. and D. W. Henderson. 1991. *Monetary Policy in Interdependent Economies*, Cambridge, MA: MIT Press.

Capie, F. and A. Webber. 1985. *A Monetary History of the United Kingdom, 1870–1982*, London: George Allen & Unwin.

Chen, Z. and A. Giovannini. 1991. "Estimating Expected Exchange Rates under Target Zones,", mimeo, Columbia University, (December).

Clark, T. A. 1984. "Violations of the Gold Points, 1890–1908," *Journal of Political Economy*, 92: 791–823.

Cunliffe Committee. 1918. *First Interim Report on Currency and Foreign Exchanges After the War*, reprinted in B. Eichengreen, ed., *The Gold Standard in Theory and History*, New York: Methuen, 1985.

De Kock, G. and V. U. Grilli. 1989. "Endogenous Exchange Rate Regime Switches," NBER Working Paper n. 3066, (August).

Dornbusch, R. and J. Frenkel. 1984. "The Gold Standard Crisis of 1847," *Journal of International Economics*, 16: 1–27.

Dornbusch, R. and A. Giovannini. 1990. "Monetary Policy in the Open Economy," in B. M. Friedman and F. H. Hahn, eds., *Handbook of Monetary Economics*, Amsterdam: North Holland.

Eichengreen, B. 1992. *Golden Fetters: The Gold Standard and the Great Depression, 1919–1939*, New York: Oxford University Press.

Einzig P. 1931. *International Gold Movements*, London: Macmillan and Co. Ltd.

Fischer, S. 1980. "Dynamic Inconsistency, Cooperation and the Benevolent Dissembling Government," *Journal of Economic Dynamics and Control*, 2: 93–107.

Flood, R. P. and P. Isard. 1989a. "Monetary Policy Strategies," *International Monetary Fund Staff Papers* 36, (September): 612–632.

Flood, R. P. and P. Isard. 1989b. "Simple Rules, Discretion, and Monetary Policy," NBER Working Paper 2924.

Flood, R. P. and P. Isard. 1990. "Monetary Policy Strategies—A Correction: Reply to Lohmann," *International Monetary Fund Staff Papers* 37 (June): 446–448.

Ford, A. G. 1962. *The Gold Standard 1880–1914: Britain and Argentina*, Oxford: Oxford University Press.

Friedman, M. 1968. "The Role of Monetary Policy," *American Economic Review* 58 (March): 1–17.

Friedman, M. and A. J. Schwartz. 1963. *A Monetary History of the United States, 1867–1960*, Princeton, NJ: Princeton University Press.

Garber, P. M. and V. U. Grilli. 1986. "The Belmont-Morgan Syndicate as an Optimal Investment Banking Contract," *European Economic Review* 30 (June): 649–677.

Gardner, R. N. 1969. *Sterling-Dollar Diplomacy*—New, Expanded Edition, New York: McGraw Hill.

Giavazzi, F. and A. Giovannini. 1989. "Monetary Policy Interactions under Managed Exchange Rates," *Economica* 56 (May): 199–213.

Giavazzi, F. and M. Pagano. 1988. "The Advantages of Tying One's Hands: EMS Discipline and Central Bank Credibility," *European Economic Review* 32: 1055–1075.

Giovannini, A. 1986. "'Rules of the Game' During the International Gold Standard: England and Germany," *Journal of International Money and Finance* 5: 467–483.

Giovannini, A. 1990. "European Monetary Reform: Progress and Prospects," *Brookings Papers on Economic Activity* 2: 217–291. Also chapter 8 in this volume.

Giovannini, A. and J. W. Park. 1992. "Capital Controls and International Trade Finance," *Journal of International Economics*, 33, no. 3/4, November, pp. 285–304.

Goodhart, C. A. E. 1969. *The New York Money Market and the Finance of Trade: 1900–1913*, Cambridge, MA: Harvard University Press.

Grossman, H. I. and J. B. Van Huick. 1988. "Sovereign Debt as a Contingent Claim: Excusable Default, Repudiation and Reputation," *American Economic Review* 78: 1088–1097.

Grubel, H. G. 1966. *Forward Exchange, Speculation, and the International Flow of Capital*, Stanford, CA: Stanford University Press.

Houthakker, H. S. 1978. "The Breakdown of Bretton Woods," in W. Sichel, ed., *Economic Advice and Executive Policy*, New York: Praeger.

Kemmerer, E. W. 1945. "The Road to Bretton Woods," *The Commercial and Financial Chronicle*, (April 19).

Keynes, J. M. 1930. *A Treatise on Money*, London: Macmillan.

Keynes, J. M. 1980. *The Collected Writings of John Maynard Keynes—Volume XXV: Activities 1940–1944 Shaping the Postwar World: The Clearing Union*, London: Macmillan.

Kindleberger, C. P. 1984. *A Financial History of Western Europe*, London: George Allen & Unwin.

Kydland, F. E. and E. C. Prescott. 1977. "Rules Rather than Discretion: The Inconsistency of Optimal Plans," *Journal of Political Economy*, 85, N. 3, (June): 473–493.

Lohmann, S. 1990. "Monetary Policy Strategies—A Correction," *International Monetary Fund Staff Papers* 37 (June): 440–445.

Macaulay, F. R. 1938. *Some Theoretical Problems suggested by The Movements of Interest Rates, Bond Yields and Stock Prices in the United States since 1856*, New York: National Bureau of Economic Research.

Madden, J. T and M. Nadler. 1935. *The International Money Markets*, New York: Prentice-Hall, Inc.

Meltzer, A. H. 1988. *Keynes's Monetary Theory*, Cambridge: Cambridge University Press.

National Monetary Commission. 1910 *Statistics for the United States, 1867–1909*, Washington: Government Printing Office.

National Monetary Commission. 1910. *Statistics for Great Britain, Germany, and France, 1867–1909*, Washington: Government Printing Office.

Obstfeld, M. 1988. "Comment on Buiter," in J. A. Frenkel, ed., *International Aspects of Fiscal Policies*, Chicago: University of Chicago Press.

Officer, L. H. 1986. "The Efficiency of the Dollar-Sterling Gold Standard, 1890–1908," *Journal of Political Economy*, 94: 1038–73.

Persson, T. and G. E. Tabellini. 1991. *Macroeconomic Policy, Credibility and Politics*, New York: Harwood Academic Publishers.

Rogoff, K. 1985. "The Optimal Degree of Commitment to an Intermediate Monetary Target," *Quarterly Journal of Economics*, 100 (November): 1169–1190.

Rose, A. K. and L. E. O. Svensson. 1991. "Expected and Predicted Realignments: The FF/DM Exchange Rate during the EMS," Institute of International Economic Studies, Stockholm, Seminar Paper n. 485.

Scammel, W. M. 1965. "The Working of the Gold Standard," *Yorkshire Bullettin of Economic and Social Research* (May): 32–45.

Svensson, L. E. O. 1991. "Assessing Target Zone Credibility: Mean Reversion and Devaluation Expectations in the EMS," Institute of International Economic Studies, Stockhom, Seminar Paper n. 493.

Temin, P. 1991. *Lessons from the Great Depression*, Cambridge, MA: MIT Press.

Tew, B. 1977. *The Evolution of the International Monetary System 1945–77*, New York: John Wiley & Sons

U.S. Treasury. 1943. *Preliminary Draft Outline of a Proposal for An International Stabilization Fund of the United and Associated Nations*, Washington, D.C.: U.S. Treasury, (Revised July 10).

White, H.D. 1933. *The French International Accounts, 1880–1913*, Cambridge, MA: Harward University Press.

White, H. D. 1945. "The Monetary Fund: Some Criticism Examined," *Foreign Affairs* 23, n. 2, pp. 195–210 (January).

Williams, J. D. 1943. "Currency Stabilization: The Keynes and White Plans," *Foreign Affairs* 21, n. 4 (July): 645–658.

Williamson, J. 1977. *The Failure of World Monetary Reform, 1971–1974*, London: Nelson.

Yaeger, L. B. 1966. *International Monetary Relations*, New York: Harper and Row.

4

The Determinant of
Realignment Expectations
under the EMS: Some
Empirical Regularities

(with Zhaohui Chen, May 1992)

4.1 Introduction

One of the central questions in the theory of international monetary regimes is whether fixed but adjustable exchange rates are a contradiction in terms. In other words, can a system of adjustable parities survive? Is it, in some sense, stable? This question has dominated the policy debate on the European Monetary Systyem (EMS), especially since the liberalization of international capital movements in the second half of the 1980's. It also characterized the debate on exchange-rate based stabilizations, started by Diaz Alejandro (1981), Dornbusch (1982) and Calvo (1983).

Recent research in international finance, in particular the work of Flood and Garber (1984) and the empirical research in the vein of Lizondo (1983), has clearly and convincingly established the linkage between the collapse of a fixed exchange rate and expectations held by actors in financial markets. In addition, the analysis of the stabilizing properties of monetary policy rules—Simons (1936), Friedman (1968) and Barro and Gordon (1983)—has shown that the crucial channel through which such rules can stabilize inflation and economic activity is the behaviour of the private sector's expectations. Hence the "strength" or "weakness" of an adjustable rate system is directly related to the behaviour of expectations under such a regime.

This chapter is an exploration of the determinants of expectations of the French franc/Deutsche mark and lira/Deustche mark parity changes during the EMS period. Such an exploration should be, in our view, the first step of a broader analysis of the stability properties of a fixed-but-adjustable rate system. More precisely, the question that we ask in this chapter is: What determines the expectations of parity changes? Are the institutional arrangements of the EMS—designed to stabilize the foreign exchange market, such as the target zone and intergovernmental coordinations—effective at all? In order to answer these questions we need to obtain reliable estimates of such expectations, and then attempt to relate them to economic and institutional variables.

The next section deals with the empirical measurement of realignment expectations, section 4.3 discusses how to select the fundamental and institution variables, section 4.4 discusses the estimation methodology, section 4.5 reports the results, section 4.6 contains some concluding remarks.

4.2   Measuring Expected Parity Changes

The first step in studying the empirical behaviour of market expectations is to find an empirical measurement of such unobservable expectations. The measurement of expected parity changes has to take into account two problems. The first is the measurement of expected changes in exchange rates. In this study, we assume interest rate parity. That is, interest rate differentials reflect expectations of exchange rate changes and that risk premia, or other sources of differences between ex-ante returns in different currencies, are insignificant. Svensson (1990) argues that in a managed exchange rate regime with target zones, given realistic distributional assumptions about fundamentals, the exchange-rate risk premium should be insignificant.

The second problem in measuring parity changes is the presence of exchange-rate bands, or target zones. Since exchange rates are flexible within these target zones, in order to estimate the expected change in a central parity it is necessary to separate the expected changes within the band and the expected shift of the central parity. In this, we extend the work of Collins (1984, 1986), who first studied realignment expectations in the EMS using interest-rate differentials.

To fix ideas, decompose the log exchange rate S into the log central parity c and the log percentage deviation from the central parity x:

$$s_t = c_t + x_t \tag{1}$$

It follows that the one-period expected change (devaluation) of the exchange rate can be decomposed into the expected central parity shift and the expected change in the percentage deviation from the central parity:

$$E[\Delta s_t | I_t] = E[\Delta c_t | I_t] + E[\Delta x_t | I_t]. \tag{2}$$

All expectations are conditional upon information available at time t, denoted by I_t. Under interest-rate parity, the left hand side can be replaced by the interest rate differential between the home country and the foreign country. Denote the differential of interest of deposits of maturity j by δ^j, the expected devaluation can be written as:

$$E[C_{t+j} - C_t | I_t] = \delta_t^j - E[(x_{t+j} - x_t)|I_t]. \tag{3}$$

With δ_t^j observed in the interest rate data, the task of measuring expected devaluation is reduced to measuring expected changes in x. Notice that the expectation is a *full information* expectation in the sense that the information set I_t should contain information concerning the possibility of both a realignment and no realignment in the next j periods, in other words, the observations on x should reflect the market's assessment of future realignment possibilities.[1] It is thus essential to make sure that the sample on x contain enough realignment observations. When the data are available, we can obtain the ex post measure of expected realignment de-valuation as

$$C_{t+j} - C_t = \delta_t^j - (x_{t+j} - x_t). \tag{4}$$

We can obtain an ex ante measure of realignment expectations by projecting the above on the current information set, as will be defined below.

4.3 Choosing the Variables in the Information Set

To determine what information variables to be included in the projection equation, it would be ideal to have a theoretical model that links the fundamental variables to expected realignment in equilibrium. It is well known, however, that the available theoretical models do not tell us what constitute the "fundamentals," so they are suggestive at best. A familiar brand of models, based on the Barro-Gordon (1983) framework of monetary policy games, describe the central bank's main objective as price stability, which can be achieved through exchange rate targeting as in the EMS. However, the central bank also has other objectives, and when those objectives are in crises, the central bank may deviate from the exchange rate targeting policy. This notion of "crises mentality" is consistent with evidence found in the Bernanke-Mishkin (1992) case study of central bank behaviour in major industrialized countries. Giovannini (1990) contains a model of this kind, known as an "escape-clause model." Instead of resorting to a particular model, we rely on the projection-equation approach. The following observations serve as background to our choice of variables in the information set.

Assume that q is the probability of a large adverse shock to the economy occurring in the next period, and that the shock is so big that it warrants a realignment attempt (the escape clause). The government may choose to devalue, or to defend the parity. Suppose the public assigns a subjective probability p to the event that the government will devalue in face of the shock, then the expected devaluation $E\Delta c$ is a probability weighted average defined as follows:

$$E\Delta c = (1 - p) \times 0 + p[q\hat{c}^{e,d} + (1 - q) \times 0], \tag{5}$$

where $\hat{c}^{e,d}$ is the expected size of devaluation if the central bank is pursuing a discretionary (devaluation) policy. Its value can be determined in the equilibrium. In general, it is positively related to the adverse shock and the weakness of the economy and the exchange rate mechanism—the stronger the economy and the better the intergovernmental coordination in defending the parity, the easier it is for the government to weather the negative shocks, and therefore the smaller the expected size of realignment. Simplifying, the above definition can be written as

$$E\Delta c = pq\hat{c}^{e,d}. \tag{6}$$

It can be clearly seen that expected realignment depends on p, q and $\hat{c}^{e,d}$. The empirical task now is to find proxies that capture the essence of these three variables.

To measure p, the public's subjective probability that the central bank will devalue the currency under crises, we need to specify a rule on how this probability is formed. One hypothesis, as suggested by the experience of many EMS countries, is that the longer the central bank manages to keep the exchange rate parity free of realignment, the smaller is p, since the public may gain more confidence on the central bank based on its past record of success. A simple way to capture this idea is to use the length of time since last realignment (we actually use $\ln(1 + t)$) as a proxy for this behaviour of p. The hypothesis suggests that we should expect to find a negative correlation between p and this measure of time. An alternative hypothesis is the so-called "honeymoon" effect commonly seen in the post-election popularity of a winning political party: the popularity surges after the election, and gradually dies out, exhibiting a hump-shaped pattern.[2] In the case of the public's perception of the central bank after a realignment, one can imagine a similar scenario: p may first decline as the public begins to be convinced that the new parity is properly in line with fundamentals so it may last into the future. But as time gets longer, uncertainty about the central bank's resolve may increase for various reasons. This hypothesis implies that p can be viewed as a U-shaped function of time. A third hypothesis, as suggested by Ghisellini (1992), assumes that there is a fixed cost of realignment, so realignment is infrequent, but the longer the time since the last realignment, the more likely a new realignment will occur. This implies a positive relationship between p and time. Combining the above discussions, we use two separate formation rules for p, one is a direct measure of time since last realignment ($t^* \equiv \ln(1 + t)$), the other is a quadratic measure ($at^* + bt^{*2}$) aimed at capturing the U-curve effect (negative a and positive b).

The probability of a large adverse shock to the domestic economy relative to the foreign counterpart, q, can be measured in terms of various fundamental variables, such as trade balance, industrial production, etc. While the expected size of devaluation, $\hat{c}^{e,d}$, can also be linked to the above variables, as well as to such fundamental positions as foreign exchange reserve, budget deficit, wages and inflation, and nominal variables such as liquidity. It should be noted that p may also depend on the government's financial positions such as deficit and foreign exchange reserves. Put together, we can actually isolate the independent effect of time since the last realignment after controlling for these fundamentals.

We also incorporate some important institutional features of the EMS and evaluate their effectiveness in reducing realignment expectations. One such institutional arrangement is the fluctuation band, or the target zone. The target zone literature has shown on both theoretical and empirical grounds that the band has a stabilizing, or mean reverting effect on expected exchange rate deviation from the central parity. In other words, the expected change in exchange rate deviation from the central parity is *negatively* correlated with the current deviation from the central parity. Although the models deal specifically with the *deviations from central parity*, the mean reverting result has been commonly interpreted in a naive way, which leads to the conclusion that the band has a stabilizing effect on *realignment* expectations. Changes in deviation from central parity and changes in central parity itself are equivalent only in the case of no realignment. So in general, when realignment is allowed, the stabilization property, at least in the form of negative correlation, may not apply. We include a variable representing the deviation from the central parity in our empirical estimation and examine whether the negative correlation holds for expected parity changes. This is crucial in evaluating the stability of the EMS.

Another feature of the EMS is the institutionalized coordination among member countries. The coordination efforts are aimed at strengthening member countries' position in preventing and counteracting crises and speculations. We focus on the effectiveness of one such coordination—

the introduction of the Basle-Nyborg agreements. Finally, the credibility and stability of the EMS can also be explored by studying the reaction of the foreign exchange market to the event of a realignment. This is done employing a "realignment dummy."

The following is a complete list and definitions of the information variables.

- **C1, C2, . . .** Constant dummies corresponding to each central parity regime. 10 regimes for IL and 7 for FF.

- **X1**   Log relative foreign exchange reserve position measured in terms of the DM.

- **X2**   The percent change in budget surplus on a cash basis (Italy or France minus Germany).

- **X3**   The difference of the trade balance surpluses (Italy or France minus Germany).

- **X4**   Relative industrial production indices. Denote foreign (German) variable with a star, the definition can be written as

$$\ln\left(\frac{IP}{IP^*}\right) \tag{7}$$

- **X5**   The position of the exchange rate within the band (x).

- **X6**   Form 1: The log of one plus the number of months since last realignment, denoted as t^*; Form 2: $at^* + bt^{*2}$.

- **X7**   An index of relative CPI's. Denote S the exchange rate measured in terms of domestic currency value of one unit of DM, the index is written as

$$\ln\left(\frac{CPI}{CPI^* \times S}\right). \tag{8}$$

- **X8**   An index of relative wages, *i.e.*:

$$\ln\left(\frac{W}{W^* \times S}\right). \tag{9}$$

- **X9   Relative liquidity,** *i.e.*:

$$\ln\left(\frac{L}{L^* \times S}\right) \tag{10}$$

- **X10**   DM/US$ exchange rate.

- **X11** Jump dummy that takes the value 1 at the first month of realignment and zero otherwise.
- **X12** X1 multiplied by the slope dummy that equals 0 before the Basle-Nyborg agreements and 1 afterward.
- **X13** X5 multiplied by the same slope dummy as in X12.

The sources for the data used are listed at the end of the chapter. The frequency of our data is monthly, and the horizons we study are 1 month and 3 months. We look at the lira/DM and French franc/DM exchange rates since the beginning of the EMS.

4.4 Estimation

In the previous sections we have argued that the estimation of the expected change in the central parity requires an estimation of the expected change in the exchange rate within the band. Our task is to explore the determinants of expectations of parity changes. To do this, we estimate the following equation:

$$\delta_t^j - (x_{t+j} - x_t) = Z_t'\beta + u_{t+j}, \tag{11}$$

where Z'_t is a vector of variables in agents' information set at time t. Here we assume Z_t consists of all the information variables listed in the previous subsection. The disturbance term u_{t+j} has two components. One is the expectations error $(x_{t+j} - Ex_{t+j})$, the other is an error due to the imprecise measurement of expectations, or the existence of variables affecting expectations that are left out from the vector Z. The former is, under the assumption of rational expectations, orthogonal to any variable included in Z, depending on the severity of specification errors. In general, the expectation error always swamps the error due to mismeasurement, because, as it is well known, the variance of the unpredictable component of exchange rates is very high. When $j > 1$ the expectation error follows a moving average process of order $j - 1$.

Equation (11) allows us to estimate, simultaneously, the expected change in the exchange rate within the band and the determinants of expected parity changes. Consider the linear projection:

$$\delta_t^j - E[(x_{t+j} - x_t)] = Z_t'\hat{\beta}, \tag{12}$$

where $\hat{\beta}$ is a consistent estimate of β. Equation (12) shows that the projection of the interest-rate differential net of the realized exchange rate changes within the band on information provides an estimate of the expected change in the central parity. The coefficient vector β will indicate the relation of the expected change in the central parity to fundamentals.

The basic strategy of this regression is inspired by the following observation. Under the assumption of linear rational expectations, the best estimate of the expectations of any economic variable is its projection on variables in the agents' information set at the time such expectation is formed. The property of this estimate is that the estimated residuals, which represent the "surprises," are orthogonal to the variables used to form expectations. In that sense, information cannot be used more efficiently to form expectations, and therefore expectations are rational.

A problem with unrestricted projection using target zone data is that it fails to explicitly specify the restrictions implied by the presence of the target zone band, which is a part of the public's information set, and is nonlinearly related to, and correlated with many other information variables. This may result in incorrect estimates of expectations. This problem is discussed by Chen and Giovannini (1992b), who propose a type of Box-Cox transformation which recovers the good properties of projection equations. This transformation cannot be used in the equation we estimate in this chapter, because it would not allow the easy joint estimation of expectations of realignments and exchange rate movements within the band. However, we have verified that, in the case of the EMS, the errors that arise from not exploiting the information on exchange-rate bands are likely to be negligible (see also Svensson, 1991).

4.5 Results

Tables 4.1 (plus 4.1A and 4.1B) and 4.2 (plus 4.2A and 4.2B) report the estimates of the projection equation over the 1-month horizon, respectively for the lira and the French franc. Tables 4.1 and 4.2 contain the estimates over the full sample (March 1979 to January 1992), tables 4.1A and 4.2A contain the estimates over the period from March 1979 to August 1987, while tables 4.1B and 4.2B contain estimates over the period from September 1987 to January 1992. The breakpoint is the date of the Basle-Nyborg agreement (September 12, 1987) of the Committee of Central Bank Governors, which strengthened the Exchange Rate Mechanism of the EMS by adopting a number of measures, including in particular an extension of the use of the Very Short Run Financial Facility to finance intra-marginal interventions.

In the case of Italy, the variables whose coefficients tend to be consistently significant are X5 (the position of the exchange rate within the

Table 4.1
One-month IL/DM expected devaluation: Full-sample regression (March 1979–January 1992)

Variable	Coefficient	t-Value	p-Value
C1	−478.1773	−0.7268	0.4686
C2	−479.8048	−0.7349	0.4637
C3	−472.0257	−0.7249	0.4698
C4	−479.6472	−0.7355	0.4633
C5	−460.6358	−0.7099	0.4790
C6	−458.5521	0.7096	0.4792
C7	−471.8912	0.7329	0.4649
C8	−459.9705	−0.7188	0.4735
C9	−467.0552	−0.7313	0.4659
C10	−460.8237	−0.7251	0.4697
X1	6.4620	−0.6659	0.5066
X2	−0.1873	−0.4917	0.6238
X3	126.6341	0.2778	0.7816
X4	−14.0219	−0.2477	0.8048
X5	0.5303	6.0541	0.0000
X6	−9.6477	−4.7456	0.0000
X7	−59.6633	−0.3861	0.7001
X8	8.5227	0.0721	0.9426
X9	−23.5367	−1.4285	0.1555
X10	19.6028	0.6498	0.5170
X11	−17.8491	−2.5136	0.0131

	Diagnostics		
	Number of observations	155	
	Standard error	16.636	
	R-squared	0.457	
	$F(21, 134)$	7.211	
	Durbin-Watson	2.320	

Table 4.1A
One-month IL/DM expected devaluation: Sub-sample regression (March 1979–August 1987)

Variable	Coefficient	t-Value	p-Value
C1	1.3754	0.0659	0.9476
C2	−11.0142	−0.8400	0.4033
C3	6.2068	0.3899	0.6982
C4	−2.0331	−0.1243	0.9014
C5	22.4409	1.1763	0.2428
C6	33.2140	1.6584	0.1010
C7	10.2432	0.6146	0.5405
C8	12.8307	1.1084	0.2709
X1	1.3248	0.0945	0.9249
X2	−0.2116	−0.4676	0.6413
X3	159.1566	0.2536	0.8004
X4	38.9896	0.4786	0.6335
X5	0.6434	4.9941	0.0000
X6	−10.5628	−3.4840	0.0008
X7	−37.4572	−0.2197	0.8266
X8	67.4376	0.4187	0.6765
X9	−39.3983	−1.6092	0.1114
X10	−35.6990	−0.7698	0.4436
X11	−15.7087	−1.6153	0.1100

	Diagnostics	
	Number of observations	102
	Standard error	19.310
	R-squared	0.509
	$F(19, 83)$	6.067
	Durbin-Watson	2.471

band), and $X6$ (time since last realignment—a variable meant to capture learning and reputation effects). The coefficient of $X5$ is always positive, indicating that a wider deviation from a central parity increases expectations of exchange rate changes. Interestingly, it is not significant at the 5% level in the period since the Basle-Nyborg agreements (table 4.1B). The strong significance and the negative sign on the coefficient of $X6$ implies that a proven tough exchange rate stance—represented by the lack of recourse to realignment for a long period—other things equal, seems to improve the credibility of the exchange rate regime. The jump dummy $X11$ has a large negative coefficient, and is sometimes significant. This

Table 4.1B
One-month IL/DM expected devaluation: Sub-sample regression (September 1987–January 1992)

Variable	Coefficient	t-Value	p-Value
C1	−2301.4348	−2.0236	0.0497
C2	−2294.3506	−2.0177	0.0504
X1	26.9352	0.0824	0.0437
X2	0.4132	0.4327	0.6676
X3	687.5019	1.2733	0.2103
X4	−45.1056	−0.8098	0.4228
X5	0.2382	1.8003	0.0794
X6	−2.9499	−1.4582	0.1526
X7	−417.4870	−1.6094	0.1154
X8	67.4277	0.4962	0.6225
X9	−5.5523	−0.4192	0.6773
X10	32.8205	1.1532	0.2557
X11	−1.9425	−0.1953	0.8462

	Diagnostics	
	Number of observations	53
	Standard error	7.856
	R-squared	0.385
	$F_{(13, 40)}$	3.236
	Durbin-Watson	1.860

suggests that the occurrence of a realignment induces sharp revisions of realignment expectations. The fact that X11 is not significant after Basle-Nyborg (table 4.1B) is not surprising: the realignment of the lira of January 1990 was only due to the narrowing of the fluctuation band of that currency vis-à-vis the ERM partners.

The results for the case of France are broadly similar to Italy's, with X5, X6 being the most significant variables, *i.e.*, the position of exchange rate within the band and the time elapsed since last realignment are the most powerful source of revision of expectations. The jump dummy X11 also exhibits negative significance in table 4.2.

Tables 4.3 and 4.4 report regression results for 1-month projections over the whole sample for Italy and France, with slope dummies on X1 and X5 to capture the effects of Basle-Nyborg on the sensitivity of realignment expectations with respect to reserves and exchange rate position within the band. Tables 4.3A and 4.4A contain regression results for the 3-month horizon. The slope dummies X12 and X13 are obtained by

Table 4.2
One-month FF/DM expected devaluation: Full-sample regression (March 1979–January 1992)

Variable	Coefficient	t-Value	p-Value
C1	317.9150	3.2361	0.0015
C2	322.2156	3.4408	0.0008
C3	321.1153	3.4300	0.0008
C4	333.0882	3.4148	0.0008
C5	331.2239	3.3702	0.0010
C6	323.2528	3.2734	0.0013
C7	317.1123	3.2861	0.0013
X1	−13.3100	−2.2929	0.0234
X2	−0.2640	−1.2067	0.2296
X3	−93.8045	−0.4467	0.6558
X4	70.5748	0.9709	0.3333
X5	0.8730	7.6783	0.0000
X6	−9.1515	−4.2937	0.0000
X7	276.7218	1.9938	0.0481
X8	−22.4749	−0.2186	0.8273
X9	−21.5987	−1.0839	0.2803
X10	−8.4588	−0.4482	0.6547
X11	−13.9427	−1.4449	0.1508

	Diagnostics		
	Number of observations	155	
	Standard error	15.916	
	R-squared	0.545	
	$F(18, 137)$	9.912	
	Durbin-Watson	2.423	

multiplying $X1$ and $X5$, respectively, by a series that equals zero up to August 1987, and one thereafter.

For Italy, the slope dummy on the position of exchange rate within the band, $X13$, is negative and significant for both one-month horizon (5.4% p-value) and three-month horizon (2.8% p-value), while the slope dummy $X12$ is not significant. The opposite holds for France: the slope dummy on the foreign exchange reserve position, $X12$, is positive and significant for both one-month horizon (5.6% p-value) and three-month horizon (0.27% p-value), while the slope dummy $X13$ is not significant. Overall, this evidence suggests that the Basle-Nyborg agreement may have indeed strengthened the central bank's ability to defend the announced parity.

Table 4.2A
One-month FF/DM expected devaluation: Sub-sample regression (March 1979–August 1987)

Variable	Coefficient	t-Value	p-Value
C1	414.2165	2.9950	0.0036
C2	413.8643	3.1375	0.0023
C3	410.6509	3.1160	0.0025
C4	416.5870	3.0512	0.0030
C5	414.2206	2.9974	0.0036
C6	412.1694	2.9652	0.0039
C7	405.4981	2.9893	0.0037
X1	−20.2068	−2.4533	0.0162
X2	−0.2537	−0.6182	0.5381
X3	−110.4367	−0.3692	0.7129
X4	89.1508	0.7758	0.4401
X5	0.9472	5.8764	0.0000
X6	−7.3715	−2.3743	0.0199
X7	237.1713	0.9697	0.3350
X8	79.2739	0.3859	0.7006
X9	−32.3508	−1.0448	0.2991
X10	28.5935	0.9969	0.3217
X11	−11.2882	−0.8933	0.3742
	Diagnostics		
	Number of observations	102	
	Standard error	19.312	
	R-squared	0.575	
	$F(18, 84)$	6.943	
	Durbin-Watson	2.415	

However, such gains in credibility appear to have been achieved through different channels in the two countries: for Italy, exchange rate deviation from the central parity less worrisome to the public (negative coefficient on $X13$) since Basle-Nyborg, probably because of the perceived availability of the Very Short Run Facility that may strengthen the central bank's ability to intervene and regulate the exchange rate within the band; For France, the gains in credibility primarily come from the strengthened exchange reserve positions.

The 3-month projections (tables 4.3A and 4.4A) contain some more interesting results. For the case of Italy, $X4$ (the relative industrial production) becomes significant, with a negative sign indicating a decline in

Table 4.2B
One-month FF/DM expected devaluation: Sub-sample regression (September 1987–January 1992)

Variable	Coefficient	t-Value	p-Value
X1	−18.8457	−2.5994	0.0127
X2	−0.3606	−3.4552	0.0012
X3	−50.9597	−0.3756	0.7091
X4	−31.7236	−0.7245	0.4727
X5	0.2597	2.1636	0.0361
X6	13.2109	2.4251	0.0196
X7	21.6307	0.3970	0.6933
X8	29.2768	0.5437	0.5894
X9	−8.6638	−0.8264	0.4131
X10	10.5750	0.7958	0.4305
	Diagnostics		
	Number of observations	53	
	Standard error	4.970	
	R-squared	0.414	
	$F(10, 43)$	3.691	
	Durbin-Watson	1.885	

realignment probabilities when Italian industrial production improves relative to that of Germany. For the case of France, $X1$ and $X9$ become significant at 5% level, with negative signs suggesting that stronger relative reserve positions and relative liquidity help reduce realignment expectations.

To visualize the projected devaluations arising from the equations we estimated, we plot the predicted values of the regressions, together with the dates of the actual EMS realignments (each indicated by the tip of a triangle). Figures 4.1 and 4.3 plot the predicted 1-month devaluation (expressed in percent per annum) for the lira/DM and the FF/DM respectively (the predictions are based on equations whose estimates are in tables 4.3 and 4.4). Interpreting the figures in terms of the model in section 4.2, we observe that they imply unambiguously a positive p (perceived probability that the government follows an escape-clause policy, and does not credibly peg the currency) throughout most of the sample. The figures also show that the market tends to anticipate a realignment in the 1-month horizon at all times, but such anticipation becomes more pronounced (indicated by large spikes in the figures) in the few months prior to actual realignments. The figures also highlight the importance of

Table 4.3
Final regression results with regime dummies: Expected one-month IL/DM devaluation
(March 1979–January 1992)

Variable	Coefficient	t-Value	p-Value
C1	−688.0799	−0.9628	0.3374
C2	−690.6784	−0.9710	0.3333
C3	−676.1609	−0.9540	0.3418
C4	−684.9434	−0.9650	0.3363
C5	−662.2425	−0.9396	0.3492
C6	−655.5832	−0.9334	0.3523
C7	−671.8954	−0.9596	0.3390
C8	−660.1667	−0.9479	0.3449
C9	−669.7942	−0.9650	0.3363
C10	−673.9213	−0.9738	0.3319
X1	2.4665	0.1594	0.8736
X2	−0.1933	−0.5125	0.6091
X3	298.6601	0.6427	0.5215
X4	−0.9510	−0.0169	0.9866
X5	0.6774	5.8305	0.0000
X6	−8.4593	−4.0102	0.0001
X7	−124.9686	−0.7844	0.4342
X8	43.1606	0.3646	0.7160
X9	−26.0058	−1.5849	0.1154
X10	−7.6254	0.2416	0.8095
X11	−11.1960	−1.4228	0.1572
X12	9.2878	0.7399	0.4607
X13	−0.4418	−1.9414	0.0543

	Diagnostics	
	Number of observations	155
	Standard error	16.471
	R-squared	0.476
	$F(23, 132)$	6.922
	Durbin-Watson	2.270

Table 4.3A
Final regression results with regime dummies: Expected three-month IL/DM devaluation (March 1979–January 1992)

Variable	Coefficient	t-Value	p-Value
C1	−205.5754	−0.7205	0.4725
C2	−200.4904	−0.7039	0.4827
C3	−184.0127	−0.6502	0.5167
C4	−184.2734	−0.6480	0.5181
C5	−174.2544	−0.6173	0.5381
C6	−175.1046	−0.6229	0.5344
C7	−183.7813	−0.6560	0.5129
C8	−187.4939	−0.6720	0.5027
C9	−197.9485	−0.7112	0.4782
C10	−205.4887	−0.7417	0.4596
X1	0.2918	−0.0401	0.9681
X2	−0.0223	−0.1902	0.8424
X3	135.2704	0.7845	0.4341
X4	−67.0406	−2.9483	0.0038
X5	1.1806	7.3367	0.0000
X6	−3.1201	−3.3994	0.0009
X7	19.9725	0.2943	0.7690
X8	−49.1452	−1.0143	0.3123
X9	−4.6889	−0.8648	0.3887
X10	−15.9043	−1.1238	0.2632
X11	0.1448	0.0476	0.9621
X12	7.3982	1.3353	0.1841
X13	−0.5789	−2.2083	0.0289

	Diagnostics	
	Number of observations	155
	Standard error	6.898
	R-squared	0.625
	$F(23, 132)$	19.330
	Autocorrelations order	2
	Autocorrelation of errors:	
	One period	0.193
	Last period	0.037

Table 4.4
Final regression results with regime dummies: Expected one-month FF/DM devaluation
(March 1979–January 1992)

Variable	Coefficient	t-Value	p-Value
C1	368.5814	3.5424	0.0005
C2	370.0584	3.7313	0.0003
C3	369.2664	3.7354	0.0003
C4	377.8181	3.6990	0.0003
C5	376.2023	3.6429	0.0004
C6	374.1967	3.5823	0.0005
C7	370.5824	3.6129	0.0001
X1	−18.2409	−2.9416	0.0038
X2	−0.2471	−1.1117	0.2682
X3	−84.2307	−0.4062	0.6852
X4	46.1439	0.6252	0.5329
X5	0.9458	7.6955	0.0000
X6	−7.5872	−3.3990	0.0009
X7	267.8869	1.9424	0.0542
X8	26.3587	0.2533	0.8004
X9	−19.6365	0.9974	0.3204
X10	−18.3181	−0.9569	0.3403
X11	−12.1930	−1.2015	0.2317
X12	14.5593	1.9234	0.0565
X13	−0.2006	−0.6343	0.5269

	Diagnostics	
	Number of observations	155
	Standard error	15.711
	R-squared	0.563
	$F(20, 135)$	9.436
	Durbin-Watson	2.344

the information about the occurrence of the realignment: after the realignment the expected devaluation of the lira and of the franc turn sharply negative.

For comparison, figures 4.1A and 4.3A report the observed 1-month interest rate differentials. While there are visible spikes they do not appear to match the timing of realignments with good precision. Another noteworthy feature of figures 4.1A and 4.3A is the familiar evidence of interest rate convergence for both countries (relative to Germany) over time. We cannot, however, find corresponding drastic decline of realignment expectations in figures 4.1 and 4.3, although the variability of the ex-

Table 4.4A
Final regression results with regime dummies: Expected three-month FF/DM devaluation
(March 1979–January 1992)

Variable	Coefficient	t-Value	p-Value
C1	195.8427	4.0488	0.0001
C2	195.1067	4.2145	0.0000
C3	195.7883	4.2517	0.0000
C4	198.5340	4.2608	0.0000
C5	191.7341	4.3632	0.0000
C6	191.2826	4.1282	0.0001
C7	187.3248	4.1287	0.0001
X1	−9.2245	−3.0188	0.0030
X2	0.0093	0.1770	0.8598
X3	28.4486	0.3100	0.7570
X4	1.7272	0.0795	0.9367
X5	1.3195	11.4652	0.0000
X6	−1.7053	−1.6346	0.1045
X7	70.1270	1.6173	0.1081
X8	75.3372	1.8853	0.0615
X9	−15.9054	−2.2699	0.0248
X10	−14.6836	−1.6717	0.0969
X11	0.8762	0.3458	0.7300
X12	6.4625	3.0575	0.0027
X13	−0.2650	−1.1693	0.2443

Diagnostics	
Number of observations	155
Standard error	6.303
R-squared	0.642
$F(23, 135)$	16.974
Number of autocorrelations	2
Autocorrelation of errors:	
One period	0.057
Last period	0.003

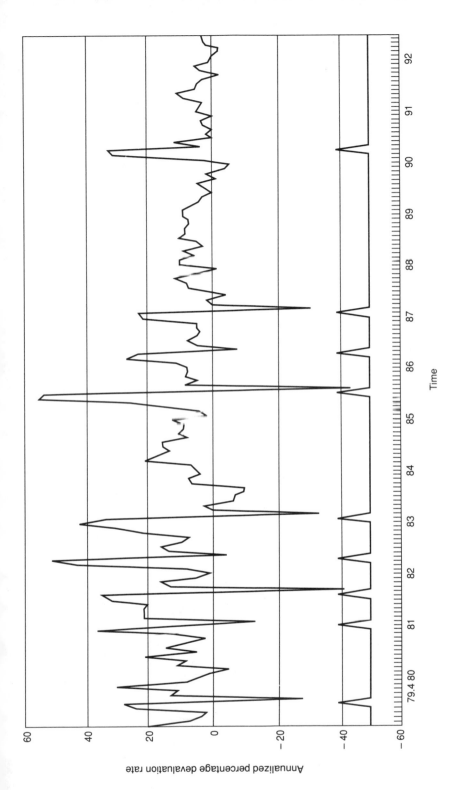

Figure 4.1
One-month expected devaluation: IL/DM

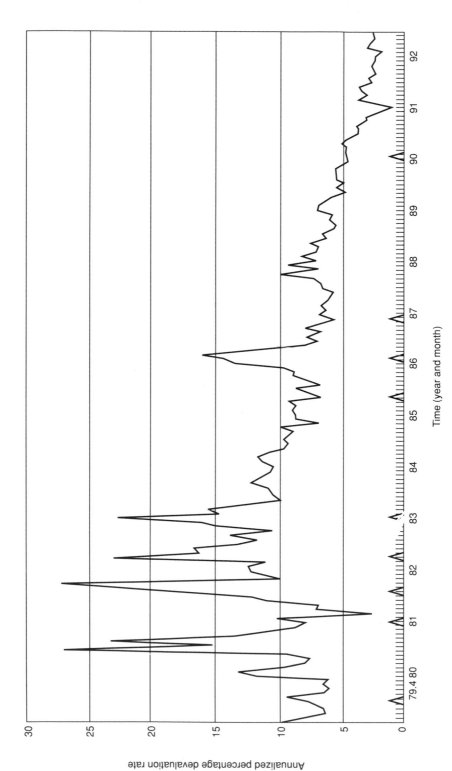

Figure 4.1a
IL-DM interest rate differential (one month)

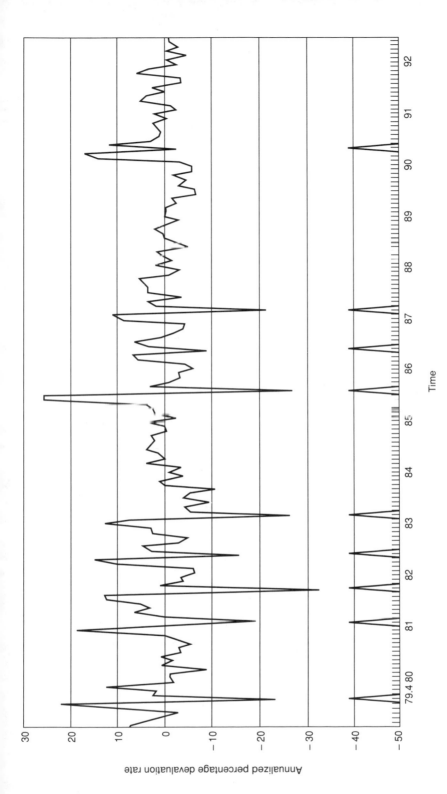

Figure 4.2
One-month vs. three-month IL/DM term premium

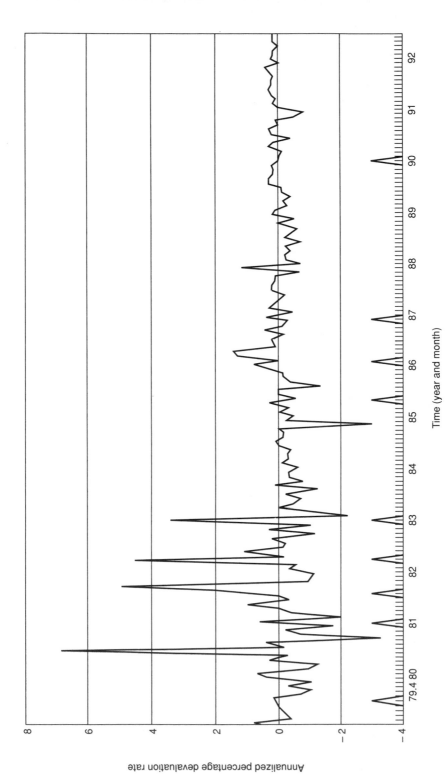

Figure 4.2a
IL/DM term premium of interest rates

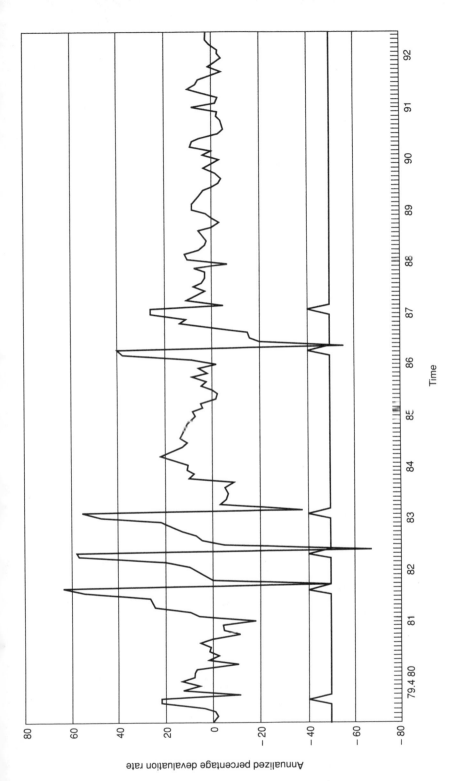

Figure 4.3
One-month expected devaluation: FF/DM

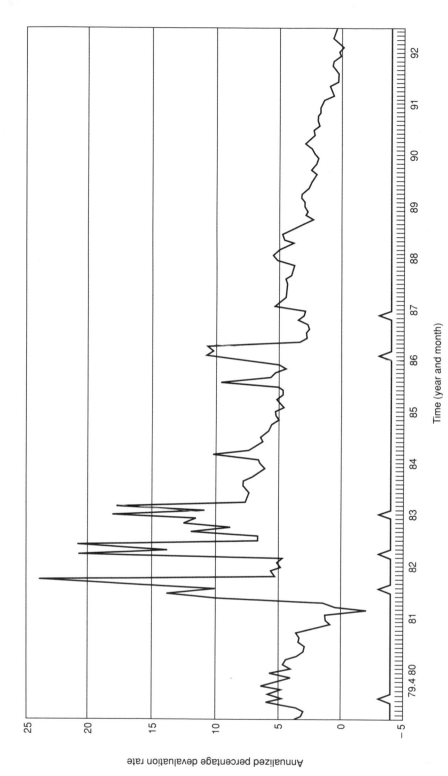

Figure 4.3a
FF-DM interest rate differential (one month)

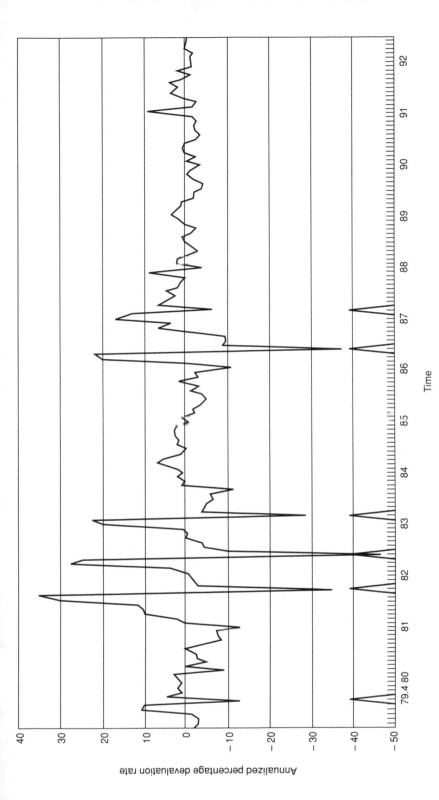

Figure 4.4
One-month vs. three-month FF/DM term premium

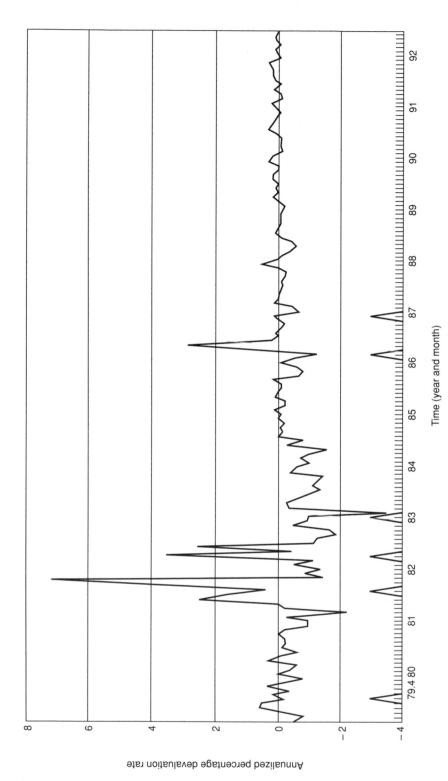

Figure 4.4a
FF-DM term premium of interest rates

pected devaluation has decreased over time. In other words, interest rate convergence is not necessarily a full reflection of a decline in expected devaluation.

In order to get a clearer indication of the accuracy of the estimated predictions about the timing of realignments, we plot in figures 4.2 and 4.4 the difference between the 1-month and the 3-month expected devaluations (the term premia). Simple intuition tells us that a positive term premium implies the estimated probability of a realignment is higher in the next month than in the two months at the long end of the horizon. Figures 4.2 and 4.4 show that the term premium tends to rise sharply one month prior to realignments, implying that the timing of realignments is correctly anticipated.

In contrast, figures 4.2A and 4.4A show the 1-month vs. 3-month term premia directly calculated from the term difference of the interest rate differentials. They do not appear to anticipate the timing of realignments with any good precision. This evidence further demonstrates that the interest rate differential is not a precise measure of realignment expectations.

Finally, our fitted data in figures 4.1, 4.2, 4.3 and 4.4 reveal large reverses of realignment expectations in the month immediately following realignments. Again, such negative expected realignments are absent in the figures constructed directly from interest rate differentials (figures 4.1A, 4.2A, 4.3A and 4.4A).

In the above report, X6 takes the form t^*. When it is replaced by the alternative form $at^* + bt^{*2}$, we find some evidence of the so-called "honeymoon" effect, or the U-curve effect. As we can see from table 4.5, the estimated coefficient $\hat{a}$ is consistently negative for both the lira and the French franc in both the one-month and three-month projection horizons. This also holds for $\hat{b}$ with an opposite sign. The coefficients in the one-month regressions are all significant at the 5% level, but they become less significant in the three-month regressions. The results indicate that lack of realignment initially helps dampen realignment expectations (negative slope of the U-curve when t^* is small), but as time goes on, this trend tends to be reversed (upward-sloping part of the U-curve). To assess which part of the effects matters more in practice, we calculate the number of months it takes to reverse the downward trend using the one-month regression results.[3] We find the turning point occurs roughly 22 months after a realignment for the case of the lira and about 42 months for the case of the franc. Time periods of such lengths are long enough for practical considerations. So we view the dampening effect of a clean realign-

Table 4.5
The "honeymoon" effect: Estimated coefficients $\hat{a}$ and $\hat{b}$ in the full projection equation with $X6 \equiv at^* + bt^{*2}$

Regression	a	b
One-month IL	−3.0357	0.0686
	(−3.8742)	(2.5591)
One-month FF	−1.4222	0.0170
	(−3.4337)	(2.1384)
Three-month IL	−0.8002	0.0144
	(−2.5606)	(1.5264)
Three-month FF	−0.2090	0.0035
	(−1.8091)	(1.3440)

Note: t-value in parentheses.

ment record on the market expectations as the dominating effect, which is consistent with the result obtained by using the proxy t^* alone.

4.6 Concluding Remarks

In this chapter we have presented a methodology to explore the relationship between expectations of parity changes and economic variables. This methodology accounts for the expectation of exchange rate changes within fluctuation bands, and therefore should in principle yield more precise estimates of expected parity changes.

Interest rate differentials are commonly used as a proxy for realignment expectations. As Svensson (1991) pointed out, the flexibility of exchange rates within the target zones, however, makes such a proxy imprecise. This is confirmed in our study with a more carefully constructed realignment expectation measurement. In addition, our estimated expectations reveal some facts about realignment expectations that are not apparent in the interest rate differential proxy, such as less than dramatic reduction in expected devaluation as implied by interest rate convergence, and more precision in expected timing of realignment than implied by interest rate differential and its term premium.

The most important finding is that expected parity changes vary over time, and appear to be significantly related to a number of variables. The variables that have consistently high explanatory power are the length of time since last realignment (measuring the reputation of the central bank) and the deviation of exchange rates from the central parity. The results indicate that in general the absence of realignments improves the central bank's reputation. Such an effect is strong in the short and medium run, but in the long run, the trend may be reversed. This is consistent with the "honeymoon" hypothesis and the presence of a fixed cost of realignments. We have also found that a change in regime is detectable after the Basle-Nyborg agreements.

In order to evaluate the performance of adjustable parity systems like the EMS it is tempting to assess whether the expectations of parity changes which we estimate in this chapter appear, according to given criteria, to be rational. Some of our observations in the previous section were indeed motivated by that question. The two most important results of our regressions are the positive significance of the variable $X5$, representing the percent deviation of the exchange rate from the centre of the band, and the large turnaround of expected parity changes following realignments. The first finding is opposite to the naive generalization of the "stabilization effect" of the fluctuation band, a hallmark of recent target zone literature. Our evidence could be consistent with herd-like behaviour in the foreign exchange markets, which however is not necessarily inconsistent with rational expectations under imperfect information.

The second finding, that the estimates of expected parity changes after realignments are always negative—the DM is to be devalued relative to the lira and the franc—and large, together with the size and significance of the dummy variable representing the recent occurrence of a realignment in some cases, is difficult to interpret. There are two potential explanations for this puzzle. One is that market participants take larger-than-necessary short positions, and find the market is over-sold after realignment. This could happen when speculators trying to bring down the parity overestimate the government's ability to defend the system.

An alternative explanation is that speculators abandon the market after having profited from the change in parity. This would be the case, for example, of fund managers who are given performance targets and do not have much of an incentive to active trading after those targets are met. As a result, information may not be efficiently used in the marketplace, with the resulting puzzling discrepancies between actual observations and predictions of models that assume rational expectations, such as ours. In general, the data at our disposal do not seem to provide evidence in support of the theory that adjustable parity systems are "stable." Indeed, two of the most significant empirical facts we have uncovered—discussed heretofore—are not inconsistent with the hypothesis that the fluctuation band generates insufficient stabilization on private realignment expectations, and that over-speculation or market inefficiency are present.

These suggestions, however, should not be taken as conclusive evidence in favour of market inefficiency. Such test requires a structural model. While our evidence cannot be considered conclusive, it adds to other empirical regularities that characterize adjustable parity systems, the most prominent of which is perhaps the so-called "capital-inflow problem" (see, for a discussion on the EMS, Giovannini, 1992). Our results, together with the empirical regularities studied in the literature on the capital-inflow problem, point to potential inherent instabilities of adjustable parity systems.

Data Sources

Exchange Rates: *Financial Times.* End of month observations.
Interest Rates: *Financial Times.* Eurodeposit rates. End of month observations.
Interest Rates:
X1:

• Germany: *Bundesbank external position. Monthly Report,* Table 12. Measured in Millions of DM.

• France: *Banque de France Quarterly Bulletin,* Table 10, Counterparties de M3. Measured in billions of FF.

• Italy: Banca d'Italia net external position, *Economic Bulletin.* Measured in billions of IL.

Budget Surplus/Deficit:

• Italy: Treasury borrowing requirement. Bank of Italy.

• Germany: Federal finance on a cash basis. Data Resources, Inc.

• France: Public authority financial deficit (national accounts). *INSEE Comptes et Indicateurs Economiques.*

Trade Balances: OECD.
Industrial Production: OECD. Index 1985 = 100.
Consumer Prices: OECD. Index 1985 = 100.
Wages:

• Italy—Contract wages. *International Financial Statistics.*

• Germany—Monthly wage and salary rate in the overall economy. Datastream Internaltional, Inc.

• France: Labor costs. *International Financial Statistics.*

X9:

- Germany and Italy—Liquidity of deposit banks, line 20, IFS.
- France—M1, IFS.

Notes

1. Svensson (1991) develops an alternative measure of expected devaluation associated with realignment expectations: $\delta_t^l - E[(x_{t+j} - x_t)|\text{no realignment}]$. The key feature of this measure is that the second term is a *conditional* expectation, conditional on an information set that is generally smaller than the full set I_t, with the realignment events excluded from the latter. While desirable in the case of few realignment observations, the conditional expectation of x can not, in general, be correctly estimated from the data even with realignment observations excluded from the sample, since the possibility of a future realignment should be "priced" by the market under rational expectations, and the sample x is conditional on both realignment and no-realignment possibilities.

2. We thank Charles Goodhart for suggesting this idea.

3. This is simply done by setting the derivatives of $at^* + bt^{*2}$ (with respect to t^*) to zero and solve for t^*.

References

Barro, R. J. and D. B. Gordon. 1983. "A Positive Theory of Monetary Policy in a Natural Rate Model," *Journal of Political Economy*, 91, No. 4, pp. 589–610.

Bernanke, B. and F. S. Mishkin. 1992. "Guideposts and Signals in the Conduct of Monetary Policy: Lessons from Six Industrialized Countries," manuscript, Columbia University.

Calvo, G. 1983. "Trying to Stabilize: Some Theoretical Reflections Based on the Case of Argentina," in Aspe Armella, P., R. Dornbusch and M. Obstfeld, eds., *Financial Policies and the World Capital Market: The Problem of Latin American Countries*, Chicago: Chicago University Press, for NBER.

Chen, Z. and A. Giovannini. 1992a. "The Credibility of Adjustable Parities," mimeo, Columbia University, presented at the Ossola Memorial Conference, July.

Chen, Z. and A. Giovannini. 1992b. "Estimating Expected Exchange Rates under Target Zones," mimeo, Columbia University.

Collins, S. 1984. "Exchange Rate Expectations and Interest Rate Parity During Credibility Crisis: The French Franc, March. 1983," mimeo, Harvard University.

Collins, S. 1986. "The Expected Timing of Devaluation: A Model of Realignment of the European Monetary System," mimeo, Harvard University.

Diaz Alejandro, C. F. 1981. "Southern Cone Stabilization Plans" in W. R. Cline and S. Weintraub, eds. *Economic Stabilization in Developing Countries*, Washington, DC: Brookings Institution.

Dornbusch, R. 1982. "Stabilization Policies in Developing Countries: What Have We Learned?", *World Development* 10, no. 9, pp. 701–708.

Flood, R. P. and P. Garber. 1984. "Collpsing Exchange Rate Regimes: Some Linear Examples," *Journal of International Economics*, 17, pp. 1–13.

Flood, R. P. and P. Isard. 1990. "Monetary Policy Strategies—A Correction: Reply to Lohmann," *International Monetary Fund Staff Papers* 37, June, pp. 446–448.

Friedman, M. 1968. "The Role of Monetary Policy," *American Economic Review*, 58, pp. 1–17.

Ghisellini, F. 1992. "Credibility and Hard Currency Options in the Transition to Economic and Monetary Union," mimeo, Ministero del Tesoro, Roma.

Giovannini, A. 1990. "European Monetary Reform: Progress and Prospects," *Brookings Papers on Economic Activity*, 2, pp. 217–292, also chapter 8 in this volume.

Giovannini, A. 1992. "The Capital Inflow Problem in the EMS," mimeo, Columbia University.

Lizondo, J. S. 1983. "Foreign Exchange Futures Prices under Fixed Exchange Rates," *Journal of International Economics*, 14, pp. 69–84.

Lohmann, S. 1990. "Monetary Policy Strategies—A Correction," *International Monetary Fund Staff Papers* 37, June, pp. 440–445.

Simons, H. C. 1936. "Rules versus Authorities in Monetary Policy," *Journal of Political Economy*, 44, 1, February, pp. 1–30.

Svensson, L. E. O. 1990. "The Foreign Exchange Risk Premium in a Target Zone with Devaluation Risk," mimeo, IIES, Stockholm.

Svensson, L. E. O. 1991. "Assessing Target-Zone Credibility: Mean Reversion and Devaluation Expectations in the EMS," University of Stockholm IIES Seminar Paper No. 493.

II

The Arguments for Monetary Union and for the European Central Bank

5   European Currency Experience

(with Francesco Giavazzi,
August 1985)

In this chapter we discuss whether changes in bilateral rates among European currencies are desirable. We compare the current system of managed rates with a currency union, i.e. a system where exchange rates are irrevocably fixed.[1] This allows us to pinpoint the motivations for using exchange rates as policy tools. A comparison of a regime of adjustable parities with a regime of irrevocably fixed parities is important, because in the intentions of its founders the European Monetary System was meant to be just a transition towards monetary unification. As argued below, it is quite clear that the present system has no tendency to converge towards a regime of irrevocably fixed rates.

5.1   Incentives to Affect Bilateral Exchange Rates

Countries that peg their exchange rates lose monetary autonomy in a world of capital mobility. As a consequence, in a system of managed rates, with n currencies and $n - 1$ bilateral parities, only one country is able to run an independent monetary policy.

Is this an adequate characterization of the European Monetary System? It would be if EMS members had to peg to one currency only, such as the Deutsche mark. Although the purpose of foreign exchange market intervention rules in the present system is precisely that of avoiding these types of asymmetries, the practice of intervening when a single currency reaches the "divergence indicator" is such that Germany never had to intervene to defend a given parity, except in very few exceptional circumstances. The working of the system so far suggests that the mark is effectively playing the role of the nth currency.[2]

Consider the case where all countries have identical macroeconomic structures. What gives rise to exchange rate changes in this world? If changes in exchange rates have real effects, one would expect them if countries are hit by asymmetric shocks. As shown in Giavazzi-Giovannini 1989, in this case they can be used as devices to share the costs of exogenous shocks among all countries. An optimal redistribution of the costs of exogenous shocks is attained if exchange rates were set in a coordinated fashion, *together with the nth country monetary policy.*[3]

The difficulties of practically implementing coordination on both exchange rates and monetary policy among European partners raise the question of whether noncooperative exchange rate setting would differ significantly. Consider the case where the *n*th country only sets its own money supply, and the other countries independently manage their exchange rates. As proved in Giavazzi-Giovannini 1989, as long as countries' inflation rates are linked through the exchange rate effect of imported goods prices, there are incentives to change exchange rates even in the face of common exogenous shocks and complete symmetry of all macroeconomies. This happens in response to supply shocks. In this case exchange rate appreciations enable countries to disinflate more easily by transmitting higher prices abroad through the exchange rate appreciation.

The possibility to help price stabilization through a real appreciation within the EMS suggests an interpretation of the recent real appreciation of the French franc and the lira in correspondence with the surge of the dollar. An appreciation of the dollar is the equivalent of a combined demand and supply shock in Europe. The positive demand shock gives no incentive to change competitiveness among European countries. In response to the supply shock, however, countries other than Germany should try to engineer a real appreciation to help price stabilization by exporting higher prices to Germany. During the years from 1979 to 1985 France, and especially Italy, have appreciated in real terms vis-à-vis Germany during the EMS period, in correspondence with the dollar appreciation. We cannot prove that the evolution of the real exchange rates was the result of a deliberate action on the part of those countries. We can conclude, however, that in the present regime such real appreciation was in the best interest of France and Italy to effectively shift part of the disinflation cost towards their European partners.

5.2   Costs and Benefits of a Currency Union

Our discussion has argued that in a system of fixed but adjustable parities, even if countries are identical there is a potential for exchange rate instability because countries have an incentive to move the exchange rate in order to shift the burden of adjustment onto their neighbors.[4] With asymmetric countries, the fragility of fixed parities further increases, because exchange rate changes are the easiest instrument to use for redistributing asymmetric shocks if short run international factor mobility is low.

Thus there is one important tradeoff which lies behind the choice of an exchange rate regime in Europe. On the one hand, the theoretical appeal of fixed exchange rates is that they eliminate in incentive to use "beggar thy neighbor" policies. On the other hand, in the absence of significant international factor mobility and of fiscal redistributions, adjustable parities can be efficient in the short run at evening out country-specific imbalances but can also be use for selfish purposes, at everybody's loss

Divergences among European countries, however, are still perhaps the feature which dominates the present system. A noticeable imbalance is the different use of the inflation tax. The ability of governments to generate revenue through seignorage attached to money creation is an important constraint of monetary policies. Countries resolve to the inflation tax not only in extreme situations when this becomes their last resort, but also in normal times, as an alternative to an often rigid fiscal decision making process. Differences in fiscal structure may therefore justify differences in the desired revenue from the inflation tax. Thus an obstacle towards the creation of a currency union arises from unwillingness to agree on the optimal inflation for all countries involved.

Table 5.1 shows the revenue from seignorage as a percentage of GDP, in several European countries, computed as in Fischer (1982). Italy is clearly the outlier, but there is some dispersion of the inflation tax also across the rest of Europe.

If adjustable parities are then perceived as the only viable alternative at the moment, we have to account for another cost of the present system. Under fixed but adjustable parities the anticipation of exchange rate realignments induces balance of payments crises if domestic monetary authorities try to minimize the volatility of short term interest rates. Although strong currencies countries can sterilize attacks in various ways, weak currencies countries can only use capital controls to stabilize domestic short term interest rates.[5] The evidence on the movements of offshore rates before EMS realignments indeed confirms that the anticipation

Table 5.1
The inflation tax (percent of GDP, average 1978–1984)

Switzerland	Germany	U.K.	Belgium	Denmark	Netherlands	France	Italy
−.08	.2	.2	.2	.3	.6	.6	2.4

Source: *International Financial Statistics*, and authors' calculations.

of realignments could move short-term domestic interest rates (overnight to one month) dramatically.[6] The likelihood of sharp increases of domestic interest rates is enhanced by the possibility that the expectation of a realignment be self-fulfilling, and that speculative attacks take place in the absence of changes in "fundamentals." In the present system weak currencies countries have to choose between the welfare losses associated with capital controls and the losses arising from the volatility of short-term domestic interest rates, and, as the evidence shows, overwhelmingly opt for the former.

The observation that countries use capital controls to prevent speculative attacks in anticipation of exchange rate realignments, suggests that capital controls tend to go together with fixed but adjustable rates. As Fischer (1985) points out, the degree of capital mobility is not independent of the exchange rate regime.[7] A system of credibly fixed parities would reduce the need to impose capital controls.

The issue of credibility is important, because under fixed exchange rates countries retain sovereign powers over their own currencies, and cannot be legally prevented from exercising it. The real issue at the center of negotiations should therefore be whether a monetary unification is desirable, and what it would look like.

5.3 All Saints' Day Ten Years Later

On November 1, 1975, nine prominent European economists issued a manifesto for European monetary union.[8] The manifesto recommended that European central banks issue a parallel currency, Europa, against national moneys. Europa's exchange rate is determined by a constant purchasing power rule, measured in terms of common European basket of goods. The purpose of this parallel currency was to substitute national moneys with a single money of stable purchasing power. According to the proponents, currency substitution would have taken place spontaneously in the markets, because Europa would have offered a more stable store of value and unit of account.[9]

The rationale of this proposal rested on the comparison of the classical arguments for and against optimal currency areas. The manifesto attributed the gains from a common currency to the informational advantages of using a common numeraire, the efficiency of a single money as a unit of account and a store of value, lower transactions cost in international trade, and the elimination of exchange rate risk. It recognized that the social costs of a monetary unification which have to be dealt with arise from the large regional diversity across Europe. It therefore suggested that the institution of a common currency be accompanied by a series of supply-side policies and fiscal reforms, designed to eliminate the causes of regional imbalances, and transitory income transfers, to alleviate the costs of sectoral shocks in the transition.

Our discussion adds a few items to this cost-benefit analysis of a monetary unification. On the benefits side, it stresses that such a system avoids potentially costly "beggar thy neighbor" policies, which are a common outcome of adjustable rates systems, where countries have an incentive to move the exchange rate to shift the burden of the adjustment upon their partners. Furthermore, a viable currency union allows avoiding the costs of capital controls, which, as we have shown, are normally associated with a system of fixed but adjustable parities.

On the costs side, we feel that fiscal policy is the core of the problem. The task of designing an efficient Europe-wide system of taxation and income redistribution is by no means solved. In the absence of such a system regional shocks would give rise to costs which probably exceed the benefits of monetary unification outlined above.

Notes

1. Most of the literature compares fixed rates with *flexible* rates rather than managed rates. For example, currency unions have recently been studied by Canzoneri (1982) and Marston (1985a, 1985b) in the context of a three-country model where the three countries represent the two union members and a nonmember country. The analysis of these authors focusses on the fact that output and employment in the countries which are members of the union depend upon their effective exchange rates, which are a weighted average of the intra-union real exchange rate, and of competitiveness vis-à-vis the nonmember country. They construct examples where stabilizing the intra-union exchange rate destabilizes the trade-weighted exchange rate of one or both countries. This is usually the case when shocks which affect member countries are asymmetric. Canzoneri, for example, discusses what can be thought of as a shift of goods or asset demands from Germany to the US. Because France and Germany are identical, flexible exchange rates insulate the French economy from the demand shift from between Germany and the US. Fixed exchange rates, however, tend to carry the disturbance to the French labor market and are therefore a source of conflict within the union. They stabilize output in Germany at the cost of destabilizing it in France. This work clearly points to the strategic aspects of exchange rate policy in Europe.

2. See, among others, the discussion of Emerson (1982) who points to the leading role of West Germany in setting European interest rate policy. Micossi (1985) provides further evidence in support of this view.

3. These exchange rate changes are the ones discussed by Mundell (1968) in his analysis of optimal currency areas.

4. In reality, real appreciations can be contrived by higher inflation countries by delaying exchange rate realignments.

5. For a theoretical analysis of the use of capital controls in a system of adjustable parities, see Wyplosz (1984).

6. The movement of longer term rates (six to twelve months) is of course less pronounced, as documented by Collins (1984).

7. This discussion suggests that capital controls in Europe are not an independent obstacle towards monetary integration, and that financial liberalization should not be considered a preliminary step towards monetary unification. Liberalization of financial markets was prominent point in the "Report on Liberalization of Internal Markets" prepared by the EEC Commissioner Lord Cockfield for the Milan Summit in June 1985.

8. The All Saints' Day Manifesto for European Monetary Union, by G. Basevi, M. Fratianni, H. Giersch, P. Korteweg, D. O'Mahony, M. Parkin, T. Peeters, P. Salin, and N. Thygesen, *The Economist*, November 1, 1975.

9. A common currency for Europe has recently been forcefully advocated by the former French President Valery Giscard d'Estaing. See *The Economist*, August, 30, 1985.

References

Canzonieri, M. B. 1982. "Exchange Intervention Policy in a Multiple Country World," *Journal of International Economics*, 13, pp. 267–289.

Collins, S. 1984. "Exchange Rate Expectations and Interest Parity During Credibility Crisis: The Franch Franc, March 1983," Harvard University.

Emerson, M. 1982. "Experience under the EMS and Prospects for Further Progress towards EMU," in M. T. Summer and G. Zis, eds., *European Monetary Union*, New York: St. Martin's Press.

Fisher, S. 1982. "Seignorage and the Case for a National Money," *Journal of Political Economy*, April, pp. 295–314.

Fisher, S. 1985. "The SDR and the IMF: Towards a World Central Bank," in G. M. von Furstenberg, ed., *International Money and Credit: The Policy Roles*, Washington, D.C.: International Monetary Fund.

Giavazzi, F. and A. Giovannini, 1989. "Monetary Policy Interactions Under Managed Exchange Rates," *Economica*, 56, May, pp. 199–213.

Marston, R. C. 1985a. "Exchange Rate Unions as an Alternative to Flexible Rates: The Effects of Real and Monetary Disturbances," in J. F. O. Bilson and R. C. Marston, eds., *Exchange Rate Theory and Practice*, Chicago: Chicago University Press.

Marston, R. C. 1985b. Financial Disturbances and the Effects of an Exchange Rate Union," in J. P. Bhandari, ed., *Exchanges Rate Management under Uncertainty*, Cambridge: MIT Press.

Micossi, S. 1985. "The Intervention and Financial Mechanisms of the EMS and the Role of the ECU," *Bank of Italy*, September.

Mundell, R. A. 1968. *International Economics*, New York: Macmillian.

Wyplosz, C. 1984. "Capital Controls and Balance of Payments Crises," INSEAD, Fontainbleau.

6   Does Europe Need Its Own Central Bank?

(with Marcello De Cecco,
August 1988)

6.1 Introduction

The initiatives to discuss the establishment of a centralized monetary authority in Europe, coming from government officials, have caught observers by surprise. The European Monetary System (EMS) has proved to the whole world to be a viable arrangement, and has been able to withstand the sizeable international financial shocks of the early 1980s: an immediate threat to the EMS is thus not evident. These initiatives, however, should all the more be applauded, since they signal the concern of governments with the fast evolution of the European economies and capital markets. The renewed debate on a European central bank reopens the questions of whether current monetary institutions will be obsolete and incapable of functioning in the face of the seemingly unstoppable trend towards market integration, and of the viability of new institutional arrangements among central banks.

In the significant body of research on the EMS there is little concern with the issue of a European central bank. Existing work concentrates on interpreting EMS experience, and evaluating the performance of that system. The purpose of this chapter is to describe the background to the question of monetary unification, the arguments according to which Europe would need its own central bank, and the problems of designing viable institutional arrangements, in the light of historical experience.

In section 6.2 we list the reasons why the institution of a central bank is viewed—at least by some—as a desirable step to take in Europe. These include a desire to further the process of monetary unification that the EMS has not contributed to accelerate, and concern with the potential disruptive effects of the complete liberalization of financial markets planned for 1992. Section 6.3 surveys the contributions of this volume to the theory of optimum currency areas. Section 6.4 discusses the historical experience, and section 6.5 considers proposals for institutional reform.

6.2 Background

It is possible to identify two separate arguments for the creation of a European central bank. The first stems from the recognition that the EMS has failed to spontaneously bring about monetary unification. This observation leads to asking the reasons for this failure: was the system ill-designed; did member countries wilfully resist monetary unification; or is the very concept of gradualism unworkable in the case of monetary reforms?

The second argument relates directly to the way monetary policy has operated during the EMS years: countries have not eliminated inflation differentials, and have resorted to periodic exchange rate realignments to avoid ever-growing divergences in relative prices. The "weak-currency" countries have preserved stability in their domestic financial markets by systematically resorting to capital controls: these capital controls have been essential for the smooth working of the EMS. The complete liberalization planned for the year 1992 would then seriously destabilize domestic financial markets, unless market participants perceived countries' commitment to a European monetary union as a credible one. According to this argument, the only credible commitment to a monetary union is the monetary union itself.

6.2.1 The EMS and the Commitment to Monetary Unification

The EMS was viewed by its creators as an intermediate step towards monetary unification. The Conclusion of the Presidency of the European Council of 4 December 1978 stated:

The purpose of the European Monetary System is to establish a greater measure of monetary stability in the Community. It should be seen as a fundamental component of the more comprehensive strategy aimed at lasting growth with stability, a progressive return to full employment, the harmonization of living standards and the lessening of regional disparities within the Community. The Monetary System will facilitate the convergence of economic development and give fresh impetus to the process of European Union.

The "transition" role of the EMS is apparent in the features that represented institutional novelties over the experiments that preceded it in the second postwar period: the Bretton Woods System and the Snake. Unlike its predecessors, the EMS is characterized by a special "money"—the European Currency Unit (ECU)[1]—and by an institution to control the issuance of this money, the European Monetary Fund (EMF).

The ECU's functions, as laid out by the Resolution of the the European Council on the establishment of the EMS (of 5 December 1978), were to serve: as numéraire for the EMS exchange rate mechanism (to establish bilateral central rates); as the basis for the indicator of divergence; as the numéraire for central bank financial operations; and as a means of settlement between monetary authorities in the European Community. The 1978 Resolution also established a two-year deadline after the start of the EMS for the full utilization of the ECU as a reserve asset and a means of settlement.

The role of the European Monetary Cooperation Fund was also much enhanced by the Resolution establishing the EMS. The Fund was supposed to provide a supply of ECU that served as means of settlement of central bank transactions, against the deposit of 20% of gold and 20% of dollar reserves held by member countries' central banks. Hence the Resolution created an embryo of a European central bank.

Has the EMS actually provided the "fresh impetus to the process of European Union "hoped for by its creators? The experience of the last ten years suggests a plainly negative answer to that question. The symptom of the inability of the EMS to boost monetary unification is the lack of any substantial role played by the European Fund and the ECU. The former remained just an account at the Bank of International Settlements, used for the clearing of the bilateral credits arranged through the Very Short Term Financing Facility. The latter never rose to perform the functions of a European money, but has been used, in official and private transactions,[2] only as an accounting unit.

Indeed, the functioning of the EMS in its first ten years strikingly resembles the functioning of other fixed exchange rates regimes:[3] the gold standard and the Bretton Woods regime. Like the earlier experiences, the conduct of monetary policy was under the control of a "centre" country—West Germany. The other countries either largely accommodated Germany's monetary policy, as did Ireland, at an allegedly high price in terms of domestic employment and welfare,[4] or achieved temporary monetary independence with the use of capital controls, as did France and Italy. This pattern also characterizes earlier experiences: monetary policy was dominated by the United Kingdom during the gold standard and—at least to some extend—by the US during the Bretton Woods years.[5] Capital controls were also used by countries other than Britain during the gold standard,[6] and by the European countries, including West Germany, during the Bretton Woods years.

Was the failed promise of the EMS due to defective design of the institutions? Analysis of the regulations governing the EMS suggests that the institutions were clearly not designed to bypass the sovereignty of individual countries' monetary authorities, as would be needed to achieve monetary unification. The rules governing the use of the ECU and the European central bank, as well as the rules governing intervention and central bank financing, were loose enough to allow independent manoeuvre by individual countries. For example, the compulsory intervention in the foreign exchange market that is required by the EMS when two currencies reach bilateral fluctuation bands does not impose any constraint on monetary policies, since countries can freely sterilize reserve flows.[7] The ECU has not functioned effectively as a common benchmark for monetary policies, since countries were not compelled to take specified corrective actions when the so-called divergence indicator reached the predetermined thresholds. These corrective actions were just presumed.[8] Similarly the EMS guidelines, while not precluding future enhancements of the role of the European Fund, do not in any way state the ultimate purpose of that institution.

In summary, the implementation of a monetary union is only a "good intention" in the rules governing the EMS. The careful exclusion from those rule of all the features that could have brought about an infringement of monetary sovereignty have prevented any further autonomous evolution of the EMS.

6.2.2   Liberalization and the Instability of Financial Markets

The second argument for a European central bank is based on the view that liberalization of international capital flows would make the EMS collapse.

The collapse of a system of fixed (but adjustable) rates with perfect capital mobility could be caused by two sets of factors. First, there is the presence of different trends in monetary growth in the member countries. Although since 1979 inflation rates and monetary growth rates have converged significantly in Europe, countries like France and Italy are still viewed as "weak" members, since their inflation rates are still roughly double those in West Germany. These countries afford higher inflation than West Germany by severing domestic financial markets from the rest of the world, and thereby preventing or minimizing the speculative attacks that take place in anticipation of the inevitable exchange rate depreciations.[9] The second set of factors which could account for the collapse of a system of adjustable parities with perfect international capital mobility is the possibility of *self-fulfilling* speculative attacks, that is runs on central banks that are not justified by divergent trends in monetary policies, relative to money demands. In the presence of self-fulfilling speculation, the very existence of different currencies—which is the implicit recognition that, at least remotely, their relative valuation can be changed—is enough to trigger speculators' activity.

What is the effect of speculation? The analysis of Euro-currency markets at times of turbulence provides a vivid illustration. When realignments of the order of 3–5% are expected to occur, short-term interest rates shoot up to 40–60% in the currencies expected to depreciate. These movements are fully consistent with the expectations about currency realignment: if the devaluation is expected to be 5% within one month, interest rate differentials on one-month deposits should be 60% (5% times 12) on a per-annum basis, to compensate for the expected capital loss. Hence it is safe to assume that, if international capital flows were fully liberalized, such short-term interest rate swings would affect domestic financial markets as well.

Supporters of the trend towards financial liberalization claim that free capital markets will force central banks to converge, without any need to unify the currencies by law. Historical experience, on the other hand, has shown that in times of crisis central banks have most frequently resorted to a temporary abrogation of the "rules of the game" imposed by international monetary arrangements: this happened during the gold standard when the Bank of England suspended the convertibility of banknotes into gold in 1847, 1857 and 1866 (as Keynes, 1930; De Cecco, 1974a, and Dornbusch and Frenkel, 1984, documented), and has happened during the Bretton Woods years and the EMS years, when countries have resorted to various forms of regulations to stem speculative inflows[10] and outflows.[11] Since liberalization of capital controls cannot strip central banks of the right to make regulations concerning financial intermediaries and the use of currency, in times of crisis central banks would still have the option of temporarily invalidating international arrangements. Thus we are led to conclude that the liberalization of financial markets does indeed present a most serious threat to the stability of the existing monetary institutions in Europe.

6.3 The Lessons of History

We now discuss the institutional feasibility of a common monetary authority. In this task, it is usually enlightening to bring back into focus some historical facts. The German and Italian experiences in the 19th century might be of interest as examples of monetary unifications, while the creation of the Federal Reserve system in the early 20th century is an example of the creation of a "federal" central bank.

The German and Italian experiences with monetary unification are deceptively similar at first glance. In both cases one state, Prussia and Piedmont, actively promoted political unity and, having achieved it through military victory, proceeded to establish its monetary system over the whole territory of the unified country.

But the similarity ends there. The Reichsbank and the Banca Nazionale nel Regno d'Italia (BNRI) managed to obtain a dominant position over bank note issue. The Reichsbank was a state institution, whose creation coincided with the proclamation of the German Reich. The BNRI, on the contrary, was a private bank (though its connections with the Government were close) while the banks of issue of the Kingdom of the Two Sicilies were public banks. This difference between the two cases helps to explain why the Italian monetary experience was much more chequered than the German one. The New Reich, moreover, started with hefty gold reparations of 5 billion francs paid by France, while the Kingdom of Italy began its life with a huge pile of public debt and an equally huge fiscal deficit. Even more important, before unification, Germany had become an integrated economic area and a united currency area, which was based on a silver standard. Italy, on the contrary, was a patchwork of economically heterogeneous states which, at the time of political unification, traded much more with foreign countries that with one another. Unlike the German states, they were not united by a network or railways. And the two main components of the new state, Piedmont and the Kingdom of the Two Sicilies, had currencies based on different standards, the former on bimetallism (like the French), the latter on a pure silver standard.

We have thus two cases that are extremely relevant for the present debate on European monetary union. The Italian case shows political and monetary unification preceding economic integration. The German case shows economic and monetary integration leading to political unification. We are the latest in a very long line of researchers believing that Italian unification was a sudden and largely unexpected event, while German unification was a long and gradual process which occupied the best part of the 19th century. This basic difference can go far toward explaining the great difficulties which the new Italian state experienced in the economic and monetary fields, and in particular the long and difficult process of building a modern banking system around a publicly controlled central bank. On the other hand, the great success of the German Reich can be attributed to the economic and monetary unification which preceded political unity. The influence of the immediate past over the present and future, both in the case of Germany and Italy, seems to have been overwhelming.[12]

Early attempts at European monetary unification, like that promoted in the Werner Report of 1970, can be likened to Italy in 1860 or even 1870. Economic and financial unity was not advanced enough in either case to justify the great step forward represented by monetary union. The economic integration of Europe in 1988 is arguably much greater than it was at the time of the Werner Report. The motorway network (which has had an impact on integration comparable to that of railways in the 19th century) is now much more complete than it was then, and it allows greater economic and social interchange (witness the much smaller size of firms engaged in intra-European trade). Total intra-European trade has stabilized for many years at a very high level, so that the interpenctration of the economies is much greater (witness the increased trade in intermediate, semiprocessed and component goods among EC countries). This evolution reminds us of Germany's experiences.

Monetary union, in its 19th century incarnation as free circulation of coins among states and in its present reincarnation as joint floating plus liberalization of capital flows, is altogether possible without political unification. A central bank to control monetary policy over the whole area of the Union, however, is the single most important step into uncharted territory, when it is not preceded by political union.

How were local interests reconciled by central monetary authorities? The Federal Reserve Charter, the Federal Reserve Act of 1913, is the expression of a much more heterogeneous economic reality that the Reichsbank foundation law, the Bank Act of 1871. The plurality of the Federal Reserve Banks witnesses that clearly, as it had been the case with the National Banking Act of 1861. But the problem of discretionary money creation was solved by the US decision to adopt the gold standard, just as it was solved by the German States by adopting silver convertibility and by the Reich by switching to the gold standard. The inelasticity of a commodity standard was, however, taken into account by the Federal Reserve Act and by the Bank Act, by allowing a possibility of exercising discretionary money creation. It is precisely that possibility that permitted the interest stabilisation which Miron (1989) attributes to the Fed and criticises as the Fed's main policy target. Interest stabilisation was one of the main policy targets of the pre-1914 Reichsbank too, widely admired, as the similar policy adopted by the Banque de France, by the members of the National Monetary Commission, and favourably contrasted with the vagaries of US and British interest rates.

Thus both the US and Germany worked on semi-automatic commodity standards, which gave central banks a wider discretionary space than is normally remembered in today's discussions. It might be useful to consider also that the Fed's regional pluralism over the conduct of monetary policy was imitated by the (American) designers of the present-day German central bank. Even this diffusion of power, however, is altogether different from what is at stake with the creation of a European Central Bank. In both the German and the US cases the greater devolution of powers over monetary policy takes place within the context of one Government and one currency. Neither has yet been achieved in Europe.

Notes

1. The ECU is defined as a basket comprising the currencies of the countries members of the European Economic Community, hence it includes currencies, like the Greek drachma and Pound sterling, which are not part of the EMS.

2. The issuance of bonds dominated in a basket of currencies identical to the ECU has boomed in recent years in the Euromarkets.

3. The fluctuation bands that characterize the EMS have also been a feature of the gold standard and the Bretton Woods regime. For example, under Bretton Woods, the maximum fluctuation of bilateral European rates was 4%, versus 4.5% in the EMS. The lira is of course an exception to the rule.

4. See Moore (1988).

5. See Giovannini (1988) for a formulation of this hypothesis, and empirical evidence supporting it.

6. In the form of manipulation of gold points, and limited convertibility of banknotes into gold for exports.

7. In fact, intervention at the fluctuation margins has been just a small fraction of total intervention.

8. In practice, the divergence indicator has a host of additional problems originating from the asymmetric weights of the different currencies. It has played no significant role in the functioning of the EMS.

9. Giavazzi and Giovannini (1989) provide a survey of Italian and French controls on international capital flows, and a formal analysis of their effects.

10. As in the case of Germany in 1960.

11. The French and Italian experience in 1968 and 1969, as well as in the more recent years, is relevant.

12. Another important factor was that the BNRI, as the first and especially the Second Bank of the United States, was a commercial bank trying to establish itself, with some backing from the government, as a central bank. The Reichsbank, by contrast, was confined to the public good by its charter. This contrast, while historically pertinent, is not useful for the present-day debate. Central banks are now firmly established as public banks, and no-one can think of giving back to them a commercial banking function.

References

De Cecco, M. 1974a. *Money and Empire*, Totowa, N.J.: Rowman and Littlefield.

De Cecco, M. 1974b. "Optimum Currency Areas and European Monetary Integration," *Journal of World Trade Law*, 8, pp. 463–474.

Dornbusch, R. and J. Frenkel. 1984. "The Gold Standard Crisis of 1847," *Journal of International Economics*, 16, pp. 1–27.

Giavazzi, F. and A. Giovannini. 1989. *Limiting Exchange Rate Flexibility: The European Monetary System*, Cambridge, MA: MIT Press.

Giovannini A. 1989. "How do Fixed-Exchange-Rate Regimes Work: The Evidence on the Gold Standard, Bretton Woods and EMS," in M. Miller, B. Eichengreen and R. Portes, eds., *Blueprints for Exchange Rate Management*, New York: Academic Press, also chapter 2 in this volume.

Keynes, J. M. 1930. *A Treatise on Money*, London: Macmillian.

Miron, J. 1989. "The Founding of the Fed and the Destabilization of the post 1914 Us Economy," in M. De Cecco and A. Giovannini eds., *A European Central Bank*, Cambridge University Press.

Moore, M. 1988. "Deflationary Consequences of a Hard Currency Peg," mimeo, Research Department, Central Bank of Ireland.

Obstfeld, M. 1988. "Competitiveness, Realignment, and Speculation: The Role of Financial Markets," in F. Giavazzi, S. Micossi and M. Miller eds., *The European Monetary System*, Cambridge: Cambridge University Press.

III

The Delors Report and the
Transition to Monetary
Union

7   The Transition to European Monetary Union

(February 1990)

7.1   Introduction

The Delors Report, prepared in 1989 by the Committee for the Study of Economic and Monetary Union, provides a broad framework for the transition toward monetary union in Europe. It does not, however, specify in detail how to manage it:

> At this juncture, the Committee does not consider it possible to propose a detailed blueprint for accomplishing this transition, as this would depend on the effectiveness of the policy coordination achieved during the first stage, on the provisions of the Treaty, and on the decisions to be taken by the new institutions. Account would also have to be taken of the continued impact of financial innovation (par. 57).

It is necessary now to consider detailed plans. In December 1990, European governments will meet to shape the institutions and make appropriate changes in the Treaty of Rome to guide the transition and manage the monetary union. Discussion of proposals now will help to establish the structure and agreements necessary to effect timely progress toward integration and to forestall problems during the transition.

This chapter describes a plan for monetary transition that both challenges and expands upon the conclusions of the Delors Report. It identifies the conditions that must be met to ensure stability of the European Monetary System (EMS) during transition and achieve agreement within the European Community (EC) regarding the role of the European System of Central Banks (ESCB) in harmonizing national and Community monetary and exchange-rate policies.

The main feature of the Delors Report is the concept of gradualism: integration is to be achieved over time in order to adapt the economies and policymaking processes to monetary union. The transition will be accomplished in stages by removing barriers to the integration of goods and financial markets while simultaneously strengthening policy coordination and progressively building up the institutions that will manage the new European money.

This chapter considers the questions raised by gradualism and the reasons why that strategy might lead to weak economic convergence that will make the transition more difficult to accomplish. It suggests several simple devices to strengthen the credibility of the gradual reforms and to forestall disruptions that could postpone monetary integration.

The chapter accepts the fundamental premise of the Delors Report that monetary union is the final objective, for the reforms European governments will be considering would, and should, be quite different if that were not the final goal. To embark upon reforms without committing to ultimate integration would create a monetary system in Europe that would be truly "half baked" (to borrow the expression, but only the expression, from an outspoken observer), prone to financial instability and inflationary pressures.

Some possible explanations for the Committee's choice of a step-by-step approach are analyzed in section 7.2 of this chapter. Section 7.3 discusses the risks of the transition. Section 7.4 presents a proposal to ease the transition and discusses in detail the institutions that could support it. The currency reform is outlined in section 7.5. Section 7.6 relates the proposal presented here to the framework of the Delors Report. And section 7.7 contains concluding observations.

7.2 Gradualism in the Delors Report

The choice of a gradual approach to monetary union in the Delors Report is not the result of an explicit analysis of alternatives. Indeed, the Report simply states that, following the 1988 deliberations of the European Council confirming the objective of economic and monetary union, the Committee has concentrated on "studying and proposing concrete stages leading towards the *progressive realization of economic and monetary union*" (par. 15).

One of the reasons for adopting a gradual approach appears to be the political difficulty of monetary integration. The Committee offers a sequence of three concrete and pragmatic stages leading toward monetary union but leaves the choice of pace to the national governments; it states that "the question of when these stages should be implemented is a matter for political decision" (par. 15).

Another likely reason for the Committee's choice is that monetary union is viewed as only one part of a much broader plan for an economic union that includes the single market, common competition and structural policies, and the coordination of macroeconomic policies. The Committee recognizes a double feedback between economic convergence and monetary convergence (see par. 42). Because economic convergence can be achieved only through a slow and lengthy series of reforms, monetary convergence should conceivably be designed to follow at the same pace. This argument is also supported by the view that monetary integration can be achieved only when the loss of the exchange-rate instrument has ceased to be serious, that is, when markets and policies are sufficiently integrated. It is likewise related to, but does not fully coincide with, the classic theory of optimum currency areas (see Kenen, 1969). Although the completion of the single European market will presumably create the conditions for Europe to become an optimum currency area, the convergence of national macroeconomic policies is not necessarily a desirable goal for such an area. The relevance of arguments relating to optimum currency areas for the transition to monetary union is discussed further in section 7.4 below.

A final explanation for the Committee's choice of a gradual transition might be the cost of adapting institutions. The management of a European currency, or even irrevocably locked exchange rates, will require a European monetary institution operating alongside other institutions. Its creation will require a change in the Treaty of Rome, and that change will have to be incorporated into national laws. This sequence will inevitably take time. In addition, because the political and administrative structure of the EC is quite different from that of a federal state, the new European central bank will operate in unprecedented political and economic circumstances. It can be argued, therefore, that the shaping of the new institutions should take time, to allow for some learning by doing and some flexibility in adapting to unforeseen problems.

In line with the gradualist approach, the Delors Report recommends that the duration of the two stages preceding the monetary union be left unspecified. The first stage, begun in July 1990, should accomplish the liberalization of financial markets, enlargement of membership in the exchange-rate mechanism (ERM) of the European Monetary System (EMS), and a change in the mandate of the Committee of Central Bank Governors (CCBG). The second stage should establish the European System of Central Banks (ESCB), which would initially operate alongside the national monetary authorities. The third stage should accomplish the irrevocable fixing of exchange rates and complete the transfer of monetary authority to the ESCB.

The Report clearly reflects an awareness of the need for substantial monetary convergence following the removal of capital controls and the increased substitutability of national currencies (par. 22), but it does not seem to have weighed appropriately the threats to monetary stability that may arise from the liberalization and deregulation of financial markets. It does not even seem to regard exchange-rate stability as an overriding requirement for the transition to monetary union; even during the second stage, exchange-rate changes are not ruled out (par. 57). Finally, the Report does not ask what would happen if the plan for monetary union were seen to be less than fully credible, but the effects of that possibility are likely to be the main problem of the gradualist approach. These threats are discussed and evaluated in the next section.

7.3 The Dangers of the Transition

The main economic problems of the transition toward European Monetary Union (EMU) stem from the uncontrollable behavior of private-sector expectations in both the financial and the goods and labor markets. These problems are discussed below.

Money Demand

Since the summer of 1990, financial capital has moved free of control among all the members of the ERM except Spain. This new freedom will create an environment for monetary policy that is dramatically different from that of the past ten years.[1]

A number of economists (including this one) believe that the EMS worked asymmetrically during its first decade, with one country at the center, the Federal Republic of Germany, serving as the "Nth country" and setting its monetary policy independently and the other members serving as the "N-1 countries" and progressively adjusting their monetary policies to accommodate those of the Bundesbank. Controls on capital flows were also important for EMS operations during its firs decade and served two main purposes:[2] (1) they allowed countries other than Germany to deviate, if only temporarily, from the monetary-policy stance followed by the Bundesbank, thus easing the convergence toward low inflation, and (2) they protected monetary policies from speculative pressures that were not dictated by fundamentals (i.e., self-fulfilling speculation).

The asymmetric structure of controls thus supported an asymmetry in monetary management. This structure has been altered, however, by the liberalization of French capital controls and the substantial loosening of Italian controls since 1985–86, and some believe that this liberalization also removed the asymmetry underlying the operations of the EMS. Whichever mode of operation, symmetric or asymmetric, will come to prevail following the full liberalization of capital movements in the summer of 1990, the conduct of monetary policy will become more difficult, not only for countries like France and Italy, but also for Germany, which will no longer be able to pursue its own objectives independently of external constraint.

In addition to the foreign-exchange pressures generated by temporary differences between national monetary policies, there is an intensified risk of "nonfundamental" speculation. It will be easier for speculators to provoke exchange-rate turbulence for their profit because it will be easier to take very large positions in European currencies. The relevance of destabilizing speculation is suggested by the behavior of the dollar exchange rate since the inception of generalized floating: to date, no sensible model of the foreign-exchange market based on fundamentals has been able to explain the extreme short-run volatility and unprecedented long-run swings of the dollar, a failure that suggests that much of the speculative activity in the foreign-exchange markets is not tightly linked to fundamentals.[3]

Further turbulence in the foreign-exchange market will come from the very substantial innovations in banking and financial markets soon to take place in Europe. The removal of barriers to competition in the banking industry (sanctioned by the Second Banking Directive) will create tremendous opportunities in the transactions-services business and in consumer banking. A first look at the data shows that the use of checks, credit cards, and automatic-teller machines is much more limited in Europe than in the United States. The potential for growth in these services is therefore significant. In addition, the currently wide divergence of reserve-to-deposit ratios suggests that the removal of competitive barriers will also put pressure on governments to lower them to a uniform standard, with very large effects on the stocks of national high-powered moneys. All of these developments will inevitably have destabilizing effects on the demand for money and will thus have repercussions in the exchange markets.

Finally, there are good reasons to expect switches in the demand for currencies. Firms and individuals are now able to hold checking accounts in any EC currency and are certainly free to choose any EMS currency to settle bilateral obligations.[4] The substitutability among currencies will be drastically increased by the ability of firms and individuals in all the EMS countries to diversify and actively manage their currency portfolios across a wide range of national moneys.

In summary, developments in financial markets during the transition will bring about (1) fluctuations in the demand for money provoked by financial innovation and deregulation in the banking industry, with ensuing instability in money markets, and (2) higher substitutability of national moneys, which will make the demand for individual currencies very responsive to rational or irrational views about the success of the transition to European Monetary Union and views about prospective movements of exchange rates.

Expectations

A second set of problems relates more directly to the adjustment of expectations. The first ten years of the EMS witnessed a very substantial, but incomplete, convergence of inflation rates. The lira and the French franc were remarkably stable in 1988 and 1989 despite the persistence of inflation differentials. As a result, the real effective exchange rates for these two currencies appreciated by between 2 to 4 percent in 1989 alone. The real appreciation of the Spanish peseta was even more significant at 5 percent. These movements in real exchange rates are the sum of two phenomena: real shocks and expectations. The Latin countries have tended to grow faster than the Federal Republic of Germany, producing differences in productivity growth, real wage pressures coming from demand pressures, and so on. These real shocks have given rise to changes in relative prices, reflected in appreciations of the real exchange rate and in the dynamics of current-account balances within the European Community. They cannot be effectively counteracted by monetary policies.

Expectations have also contributed to inflation differentials. Price setters, producers and unions, embody in their pricing and bargaining policies expectations about exchange-rate changes. These expectations are influenced by the credibility of the bilateral parities in the ERM, and they represent the most difficult obstacle to convergence. If, for example, producers and unions expect a devaluation of the national currency, and they raise prices and wages in light of that expectation, the rate of inflation will rise. The central bank can either refuse to devalue and thus accept a real appreciation and a current-account deficit, or it can accommodate inflation by devaluing the currency and thus validate the expectations.

The pressure to devalue will come not only from domestic exporters, but also from ERM partners, who would otherwise suffer from imported inflation. An example of this is provided by the debates throughout 1989 between the Bundesbank, on the one hand, and the Banque de France and Banca d'Italia, on the other, concerning the desirability of a devaluation of the lira and the French franc. Because inflation differentials had not been eliminated in 1989, fixed parities meant that Germany was importing inflation from her neighbors. For this reason, the Bundesbank advocated a devaluation of the franc and the lira, giving as the official justification the need to balance current accounts. France and Italy resisted these pressures, however, stating that devaluation would not by itself reduce current-account imbalances, but would simply give an extra push to domestic inflation.

This sequence illustrates a general phenomenon: even a slight probability of a devaluation prompts wage and price setters to hedge and therefore increases the domestic inflation rate. The resulting appreciation of the real exchange rate induces tensions with the partners in the ERM, because it exports inflation to the country that has exercised monetary restraint the most. Yet, changes in exchange rates to accommodate inflation differentials and angry partners amount to a declaration that public expectations were right, and that fixed rates are not sustainable. These devaluations also make the inflation differentials permanent, because they return relative prices to equilibrium. Thus, exchange-rate realignments defeat the purpose of the transition to monetary union. Only the fixing of bilateral parities can induce the convergence of expectations that is necessary to eliminate inflation differentials and—with the help of the full liberalization of capital movements—the convergence of national currencies. The achievement of these objectives will ease the final steps toward a single currency.

7.4 A Proposal for the Management of the Transition

The foregoing discussion leads to the first pillar of this proposal: no meaningful gradual transition to monetary union can allow exchange-rate parities to be changed during the process. As argued above, the fixity of central rates is necessary because any change in parities would accommodate permanent differences in inflation rates, recognize differences across

European currencies, and indefinitely postpone monetary convergence. To convey a clear message of commitment to the public, irrevocably fixed parities could be accompanied by some narrowing of the bilateral bands that limit fluctuations around the fixed parities.

The most important economic effect of fixed parities is, of course, to relinquish completely the advantages of changing the exchange rate to off-set relative price changes. Forsaking these advantages, which are most prominently discussed in the literature on optimum currency areas, is the most serious cost of the transition. There are reasons to believe, however, that the stability of exchange rates might by itself bring about the closer integration of goods and factors markets that provides the backbone of an optimum currency area. This argument is presented by Bertola (1989) and relies on the observation that the reactions of producers and consumers to price incentives can be significantly less elastic in the presence of exchange-rate uncertainty than in its absence. This important modification of the original theory of optimum currency areas might substantially diminish the cost of relinquishing exchange-rate changes from the beginning of the transition period. Eichengreen (1990), in a thorough and highly valuable analysis of the experience of the United States as a currency area, suggests that capital mobility is the most likely absorber of country-specific imbalances. He concludes, along the lines of Bertola, that the mobility of productive capital is likely to be enhanced by the disappearance of exchange-rate risk.

Because bilateral parities should not be changed during the transition, the gradualist approach cannot solve the fundamental problem of all fixed-rate regimes: disagreements among member countries about the appropriate stance of monetary policy cannot persist without bringing down the system. Even involuntary errors by central banks, such as errors in forecasting velocity, can seriously jeopardize exchange-rate parities by triggering large capital flows. Indeed, the tradeoff to be faced by European governments aiming at more stable exchange rates and more integrated financial markets is between credibility and flexibility. It is necessary to create a system in which exchange-rate parities are fully credible, but which allows enough flexibility for the monetary authorities both to adapt to changing conditions in national money markets, and, as the Delors Report suggests, to learn by doing.

To achieve this, I propose a modification in the mechanics of gradualism described in the Delors Report and suggest a structure for the European System of Central Banks (ESCB) that would allow flexible and credible management of the transition.

Gradualism Rescued

The Delors Report neither rules out exchange-rate changes nor specifies deadlines for the completion of stages one and two. These two omissions account for the weakness of the proposed transition plan. Recurrent instability in foreign-exchange markets and inflationary expectations could force governments into a series of exchange-rate realignments that would ultimately bring about a de facto dismemberment of the zone of monetary stability successfully created by the EMS. For this reason, realignments of central parities should be categorically ruled out during the transition.

An official pledge not to change bilateral parities, however, is not enough to ensure the credibility of the plan and smooth progress toward monetary union; ostensibly fixed exchange rates have been changed before in history. What is needed is a mechanism that automatically prevents destabilizing speculation from being successful and yet preserves the virtues of gradualism.

This mechanism would be a declaration by all governments embarking on stages one and two that disruptions in the foreign-exchange and money markets would be met, not by realignments, but by an acceleration instead of the final monetary reform and the creation of the single currency ahead of time. This option to accelerate the monetary union would give full credibility to the fixed bilateral parities during the transition.

What would be the cost of exercising this option? As argued in section 7.2, the advantages of gradualism appear to be associated with the political difficulties of a sudden monetary reform, the desire to achieve more integration of goods and financial markets (the optimum-currency-area argument) and the costs of adapting institutions.

If the acceleration of the monetary union were prompted by monetary disruptions during the transition, and if the alternative were the sure postponement of the union and the likely undoing of monetary integration (and consequent delay in the completion of the single market), the political obstacles to acceleration would probably be reduced to a minimum.

The sudden adoption of a single currency during the transition should not be of great concern from the standpoint of the optimum-currency-area argument. The opportunity cost of jumping from a system of irrevocably fixed rates to a single currency would be zero, because changes in bilateral parities would have been ruled out during the transition. Furthermore, central bankers in ERM countries are already using parity changes extremely sparingly, so that the loss of flexibility would be minimal.

The third argument for gradualism, the cost of adapting institutions, would still apply. It is plausible, however, that, given the substantial preparatory work governments are doing for the intergovernmental conference to be held in December 1990, they will have worked out most of the technical details for the creation of a European central bank: accelerating its creation should not require a large additional investment of technical resources.

Finally, it should be pointed out that the option of accelerating the monetary union has a very small probability of being exercised in a world of rational agents and well-working markets. The arguments presented above suggest that inflation differentials and exchange-rate realignments cannot disappear if governments have no credible means of convincing the public of the fixity of exchange rates. Rational price setters and foreign-exchange speculators would continue to expect realignments and would continue to behave in ways that brought them about, thereby validating their expectations. By contrast, rational agents would have no incentives to raise prices and stage runs on the central bank if they knew that the only effect of their activities would be to trigger immediately the "bear squeeze" of the currency reform.

Unfortunately, financial markets are not driven exclusively by rational behavior and do not always work flawlessly. It is therefore necessary to safeguard the option of acceleration by creating institutional arrangements that can absorb nonsystematic shocks and facilitate the coordination of national monetary authorities prior to the achievement of full monetary union. These institutional arrangements are described below.

How Should the European System of Central Banks Work?

To facilitate the transition to a common central bank, the ESCB could begin operations through two agencies an Exchange-Rate Stabilization Authority (ERSA) and the Board of Central Bank Governors (BCBG). This would allow for a clear separation of its responsibilities for bilateral exchange-rate intervention and for regulation of the money supply, and would distinguish them in turn from those of the national central banks, which would continue to be responsible for the supplies of the national currencies. Only the bilateral European exchange rates and foreign-exchange operations affecting the dollar rate would be delegated to ERSA. ERSA's dollar position, however, would be strictly limited by the member countries' central banks through the BCBG, which would act as a consulting body to help central bank governors coordinate national monetary policies. This institutional structure would meet three criteria necessary for a relatively easy convergence of monetary policies leading to European monetary union:

1. Transparency. When operating on intra-European exchange rates, ERSA would by definition be unable to affect the value of the aggregate stock of money of the countries in the system. It could only change the composition so as to accommodate shifts in demand among national currencies and thus stabilize exchange rates. Its positions in European currencies would therefore be limited by the size of its total resources. Its dollar operations, however, could change the total stock of money in Europe, and its dollar positions would therefore be strictly limited by the BCBG.

Under the plan proposed here, money creation during the transition would be left to the national central banks. The BCBG, however, would provide the ideal setting for monitoring the policy stances of member countries and for facilitating the reconciliation of national policies with the overall objective of fixed exchange rates. The BCBG would work in conjunction with ERSA, as its operations would indicate which currencies were "scarce" and which were "abundant." This working relationship is explained in more detail below.

Because ERSA would act independently and the BCBG would periodically evaluate the policies of individual countries in the light of ERSA's operations, the proposed separation of money creation from exchange-market intervention would make it comparatively easy for the BCBG to identify instances in which national central banks were sterilizing the effects of ERSA operations on their money stocks and thus to identify inconsistencies between national policies and the viability of the fixed exchange rates. This increased transparency would significantly facilitate the process of coordinating monetary policies so as to sustain the fixed rates.

2. Credibility. As argued above, bilateral parities should remain fixed during the transition to a single currency. The structure proposed here is very likely to enhance the credibility of fixed exchange rates for three reasons. First, it would provide a strong signal to foreign-exchange markets that fixed rates had become the overriding objective in the transition; an independent agency would act on behalf of the member countries in the foreign-exchange markets. Second, it would facilitate the coordination of monetary policies by separating the function of money creation from the pegging of exchange rates (more on this below). Third, it acknowledges that financial markets are not always correct and that they can be the source of serious disruptions; the proposed institutions would

strengthen the system of fixed rates by facilitating the absorption of fluctuations in currency demand that are not justified by changes in the economic fundamentals, rather than forcing countries to adjust to them immediately and passively.

3. Flexibility. The proposed system would be flexible both because it would permit learning by doing, without unduly exposing the fixed parities to speculative pressures, and because it could easily adapt to the changes required for the subsequent transition to a single currency and a common central bank.

Day-to-day operations under the new system would be facilitated by the ability of ERSA to absorb currency-specific shocks without compelling countries to adjust to them immediately. This flexibility would be essential in the initial phases of union, when the central banks of the individual countries would be learning how to operate the new system and possibly making errors that should not be permitted to jeopardize the system itself.

ERSA and the BCBG are well suited to become the two arms of the permanent European central bank in the final phase of monetary union. The BCBG could easily evolve from a purely monitoring and consulting organization into a decisionmaking body; it would be composed of the governors of the member countries' central banks, and it would have the institutional experience accumulated as a regulatory and advisory body. ERSA could become the principal foreign-exchange (dollar) intervention agency for the new system and even the principal agent for open-market operations, playing a role similar to that of the Federal Reserve Bank of New York in the Federal Reserve System.

The proposed system can be viewed simply as a strengthening of the current EMS institutions, and, seen in that light, it should be easy for member countries to accept. ERSA would be a stronger version of existing financing facilities and not very different from the original concept of the European Monetary Cooperation Fund (EMCF). The crucial change required would be to grant it independent status. Similarly, the BCBG resembles the Committee of Central Bank Governors, especially since the recent reform of November 1989. Under the proposed system, however, the BCBG would have a very precise role, defined by the nature and operations of its companion institution, ERSA.

More on the Exchange-Rate Stabilization Authority

ERSA would be physically and operationally distinct from the national central banks, which would give it the resources required to intervene in the foreign-exchange markets. Its foreign-exchange operations would be mainly for the purpose of pegging intra-European exchange rates. Specifically, at the beginning of its operations, ERSA would issue its own obligations to the national central banks in exchange for national currencies and foreign-exchange reserves. After that, the monetary policy of the national central banks would be limited to domestic operations and discount-rate changes.

In its intra-European operations, ERSA would be subject to no restrictions other than its own balance-sheet constraints. By contrast, its dollar operations would be strictly limited by position ceilings determined by the BCBG. To the extent that its transactions were aimed at maintaining fixed exchange rates among European currencies, its dollar portfolio would be unaffected by any operation involving a bilateral European rate.

ERSA would serve two fundamental roles:

1. It would be a buffer stock of currencies. ERSA would rebalance its portfolio in response to fluctuations in the demand for European currencies in the foreign-exchange markets. These fluctuations might be due either to a lack of synchronization between private demands and supplies of moneys (changes in velocity that cannot be perfectly forecast by national authorities) or to the less-than-smooth working of the foreign-exchange markets. The ability of ERSA to respond quickly to market fluctuations would relieve the national central banks of the need for an immediate response, thus strengthening the system.

2. It would be a thermometer. The evolution of ERSA's portfolio would reflect trends in imbalances between supplies of national currencies and the demands for them. If there were no such imbalances on average, the composition of ERSA's portfolio would tend to be stable.

Pronounced and persistent imbalances in the portfolio would, therefore, constitute a warning that national monetary policies were not consistent with the maintenance of fixed exchange rates. These portfolio imbalances would be brought to the attention of the BCBG, which would propose and facilitate the choice of strategies to eliminate inconsistencies among national monetary policies.

Operations in the intra-European foreign-exchange market would necessarily leave the value of ERSA's portfolio unchanged; in the absence of changes in intra-European exchange rates, the value of its purchases would always equal the value of its sales. If its operations could not change its total holdings of European currencies, however, then ERSA could not affect the total value of European currencies held by the public; it could only affect the composition.

The size of possible profits and losses from intra-European currency management would be limited by the bilateral bands limiting currency fluctuations relative to the bid-ask spreads. By contrast, the size of profits and losses on dollar operations would be determined by the size of the dollar positions ERSA was allowed to take and the horizon over which it was given independence. These parameters could be fine-tuned by the member countries. In general, the more stable the intra-European exchange rates, the more profitable would be ERSA.

The last problem to be addressed pertains to the optimal size of ERSA—the total value of its currency portfolio. Because the objective of ERSA would be to carry out operations in the foreign-exchange market independently and efficiently, thus lending credibility to the exchange-rate targets, it would be necessary to ensure that it had sufficient resources without borrowing any of the currencies of the member countries. It should never run out of any currency in its portfolio. To measure sufficiency, it would be necessary to estimate the likely fluctuations in money demand relative to supply, a procedure complicated by two sets of problems. First, expectations about the credibility of the fixed exchange rates would be a crucial determinant of the demand for individual moneys; the more credible the parities, the less likely the occurrence of large relative switches in money demand. Second, fluctuations in money demand would depend on the degree of substitutability among European currencies, as well as the effects of financial innovations that are currently underway and will accelerate in the next few years. It is nevertheless possible to compute a range of estimates for the optimum size of ERSA under a wide array of assumptions about the behavior of money demands and of national money supplies. Preliminary experiments suggest that a portfolio comprising about 10 percent of the total money supply of each member country would enable ERSA to operate without borrowing resources, even in the presence of large short-run fluctuations in relative money supplies. This would undoubtedly lend credibility to the system, provided of course that member countries were to achieve long-run consistency in their national monetary policies.

Because estimates of the evolution of money demands are subject to error, it would be desirable to supplement the actual resources of ERSA with a provision allowing it to draw on participating central banks in case of sudden and unavoidable need. This provision would be invoked only as a last resort, but its existence would reflect the strength of the commitment to the fixed-rates system; it would not entail any transfer of national currencies or foreign-exchange reserves.

More on the Board of Central Bank Governors

Under the proposed plan, the BCBG would have three tasks: (1) It would review the operations of ERSA, the composition of its portfolio, and its operations vis-à-vis third currencies. (2) It would determine whether the current and recent policy stances of member countries were consistent with the fixed parities, and if not, to single out the divergent policies (easily accomplished by an analysis of ERSA's portfolio). (3) It would prepare for each member country alternative monetary-policy targets consistent with fixed exchange rates and would facilitate and encourage the choice among these targets by the member central banks.

It should be emphasized that the BCBG would not determine national monetary policies or make collective decisions; it would be limited to identifying viable alternatives and facilitating international monetary cooperation. For this reason, it should be granted maximum independence from outside bodies like national governments. Its independence, as well as the political weight it would carry as the collective voice of the national central bank governors overseeing ERSA and the management of fixed exchange rates, should help the individual central banks to implement national monetary targets consistent with exchange-rate stability, even though those targets might conflict with the desires or objectives of domestic constituencies. By their very nature, then, the operations of the BCBG would be more conducive to sound anti-inflationary policies than are the current informal bargaining processes among EMS members, in which there is always the possibility of devaluation and thus the validation of inflation-rate differentials.

7.5 The Currency Reform

The ultimate objective of European monetary integration is the currency reform, which would occur after successful refinement of the rules governing ERSA and the BCBG or by the exercise of the option to accelerate if the transition proved to be too vulnerable to financial instability.

A currency reform is preferable to fixed exchange rates for two reasons. (1) The odd exchange rates linking European currencies significantly complicate transactions and in themselves make national moneys different from each other and monetary integration incomplete. (2) A one-to-one exchange rate would be a clear message that the monetary union is permanent. To convince the public that there is no remaining difference among national currencies, the symbol of the European Currency Unit

Table 7.1
Exchange rates relative to the ECU on January 31, 1990 (rounded to the hundredth point)

Currency	Rate
Belgian/Luxembourg franc	42.67
Danish krone	7.89
German mark	2.04
Dutch florin	2.30
French franc	6.93
Greek drachma	190.90
Irish pound	0.77
Italian lira	1515.00
Portuguese escudo	179.10
Spanish peseta	131.80
U.K. pound	0.72

(ECU) should be added to the currency notes of each member nation (for example, the new deutsche mark note would carry both the DM and ECU logos). Introducing the ECU as the European currency in this manner would forestall the monetary instabilities associated with its introduction as a parallel currency.

The currency reform would involve a simple redefinition of units, and, without an attendant realignment of exchange rates, would not affect the real values of existing assets and liabilities. To see how the currency reform could be carried out in practice, consider the ECU rates prevailing on January 31, 1990 for the eleven European currencies (see table 7.1).

The reform would involve a joint declaration by the twelve governments that a new Belgian franc would be worth 42.67 old francs, a new deutsche mark worth 2.04 old marks, and so forth (alternatively, the ECU central rates could be used). Each new national currency would be equal to one ECU, and new banknotes would be printed by the national central banks.

Immediately after the declaration, contracts could be cleared in either ECUs or the old currencies. The value of the stock of new banknotes would be equal to the value of the stock of old banknotes being retired. This arrangement would eliminate all losses or gains that holders of old banknotes and coins might experience as a result of the redefinition of units.

Undoubtedly, this reform would produce a dramatic one-time increase in the use of pocket calculators and a considerable but short-lived nuisance, for it would require the recalculation of all prices and all outstanding assets and liabilities. Those costs, however, should be compared with the present discounted value of all gains to be obtained from moving to a permanent regime whereby all European currencies would have the same values and all transactions across Europe would be enormously facilitated—in particular, the management and control of Europe-wide businesses.

Immediately after the currency reform, the ESCB would be permanently empowered to determine the common European monetary policy. ERSA would be relieved of its initial tasks with the disappearance of the national currencies and would transform itself into the operating agency of the monetary system, carrying out both foreign-exchange and domestic open-market operations.

7.6 Relating This Proposal to the Delors Report

The plan offered in this essay provides the details left out of the Delors Report: an exact description of the structure and operations of the ESCB during stage two and a description of the currency reform that would establish full monetary union. The plan also suggests two slight, but crucial, modifications of the original framework proposed by the Delors Report: (1) the announcement that existing bilateral parities are not to be changed during the transition to monetary union, and (2) the commitment to accelerate progress toward union whenever speculative pressures in the money markets would make it difficult to preserve existing parities.

The approach taken in developing this plan was to design institutions that could cope effectively with the most important economic problems of the transition, the instability of financial and foreign-exchange markets, the likelihood of wide fluctuations in demands for national currencies, and the adjustment of expectations of price setters regarding inflation and exchange-rate changes.

The necessity of strengthening EMS institutions after the liberalization of capital flows was recognized by the Delors Committee's French delegation, which proposed that a European Reserve Fund (ERF), similar in many ways to ERSA, be created during stage one (see, in particular, de Larosière, 1989). The Report explicitly advocates the pooling of foreign-exchange reserves during stage two (par. 57).

A detailed comparison of ERSA and the proposed ERF can be made by comparing part two of Section 4 above with de Larosière's paper. It is important to stress that, unlike the ERF, ERSA would have competence only in the foreign-exchange sphere. It would not foreshadow the final European central bank, but would become one of its departments; it would not exercise surveillance over monetary trends (the task of the BCBG); and it would not supplement the actions of individual central banks, but would, instead, carry out foreign-change operations for all the participating central banks.

7.7 Concluding Remarks

The EMS has helped to fight inflation in Europe and has improved cooperation among central banks, but it is not the right institution to effect the transition to monetary union. What is needed is a structure that will encourage more cooperation among central banks and impart greater credibility to the commitment to fixed exchange rates.

Because acceptance of the first stage of the Delors plan amounts to acceptance of the ultimate aim of monetary union (par. 39), this chapter assumes that a single currency is the ultimate objective for Europe. It is essential that the transition toward one currency be sustained by institutions that are credible to the markets, allow some flexibility, and ensure that sound policies will be carried out. The institutions proposed here were designed to meet these three objectives.

Notes

1. For a discussion of the possible effects of the removal of capital controls, see Giavazzi and Spaventa (1990).

2. This theory is presented in Giavazzi and Giovannini (1989).

3. For a recent critical appraisal of the experience with floating exchange rates, see Rolnick and Weber (1989).

4. Until very recently, residents of most EC countries were effectively limited to checking accounts denominated in their own currencies.

References

Bertola, G. 1989. "Factor Mobility, Uncertainty and Exchange Rate Regimes," in M. De Cecco and A. Giovannini, eds., *A European Central Bank? Prospectives on Monetary Unification After Ten Years of EMS*, Cambridge University Press, 1989, pp. 95–119.

Eichengreen, B. 1990. "One Money For Europe? Lessons from the U.S. Currency Union," *Economic Policy*, 10 April, pp. 117–187.

Giavazzi, F. and A. Giovannini. 1989. *Limiting Exchange-Rate Flexibility: The European Monetary System*, Cambridge, MA, MIT Press.

Giavazzi, F. and L. Spaventa. 1990. "The New EMS," Working Paper No. 369, London, Centre for Economic Policy Research.

Kenen, P. 1969. "The Theory of Optimal Currency Areas: An Eclectic View," in R. Mundell and A. Swoboda, eds., *Monetary Problems of the International Economy*, Chicago, University of Chicago Press, pp. 41–60.

Rolnick, A. and Warren E. Weber 1989. "A Case for Fixing Exchange Rates," *Federal Reserve Bank of Minneapolis Annual Report*.

8

European Monetary Reform: Progress and Prospects

(August 1990)

8.1 Introduction

In the past two years, a new plan for monetary union in Europe has gained widespread popularity and has given new strength to the initiative to build a single currency area among European Community (EC) countries—an initiative that has been a recurrent feature of the debate on European monetary policy during the second postwar period. Indeed, many observers believe that now the achievement of a monetary union is a highly likely event: C. Fred Bergsten (1990) states that Western Europe is *"almost certain* [emphasis added] to go beyond 'completion of the internal market' to an Economic and Monetary Union, or EMU."

The policy problems of a monetary reform among EC countries are determined by the way such a reform is approached. The two alternative strategies available had been the subject of considerable debate in the late 1960s, but, surprisingly, they had not been much discussed now. They are:

• The gradualist strategy (whose supporters in the 1960s were labelled "economists"), relying on progressive removal of barriers to goods markets integration, convergence of inflation rates and progressive stability of exchange rates, and a parallel modification of monetary policies and institutions.

• The strategy of a currency reform (whose supporters in the 1960s were labelled "monetarists"), which amounts to either an irrevocable locking of exchange rates with elimination of target zones or to a replacement of national currencies with a single currency, to occur once a central banking system to manage either system is in place.

The current plan for monetary union, the Delors plan, largely reflects the "economists'" view. Significantly, the Delors plan does not set deadlines for the progress to monetary union, nor does it supply criteria or conditions to be satisfied for moving from stage to stage in the institutional reform. As a result, and despite the early show of support, it is not clear how much of a commitment for this plan there is, even among the "continental" governments, whose currencies are members of the European Monetary System (EMS).

How could the current plan for monetary union become successful? In the absence of new institutional developments, the convergence of inflationary expectations and its dual, the stability of exchange rates, are the necessary conditions for any progress of the gradualist strategy. This chapter discusses the problem of achieving and sustaining these twin objectives and, more broadly, the chances of success of the plan for monetary union. For this purpose I consider the historical and institutional background (the monetary arrangements in the second postwar period, the earlier attempts at achieving monetary cohesion and the characteristics of the Delors plan), the extent to which convergence of expectations has occurred among Germany, France and Italy, and the implications for the question of the monetary reform.

The historical precedents are analyzed in section 8.2. Western European countries have been talking about monetary union since the 1960s, and the nature and chances of success of the current initiative can best be understood after discussing the motivations and the experience of the earlier attempts. Section 8.3 reviews the evidence on the three largest countries that are involved in the debate on monetary union and were members of the EMS since its inception: France, Germany and Italy. The section focuses on the question of convergence of inflationary and exchange-rate expectations, which can be gauged from the behavior of wages and, especially, interest rates.

Section 8.4 examines the empirical evidence presented in section 8.3 using alternative models. The main questions are, first, how much can a policy of exchange-rate pegging achieve convergence of inflation and interest rates; and second, how credible is a plan of monetary union that hinges on exchange-rate pegging. One noticeable result of this section—with potentially important implications for the theory of alternative exchange-rate regimes and optimum currency areas—is that announcing fixed exchange rates might not eliminate distortions in real interest rates and real wages. Section 8.5 discusses, in light of the conclusions of the previous section, the problems and chances of success of the current plan for monetary union. Section 8.6 contains a few concluding observations.

Throughout the chapter, I assume that the objective of the monetary union is to converge to the low level of inflation in Germany. This common attitude towards inflation is widely reflected in all official documents (see, for example, the Delors Report), and has arguably justified the cohesion of the EMS.

8.2   The Renewed Momentum to Monetary Union

Europeans have been discussing monetary union at least since the signing of the Treaty of Rome. The accelerating pace of negotiations of the last 18 months should be set against the background of these recurring attempts at achieving monetary cohesion. This exercise should also help at assessing the prospects of the current efforts, in light of the earlier failures.

Figure 8.1 shows the real bilateral exchange rates of one Deutsche mark relative to the U.S. dollar, the French franc, and the lira and summarize the monetary arrangements of the three European countries in the last 30 years. The Treaty of Rome advocated, together with the creation of a common market for goods, the removal of exchange controls in tandem with the liberalization of goods markets. The Treaty also recommended that exchange-rate changes by member countries be elevated to the status of "matters of common interest." These statements of principle, however, proved ineffective in practice. The exchange-rate realignments of the Deutsche mark in March 1961, the French franc in August 1969, and the Deutsche mark again in October 1969 were unilateral decisions.[1] Except in these case, the stability of intra-European exchange rates before 1971 was assured by pegging each currency to the dollar.

8.2.1   The First Attempt

The response of the European Community to these events, and to the unfolding of the crisis of the Bretton Woods regime, was a solemn statement by the Heads of State at the European Summit held at The Hague on December 1 and 2, 1969. The statement was a wish to see the Community develop into an economic and monetary union through the implementation of a phased plan. Some of the views expressed at that time on the most appropriate course of action for the monetary reform are in part still reflected in the current debate: the French advocated a sudden locking of parities and an elimination of fluctuation bands, while the Germans preferred a gradual approach, where the convergence of macroeconomic

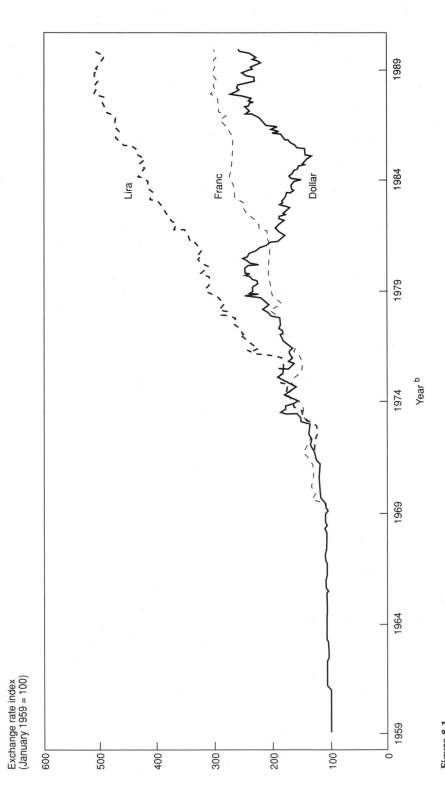

Figure 8.1
The Italian lira, French franc, and U.S. dollar relative to the Deutsche mark, 1959–1989

structure and performances was a precondition to proceed into monetary union.[2]

The Summit appointed a Committee headed by Pierre Werner (Prime Minister and Finance Minister of Luxembourg) to produce a report on the practical steps to achieve economic and monetary union. The Werner Report indicated that the achievement of monetary union had to be a three-stage process. During the first and second stages coordination of economic policies had to be strengthened. The process of coordination entailed prior consultations together with ex-post monitoring. The second stage was further characterized by the creation of a "European Fund for Monetary Cooperation" which would "progressively manage Community reserves" and manage intra-European balance-of-payments financing. This Fund would be integrated, in the third stage, into the system of Community central banks. Parity readjustments were ruled out for the second stage. In particular, the Werner Committee concluded that:

The ultimate objective,...., appears to be one that can be attained within the present decade, provided that it continues to enjoy the political support of the governments.

... The adoption of a single currency could be the final stage of this union, ensuring the irreversibility of the process.

The first stage would start in January 1971 and last no more than three years.

The Werner Report was the outcome of heated debates which saw, on one side, the French government, with a strong aversion to any institutional changes that would limit its own national sovereignty, and on the other side the five remaining countries, who favored some transfer of power to European institution, and changes in the Treaty of Rome. The outcome of these disagreements was a final document which left unspecified many details about intermediate stages, and focused mostly on the final objective (safely distant in the future) and the first stage.

On March 22, 1971 the EC Council of Minister signed a resolution adopting the conclusions of the Werner Report, and laying down a timetable of reforms necessary to enhance the integration of goods (starting January 1st, 1974, harmonization of tax bases for VAT and excises, harmonization of taxes on dividends and interest and "those kinds of tax which are likely to have a direct influence on capital movements within the Community," "further harmonization of taxation of companies and firms"), and financial markets (adopt a Directive to start progressive liberalization of capital markets, support the coordination of regulatory activities). On the policy side, the resolution advocated more power for the Monetary Committee and the Committee of Central Bank Governors, and a narrowing of fluctuation bands for exchange rates.

Two months later, in May 1971, foreign exchange markets provided the conditions for the effective meltdown of the Werner plan. Germany called an emergency meeting of the EC finance ministers to propose the floating of the Deutsche mark. The French opposed it, and advocated tighter capital controls. No agreement was reached at the meeting, so that the mark and the guilder were floated, while all other countries tightened capital controls. Ironically, some of the tax reforms called for by the March 1971 Council still have to be tackled by the Community (capital income taxation, corporation taxes).

8.2.2 Monetary Initiatives in the 1970s

Figure 8.1 also shows that the collapse of the "North Atlantic" Bretton Woods system was followed by a period of dramatic exchange-rate fluctuations, during which the franc and the lira progressively diverged from the dollar. Neither of the currencies has regained its stability, relative to the dollar, that characterized the dollar-based regime of the 1960s. The European monetary initiatives of the rest of the 1970s are better known. From April 1972 to March 1973 there was the "snake in the tunnel," where the tunnel was represented by the bilateral fluctuation margins of the dollar (4.5 percent) and the snake by the narrower margins of intra-European rates (2.25 percent). After March 1973 European currencies floated freely against the dollar. The only stable members of the snake were Germany, Belgium, the Netherlands and Luxembourg. The large EC countries, France and Italy, left it soon (January 1974 and February 1973, respectively. France rejoined from July 1975 and March 1976.).

The European Monetary System was set up in December 1978, and included, in its exchange-rate mechanism, all EC members except the United Kingdom. As Delors (1989) notes, it was based on intergovernmental agreement rather than on Community law. While explicit references to economic and monetary union appeared absent, the EMS was regarded instrumental to further integration in the Community. The success of the EMS has certainly contributed to the serious consideration being given to extending the reach and the depth of the experiment. But—as De Cecco and I note (chapter 6)—the EMS, by itself, has induced changes in monetary institutions to sustain closer cooperation: two of its technical features that were designed with that objective—the European Monetary Cooperation Fund and the ECU—did not achieve the status originally envisaged by their supporters.[3]

8.2.3 The Delors Report

The roots of the most recent project for monetary union—the Delors Report—are not in the monetary area. Unlike the initiative that led to the Werner Report, which could be viewed as a last-resort effort of European governments to brace together in front of a collapsing monetary system, the Delors Report grew out of the White Paper on the completion of the internal market of June 1985 and the Single European Act of January 1986. The former laid out the "1992" plan, the latter was the outcome of an intergovernmental conference held in Luxembourg in December 1985 to modify the Treaty of Rome. The Treaty now includes a formal commitment to complete the 1992 plan, and a number of institutional changes to facilitate that—including extension of qualified-majority voting to about two-thirds of the draft directives that make up the 1992 plan—and increased involvement of the European Parliament. A crucial pillar of the single market program is the liberalization of capital flows within the Community. This was achieved very early, with the adoption by the Council of Economic and Finance Ministers (ECOFIN) of June 1988 of a draft proposal on the creation of a European financial area. In the same month, the Heads of State commissioned a study on the achievement of economic and monetary union to a group of central bankers (and three outside experts) headed by Jacques Delors. The results of that study had to be presented at the European Council Meeting of Madrid in June 1989.

The Delors Report refrains from specifying explicit deadlines. The developments of the last year, however, have provided some of them. At the European Council of June 1989 in Madrid, Heads of State agreed to embark in the first stage of the Delors plan. This was a significant step, since "Although this process is set out in stages which guide the progressive movement to the final objective, the decision to enter upon the first stage should be a decision to embark on the entire process." (Delors Report, para. 39). At the Strasbourg Summit of December 1989 it was agreed to convene two intergovernmental conferences by December 1990. One conference will prepare the changes of the Treaty of Rome that are necessary to set up the institutions of the monetary union. The other conference will deal with political union. At the European Summit of Dublin of April 28, 1990, Heads of State declared that the changes of the Treaty related to economic and monetary union will have to be ratified by national governments before the end of 1992. Hence stage two of the Delors plan could start in January 1993.

8.2.4   What Motivated the Delors Report

Significantly, the Delors Report is not motivated by an analysis of the costs and benefits of a monetary union in Europe. Tommaso Padoa Schioppa (1989), when proposing the idea of a monetary union in the 1990s, argues that the forthcoming integration of goods and financial markets requires an institutional change of the EMS because the present system would be too vulnerable to speculative attacks.

A catalog of the economic effects of EMU has in fact *followed* the Delors Report in a study of the European Commission: (*The Economics of the EMU*). The economic impact of the EMU is looked at from five different angles, including the elimination of transactions costs and foreign exchange risk premia, the achievement of price stability through the setup of an independent central bank, the G7 exchange-rate coordination process and the distribution of world foreign exchange reserves and seigniorage gains, budgetary policies, and the loss of the exchange-rate instrument to offset country-specific shocks. The study appropriately refrains from producing a single summary quantification of the effects of a monetary union, because it relies on a series of partial equilibrium analyses of different markets.

Estimates of the welfare effects of a single currency, a classic question in international economics (Mundell, 1968, McKinnon, 1963, Kenen, 1969, Cooper, 1976), heavily hinge on our knowledge of the determinants of the demand for different currencies in an integrated area, which is, at best, limited. While this is a quite active area of investigation (see in particular the studies by Bertola, 1989, and Canzoneri and Rogers, 1990, both applied to the European monetary union), it seems that a comprehensive analysis is still well beyond reach.[4] In addition, and probably for this reason, political considerations play an important role in the discussion of the desirability of a monetary union. Triffin in 1960 writes:

It must be emphasized that the desirability of a merger of members' national currencies into a single currency as well as its difficulties are essentially political rather than economic.

Hence this chapter focuses on the process towards monetary union, taking as given the desirability of the final objective.

8.2.5   1990 versus 1970: What Are the Differences?

To an observer with no training in the language of diplomacy, the Delors Report looks extremely similar to the Werner Report. The latter is also made up of three stages. During the first stage policy coordination would be enhanced. During the second stage a "European Monetary Fund" would be set up. The third stage would be characterized by irrevocable locking of exchange-rate parities. During the first two stages, exchange-rate adjustments would be allowed, but should be unnecessary by the second stage. The Werner Report also contains a number of measures in the economic field, including: (i) joint setting of medium-term objectives for macroeconomic policies, and joint setting of the broad outlines of short-term policies; (ii) common agreement on the margins within which the national budget aggregates would be held, and on the method of financing deficits. Finally, both reports discuss the need to set up a European central bank.[5]

These marked similarities suggest two questions: Is the Delors Report any "better" than the Werner Report? Why has the more recent plan for monetary reform enjoyed (so far) greater success?

The first question must have been raised also within the Delors Committee. The first paper of the collection published with the Report (Baer and Padoa Schioppa, 1989) addresses precisely this question. The authors do point out a number of technical problems of the Werner Report, including a "lack of safeguards against lapses in policy consensus," "institutional ambiguities" and "lack of internal momentum." But the differences in the political and economic environment, as Baer and Padoa Schioppa also claim, must have played a major role.

8.2.5.1   Political Factors

Consider first the evolution in the international political scenario. The increase in economic integration of the European Community has, until last year, preceded stronger political cohesion. The slow buildup of political cohesion was itself the mirror of the progressive loosening of the strong North Atlantic ties of all large Western European countries—which were justified by the emergencies of the immediate second postwar, and by the cold war.[6] The Single European Act was the peak of this process: observers noted that the 1992 program was going to have important political consequences, as evidenced by the sometimes heated debate between the government of the United Kingdom on one side and the Community and the other European governments on the other side, regarding the way to manage the completion of internal market.[7]

With the events of the last year, political cohesion is no more just an implication of the stronger economic ties, but has gained a status of its own. The dismembering of the communist world has decreased the strategic significance of the ties with the United States, and provides the conditions for an acceleration of European integration. An anecdote on the way the convening of the intergovernmental conference was decided provides a useful illustration of the new interplay of political and economic elements in the negotiations:[8] until the day before the start of the Strasbourg Summit, German economic officials were not willing to see an intergovernmental conference on monetary union called during the following three years; yet, at the end of the meeting, the monetary conference was convened for December 1990. This drastic anticipation was most likely obtained with the support of German unification by the Community governments.

In summary, the differences in the world strategic scenario, and in particular the difference in the political relations among European states, might provide a more favorable environment to initiatives aimed at a European monetary reform than was the case in the early seventies. The risk, of course, is that increased cross border competition arising from the removal of controls will amplify political frictions among Western European governments, and bring the integration plan to a halt (this could be labelled the "Ridley scenario").

8.2.5.2   Economic Factors

The differences between the economic conditions of the European Community in the 1990s versus the 1970s have to do with two types of phenomena. The first is economic integration. Table 8.1 reports the composition of trade of the 6 original members of the EC: imports and exports to Community countries as a fraction of imports and exports to the rest of the world. The only countries for which intra-Community trade has not swamped external trade by 1989 are Germany (intra-Community imports 110 percent of imports from the rest of the world, exports 120), and Italy. For all countries, the growth of intra-Community trade has been steady since the 1960s. The differences between 1970 and 1989 are however not dramatic, except perhaps for France and Italy. Economic integration will further be boosted by the completion of the internal market. Indeed, the Commission suggests the presence of a double feedback between the single market program and monetary union (a sin-

Table 8.1
Intra-Community trade relative to trade with the rest of the world, original EC countries, 1960, 1970, 1989 (percent)

	1960	1970	1989
Exports			
Belgium and Luxembourg	154.5	302.7	303.1
France	63.0	139.6	162.7
Germany	67.0	98.9	120.2
Italy	66.7	107.1	144.6
Netherlands	158.2	266.3	309.6
Imports			
Belgium and Luxembourg	131.0	196.0	239.1
France	53.5	126.7	189.0
Germany	66.3	106.3	109.8
Italy	58.1	91.3	133.3
Netherlands	118.1	172.7	158.9

gle currency would help achieve more integrated markets). Yet, whether the Europe of 12 countries of 1990 is a more integrated economy of the Europe of 6 countries in 1970 is an open question.[9] The second economic phenomenon which differentiates the 1990s from the 1970s is of course the liberalization of financial markets. Historical experience suggests that all fixed-exchange-rates regimes were characterized by extensive use of capital controls.[10] These controls were justified by the desire to stem speculative attacks on central banks' reserves. The complete removal of capital controls will force European countries to create some new institutional arrangement to ensure closer monetary policy cooperation, since in its absence fixed parities would be very likely to collapse: this is the argument advanced by Padoa Schioppa (1989).

In summary, there are reasons to believe that, even though the Werner Report and the Delors Report have many similarities, the chances for monetary reform in Europe in the 1990s are—relative to the 1970s—significantly better. In the following section I introduce the economic problems raised by this project, by reviewing the experience of the EMS, with special focus to the last three years.

8.3   A Review of the Recent Experience

This section presents the empirical evidence on the behavior of inflation and interest rates relative to exchange rates, with special attention to the last three years. The discussion is limited to the experience of France and Italy (relative to Germany), for a number of reasons:

• they are the two largest partners of Germany, and therefore they carry a very high political weight in the current negotiations on monetary reform;

• they embarked into the exchange-rate arrangement since its inception (unlike Spain and the UK, for example), and started from rather divergent initial conditions;

• they are unlike the small countries, whose openness vis-à-vis the rest of the EC is so high to make the monetary reform less questionable;

• their recent experience contains a number of features that are also observed, to a different degree, in the other countries.

Figures 8.2 and 8.3 plot the French franc/Deutsche mark and lira/ Deutsche mark exchange rates during the EMS, together with their respective bilateral fluctuation margins. The discrete movements of the bilateral fluctuation margins occur at the dates of realignment of central parities.[11] Figure 8.4 plots the monthly percent changes in these bilateral exchange rates since June 1973.

The figures reveal a number of facts. First, the EMS period is characterized by trends in bilateral exchange rates. These trends are somewhat broken in the case of the franc, but appear largely accommodated by adjustments in bilateral parities in the case of the lira. Only in the last three years the tendency of the franc and the lira to depreciate relative to the mark appears to have subsided. Correspondingly, the frequency of realignments is shown to have decreased recently.

Despite the presence of trends, especially in the first years of the EMS, figure 8.4 highlights a second empirical regularity: the variability of bilateral exchange rates has decreased since the start of the EMS (the vertical line ar March 1979 marks the start of the EMS). This impression is confirmed by statistical tests. Non-parametric tests indicate that the volatility of total and unanticipated exchange-rate changes has decreased after the EMS (see Giavazzi and Giovannini, 1989; this is not the case of currencies outside the ERM, like the British pound).

Finally, the three figures suggest that both volatility and the tendency of the franc and the lira to depreciate relative to the mark have decreased since 1987. Some observers (in particular, Giavazzi and Spaventa, 1990) claim that 1987 marks the beginning of a change in regime in the EMS, after which France and Italy have resolutely avoided exchange-rate de-

Francs per deutsche mark

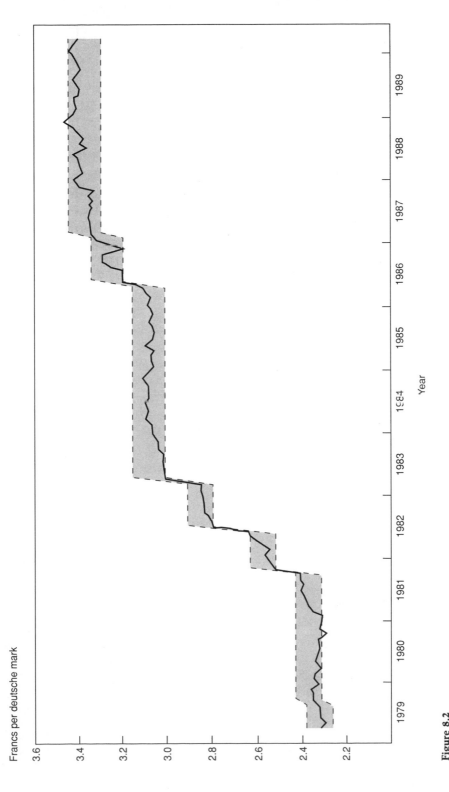

Figure 8.2
The French franc in the EMS, March 1979–December 1989

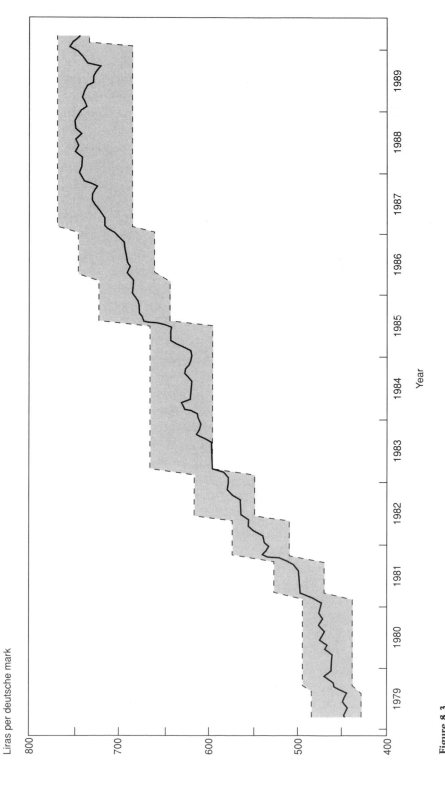

Figure 8.3
The Italian lira in the EMS, March 1979–December 1989

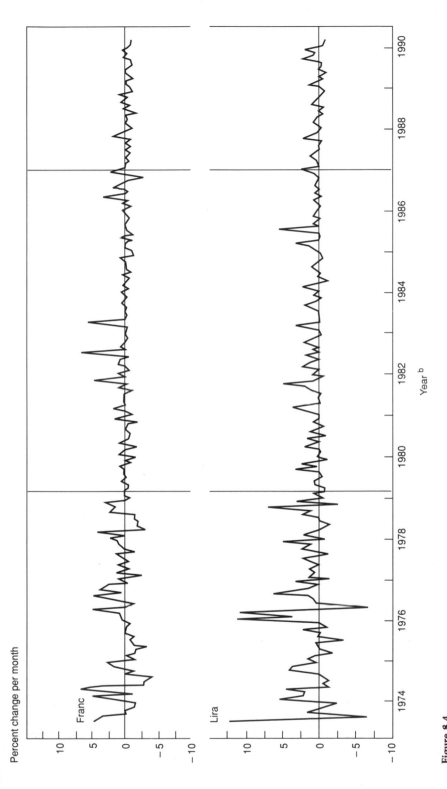

Figure 8.4
Fluctuations in the lira-mark and franc-mark exchange rates, June 1973–December 1989

preciations. A change in attitudes of the Banque de France and the Banca
d'Italia was noticeable especially in 1989, when both central banks resisted pressures for devaluation from the Bundesbank by further tightening domestic credit.

8.3.1 Exchange Rates and Inflation

Figure 8.5 reports consumer price index (CPI) inflation rates for France,
Germany and Italy since 1958. The figure shows that inflation rates in
France, Italy and Germany began to diverge significantly after the first oil
shock; these divergences have not been completely eliminated. The EMS
was created right before the second oil shock, and significant reduction
and convergence of inflation rates is not observed until the second half of
the 1980s. The most recent data indicate almost complete convergence of
French and German inflation, while Italy maintains a differential of about
3.5 percent with the partners. The experience of the other EC countries is
similar to that of France and Italy, except for Greece and Portugal, whose
inflation rates exceed 10 percent in the past year.

Whether the EMS has significantly helped its members in fighting inflation has been the subject of some controversy. The view that I have
taken elsewhere (Giavazzi and Giovannini, 1989) is that the evidence in
favor of the hypothesis that the EMS made a difference is very weak.
There has been a shift in the stochastic process governing wage- and
price-inflation and output in France, Denmark, Germany, Ireland and Italy.
The shift has been in the direction predicted by the theory, that is the
relation between output and inflation has worsened in Germany and
improved in all other countries. However, the shift is not statistically
significant, even though lack of significance could well be due to small
sample problems. Furthermore, a similar shift is observed for the United
Kingdom, which was floating at the time. And finally, the shift does not
occur at the inception of the EMS, but only after 1983. In conclusion, the
"credibility boost" of the EMS has been rather limited, but for this reason
it should not be dismissed.

The interaction of exchange-rate changes and inflation is reported in
table 8.2, which reports the annual rates of change in unit labor costs and
the annual rates of changes in the franc-mark and lira-mark exchange
rates. The table underscores the differences within the EMS period during
1980s. Until 1986 large exchange-rate depreciations in France and Italy
accompanied large divergencies in the rate of growth of unit labor costs
relative to Germany. Notice that in the early 1980s the rate of deprecia-

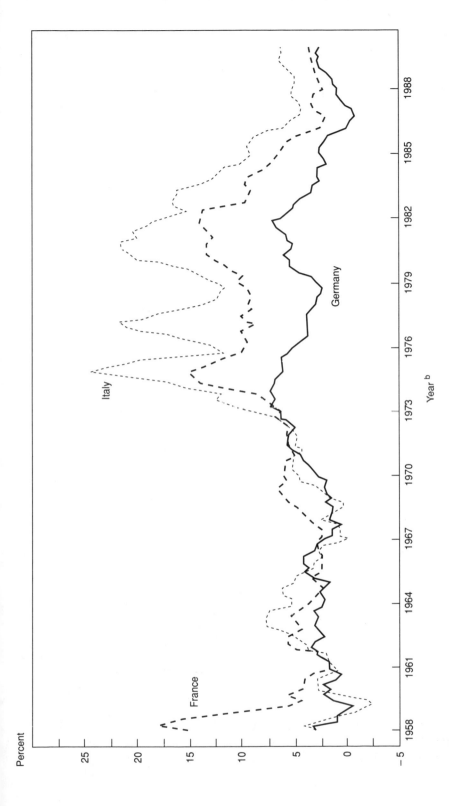

Percent

Figure 8.5
Inflation in France, Italy, and Germany, January 1958–March 1989

Table 8.2
Growth in relative unit labor costs and exchange-rate depreciations

Year	France vs. Germany		Italy vs. Germany	
	Relative U.L.C.	Exchange rate	Relative U.L.C.	Exchange rate
1980	6.9	−0.7	12.3	2.3
1981	8	10.6	16.9	12
1982	8.3	11	13.4	8.3
1983	8.3	8.3	14.9	5.7
1984	5.2	−0.6	8.1	0.9
1985	2.8	0.8	6.4	10.9
1986	−0.4	8.3	2.9	2.6
1987	−0.1	1.5	4.3	5.7
1988	0.8	0.8	5.9	−0.8
1989	1.5	0.2	5.9	2
1990	0.8	−1.7	4.2	−2.2

Source: *European Economy*. Growth in relative unit labor costs is the difference between the growth rate of unit labor costs in each country and that in Germany.

tion of the exchange rate in France exceeded the rate of change of relative labor costs, while in Italy the opposite was true. This difference is probably a reflection of the well-known decision of Italian authorities to enter the EMS with a "depreciated" currency, which allowed them to help the domestic disinflation efforts with appreciations of the *real* exchange rate.

After 1987 exchange rates have stopped depreciating, and yet, especially in the case of Italy, the rate of growth of unit labor costs exceeds that of Germany. Table 8.3 reports rates of growth of real compensation per employee, measured in terms of the CPI. In the past three years, despite the persistence of inflation differentials, real wages have grown significantly in Italy, whereas France appears broadly in line with Germany. Finally, table 8.4, reporting growth rates of productivity, shows that the performance in the three countries has been similar: adjusting for growth in productivity would not significantly change the pattern in competitiveness shifts reflected by the growth rate of relative wages.

The effects of inflation differentials on international competitiveness are summarized in table 8.5. The table reports the levels of wages adjusted for productivity in France and Italy relative to Germany, and the terms of trade of the two countries, also relative to Germany. Adjusted relative wages are obtained by multiplying the ratio of wage shares in GDP times the relative GDP deflator. Terms of trade are export unit values divided by import unit values. The table highlights the differences between France

Table 8.3
Real compensation per employee

Year	Germany	France	Italy
1979	1.8	2	2.4
1980	1	1.8	1.9
1981	−0.8	1.1	3.9
1982	−0.5	2.3	0.2
1983	0.5	0.4	0.8
1984	1	0.5	0
1985	1	0.8	1
1986	4.1	1.4	1.6
1987	2.2	0.6	4
1988	2	1.1	3.8
1989	0	0.5	2.7
1990	0.7	1.3	1.9

Source: *European Economy*. Annual growth rates. Deflated by the consumer price index.

Table 8.4
Productivity

Year	Germany	France	Italy
1982	1.1	2.4	−0.3
1983	3.1	1.1	0.4
1984	2.7	2.3	2.8
1985	1.3	2	2
1986	1.3	1.9	1.9
1987	1.2	2.1	2.9
1988	3	2.8	2.5
1989	2.3	1.8	2.6
1990	2.4	2	2.4

Source: *European Economy*. Annual growth rates.

and Italy. The former country succeeded in correcting its own losses in competitiveness with the devaluations of 1983 and 1986, while Italy's adjusted relative wage has steadily increased—except for a small correction in 1986—throughout the last ten years. Relative terms of trade, which include the effects of fluctuations of dollar prices on the import and export baskets of these countries, broadly reflect the behavior of relative wages.

In summary, the drastic stabilization of exchange rates since 1987 has occurred at a time when inflation rates had not fallen to the German levels, especially in Italy, and as a result has been accompanied—in both

Table 8.5
Adjusted relative wages and terms of trade

Year	France		Italy	
	Relative wage	Terms of trade	Relative wage	Terms of trade
1979	98.6	103	90.5	97.5
1980	104.8	100	97.8	100
1981	108.7	101.2	106.1	98.9
1982	105.1	100.3	108.5	101.3
1983	102.8	100.2	117.4	103.4
1984	105.3	100.9	122.2	104.2
1985	109.3	103	123.6	104.1
1986	104.1	102	121.3	105.7
1987	99.7	98.4	121.4	104.3
1988	99.9	98.8	126.9	104.5
1989	101.1	99.3	137.2	105.6
1990	102.6	99.5	144.1	106.6

Source: *European Economy*. Adjusted relative wages are obtained from the ratio of adjusted wage shares (total economy) in GDP, multiplied by the (exchange-rate adjusted) ratio of GDP deflators). Terms of trade are the ratio of export unit values to import unit values.

countries—by losses in competitiveness relative to Germany. In the case of Italy, this loss in competitiveness adds to a sustained trend of real appreciations, which has produced an increase in adjusted relative wages of as much as 45 percent since 1980. The repercussions of these policies on external accounts is shown in table 8.6, reporting current account balances and international capital flows. The French and Italian losses in competitiveness of the last three years are reflected in widening current account deficits, which however are *overfinanced* by capital inflows in both countries. The balance-of-payments surpluses of France and Germany in the last three years are an indication that the stance of monetary (domestic credit) policies in the two countries has been tighter than Germany's. Table 8.7, reporting data on output growth and unemployment, shows that since the mid-1980s the three countries have had—somewhat surprisingly—similar performances. Sustained growth and high unemployment characterize the recent experience of Italy and Germany, while in France the unemployment rate decreases slightly after 1988. The large movements in relative prices have had a small impact on output growth because of strong domestic demand in Italy and France. The increase in unemployment both in Italy and Germany cannot be explained by the movement in relative wages in those two countries.

Table 8.6
Balance of payments

Year	Germany		France		Italy	
	CA.	CAP.	CA.	CAP.	CA.	CAP.
1983	5.11	−1.24	−5.17	1.08	1.38	−5.53
1984	9.75	−7.63	−0.88	0.57	−2.5	1.58
1985	17	−22.64	−0.04	−5.64	3.54	1.34
1986	40.09	−49.43	2.43	−7.29	2.91	−8.01
1987	46.12	−73.34	−4.45	2.82	−1.66	−7.67
1988	50.47	−31.08	−3.55	11.23	−5.45	10.47
1989	55.48	−58.43	−4.3	5.03	−13.50	26.33

Source: *International Financial Statistics*. Billions of U.S. dollars. Lines 77ad and 79cd−77ad. The 1989 Italian data refers to the period January−October (source: Bank of Italy).

Table 8.7
Output and unemployment

Year	Germany		France		Italy	
	GDP	Unemployment	GDP	Unemployment	GDP	Unemployment
1983	1.5	6.9	0.7	8.3	1.1	9
1984	2.8	7.1	1.3	8.2	3.2	9.5
1985	2.0	7.3	1.7	9.9	2.9	9.4
1986	2.3	6.5	2.1	10.3	2.9	10.6
1987	1.9	6.4	2.2	10.4	3.1	10.1
1988	3.7	6.4	3.4	10.5	3.9	10.6
1989	3.8	7.4	3.3	9.5	3.5	10.5
1990	3.5	7.6	3.2	9.1	3.0	10.6

Source: *European Economy*. GDP annual growth rates. Unemployment percent of civilian labor force.

8.3.2 Exchange Rates and Interest Rates

The relative levels of interest rates are measured by the differential of nominal interest rates adjusted by the realized change in the nominal exchange rate:

$$rd = R - (R^* + \hat{s}) \tag{1}$$

where R and R^* represent the domestic and foreign rates of interest, respectively, and $\hat{s}$ is the proportional change in the price of foreign currency in terms of the domestic currency.[12] From the viewpoint of an investor, these are realized nominal *and* real return differentials, since the foreign rate of interest R^* is translated into domestic currency terms by the change in the exchange rate, and hence the price deflator applied to the two returns is the same.

Let r represent the ex-ante (required) rate-of-return differential:

$$r = R - (R^* + \hat{s}^e) \tag{2}$$

where $\hat{s}^e$ is the expected rate of depreciation of the franc relative to the mark. The realized return differential can thus be decomposed as follows:

$$rd = r + (\hat{s}^e - \hat{s}) \tag{3}$$

That is, ex-post rate-of-return differentials are the sum of two components: ex-ante, or expected, rate-of-return differentials and unexpected changes in exchange rates, or exchange-rate surprises. The surprises are only in exchange rates because both the domestic and foreign interest rates are known with certainty at the time the investment is made. In other words, the nominal interest rates are assumed free of default risk. In what follows, I report evidence on rd, and provide estimates of the decomposition in (3). The decomposition is carried out by computing plausible estimates of the ex-ante rate-of-return differentials: estimates of exchange-rate surprises are the residuals.[13]

8.3.2.1 Ex-post Rate-of-Return Differentials
Ex-post rate-of-return differentials are obtained computing the net profit from two strategies:

• borrow liras or francs, buy marks spot, lend marks, sell marks spot at maturity;

• borrow marks, buy liras or francs spot, lend liras or francs, repay the mark loan with liras or francs obtained spot at maturity;

profits for both strategies are computed in dollars.

Since during the first half of the 1980s Italy and France have imposed controls on international capital flows, effectively isolating the domestic and international money markets in their currencies, I use the offshore (Euro) market in French francs, Deutsche marks and liras. An added advantage of these data is that money market instruments denominated in different currencies are practically identical as far as reserve, insurance, and tax provisions are concerned.

The calculation of speculative profits takes explicit account of the transactions costs. Specifically, the profits on a long position in marks are:

$$\tau \left[(1 + R_t^{*B}/\tau) \frac{S_{t+12/\tau}^{*B}}{S_t^{*A}} - (1 + R_t^A/\tau) \frac{S_{t+12/\tau}^A}{S_t^B} \right] \tag{4}$$

where τ equals 12 or 1, depending on whether interest rates are monthly or annual (the subscript t is monthly), R^* is the DM interest rate (in annual terms), R is the interest rate on franc or lira deposits, S^* is the US dollar/ DM exchange rates, while S is the price of 1 lira or 1 franc in dollars. The superscripts B and A denote bid and asked rates, respectively. The profits on a short position in DM are obtained by changing signs in equation (1), and substituting bid rates for asked rates, and vice versa.

Figures 8.6 and 8.7 report the profits thus computed over the period from January 1981 to May 1990 on one-month investments. The figures are obtained by applying the formula above. To economize space, I report on each graph the profits from a strategy of borrowing francs or liras and lending marks, and a strategy of borrowing marks and lending francs or liras. The former is represented by the solid line, the latter by the dotted line. When borrowing francs or liras to lend marks is profitable, the solid line is below zero. Conversely, when the opposite strategy is profitable, the dotted line is above zero. The data are sampled at the end of the month from daily series.[14] The distribution of ex-post returns are very similar for both currencies: shorting the franc and the lira vis-à-vis the mark has been profitable less than 25 percent of the time in the last ten years, and almost never since the beginning of 1988. However, when profitable, shorting the franc and the lira has yielded high returns.

By contrast, the figures show that shorting the DM in favor of the franc or the lira has yielded lower, but much more consistent returns. Indeed, this strategy has been profitable 65 percent of the time in the case of the franc, and 75 percent in the case of the lira. Figure 8.8, which plots the distribution of returns from shorting the mark and lending francs, illustrate its skewness.[15] The distribution of lira returns is approximately the same, with the highest frequency of small positive realizations, and a very low frequency or large and negative realizations.

The profitability of investments in 1-year deposits—plotted in figures 8.9 and 8.10—has followed a very similar, but even more marked, pattern as the profitability of 1-month investments. Shorting the franc in favor of the mark has been profitable only 30 percent of the time, while the opposite strategy was profitable 70 percent of the time.[16] Contrary to the evidence from 1-month interest rates, the order of magnitude of speculative

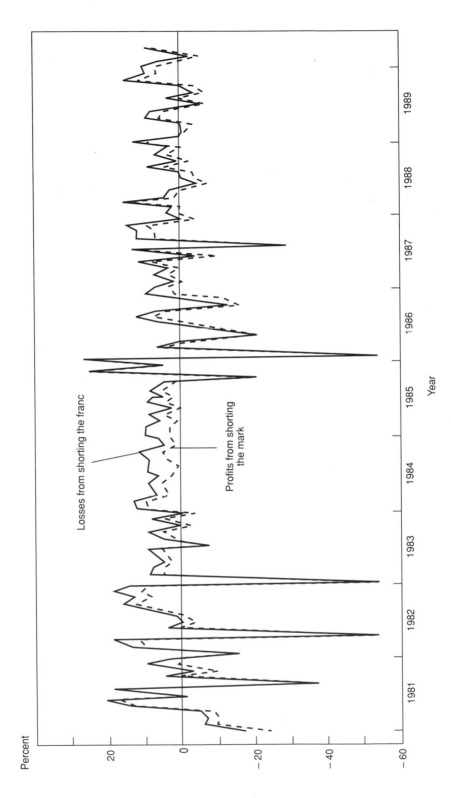

Figure 8.6
Profitability of one-month investments: The franc relative to the mark, January 1981–May 1990

Percent

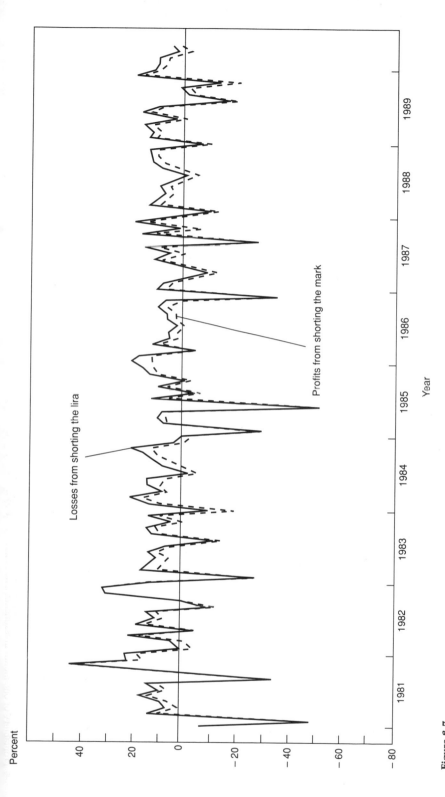

Figure 8.7
Profitability of one-month investments: The lira relative to the mark, January 1982–May 1990

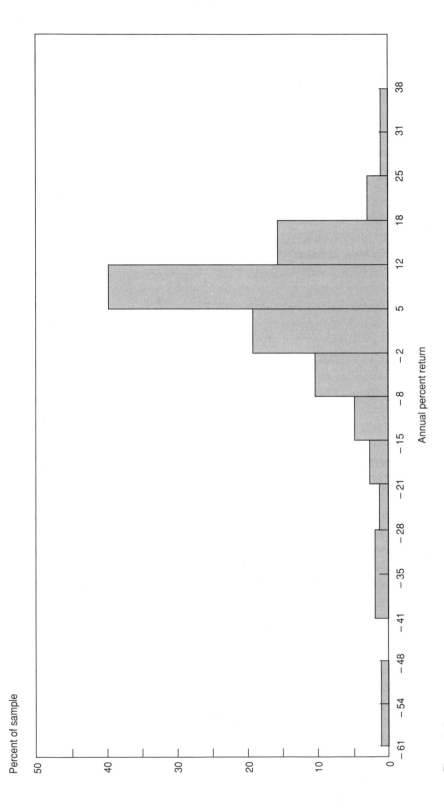

Figure 8.8
Distribution of lira returns on shorting the mark: January 1981–June 1990

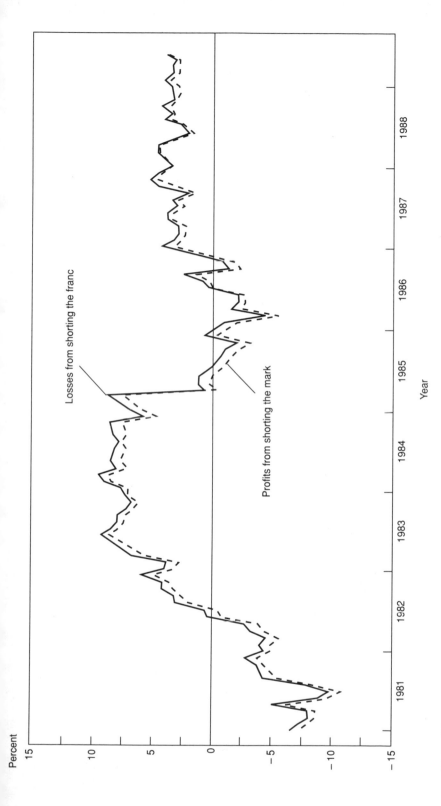

Figure 8.9
Profitability of one-year investments: The franc relative to the mark, January 1981–June 1989

Percent

Losses from shorting the franc

Profits from shorting the mark

Year

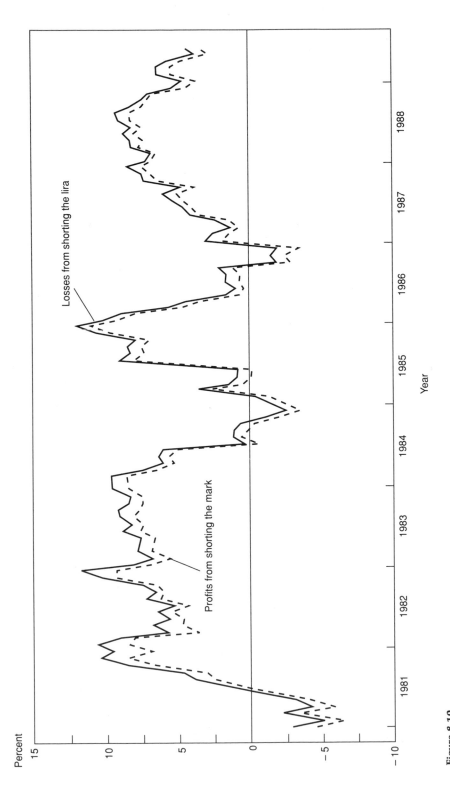

Figure 8.10
Profitability of one-year investments: The lira relative to the mark, January 1981–June 1989

returns is similar for both strategies. In the case of the lira, speculation against the mark has been profitable 86 out of 102 months, while the opposite strategy has been profitable only 13 out of the 102 months in the sample. An investor would have made money consistently, every month from June 1981 to June 1984 and from January 1987 to June 1990, had he simply borrowed marks to invest liras. More strikingly, the size of the "short-mark" positive profits is much larger than that of the "short-lira" positive profits.

8.3.2.2   Interest Rate Differentials and Exchange-Rate Margins

The analysis of bilateral exchange-rate margins provides additional evidence relevant to the decomposition of realized rate-of-return differentials.[17] In March 1979, France and Italy declared that they would not allow their exchange rates with the mark to cross given margins, without an official modification of the margins. Suppose for the moment that the required ex-ante rate-of-return differential between, say, marks and francs were zero. If the upper margin of fluctuation of the two currencies (of the franc/mark exchange rate) were fully credible, the franc interest rate at every time t could never exceed the following value:

$$\bar{R}_t = \left[(1 + R^*) \frac{\bar{S}^{ff,dm}}{S_t^{ff,dm}} - 1 \right], \tag{5}$$

where for simplicity I consider only interest rates on one-year investments, and $\bar{S}^{ff,dm}$ denotes the upper bilateral fluctuation margin for the franc/DM exchange rate, while $S_t^{ff,dm}$ is the spot franc/DM exchange rate at time t. Similarly, the franc interest rate can never be lower than:

$$\underline{R}_t = \left[(1 + R^*) \frac{\underline{S}^{ff,dm}}{S_t^{ff,dm}} - 1 \right], \tag{6}$$

where $\underline{S}^{ff,dm}$ is the lower bilateral fluctuation margin for the franc/DM exchange rate.

$\bar{R}_t$ and $\underline{R}_t$ are observable at every time t. If the franc interest rate at t is outside of these two bounds, either the margins are not credible—that is, agents expect that, *over the maturity of the interest rates considered*, the exchange rate can cross the margins—or required (ex-ante) rate-of-return differentials are non-zero (we assumed them to be zero to derive the upper and lower bounds for the interest rates).

Figures 8.11 and 8.12 compare the actual 1-year and franc and lira interest rates with the upper and lower bounds implied by the spot exchange rates,

Percent

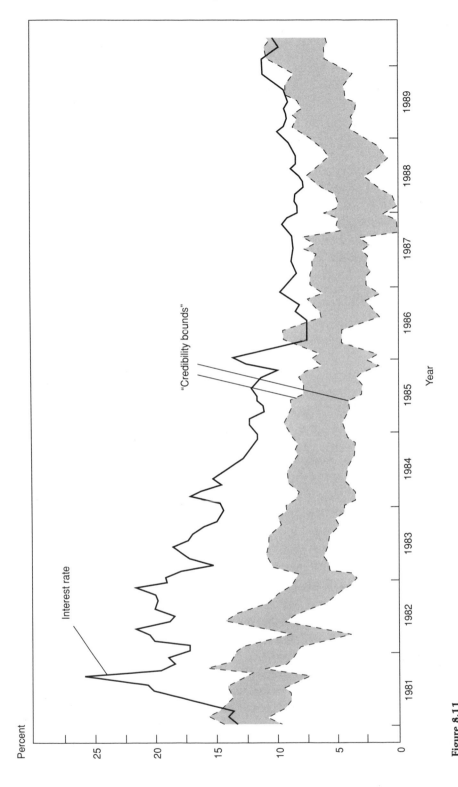

Interest rate

"Credibility bounds"

25

20

15

10

5

0

1981   1982   1983   1984   1985   1986   1987   1988   1989

Year

Figure 8.11
Franc interest rate and its "credibility bounds," January 1981–June 1990

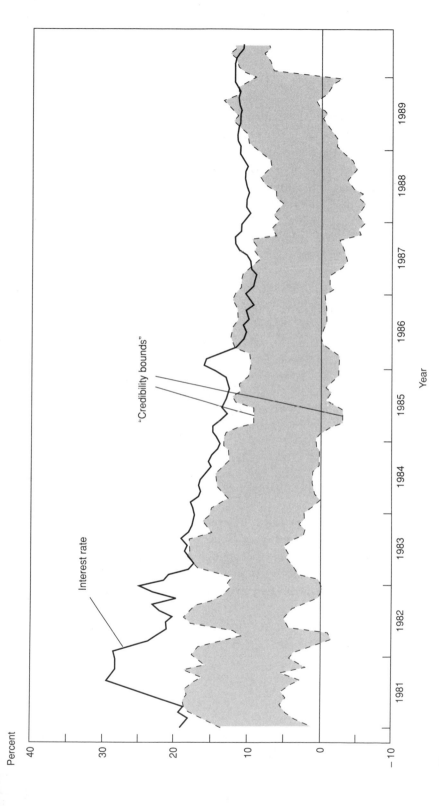

Figure 8.12
Lira interest rate and its "credibility bounds," January 1981–April 1990

the exchange-rate margins, and the Deutsche mark interest rates. Both the franc and the lira interest rates are consistently above the upper bound. The evidence confirms the evidence on the systematic biases on realized returns discussed above. If risk premia are second-order, figures 8.11 and 8.12 indicate that the perceived probability of realignments is quite high, since the *expected value* of the exchange rate exceeds the upper bound. The highest values in the range of the distribution of exchange rates one-year hence has to significantly exceed the upper bound for the mean to be greater than the upper bound. Notice, however, that the divergence between the actual interest rates and the upper bounds has decreased over the last three years.

8.3.2.3 Long-Term Interest Rates

To complete the analysis of interest rates, I report in table 8.8 nominal long-term rates. These are long-term government bond yields from IFS. A number of problems with the data do not allow to carry out the precise calculations presented above: First, the maturity of these bonds is not reported, and might not be matching. And second, domestic government bonds were not as freely tradeable as Eurodeposits, especially during the first half of the 1980s.

The decomposition of return differentials on long-term interest rates is as follows:

$$\frac{1 + R_t^L}{1 + R_t^{*L}} = (1 + r^L) \left[\prod_{i=0}^{L} (1 + \hat{s}_{t+i}^e) \right]^{1/L} \tag{7}$$

where L represents the maturity (in years) of the bonds, and R^L and R^{*L} are the rate of interest for bonds of maturity L. r^L is the risk premium, and $\hat{s}_t^e$ is the expected annual rate of change in the exchange rate from year t to year $t + 1$. Equation (7) says that, net of the risk premium, interest-rate differentials represent the *average* expected rate of depreciation of the ex-

Table 8.8
Long-term government bond yields

	Germany	France	Italy
1979:3–1986:12	7.99	12.28	16.06
1987:1–1989:12	6.34	9.09	10.19
1990:1	8.07	9.52	11.52
1990:6	8.86	9.76	n.a.

Source: *International Financial Statistics*, line 61.

change rate over the maturity of the bonds. Viewed from this perspective, the large differentials among nominal bond rates observed in January 1990 suggest rather large expectations of exchange-rate adjustment. In order to verify this guess, however, it is necessary to evaluate the magnitude of risk premia, to which I turn next.

8.3.3 Alternative Explanations for the Interest-Rate Differentials

Equation (3) has provided a breakdown of the observed ex-post excess returns of franc and lira assets relative to mark assets. It says that realized rate-of-return differentials equal the sum of ex-ante rate-of-return differentials and exchange-rate surprises. To determine whether the long strings of large return differentials is a long string of exchange-rate surprises, I present a discussion of the determinants of the first term on the right-hand-side of (3), and its plausible magnitude. An attempt at quantifying ex-ante rates of return should consider three possible sets of determinants: transactions costs, capital-market segmentations (capital controls), the pricing of risk with perfect capital markets, and the pricing of risk with imperfect capital markets.

8.3.3.1 Transactions Costs
In the presence of transactions costs and uncertainty about returns on foreign-currency deposits, traders' strategies can be characterized an "inactivity" band, whose size is determined by the magnitude of the costs of transactions in the foreign exchange markets, and the uncertainty in expected rates of return (see, for example, Baldwin, 1990). An increase in the expected return on, say, lira deposits, might not be accompanied by a shift in portfolios if traders believe that the costs of adjusting the portfolios and closing-out their position in the future exceed the expected return on the lira investment. Uncertainty and transactions costs therefore induce traders not to eliminate expected rate-of-return differentials unless they reach sufficiently high values, or are expected to persist.

What is the implication of this observation for equilibrium returns? If all market participants behave according to the same trading rules it is possible that, even in the absence of risk aversion,[18] ex-ante rate-of-return differentials will be positively autocorrelated. With rational expectations, ex-post rate-of-return differentials would also be positively autocorrelated. Autocorrelation of returns however does not imply the biases that seem to characterize excess returns on lira and franc deposits, and therefore the effects of transactions costs are not likely to be the explanation of the evidence reported in figures 8.6 to 8.10.

8.3.3.2 Capital Controls

The segmentation of national capital markets prevents efficient portfolio diversification, and induces ex-ante rate-of-return differentials on assets located in different countries. In Europe, France and Italy had adopted controls preventing full arbitrage between domestic and foreign capital markets at least until 1986. These controls have typically generated large differentials between domestic and offshore interest rates on the same types of interbank deposits.

The evidence in figures 8.6 to 8.10 is constructed using interest rates on Eurodeposits, that is, rates on deposits denominated in francs, marks and liras, but all located outside of the three countries. In principle, Eurorates should simply reflect the market's assessment of risk and exchange-rate changes.

Yet capital controls might affect interest rates in the offshore markets through two channels: first, the lack of transfer of funds from onshore to offshore might give rise to liquidity or premia due to offshore market thinness; second, all transfers of funds in the Euromarkets are cleared in the countries of the currencies traded: high political risk might be reflected in an unwillingness to trade and probably additional liquidity premia. Neither argument seems to apply to the currencies considered. Funds do not need to be transferred from onshore to offshore for agents to take advantage of the profit opportunities documented above: it is sufficient to purchase liras or francs in the foreign exchange market, and then lend them in the deposit market. As far as political risk is concerned, restrictions that prevent clearing of funds related to offshore transactions would be extremely severe, and are very unlikely to be imposed in countries like France and Italy, even after all types of transfers of funds between domestic residents and foreigners have been prohibited.

Finally, the evidence discussed above indicates that ex-post return differentials have persisted well after the liberalization of capital controls of 1986. During that period the wedges between onshore rates and offshore rates have disappeared and in some instances domestic interest rates have been higher than offshore rates.[19]

8.3.3.3 Equilibrium Pricing of Foreign Exchange Risk

The next potential explanation of ex-ante rate-of-return differentials is the equilibrium pricing of foreign exchange risk. In order to assess the importance of foreign-exchange risk premia it is necessary to rely on some version of the capital asset pricing model (CAPM). This exercise is complicated by the fact that empirical evidence has repeatedly rejected various specifications of the international CAPM, and precisely on the grounds that risk premia generated by these models are significantly smaller and less volatile than empirical risk premia.[20]

The main potential sources of empirical failure of the CAPM are two. First, if the pattern of returns in the foreign exchange markets is such that large adjustments occur infrequently, standard tests of the CAPM are biased in small samples: this is the "peso" problem (see Krasker, 1980). In the presence of a peso problem, even if expectations are rational, the probability that sample averages match agents' expectations of rates of return is very low in small samples. As I will argue below, while sample averages might be a biased estimate of risk premia if there is a peso problem, sample covariances should not be, if markets allow sufficient portfolio diversification. Thus, rather than computing risk premia from sample estimates of the first moments of returns, I compute them from sample estimates of second moments, and a range of hypothesized parameters' of investors' utility functions—given maintained hypotheses on the equilibrium determinants of asset prices.

The second reason why statistical tests have rejected the CAPM might be specification error. In particular, it might be that agents are not all alike, either because they have different attitudes towards risk, or because they cannot use financial markets to diversify away certain types of risk. In both cases the "representative agent" paradigm does not apply. As the following discussion will make clear, the computation of risk premia can, to some extent, allow for these problems.

To start with, consider the standard representative-agent CAPM. From the investor's optimization problem, the model yields equilibrium relations between conditional expectations and conditional covariances of asset returns. As a general framework I adopt the version of the CAPM derived by Giovannini and Weil (1989). When rates of return on the assets in the portfolio and consumption growth are jointly lognormally distributed,[21] the equilibrium relations between ex-ante returns on deposits denominated in francs, liras and marks is:

$$\ln\left[\frac{E(\tilde{R}^{ff})}{E(\tilde{R}^{dm})}\right] = \rho\frac{1-\gamma}{1-\rho}(\sigma_{ff,c} - \sigma_{dm,c}) + \frac{\gamma-\rho}{1-\rho}(\sigma_{ff,M} - \sigma_{dm,M}) \qquad (8)$$

$$\ln\left[\frac{E(\tilde{R}^{lit})}{E(\tilde{R}^{dm})}\right] = \rho\frac{1-\gamma}{1-\rho}(\sigma_{lit,c} - \sigma_{dm,c}) + \frac{\gamma-\rho}{1-\rho}(\sigma_{lit,M} - \sigma_{dm,M}) \qquad (9)$$

Where the term on the left-hand-side is the log of the ratio of expected gross returns measured in dollars. ρ represents the reciprocal of the coefficient of intertemporal substitution, while γ is the coefficient of relative risk aversion. The equations are defined for $\rho \neq 1$. $\sigma_{i,M}$ is the covariance of the log of the gross rate of return on asset i with the log of the gross return on the market portfolio, while $\rho_{i,c}$ is the covariance of the log of the gross rate of return on asset i with the log of the gross rate of growth of consumption.

These equations embed traditional asset pricing models as special cases. For example, under logarithmic risk preferences ($\gamma = 1$) equations (8) and (9) collapse to the so-called "static" asset pricing equations, where only the covariance of an asset with the market rate of return determines its expected return in equilibrium, while in the case where risk aversion equals intertemporal substitution ($\gamma = \rho$: the case of Von-Neumann preferences) the two equations reduce to the "consumption-based" asset pricing model.

Equations (8) and (9) highlight the reasons why the presence of a "peso problem" might not significantly bias an evaluation of risk premia that rely on sample information for the covariances with the market and consumption. The occurrence of large exchange-rate changes can change significantly the covariances in (8)–(9) if those exchange-rate changes were associated with large changes in either consumption, or the market return, or both. This is unlikely to occur if the world portfolio and the representative investors' consumption on which the asset pricing equation is based are well diversified.

To obtain some rough estimates of the order of magnitude of risk premia from the CAPM I estimate average covariances of franc, lira, and mark returns on 1-year Eurodeposits over the 1980s (using non-overlapping data) with a market index and a consumption index. In Giovannini and Weil (1989) all moments, first and second, are conditional on information available every period (subscripts are here omitted for simplicity). The calibration, instead, uses average data. The error-in-variables problem is negligible if the covariance between the time-varying first and second moments is second-order.[22]

Calibrating the model requires choosing the relevant consumption index and market index. Under the representative-agent assumption, the market index should be an average of national market indices, and the consumption index an average of national consumptions. The indices I chose are, respectively, Capital International Perspective's World market index (Source: Morgan Guaranty),[23] and consumption growth of OECD countries (Source: OECD Main Economic Indicators). There are, however, reasons to believe that the representative agent assumption does not hold, because individual countries' attitudes towards risk may not be the same. First, consumption is not highly correlated across countries, and second, as Adler and Dumas (1983) point out, deviations from purchasing power parity and the law of one price indicate that the conditions for aggregation of national indices are not met. For these reasons, it is useful to compute risk premia from the perspective of national investors. While no general asset pricing model allows aggregation, it is useful to explore whether the predictions of rate-of-return differentials from the perspectives of different national investors differ significantly.

For these reasons I compute equilibrium relative returns also from the viewpoint of a UK investor (using the UK stock market index and the rate of growth of UK consumption[24]) and a Japanese investor (Same sources as for the UK).

Table 8.9 reports the results of this exercise. The top section of the table contains the average relative returns (the terms on the left-hand side of equations (8) and (9) express in percent) as measured from the data, together with the relevant average covariances, also from the data. The bottom section contains the implied relative returns from the model, and concentrate on a number of specific cases: the case of the "static" CAPM ($\gamma = 1$), the case of the consumption CAPM, ($\gamma = \rho = 2$ and 10, respectively), and a general case where I assume high risk aversion ($\gamma = 10$) but intertemporal substitution equal to 0.5 ($\rho = 2$). All reported numbers are in terms of dollars (first column), pounds (second column) and yen (third column).[25]

Except for the case of the Japanese investor, the table indicates that the average risk premia consistent with asset pricing models tend to be smaller than those observed in the data. Often, the models predict higher ex-ante returns on DM assets than on franc or lira assets. In the case of the Japanese investor, the static CAPM produces risk premia that resemble the observed data, but a change in parameters generates very large differences between the data and the model's predictions

I now turn to the second reason why asset pricing models are rejected: the peso problem. The potential of large and rare devaluations might explain the evidence from table 8.9. The table suggests that the risk premium do not seem to account for the average rate-of-return differentials between marks, francs, and liras. Yet this evidence is not necessarily inconsistent with rational expectations. It could indicate that investors had been expecting exchange-rate changes that never occurred, but that, given policymakers' objectives and constraints and the distribution of exogenous shocks to Germany, France, and Italy, changes are not to be ruled out. The presence of a "peso problem" should not significantly bias

Table 8.9
Calibration of risk premiums, for investors in selected currencies, 1981–1989

	World investor (U.S. dollar)	U.K. investor (pound)	Japanese investor (yen)
	Sample data		
Average rate-of-return differentials			
Franc	1.44	1.05	1.05
Lira	4.30	4.14	4.14
Covariance with market			
Mark	0.0200	0.0173	−0.0061
Franc	0.0192	0.0212	0.0322
Lira	0.0220	0.0211	0.0321
Covariance with consumption			
Mark	0.0005	0.0003	−0.0009
Franc	−0.0000	−0.0000	0.0010
Lira	0.0013	0.0000	0.0011
	Theoretical risk premiums		
Static CAPM ($\gamma = 1$)			
Franc	−0.09	0.39	3.84
Lira	0.20	0.39	3.83
Consumption CAPM ($\gamma = \rho = 2$)			
Franc	−0.12	−0.06	0.38
Lira	0.15	−0.03	0.15
Consumption CAPM ($\gamma = \rho = 10$)			
Franc	−0.61	−0.30	1.87
Lira	0.74	−0.15	2.02
General CAPM ($\gamma = 10, \rho = 2$)			
Franc	−0.41	−0.62	−27.29
Lira	−0.23	−3.40	−27.00

risk premiums because it should not affect covariances with the market
and consumption. The occurrence of large exchange-rate changes can significantly change the covariances in equations (8–9) if those exchange-
rate changes are associated with large changes in either consumption,
market return, or both. This is unlikely to occur if the world portfolio and
the representative investor's consumption, both on which the asset pricing equation is based, are well diversified. Errors can, however, occur in
small samples if the large realization of exchange-rate changes are either
overrepresented or underrepresented in the sample. Since my interpretation of the evidence is that, if anything, these large exchange-rate
changes are underrepresented in the sample used for my computations,

and since population covariances should be unaffected by their potential occurrence, my computation should be little affected by the peso problem. Hence the results reported in table 8.9 lead me to conclude that standard asset pricing models do not seem to consistently explain average excess returns on lira and franc deposit relative to deposit in marks. Theoretical risk premiums appear to be small, or, more seriously, of the opposite sign than observed average rate-of-return differentials.

8.3.3.4 Foreign Exchange Risk Premia with Non-Market Risk

One reason why the CAPM fails empirically might be, as I pointed out above, the presence of risk that cannot be efficiently diversified away in financial markets. While in the previous section I have argued that, in the presence of well diversified international portfolios, the rare and large depreciations of the lira and the franc relative to the mark should not affect significantly covariances with consumption and the market, this might not occur in the presence of non-marketable risk.

To illustrate this possibility, consider the optimization problem of an individual investor, assuming—for simplicity—expected utility maximization. The efficiency condition is that, at every time and conditional on information available, the expectation of the product of the gross return on asset i and the marginal rate of substitution in consumption has to equal unity:

$$E[\eta \tilde{R}_i] = 1, \tag{10}$$

where η is the ratio of marginal utility of consumption at the time of the payoff of asset i and current marginal utility of consumption. Following Weil (1990), consider a two-period setup,[26] where at the start of the first period agents are all identical as far as their endowments and risk characteristics are concerned. Their total income is the sum of two components, a marketable and a non-marketable component. The non-marketable component is distributed identically across investors.[27] Using the definition of the riskfree rate of return, $R^F = 1/E(\eta)$, and the relation $E[\eta \tilde{R}_i] = E(\eta)E(\tilde{R}_i) + \text{Cov}(\eta, \tilde{R}_i)$, we obtain:

$$E(\tilde{R}_i) = R^F(1 - \text{Cov}(\eta, \tilde{R}_i)) \tag{11}$$

for any i, and thus:

$$\frac{E(\tilde{R}_i)}{E(\tilde{R}_j)} = \frac{1 - \text{Cov}(\eta, \tilde{R}_i)}{1 - \text{Cov}(\eta, \tilde{R}_j)} \tag{12}$$

The expression within parentheses in equation (11) is greater than 1, since $\text{Cov}(\eta, \tilde{R}_i)$ is negative: an increase in the rate of return on an asset in the portfolio increases future consumption, and therefore decreases its marginal utility. Equations (11) and (12) are of course formally identical to standard asset-pricing equations, like those from which (8) and (9) are derived. The important difference is the presence of non-marketable risk in the marginal rate of substitution, η: in this model risk premia can diverge from those in the standard asset-pricing model if returns in different assets have different covariances with the marginal rate of substitution, because of the presence of non-marketable risk.

From the analysis above, it can be shown that the order of magnitude of the theoretical risk-free rate and the empirical rate-of-return differentials is such that the covariance between the marginal rate of substitution and the rate of return on francs and liras should be about double the one computed assuming perfect risk pooling. However, it is once again difficult to find convincing reasons why large exchange-rate changes should affect the covariances of franc and lira assets more than that of mark assets. The most plausible forms of non-marketable risk in international financial markets are those related to the problems of asymmetric information (see Diamond and Dybvig, 1983), and those arising from legal constraints on financial intermediaries. Large exchange-rate changes produce potentially large transfers of wealth among financial intermediaries in the Euromarkets, and can give rise to liquidity problems and bankruptcies. However, the mechanics of these liquidity crises do not depend on the specific currency composition of bank portfolios. For these reasons, the covariance of returns on lira and franc assets with the marginal utility of consumption (or with any other benchmark) should not be significantly affected large changes in the franc/DM or lira/DM exchange rates. Therefore, the kind of non-marketable risks that characterize international financial markets should not affect ex-ante rates of return on deposits denominated in different currencies.

8.4   What Might Explain High Real Wages and High Real Interest Rates?

The evidence presented in section 8.3 can be summarized as follows:

• The last three years have been characterized by increased stability of exchange rates within the EMS: both volatility and trends in the franc/mark and lira/mark exchange rates have decreased noticeably;

• The decrease in inflation differentials between Germany, France and Italy has been achieved, especially in the case of Italy, through a substantial increase in real wages and relative prices. The last three years have witnessed some worsening of the competitive position of both France and Italy;

• Persistent interest differentials between franc, lira and mark assets do not appear explainable by risk premia and capital-market imperfections;

• The mirror image of high ex-post real interest rates and high real wages were current account deficits and capital account surpluses (often more than offsetting the current account deficits) in Italy and France. In Germany, by contrast, there have been large current account surpluses matched by capital account deficits.

What underlies the persistence of real-wage and real-interest differentials at low levels of inflation and well after the dramatic reduction of inflation differences of the mid-1980s?[28] This section reviews alternative explanations.

8.4.1 "Pure" Wage and Price Stickiness

The first natural candidate is the traditional wage-price stickiness story.[29] With credible exchange-rate targeting high real wages and a loss in competitiveness have to be observed in the transition since only a fraction of existing prices and wages in the economy are reset every period.

The first problem with this approach is that the change in regime has occurred for some time now. Some claim that France and Italy dramatically altered their domestic policies in response to the discipline of the EMS in the mid-1980s; others regard January 1987 as the date when these two countries have pledged not to use parity changes any more. The persistence of wage and real-interest differentials three years after the hypothesized change in regime presumably occurred is hard to square with the standard models of overlapping wage contracts, since in these models inertia lasts only for the maximum length of wage contracts.[30] What would then be needed is some type of protracted price stickiness of the type discussed, for example, by Blanchard (1983).

Even if protracted nominal sluggishness is present, however, these models would still not be able to explain the persistence of interest-rate differentials documented in section 8.3. If the exchange rate is credibly fixed the increase in money demand coming from the fall in inflationary expectations after the change in regime would be automatically accommodated by balance-of-payments surpluses, and the nominal interest rate need not go up.[31] In order to explain the observed interest-rate differential one should rely on slow adjustment in international asset markets, or risk premia, a hypothesis that has been ruled out above.

In conclusion, there are a number of reasons to believe that nominal stickiness might not be the exclusive explanation of the observed behavior of real interest rates and real wages in France and Italy relative to Germany. This is of course not to say that nominal inertia is irrelevant, but only that it is useful to search for additional explanations of the facts.

8.4.2   Credibility Problems

The next hypothesis to evaluate is the lack of credibility of the policy change. In order to illustrate that hypothesis, it is useful to adopt the standard model of interaction between the government and the private sector, which follows Barro and Gordon (1983a,b).[32] The assumptions of the model are the following:

1. Unanticipated changes in nominal exchange rates have real effects;

2. Monetary authorities perceive a cost in exchange-rate changes, which under a managed floating regime can represent the cost of the induced higher inflation, and in a regime like the EMS could represent, together with the higher inflation cost, the political cost of exchange-rate changes;

3. There are distortions in the economy which could be corrected, even if temporarily, by exchange-rate changes. The best example for European countries is the monopoly power of (some) trade unions;

4. Monetary authorities can respond to events faster than the aggregate private sector;

5. The state of the economy is represented by the realization of an exogenous disturbance which affects the real economy. In other words, slow (multiperiod) adjustment of prices or wages is ruled out for the sake of tractability.

The unanticipated exchange-rate changes and the exogenous disturbance affect the economy as follows:

$$y = (\hat{s} - \hat{s}^e) - \varepsilon, \tag{13}$$

where ε is the exogenous real shock discussed in 5: an i.i.d. random variable with zero expectation.

The preference of monetary authorities are represented by the following loss function:

$$L = E[\hat{s}^2 + \phi(y - K)^2],\tag{14}$$

where the first term represents the costs of exchange-rate changes discussed in 2, and the second term, $K > 0$, is the distortion in 3.

The ability of monetary authorities to respond to events faster than the aggregate economy is captured in the assumption that monetary authorities set the rate of change of the exchange rate after observing ε, while the private sector forms expectations on monetary policy before the realization of ε. Under these assumptions, a regime of managed floating would be one where $\hat{s}$ is the solution of the following problem:

$$\min \hat{s}^2 + \phi(y - K)^2\tag{15}$$

subject to:

$$y = (\hat{s} - \hat{s}^e) - \varepsilon,\tag{16}$$

$$\hat{s}^e \quad given\tag{17}$$

The equilibrium change in the exchange rate, level of activity and expectations of exchange-rate changes are, respectively:

$$\hat{s} = \phi K + \frac{\phi}{1 + \phi}\varepsilon\tag{18}$$

$$y = -\frac{1}{1 + \phi}\varepsilon\tag{19}$$

$$\hat{s}^e = \phi K.\tag{20}$$

These (familiar) results highlight the inflationary bias in a regime where the central bank is unable to credibly commit to a fixed exchange-rate target.

8.4.2.1 Learning about the Change in Regime

Consider now the case where the monetary authorities, for reasons that are not explicit in the model (like for example the desire to accelerate economic and political integration with the rest of Europe) abandon any attempt to correct domestic distortions with the exchange rate, and stick to the fixed exchange-rate parity: $\hat{s}$ is equal to zero independently of the state.

The private sector, not fully aware or convinced by this change in regime, believes that the authorities could revert to the discretionary management of the exchange rate described above. The public assigns a probability p that the monetary authorities will not follow the fixed-exchange-rate rule. Every period, this probability is revised optimally based on the observed behavior of the monetary authorities. That is, p_{t+1} is decreased if $\hat{s}_t = 0$. The expectation of the exchange-rate change is thus:

$$\hat{s}^e = p\hat{s}^{e,d} + (1 - p) \times 0 \tag{21}$$

where $\hat{s}^{e,d}$ is the expectation of the depreciation of the exchange rate in the case the authorities followed discretionary exchange-rate management. Assuming rational expectations, $\hat{s}^{e,d}$ is formed using the knowledge of the authorities incentives, i.e. of the first-order condition for the problem (15)–(17):

$$E[\hat{s}^e + \phi(\hat{s}^e - p\hat{s}^{e,d} - \varepsilon - K)] = 0 \tag{22}$$

This implies:

$$\hat{s}^{e,d} = \frac{1}{1 - \phi(1 - p)}\phi K, \tag{23}$$

$$\hat{s}^e = \frac{p}{1 - \phi(1 - p)}\phi K, \tag{24}$$

If the authorities adhere to the exchange-rate parity, p is progressively decreased, until it reaches zero. The transition, however, is characterized by a series of prediction errors. This would generate data resembling the phenomena described above.

Consider interest-rate differentials. Equation (3) indicates that realized interest-rate differentials would be high, even if ex-ante real interest differentials were zero. Negative exchange-rate surprises also depress economic activity:

$$y = -\hat{s}^e - \varepsilon = -\frac{p}{1 - \phi(1 - p)}\phi K - \varepsilon \tag{25}$$

The intuition behind this result can be provided with reference to the evidence on real-wage differentials discussed in section 8.3. Wages are set with an expectation of a positive exchange-rate depreciation. As the exchange-rate depreciation is not realized, the loss in competitiveness is reflected in a fall in economic activity.

The model of slow adjustment of expectations presented above raises two questions. The first regards the speed of adjustment of expectations. The model predicts that expectations of exchange-rate changes would asymptotically converge to zero. This convergence has not occurred in countries like France and, especially, Italy. More strikingly, this convergence does not seem to occur in countries with an experience of much more stable exchange rates.

The case of Austria provides an interesting example. Until the early seventies the schilling and the DM were tied together by the Bretton Woods System: both currencies were pegged to the dollar (hence the March 1961 revaluation of the mark is reflected in a devaluation of the schilling). With the collapse of the Bretton Woods regime, the schilling was pegged to a basket of currencies, where the Deutsche mark gained an increasing weight. Finally, in 1981 the schilling was tied to the mark exclusively. Notice that the only sizeable change in the schilling/mark rate is the one occurring at the end of 1969, when the price of the mark increased progressively from about 6.5 to 7 (a depreciation of 7.5 percent). In contrast to the franc and the lira, the schilling has kept remarkably stable relative to the mark throughout the 1980s.

In the years after 1986, the period for which reliable data are available, Austrian short-term interest rates exceeded German short-term interest rates by an average of about 50 basis points. The experience of the Netherlands, a country member of the EMS which has kept is currency and monetary policy tightly linked to Germany's, broadly matches the evidence for Austria.

This evidence raises the possibility of permanent interest-rate distortions, which suggest that the government commitment to the given parity might be less than fully credible, even in the long run. The lack of full credibility of bilateral parities in the long run is well justified by the observation that the maintenance of different currencies is just the preservation of the governments' right to change their relative value. Given that exchange-rate changes have real effects, governments might be reluctant to give this instrument up.

8.4.2.2 Exchange-Rate Changes as "Escape Clauses"

An alternative to the "learning" model presented above is thus a model where the public is aware that there will always be instances when the monetary authorities will want to use the exchange rate.[33]

The government strategy is this time a mixture of the simple rule of fixing the exchange rate ($\hat{s} = 0$), and discretionary policy (for this reason the model is labelled "escape clause"). Discretionary policy is chosen whenever the exogenous shock ε exceeds a given range. The public fully understand this. It bases its own expectation about the government's behavior on the probability of large realizations of ε, the instances when the escape clause will be invoked. Given that ε is serially independent, these probabilities are constant.

The solution of this model is formally identical to that of the "learning" model, except that now p represents the probability that ε lies beyond the "normal" range and is constant. Hence, as long as ε keeps in the normal range there will be high ex-post real interest rates and high real wages. When the large realizations of ε occur, the government discretionary exchange-rate changes will be more effective, because the public will be more surprised than under a managed exchange-rates regime. Thus, it can be easily shown, (see Flood and Isard, 1989, and Persson and Tabellini, 1990) that there are parameter values such that this strategy would be preferred by the government to both fixed exchange rates and managed floating. The mixed strategy is thus believable by the public.[34]

8.4.2.3 Extensions and Implications

An important difference between the models presented above and reality is that the state of the economy is not serially independent. Because of sluggishness of prices and wages, and slow response of employment to real wages, the loss in competitiveness builds up over time. In other words, for a given stream of realizations of the exogenous disturbance the monetary authorities' incentives to change the exchange rate increase over time, since the losses in competitiveness due to past increases in prices are still there in the present. In the models this does not occur because the losses in competitiveness result in an immediate fall in economic activity.

An extension of the models that accounts for a larger state space is beyond the scope of this chapter. My conjecture is that in this case the "escape clause" equilibrium, if it is at all viable, might be subject to more frequent exchange-rate realignments, and larger biases of ex-post real interest rates when the realignments do not occur. An additional, more manageable extension of the model is to mix learning with the "escape clause" parable. It seems that elements of both stories should be relevant to interpret the experience of European countries. The public is not sure how serious is the commitment to monetary convergence, and might revise its views as years go by; yet, there is always a belief that governments might use the exchange rate under extreme circumstances. Even the probability that the government resorts to exchange-rate changes might be subject to revisions.

An implication of the analysis above is an interesting extension of the theory of optimum currency areas. A regime of fixed exchange rates with separate currencies is not equivalent to a single currency, since the public understands the motivations of monetary authorities to use exchange rates for the purpose of correcting distortions. This awareness induces biases on rates of return to productive factors, whose welfare effects are estimable.

A calculation of the welfare effects of the interest-rate distortions described above should take into account uncertainty, and in particular the fact that in the "escape clauses" model large realizations of the exogenous shock occur once in a while. Two types of effects should be relevant in this calculation. First, the long-run rate of return might be tied down, either by a modified golden rule condition, or, in the case of a small open economy, by the world rate of interest. In this case the wedges discussed here might have large welfare effects, similar to those arising from taxing savings. And second, accounting for uncertainty should allow for a more precise estimate of the investment distortion.

8.5   The Transition to Monetary Union

What are the implications of the analysis for the current policy discussion? This section examines the policy debate in light of the evidence and the interpretations presented above. What follows, however, is necessarily an attempt to interpret a snapshot of a fast sequence of diplomatic exchanges among EC countries. These exchanges have accelerated in the very recent past, possibly due to the forthcoming intergovernmental conference (December 1990) whose scope is to change the Treaty of Rome to allow for the creation of a common European central bank. Hence this section can at best help to identify the main lines of the debate and offer some guarded predictions on the likely outcomes of imminent important joint decisions of EC governments.

The section is divided in three parts. First I discuss the feasibility—and indeed the desirability—of gradualism as a strategy to achieve a monetary union. Next I turn to the problems that are perceived to hinder further progress of the monetary union: the budgetary and debt problems and the question of "two speed" EMU, with a core group of countries moving towards a single currency before the rest of the EC. Finally, I characterize the likely differences in the positions of the major negotiators at the forthcoming intergovernmental conference.

8.5.1   Can Gradualism Work?

In section 8.3 I have presented evidence that exchange-rate targets in the EMS have not been credible in the beginning of the experiment and are still not fully credible now. The lack of credibility of exchange-rate targets is the curse of gradualism. In section 8.4 I have shown that, if the incentives to change exchange rates remain intact, expectations of their occurrence will never go away. The question is then whether the incentives for France and Italy to devalue their currencies relative to the DM have been significantly affected by the Delors plan. These incentives are a combination of the real effects of surprise realignments and the (political and economic) costs of these realignments.

As I pointed out above, some observers believe that the political costs of devaluations as perceived by French and Italian authorities are higher now than, say, five years ago. This might well be just a reflection of these two countries' greater political enthusiasm towards the idea of creating in the European Community an integrated economy with a single currency. Resistance from other EC partners, as well as problems raised by external economic shocks, might however suddenly lower the perceived political costs of exchange-rate changes. In addition, the intrinsic dynamics of wages and prices can also lower the perceived costs of devaluations, since in the absence of full convergence of inflation rates exchange-rate misalignments build up. Finally, the lack of credibility of exchange-rate targets is further justified by the present institutional setting. Nothing prevents monetary authorities from using changes in bilateral parities to accommodate price imbalances. Indeed, the Delors Report views this strategy as acceptable—or even desirable (at least according to the interpretation of this plan by German authorities)—in the transition, since it allows exchange-rate realignments during stage one, and possibly even during stage 2.

The model discussed in section 8.4 implies that, when exchange-rate targets are not fully credible, convergence can never be complete.[35] For this very reason it is quite unlikely that monetary authorities would be able to maintain exchange-rate targets throughout the whole adjustment period and gradualism fails. The policy implication is that the elimination of small inflation-rate differentials is a faulty criterion to guide a monetary reform. The stubbornness of small inflation differentials does not allow monetary authorities to decide when maximum inflation convergence is reached.

These observations are based on the implicit assumption that real shocks are absent. Under this assumption, and absent the nonneutralities arising from credibility problems under fixed exchange rates, all relative prices between the low- and the high-inflation countries would be equal to unity. Indeed, this implicit assumption provides the benchmark for the inflation-convergence criterion. In reality, however, real shocks are present, and therefore the criterion of inflation convergence becomes even less reliable, because it requires the knowledge of equilibrium relative prices. The difficulties in computing equilibrium relative prices are due to the well-known uncertainties on the relevant economic model and its parameters, discussed, for example, by Frankel (1988).

In conclusion, economic theory suggests that gradualism is not an effective strategy to pursue in a monetary reform. The very recent increases in the price of oil will almost surely bring out the weaknesses of gradualism to the open. First of all, the increase in the price of oil is a real shock, and EC countries might regard it necessary to allow intra-European real exchange rates to be changed. This would imply giving up the twin objectives of exchange-rate stability and inflation-rate convergence. In addition, the increase in the price of oil will affect inflation and inflationary expectations. Calculations I performed with Francesco Giavazzi using 1980 input-output tables (Giavazzi and Giovannini, 1987) show that the aggregate effect of a 10 percent increase in the price of energy products ranges from 1.3 percent (in France) to 1.9 percent (in the Netherlands) assuming constant nominal wages and letting all other prices adjust, and from 6.6 percent (in the Netherlands) to 7.2 percent (in Germany and the U.K.) assuming constant real wages in all the countries. These numbers are computed taking into account the effects of intra-European input-output interactions. They indicate that the structure of production in EC countries does not necessarily disadvantage the "high inflation" countries. However, the large differences among constant-nominal-wages and constant-real-wages simulations suggest that, despite the technological homogeneity of European economies, an energy shock can have sizeable destabilizing effects if it affects price-setters' expectations unevenly.[36]

The pitfalls of the gradualist approach lend support to the alternative, "monetarist" strategy. The monetarist strategy calls for a sudden and permanent change in the monetary regime. Elsewhere (Giovannini, 1990) I have argued that the best way to achieve a monetary union, once the common monetary authority is in place, is a currency reform. A currency reform is a replacement of national currencies either by a single currency (say, the ECU), or by new national currencies that exchange at par (1 Deutsche mark equals 1 franc, equals 1 lira, and so on).[37] This exchange is carried out over a specified period of time, during which residents of each country will swap old banknotes for new banknotes at a prespecified rate. Bank accounts are automatically converted. As a result, the stock of money in circulation is unaffected. During the same period, all outstanding assets and liabilities in the economy have to be recalculated, requiring considerable expense: all accounting and control systems—both private and public—have to be translated.

While the two alternatives (1-to-1 exchange rates versus ECU) produce the same effects on prices (aligning nominal prices of goods of all countries in the union), they are not exactly equivalent for two reasons. On one hand, some countries might be unwilling to give up their national currency's name and symbol in exchange for the ECU: these countries would find it more desirable to change units keeping national currencies alive. On the other hand, the persistence of banknotes with the old names and symbols might make those of the countries with previously higher inflation somewhat less desirable, especially in retail transactions. A compromise solution would be to print new banknotes with the ECU name together with the names of all the currencies in the union.

The advantages of the currency reform are many. First, by eliminating exchange rates, it eliminates the distortions arising from expectations of exchange-rate changes. Second, it solves unit-of-account problems, by cutting down on the calculations necessary to translate prices in different currencies (with N currencies, the number of relevant bilateral exchange rates is $\frac{N^2}{2} - \frac{N}{2}$).[38] Third, it allows final adjustments of exchange rates without inducing any changes in inflationary expectations. Finally, and most importantly, it is the only reform that is fully credible, since it does not allow reversals to the old regime.

However, a currency reform is a politically costly undertaking because it requires full and immediate commitment by all countries deciding to join; it forces to set up a common European central bank, and to resolve the issues related to its management, accountability, and tasks.[39] These problems are discussed in detail below.

8.5.2   Obstacles to a Currency Reform

The economically more sensible strategy for a monetary union, a currency reform, faces two important obstacles. The first is the creation of a common central bank that is independent of national fiscal authorities, and can carry out its own objectives without undue pressures or influence from national governments. The second obstacle is the question of the participation to the monetary union.

Table 8.10
Interest-rate differentials: Austrian schilling minus Deutsche mark

	Mean	Minimum	Maximum
Money market rate	0.49%	−0.30%	1.70%
Eurodeposit rate	0.46%	−0.86%	1.31%
Memorandum: Exchange rate	7.0375	7.0149	7.1135

Sample: October 1986 to June 1990.
Sources: Exchange rate, *International Financial Statistics*; Interest rates, DRI.

Table 8.11
Debt GNP ratios: 1989

Country	Debt/GNP (percent)
Belgium	127
France	35
Germany	43
Italy	99
Netherlands	78
United Kingdom	44
EC12	58

Source: Salomon Brothers.

One of the sources of pressure on the European central bank that has been most frequently debated in the past year is divergences in fiscal stances in individual countries. Table 8.11 shows debt/GDP ratios and primary deficits for EC countries. The table highlights the nature of the divergences. Primary deficits are of the same order of magnitude, whereas differences in debt/GNP ratios induce large differences in the recourse of national governments to financial markets, both as *net* absorbers of savings and as primary borrowers.[40]

The data in table 8.10 raises two questions:

• Can a monetary union function without a central fiscal authority?

• What threats do independent fiscal authorities as currently in place provide to the well-working of a European central bank?

The first question is raised by those who regard central banks as fiscal agencies of the government in charge of managing the government debt, either by selling securities to the market or by purchasing government securities directly in exchange for high-powered money. Over the years, central banking has progressively moved away from these functions, for which the private banking sector is perfectly equipped. Currently central banks are mostly concerned about the soundness of financial intermediaries, the stability of interest rates and the exchange rate, and the control of inflation.[41] An additional aspect of the first question regards the optimum-currency-area tradeoff between monetary and fiscal policy, stressed, for example, by Kenen (1969). The creation of a single currency area might give a role to a centralized fiscal authority to redistribute income in response to region-specific shocks.[42] The current policy sentiment, especially in the EC countries, is that a centralized and permanent system of income transfers might be plagued by inefficiencies. Financial intermediaries and development banks, perhaps under the explicit delegation from national governments, are probably best suited in identifying the relevant development opportunities, in selecting the most socially efficient projects, and in monitoring their progress.

The second question raised by the current structure of fiscal authorities and their divergent imbalances regards the spillovers of national fiscal shocks onto the whole Community, and the effects of these spillovers on the operations of a common central bank.[43] Three types of spillovers are relevant in this case. The first are the traditional Keynesian spillovers, associated with the export of crowding out in a region characterized by integrated financial markets and a single currency. The bias in this case is expansionary, and the effects are an increase in the real interest rate and an appreciation of the region's real exchange rate relative to the rest of the world. Hence the pressures on a central bank would be to offset these biases via monetary expansion.[44] The second type of spillover comes from the interaction of distortionary taxation in the presence of increased mobility of goods and factors within the area. Uncoordinated tax policies lead to tax competition and undertaxation of the mobile factors, with adverse effects on national budgets. If national governments are unable to either decrease spending or increase taxation of the immobile factors by the required amounts, tax competition increases net borrowing by national governments, and might induce pressures on the common central banks to monetize part of the deficits. In addition, higher government borrowing increases the stocks of government debt. The third type of spillovers is related to the dynamics of debts and deficits, and to the systemic effects of funding crises of individual governments. In countries with large stocks of debt, questions are raised as to the ability of the national government to adhere to its intertemporal budget constraints without debt repudiation or other forms of extraordinary taxation. The impact of these crises on financial markets might be very significant, especially if the *absolute* size of the government debts whose value is put in question is large. The incentives for a common central bank would be to inject liquidity into financial markets to avoid the negative effects of a systemic crisis, associated with multiple collapses of financial intermediaries.

Spillovers of the first kind are not to be considered a source of great concern, since differences in private savings rates across EC countries largely offset the differences in government budget deficits, especially as far as the largest countries are concerned. Spillovers of the second kind are potentially more serious, although to date there are no reliable numbers of the impact of the single market on tax revenues—assuming no change in national tax structures and policies—and at the same time the Community has practically abandoned attempts at comprehensively overhauling tax coordination. Concerns about the ability of the government of Italy to stabilize its debt/GNP ratio makes the spillovers of the third kind become most significant and most urgent.

The attitudes of official institutions towards the problem of coordination of national fiscal authorities with the common central bank are a mixture of concerns about stability in the transition (i.e. concerns to eliminate the incentives that countries might have to depreciate their currencies in the transition) and concerns about the operation of the monetary union. The Delors Report considers convergence of fiscal deficits a crucial condition for monetary union to be feasible, and advocates concerted budgetary actions during stage one including "quantitative guidelines and medium-term orientations." In the second stage the Report calls for "precise, although not yet binding, rules relating the size of annual budget deficits and their financing." In the third stage, budgetary rules would become binding. The EC document on Economic and Monetary Union (European Commission, 1990) advocates the adoption of "binding procedures," whereby during the transition member states submit rules or guidelines for their budgetary laws, whose adequacy would have to be discussed at the Community level. In the final stage, the Community proposes monitoring, adjustment and enforcement through peer pressures. Finally, the EC Monetary Committee (1990) spells out even in greater details "principles of sound budgetary policies," which include the elimination of governments' access to direct financing by central banks, no cross-government "bail out" rules, and the correction of excessive deficits, together with, if possible, incorporation of criteria to determine acceptable levels of budget deficits into the Treaty of Rome.

It is not clear which specific externalities would be corrected by the proposed rules, especially the rules relating to ceilings in national budget deficits. These rules have been criticized on the grounds that budgetary ceilings might eliminate the flexibility that national governments will need in order to supplement the loss of the monetary instrument to offset regional shocks in the union (see especially Buiter and Kletzer, 1990), that the U.S. experience with similar rules has been a proliferation of artificial accounting devices to bypass them with little substantial results, and that it is very difficult to build sanctions for the countries that break the rules that are actually credible. More importantly, none of the proposed rules directly attacks the most serious threat to the stability of a fledgling European monetary union: the occurrence of fiscal crises. In principle, a more satisfactory solution to the problem of insuring the minimization of the risks of fiscal crises while at the same time avoiding a slow-down of the monetary union would have been the definition of fiscal preconditions for countries to join the union. These preconditions could include requirements to convincingly stabilize—or indeed reduce—the debt/GNP ratio before joining the union. These preconditions are however politically very costly both for the countries "in trouble" and for the "virtuous" countries, which tend to resist accelerations in the progress towards monetary union. The former would in fact have to engineer large fiscal stabilizations fast, without the options of delaying adjustment, or the hope of exporting the political costs of the adjustment to the rest of Europe. The latter would have to accept to proceed immediately to the next step of the union, either together with the countries which have completed the fiscal stabilization, or without them, but sooner.

These observations highlight the second important obstacle to the currency reform, that is the question of the participation to the monetary union, or the "two-speed" EMU. The Delors Report does not impose the constraint of full participation to all the stages of the monetary union, yet the importance of this reform is such that several governments have expressed uneasiness with informal proposals of starting the monetary union with a small number of EC countries to be increased progressively. These proposals have been prompted by the observations of the sizeable inflation differentials between Germany and, say, Greece and Portugal, or the apparent difficulties that Spain and Italy are having in keeping their inflation rate low without losing external competitiveness. The debate on a "two-speed" EMU has been very similar to the debate on fiscal policy problems. In both cases the concern was that the "weak" countries will impart an inflationary bias on the union's central bank. If the cause of higher inflation is fiscal policy, the discussion above applies. By contrast, if the source of high inflation is simply lack of reputation of the monetary authorities, it is unclear that a monetary union would damage seriously the "hard core" countries, except in the case where the public perceives that the reputation of the new European central bank is a weighted average of the reputation of the central banks of its member countries. Concern by the low inflation countries about these risks, as well as resistance by the high inflation countries to any project aimed at speeding up the monetary union for only a subset of the European Community,[45] are additional sources of procrastination of the monetary reform.

8.5.3   The Next Step: The December 1990 Intergovernmental Conference

On October 8, the UK government decided to have the pound join the exchange-rate mechanism of the EMS.[46] Despite a long series of official statements that the pound will join the EMS only when the UK rate of inflation converges with that of Germany (the current differential is about 6 percent), this decision has not surprised those who expected that England will make sure it will play a crucial role at the intergovernmental conference. The entry of the UK into the active negotiations on EMU will crucially determine their outcome because the British position on EMU could become the "swing factor" in the collective decisions, since it is not the natural ally of either the "monetarists" or the "economists."

The two extremes of the spectrum of political attitudes towards EMU are represented by Germany—the "economist"—on one side and France and Italy (together with Belgium)—more "monetarists"—on the other. The latter three countries favor steady progress of monetary union, and would likely not oppose the idea of a currency reform outlined above. They support the concept of an independent central bank model after the Bundesbank and the Federal Reserve System. They acknowledge the important role of the EMS in their own disinflation experience.

On the other end of the spectrum, Germany is the champion of the "economists" view on monetary union.[47] It strongly resists initiatives that might accelerate the process. It fully believes that, with the appropriate adjustment, inflation and inflationary expectations can fully converge. It regards the convergence of inflationary expectations an absolute precondition for embarking on the next stages of the monetary union.

It is very difficult to determine where does the UK position fits relative to the two extremes of France, Italy and Belgium on one side and Germany on the other. The UK has been consistently opposing all the recent major initiatives to increase economic integration in Europe, including the completion of the single market, EMU and the forthcoming inter-governmental conference. The rationale for this opposition is well explained by the following interpretation of Thatcher's thought:

... But part of this function [of the Conservative Party] is "external vigilance as a condition of our liberty", and, has she [M. Thatcher] has also trenchantly indicated—the Government has not labored arduously since 1979 to eject social-ism in the UK only to find it entering through the back-door via Brussels; thus any intention that the European Commission's writ should extend to the minutiae of economic and social policies must be firmly rejected. (Foreword by Harold A. Taylor to Minford, 1989)

The position of the UK government is a blend of a vigorous anti-regu-lation and anti-socialist sentiment with a strong desire to preserve na-tional sovereignty and national identity.[48] This special position of the UK government makes its own contributions to the debate on EMU some-what orthogonal to the rest of the debate. The UK government has in the past year presented two related proposals. The first (HM Treasury, 1989) called for an "evolutionary" approach to monetary union that would ex-ploit to the maximum the virtues of competition. According to the pro-posal, the best way to manage the transition to monetary union is to remove all those obstacles that prevent private agents from effectively diversifying their currency portfolios. The effects of deregulation would be to increase the pressures on "deviating" monetary authorities, and force convergence to the "best" regime, characterized by stable purchas-ing power and an efficient payments system. The Treasury document sug-gested instead that the move to a single currency could happen as a result of "natural evolution" resembling the law of the survival of the fittest.

More recently, the UK government has circulated a follow-up to the 1989 document (HM Treasury, 1990) stressing the need to give in-dependent status to the ECU (for this reason the latest proposal is some-times labelled the "hard ECU" proposal), to ensure that, if the markets will decide to adopt a single currency, it will be the ECU.[49] Thus, on the issue of the relevant horizon for EMU, it is difficult to see the UK becoming an ally of Italy, France and Belgium—given its opposition to the idea of a government-directed monetary reform—but it is also difficult to see it become an ally of Germany—since it would imply acceptance of the EMS status quo, which is characterized by a distribution of monetary sover-eignty biased in favor of Germany's monetary authorities. In sum, the divergences of the positions of the EC governments at the start of the inter-governmental conference seem to suggest that the conference is not poised to provide significant impetus to a monetary union among EC countries.

8.6 Concluding Remarks

This chapter has discussed the problem of a monetary reform in Europe. The current initiative of EC countries to move towards a single currency is very similar to the Werner plan, discussed and approved in 1970. That plan was quickly discarded in front of an exogenous shock: international capital flows towards the Deutsche mark in anticipation of a collapse of the Bretton Woods system. Twenty years later, the second plan for monetary union is challenged by another exogenous shock: the increase in the price of oil caused by the invasion of Kuwait and the tension in the Gulf area. The results of my analysis suggest that the gradualist strategy is little credible and thus too vulnerable.

Partly because of the oil shock the European currency reform has now reached a deadlock. The strategy currently pursued, gradualism, could mask lack of commitment by national governments, and for that reason is little credible. The alternative strategy, a currency reform, requires the solution of the difficult political problems of setting up a multinational central bank, and forcing the substitution of national currency with a new money at odd exchange rates. In the absence of strong political leadership, a currency reform is unlikely to be undertaken in the near future. The current halfway house, characterized by complete capital mobility, tight exchange-rate targets, and lack of institutional coordination of national monetary authorities, could easily collapse.

The recurrence of similar difficulties 20 years after the failure of the Werner plan suggests one basic problem faced by European countries with respect to currency reform: they understand and seek the benefits of a single currency, but they face considerable political difficulties and adjustment costs of a sudden reform. As a result, they tend to adopt strategies with a very high risk of self-defeat.

Notes

1. Sterling was devalued in November 1967, but at the time the United Kingdom was not a member of the European Community.

2. At that time the "monetarist" and "economist" labels were created to characterized these two polar views. See Tsoulakis (1977).

3. By contrast, Michael Emerson (1982) claims that the EMS has significantly affected the institutional development of the Community, in that it has "brought a major policy function back into the Community setting, as compared to the snake mechanism that had left it. It has linked together Community monetary and public finance mechanisms, and its economic policy coordination procedures."

4. A wide-ranging discussion of the economic effects of EMU is in Eichengreen (1990).

5. "Community System for the Central Banks" in the former, "European System of Central Banks" in the latter.

6. In the 1960s the political issues tended to surface in the context of economic discussions. A good example is the defence of European monetary independence by Giscard d'Estaing (1969), which was based on the desire to take away seigniorage from the United States, and, before him, Rueff (1967).

7. See, for example, Wolf (1989).

8. This anecdote is based on discussions with members of the German delegation.

9. This last question gives relevance to the "two speeds" project for monetary union, according to which a "core" of countries can proceed fast towards monetary reform, while the others should join when conditions are, according to some criterion, appropriate.

10. See, for example, Giovannini (1989, chapter 2 in this volume).

11. In the case of the lira—appearing in figure 8.4—the January 1990 narrowing of the band (from 6 percent to 2.25 percent on both sides) was accomplished together with an adjustment of the central parity: the central parity was changed so that the upper fluctuation limit before and after the realignment remained the same.

12. This relation is an approximation. It is exact for continuously compunded rates.

13. For an analysis of interest-rate differentials between Spain, Portugal and Germany see de Macedo and Torres (1989).

14. For both deposit rates and exchange rates the source is Reuters, and all series are sampled at London close.

15. Every bar represents the frequency of observations between the corresponding value and the value to the right.

16. I report both statistics because there could well be several instances when, due to transactions costs, neither strategy is profitable.

17. See Svensson (1990) for an application of this analysis to the Swedish krona.

18. That is in a world where ex-ante rate-of-return differentials would be zero in the absence of transactions costs.

19. See Giavazzi and Spaventa (1990). These phenomena reflected liquidity problems onshore rather than offshore, and restrictions on capital inflows.

20. In particular, risk premia generated by the CAPM do not match those obtained from atheoretical projection equations. The discussion below, however, suggests that estimates that rely on projection equations might be biased. The empirical literature on the CAPM is vast. For a critical survey of international models, see Frankel and Meese (1987).

21. This assumption can of course only hold approximately. Giovannini and Jorion (1990) argue that the approximation is satisfactory.

22. From the beta-representation of expected returns, note that the conditional expected return on an asset is equal to the product of the conditional beta, times the conditional expected return on the benchmark portfolio. If the time-covariance of the conditional betas

and the conditional expectations of the return on the benchmark-portfolio is negligible, the expectation of that product is approximately equal to the product of expectations.

23. National stock markets are aggregated using as weights their relative capitalization.

24. Sources: Columbia Center for International Business Cycle Research and OECD Main Economic Indicators, respectively.

25. While relative real returns are in principle more appropriate than nominal returns, in practice inflation uncertainty is so small relative to exchange-rate uncertainty that the difference between real and nominal calibration is negligible.

26. If returns and nonmarketable risk were i.i.d., this model would be applicable to a multiperiod setup.

27. When all investors are alike, they all hold the same porfolio of tradeable securities, which in equilibrium equals the market portfolio.

28. The problem of high real interest rates in the EMS, and its relation with the credibility of exchange-rate targets, is discussed in Dornbusch (1991).

29. Analyses of inflation stabilization with exchange-rate targeting are carried out in Cukierman (1988) and Fischer (1988). Wage and price dynamics under alternative exchange regimes are discussed in Dornbusch (1982) and Alogoskoufis (1990).

30. In addition, empirical evidence suggests that in Europe nominal wage stickiness is significantly less important than in the United States: see, for example, Sachs (1979), Branson and Rotemberg (1980) and Grubb, Jackman and Layard (1982, 1983).

31. Of course the real interest rate in terms of domestic goods would increase. This would occur because the differential between own-good interest rates is approximately equal to the expected change in the relative price of the two goods. But the relative price of the domestic good is expected to fall as the transition period draws to a close.

32. In this section I follow closely the excellent treatment of these models by Persson and Tabellini (1990).

33. This model has been recently developed by Flood and Isard (1989). See also Cukierman (1990) for a discussion applied to the Delors plan.

34. Another virtue of the "escape clause" model is that it could be sustained in a multiperiod setting, where this game resembles the one studied by Rotemberg and Saloner (1986).

35. The model shows that nominal interest rates will never converge. In the model the rate of inflation does not appear, but it is reasonable to assume that price inflation is equal to $\hat{s}$, whereas wage inflation is equal to $\hat{s}^e$. Therefore price inflation converges, but wage inflation does not: the result is a fall in economic activity. The general lesson is that, in the absence of exchange-rate adjustments, inflation-rate differentials may persist for prolonged periods before the disruptions brought to the external balance and employment lower real wages.

36. Of course, these calculations do not account for the impact of the oil price increase on wealth and aggregate demand.

37. Triffin (1960) advocated a reform that locked intra-European exchange rates at parity.

38. The advantages of a single currency are discussed in detail by Ernst & Young (1990) and Gros and Thygesen (1990).

39. For a discussion of the problems of ensuring the independence of a European central bank, see Neumann (1990).

40. In other words, government debt accounts for possibly large fractions of total assets, and, depending on the maturity of debt instruments, they take up a large fraction of the total turnover in primary markets.

41. See Goodhart (1988) for a historical and comparative perspective on the evolution of central banking. Goodhart stresses the role of central banks as public insurers of systemic risk, and traces it back to the birth of the Bank of England. Barro (1989) discusses the concerns of central banks with interest-rate stability.

42. See Sachs and Sala-y-Martin (1989) for evidence on the U.S.

43. See Begg and Wyplosz (1989) and Buiter and Kletzer (1990) for discussions of externalities associated with non-cooperative fiscal policies.

44. Alternatively, some central bankers would find it more appropriate to offset the aggregate spending biases by monetary contraction, which would further increase interest rates.

45. The outright opposition to the idea of a "two speed" monetary union by the high-inflation countries (see, for example, "Spain Counts Cost of Joining the Club," interview to Mariano Rubio Jimenez, Governor of the Bank of Spain, in the *Financial Times* of June 20, 1990) stems from the perception that the reputation cost of being left behind is very high, and its political effects might be equally serious.

46. The fluctuation bands chosen by the U.K. government are 6 percent on both sides of central parities.

47. For an excellent exposition of the position of German monetary authorities, see Deutsche Bundesbank (1990).

48. Two useful discussions of the political aspects of the debate on EMU are in Spaventa (1990) and Wolf (1989).

50. While it is not the purpose of this section to analyze the theoretical underpinnings of the different countries' views, it might be useful to point out that the circulation of the ECU in parallel to national currencies—even with all the features that are proposed to ensure the stability of its purchasing power—does not necessarily induce its adoption as the single European currency. This question hinges on the existence of multiple equilibria in an economy of competing currencies. The "thick market" externalities associated with the use of a widely circulating media of exchange can generate many self-sustaining equilibria, and it is not clear what it takes to move from one to the other.

References

Alogoskoufis, G. 1990. "Exchange Rate Regimes and the Persistence of Inflation," CEPR Working Paper 390.

Baldwin, R. E. 1990. "Hysteresis Bands and Market Efficiency Tests," mimeo Columbia University.

Barro, R. J. and D. Gordon. 1983a. "Rules, Discretion and Reputation in a Model of Monetary Policy", *Journal of Monetary Economics*, 12, pp. 101–22.

Barro, R. J. and D. Gordon. 1983b. "A Positive Theory of Monetary Policy in a Natural Rate Model," *Journal of Political Economy*, 91, pp. 589–610.

Bergsten, C. F. 1990. "The World Economy After the Cold War," *Foreign Affairs*, Summer, pp. 96–112.

Bertola, G. 1989. "Factor Flexibility, Uncertainty, and Exchange Rate Regimes," in M. De Cecco and A. Giovannini (eds.) *A European Central Bank?* Cambridge: Cambridge University Press.

Blanchard, O. J. 1983. "Price Asynchronization and Price Level Inertia" in R. Dornbusch and M. E. Simonsen, eds., *Inflation, Debt and Indexation*, Cambridge, MA: MIT Press.

Branson, W. H. and J. J. Rotemberg. 1980. "International Adjustment with Wage Rigidity," *European Economic Review*, 13, pp. 309–322.

Buiter, W. H. and K. M. Kletzer. 1990. "Reflections on the Fiscal Implications of a Common Currency," in A. Giovannini and C. Mayer, eds. *European Financial Integration*, Cambridge: Cambridge University Press.

Canzoneri, M. B. and C. A. Rogers. 1990. "Is the European Community an Optimal Currency Area? Optimal Taxation Versus the Cost of Multiple Currencies," *American Economic Review*, 80, no. 3, pp. 419–433.

Cohen, Daniel and Charles Wyplosz. 1989. "The European Monetary Union: An Agnostic Evaluation," in Ralph C. Bryant, David A. Currie, Jacob A. Frenkel, Paul R. Masson and Richard Portes, (eds.), *Macroeconomic Policies in an Interdependent World*, Washington, D.C.: The Brookings Institution, Centre for Economic Policy Research and International Monetary Fund.

Cooper, R. N. 1976. "Worldwide vs Regional Integration: Is there an Optimal Size of the Integrated Area?", in F. Machlup, ed., *Economic Integration: Worldwide, Regional, Sectoral*, New York: St. Martin's.

Cukierman, A. 1988. "The End of the High Israeli Inflation: An Experiment in Heterodox Stabilization, in M. Bruno *et al.*, eds., *Inflation Stabilization: The Experience of Israel, Argentina, Brazil, Bolivia and Mexico*, Cambridge, MA.: MIT Press.

Cukierman, A. 1990. "Fixed Parities versus a Commonly Managed Currency and the Case Against 'Stage Two,'" mimeo, June 1990.

De Cecco, M. and A. Giovannini. 1989. "Introduction", in M. De Cecco and A. Giovannini, eds., *A European Central Bank? Perspectives on Monetary Union After Ten Years of EMS*, Cambridge: Cambridge University Press.

de Macedo, J. B. and F. Torres. 1989. "Interest Differentials, Financial Integration and EMS Shadowing: Portugal and a Comparison to Spain," mimeo Commission of the European Communities.

Delors, J. 1989. "Economic and Monetary Union and Relaunching the Construction of Europe," in Committee for the Study of Economic and Monetary Union, *Report on Economic and Monetary Union in the European Community*, Luxembourg: Office of Official Publications of the European Communities.

Deutsche Bundesbank. 1990. "Statement of the Deutsche Bundesbank on the Establishment of an Economic and Monetary Union in Europe," Frankfurt am Main: Deutsche Bundesbank Presse und Information, September.

Diamond, D. and P. Dybvig. 1983. "Bank Runs, Deposit Insurance and Liquidity," *Journal of Political Economy*, 91 3, pp. 401–419.

Dornbusch, R. 1982. "PPP Exchange Rate Rules and Macroeconomic Stability," *Journal of Political Economy*, 90, pp. 158–165.

Dornbusch, R. 1991. "Problems of European Monetary Integration," in A. Giovannini and C. Mayer, *European Financial Integration*, Cambridge: Cambridge University Press.

Drèze J. and C. Bean. 1990. "European Unemployment: Lessons from a Multicountry Econometric Study," *The Scandinavian Journal of Economics* 92, no. 2, pp. 135–165.

EC Monetary Committee. 1990. "Economic and Monetary Union Beyond Stage 1: Orientations for the Preparation of the Intergovernmental Conference," Brussels, March.

Eichengreen, B. 1990. "One Money For Europe? Conceptual Issues and Lessons from the U.S. Currency Union," *Economic Policy* 10.

Emerson, M. 1982. "Experience under the EMS and Prospects for Further Progress towards EMU" in M. T. Sumner and G. Zis, (eds.), *European Monetary Union*, New York: St. Martin's Press.

Ernst & Young. 1990. *A Strategy for the ECU*, London: Ernst & Young and National Institute of Economic and Social Research.

European Commission. 1990. "Economic and Monetary Union. The Economic Rationale and Design of the System," Brussels, March.

Fischer, S. 1988. "Real Balances, the Exchange Rate, and Indexation: Real Variables in Disinflation," *Quarterly Journal of Economics*, February, pp. 27–49.

Flood, R. and P. Isard. 1989. "Simple Rules, Discretion and Monetary Policy" *National Bureau of Economic Research* Working Paper No. 2934, April.

Frankel, Jeffrey A. 1988. *Obstacles to International Macroeconomic Policy Coordination*, Studies in International Finance no. 64, Princeton: Princeton University.

Frankel, J. A. and R. Meese. 1987. "Are Exchange Rates Excessively Variable?" *NBER Macroeconomics Annual*, pp. 117–162.

Giavazzi, F. and L. Spaventa. 1990. "The 'New' EMS," CEPR Working Paper.

Giavazzi, F. and A. Giovannini. 1987. "Exchange Rates and Prices in Europe," *Weltwirtschaftliches Archiv* 123, n. 4.

Giavazzi, F. and A. Giovannini. 1989. *Limiting Exchange Rate Flexibility: The European Monetary System*, Cambridge, MA: MIT Press.

Giovannini, A. 1989. "How Do Fixed-Exchange-Rates Regimes Work? The Evidence from the Gold Standard, Bretton Woods and the EMS," in M. Miller, B. Eichengreen and R. Portes, eds., *Blueprints for Exchange Rate Management*, New York: Academic Press, also chapter 2 in this volume.

Giovannini, A. 1990. "The Transition Towards Monetary Union," *CEPR Occasional Paper* n. 2, May, also chapter 7 in this volume.

Giovannini, A. and P. Jorion. 1990. "Time-Series Tests of a Non-Expected-Utility Model of Asset Pricing," mimeo, Columbia University.

Giovannini, A. and P. Weil. 1990. "Risk Aversion and Intertemporal Substitution in the Capital Asset Pricing Model," *National Bureau of Economic Research* Working Paper No. 2824, January.

Giscard d'Estaing, V. 1969. "The International Monetary Order," in R. A. Mundell and A. K. Swoboda (eds.) *Monetary Problems of the International Economy*, Chicago: Chicago University Press.

Gros, D. and N. Thygesen. 1990. "From the EMS towards EMU: How to Manage in the Transition?" mimeo CEPS, Brussels.

Grubb, D. R. Jackman and R. Layard. 1982. "Causes of the Current Stagflation," *Review of Economic Studies*, XLIX, pp. 707–730.

Grubb, D. R. Jackman and R. Layard. 1983. "Wage Rigidity and Unemployment in OECD Countries," *European Economic Review*, 21, pp. 11–39.

HM Treasury. 1989. *An Evolutionary Approach to Economic and Monetary Union*, London: HM Treasury, November.

HM Treasury. 1990. "Economic and Monetary Union: Beyond Stage 1," Chancellor's Speech to German Industry Forum, June 20, London.

Hochreiter, E. and A. Törnqvist. 1990. "Austria's Monetary and Exchange Rate Policy—Some Comparative Remarks with Respect to Sweden," mimeo Austrian National Bank and Sveriges Risksbank.

Kenen, P. B. 1969. "The Theory of Optimal Currency Areas: An Eclectic View," in R. A. Mundell and A. K. Swoboda (eds.), *Monetary Problems of the International Economy*, Chicago: University of Chicago Press.

Krasker, W. S. 1980. "The 'Peso Problem' in Testing the Efficiency of Forward Exchange Markets," *Journal of Monetary Economics*, 6, pp. 269–276.

McKinnon, R. I. 1963. "Optimal Currency Areas," *American Economic Review*, 53, pp. 717–725.

Minford, Patrick. 1989. *European Monetary Union and 1992*, London: Selsdon Group Special Papers.

Mundell, R. A. 1968. *International Economics*, New York: Macmillan.

Neumann, M. J. M. 1990. "Central Bank Independence as a Prerequisite to Price Stability," mimeo University of Bonn.

Padoa Schioppa, T. 1989. "The European Monetary System: A Long-Term View," in F. Giavazzi, S. Micossi and M. Miller (eds.) *The European Monetary System*, Cambridge: Cambridge University Press.

Persson, T. and G. Tabellini. 1990. *Macroeconomic Policy Credibility and Politics*, mimeo.

Rotemberg, J. J. and G. Saloner. 1986. "A Supergame Theoretic Model of Price Wars During Booms," *American Economic Review*, 76, June, pp. 390–407.

Rueff, J. 1967. "The Rueff Approach," in R. Hinshaw (ed.) *Monetary Reform and the Price of Gold*, Baltimore: Johns Hopkins University Press.

Sachs, J. A. 1979. "Wages, Profits and Macroeconomic Adjustment: A Comparative Study," *Brookings Papers on Economic Activity*, no. 2, pp. 269–333.

Spaventa, Luigi. 1990. "The Political Economy of European Monetary Integration," *Banca Nazionale del Lavoro Quarterly Review* n. 172, March, pp. 3–20.

Svensson, L. E. O. 1990. "The Simplest Test of Target Zone Credibility," *National Bureau of Economic Research* Working Paper No. 3394, June.

Triffin, R. 1960. *Gold and the Dollar Crisis*, New Haven: Yale University Press (Reprinted by Garland Publishing Inc., New York & London).

Tsoulakis, L. 1977. *The Politics and Economics of European Monetary Integration*, London: George Allen & Unwin LTD.

Weil, P. 1990. "Equilibrium Asset Pricing with Undiversifiable Labor Income Risk," mimeo, Harvard University.

Wolf, M. 1989. "Global Implications of the European Community's Programme for Completing the Internal Market," mimeo, The Lehrman Institute.

9 Fiscal Rules in the European Monetary Union: A No-Entry Clause

(with Luigi Spaventa,
November 1990)

9.1 Facts and Issues

It is a known fact that countries participating in the exchange rate agreements of the EMS have achieved a significant reduction of inflation differentials. Their monetary policies have tended to converge and in the recent phase of more fixed exchange rates and freedom of capital movements also interest rate differentials have narrowed considerably. It is equally well known that the record is far less impressive in the fiscal field (table 9.1). Though the general trend since the mid-eighties has been towards an improvement of primary balances, there are still countries running primary deficits. The ratios of overall deficit and debt to GDP present a very wide dispersion amongst countries. While the debt ratio has stabilized or is declining in many countries, it is still rising in others.

"Excessive" deficits have been a customary object of discussion, criticism and recommendations in the exercises of multilateral surveillance performed both at the European level and in international organizations such as the IMF and the OECD. Never had the problem acquired political relevance, however, before the European twelve decided first to examine the possibility of, then to move the first step towards some form of monetary union.

In designing the blue-print for a Union the Delors Report stated that:

it would seem necessary to develop both binding rules and procedures ... involving respectively:

• effective upper limits on budget deficits of individual member countries; exclusion of access to direct central bank credit and other forms of monetary financing; limits on borrowing in non-Community currencies;

• the definition of the overall stance of fiscal policy over the medium term, including the size and financing of the aggregate budgetary balance, comprising both the national and the Community positions. [1989, para. 33]

Table 9.1
Ratios of gross public debt to GDP, 1989

	1981–5	Changes 1985–7	1987–9	Level 1989
Belgium	+28.3	+10.8	−0.4	128.4
Denmark	+22.6	−10.7	−0.4	63.5
France	+9.3	+1.9	+0.4	35.5
Germany	+6.2	+1.3	−0.8	43.0
Greece	+28.3	+9.0	+14.7	86.2
Ireland	+23.0	+13.8	−13.6	104.9
Italy	+22.9	+9.0	+5.3	98.3
Luxemburg	−0.4	−2.0	−3.0	9.0
Netherlands	+19.4	+5.6	+3.1	78.4
Portugal	+22.9	+2.1	+1.4	73.1
United Kingdom	+5.2	−2.9	−10.3	44.3
Spain	+24.2	+1.1	−4.5	43.8
EC (a)	+17.7	+3.2	−0.6	67.4
(b)	+13.6	+2.6	−1.2	58.3

These objectives would be implemented gradually: "a new procedure for budgetary policy coordination, with precise quantitative guidelines, in stage one; "precise—although not yet binding—rules relating to the size of overall budget deficits and their financing," in stage two; "constraints on national budgets to the extent to which this was necessary to prevent imbalances that might threaten monetary stability," in the final stage.

The precision of these prescriptions is only apparent. The Report fails to specify which criteria should underly the definition of the rules and the constraints. But this failure stems from a more basic ambiguity regarding the motivations for the imposition of explicit limits to national budgets in a future monetary union. True, the Report refers to the need for "mutually consistent and sound behaviour by governments;" states that "uncoordinated and divergent national budgetary policies would undermine monetary stability and generate imbalances in the real and financial sectors of the Community;" and observes that coordination of national policies is essential "to establish a fiscal/monetary policy mix appropriate for the preservation of internal balances, or for the Community to play its part in the international adjustment process" [1989, para. 30]. But there are so many different arguments—and models—explicitly or implicitly mixed in this list, that the main question remains unanswered: what is the source of actual or potential contradiction between twelve independent national budgets and a common monetary policy having price stability as its major objective?

One possibility is that uncoordinated national *discretion* in setting budgetary policies may have undesirable spillover effects: the existence of such effects in open economies has been the source of a vast literature on the possible inferiority of uncoordinated outcomes. Three related considerations bear on this argument. First, a monetary union may provide a greater incentive to competitive discretionary behaviour. Second, considering that the Union's currency will float with respect to third currencies, externalities may be greater, as national fiscal policies will affect the Community's external balance with the rest of the world. Third, the tiny size of the Community budget relative to national budgets makes the problem be more relevant than in known experiences of federal states.

The last, factual, consideration may justify a different reason for concern. Under a monetary union the task of cushioning the effects of asymmetric regional shocks falls upon fiscal policy. This role should be performed by the federal budget by means of offsetting changes of federal revenues and expenditures in the region hit by the shock, as shown by the experience of existing federal states. Given the size and the structure of the Community budget, however, the automatic transfers induced by a country-specific shock would be negligible (Sachs and Sala i Martin [1989], Eichengreen [1990]); if national fiscal policies are to retain their importance as shock absorbers, they must be coordinated to that end.

Finally, Delors' plea for rules may find its motivation in a different set of reasons, quite unrelated in principle to the externalities of national discretionary fiscal management or to arguments of fiscal federalism. *Structural* fiscal imbalances in countries joining the union may jeopardize the union's monetary stability in the long run.

To understand what the rules are about is not an academic question. First, if they are to go beyond the usual recommendation to pursue "sound" budgetary policies, rules and constraints must refer to some quantifiable indicator. But no unique multi-purpose indicator can give meaningful and suitable answers to problems as different as those listed above (see Blanchard [1990], OECD [1990]). Second, different problems may not, and do not in recent experience, overlap: structural imbalances, being more a heritage of the past, are often unrelated to the current fiscal policy stance; on the other hand the spillover effects of a country's discretionary budgetary action are quite independent of that country's structural fiscal position.

In what follows we shall neglect the issues of fiscal federalism and of the role of domestic policies in dealing with country-specific shocks and consider instead the other two sets of problems: those of externalities and especially those of structural fiscal imbalances.[1] In the next section we shall briefly examine first whether coordination problems can receive a meaningful solution in terms of budget rules and then whether they are after all relevant in Europe. Our answer being negative on both counts, we turn to structural imbalances. In section 9.3 we discuss the notion of "unsustainable" fiscal positions, consider the available evidence for the 12 EEC members and conclude that for a small number of countries sustainability appears to be a potentially serious issue. In section 9.4 we argue that, while EMU may make the problem more severe, membership of countries with structural fiscal imbalances may represent a risk for the stability of the Union. We do not believe on the other hand that monetary discipline enforced by a sufficiently "conservative" European Central Bank, accompanied by enhanced market discipline, will by itself impose fiscal discipline or at least insulate the Union from the consequences of indiscipline (section 9.5). Specific sanctions and threats are instead needed, of which the most effective would be a no-entry clause announced in advance: membership of the Union should be made contingent upon changes in the fiscal position specifically defined for each of the countries concerned.

9.2   Coordination: Does It Really Matter?

Following the Delors Report and the acceptance of EMU by the EC Council of Ministers in June 1989, the issue of fiscal rules has received much attention both in the academic literature (Buiter and Kletzer [1990], Bovemberg, et al. [1990], Davies et al. [1990], De Grauwe [1990] Glick and Hutchison [1990], van der Ploeg [1990], Wyplosz [1990] to quote some) and in public statements and informal debate by officials in preparation to the intergovernmental conference of December 1990. Padoa Schioppa (1990) draws the distinction between issues relating to fiscal coordination and issues relating to fiscal discipline and observes that, while scientific literature has mostly focussed on the former, the debate at the political level has concerned the feasibility of a monetary union in presence of structural fiscal imbalances. The practitioners' choice is in our view the right one. A problem of coordination arises if there are aggregate demand spillovers. Traditional analyses of the effects of fiscal policy on aggregate demand stress the connection between fiscal expansions and changes in real interest rates or real exchange rates that might partially or completely crowd out the initial impulse. If however markets are fully integrated, as they must be in a monetary union, national fiscal authorities can avoid this outcome by tapping foreign savings.

With integrated capital markets an aggregate demand externality arises because there is a discrepancy between the *perceived* and the *equilibrium* response of a country's real interest rate and real exchange rate to a fiscal expansion. The response of the real interest rate depends on the size of the country and on it financial integration with the rest of the Union and the rest of the world. If the country is small within the European community, the *perceived* response of the real interest rate is small. The *equilibrium* response of the EC interest rate depends on the other hand on the integration of EC capital markets with the rest of the world, and on the relative size of the EC and the rest of the world. The response of the exchange rate depends on the nature of the aggregate demand increase (whether more on domestic goods than foreign goods) and on the substitutability of goods in different countries.

An expansionary bias occurs whenever there is a significant discrepancy between the perceived and the equilibrium effects of fiscal expansions. This spillover may affect the common central bank, if the latter feels forced either to expand the supply of money in order to decrease the pressure on interest rates and the real exchange rate, or to contract money supply to offset expansionary fiscal policies.

Before concluding that binding rules on deficits are required to prevent the occurence of these effects in the Union, we must answer two questions. First, are budget deficits satisfactory indicators of the spillovers arising from discretionary expansionary policies? Second, do such externalities pose a relevant problem to European policymakers?

9.2.1   Budget Deficits and Aggregate Demand Externalities

Suppose that aggregate demand externalities are considered a relevant problem by European policymakers. The aggregate demand effects of fiscal policy are conventionally measured by changes in the budget balance— actual or suitably adjusted to allow for the cycle and for inflation. But are budget changes a suitable indicator of actual or potential spillovers?

The economic significance of budget deficits has in the past been attacked by proponents of the neo-Ricardian view, on the grounds that the intertemporal shifts of taxation and spending as caused by changes in the budget deficits are offset by private markets, do not alter permanent income of the private sector, and therefore leave aggregate demand unaffected. The relevant point of this view is not so much the neutrality proposition, which can be disputed on several grounds, as the unobjectionable argument that, for fiscal policy to have effects on aggregate demand, it has to redistribute wealth across agents with different spending propensities.

Precisely for this reason, even absent Ricardian neutrality, the economic significance of budget deficits as indicators of aggregate demand can be seriously questioned: different patterns of government budget balances can produce an identical redistribution of wealth between current and future generations, and hence an identical impact on demand. The following example (from Kotlikoff [1990]) illustrates the general problem. Suppose that, with stationary population, the government starts a social security program, by taking a given sum from the young generation, giving it to the old generation, and repeating the operation in the future. It can be easily shown that this policy unambiguously increases aggregate demand because it redistributes wealth from the current and future young generations (with propensity to consume less than one) to the current old generation (with propensity to consume equal to one). Yet the effects on the government budget cannot be determined *a priori*, as these transfers can be effected by a number of alternative packages. If the initial sum is borrowed from the young generation and future interest payments are financed with taxes on the young, there will the be an initial deficit, followed by a string of balanced budgets. If however the current young generation can be taxed for the amount of the transfer, the budget will be balanced throughout. Alternatively taxes and transfers may be allocated so as to change the future pattern of deficits. Thus, as the example vividly illustrates, the government budget might be a very poor indicator of aggregate demand and is not a reasonable candidate as a divergence indicator for the purpose of minimizing aggregate demand externalities.

As an empirical illustration of this point, figures 9.1 to 9.4, report scatter diagrams of national savings ratios on government savings ratios for the 12 EC member countries, over the 1980–84 and 1985–89 periods. The figures show that a reliable positive relation between national savings and government savings is observable only when Luxembourg (with 55 percent national savings ratio and about 9 percent government savings) is included. If it is excluded, any relation between the budget and national savings seems to disappear.

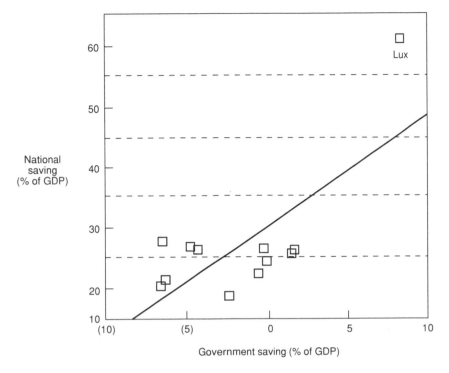

Figure 9.1
Government saving and national saving, 1980–1984

We thus conclude that rules on budget deficits would not be the adequate solution to a problem of fiscal policy externalities. But is this problem really relevant?

9.2.2   Is Coordination a Relevant Problem?

Three sets of reasons lead us to submit that the externalities-coordination problem is of little relevance, at least within Europe. We first note that, at least since the mid-eighties, the common orientation in Europe has been towards a reduction of public sector deficits, or at least towards an improvement of primary balances. Fiscal policy management in view of macroeconomic objectives has been conspicuously absent. The experience of France in 1981–83 was the last attempt to expand in one country. The ill-fated experiment of 1978 was the first and last experiment of international fiscal policy coordination. For many years now the explicit target of all EC governments has been the reduction of deficits and the increase in public savings. While coordination has appeared neither necessary nor

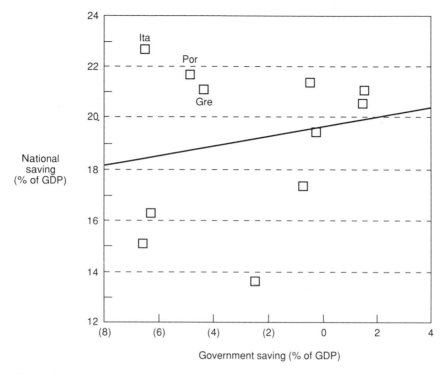

Figure 9.2
Government saving and national saving, 1980–1984, excluding Luxembourg

desirable, convergence to "sound" budget positions has been the commonly accepted objective: if some countries have been less successful than others, this is due to political weakness in implementation rather than to different convictions as to the role of fiscal policy. Thus while in the literature games between governments and central banks and between governments of different countries are still being actively played, in practice fiscal activism has been abandoned and the issue of coordination has lost its glamour.

Another reason for disregarding the issue is that Europe comprises at least four large countries. For a large country the difference between the perceived and the equilibrium response of real interest rates is small: it is therefore less convenient for them to play a game of expansionary fiscal policies at the expense of others.

A third reason behind the practitioners' lack of interest for problem of macro-policy coordination is that the relevant literature, no matter how sophisticated, builds upon extremely simple models of the open economy (usually of the Mundell-Fleming variety), where the signs of the impact effects of discretionary fiscal policy changes are usually unambiguous.

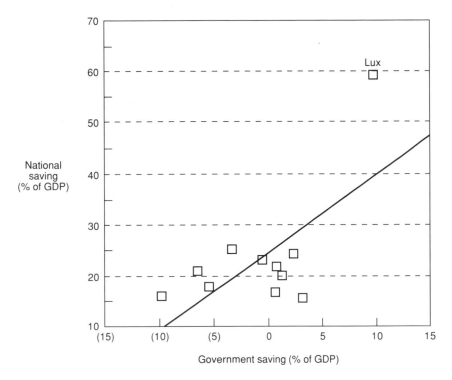

Figure 9.3
Government saving and national saving, 1985–1989

Empirical research and the analysis of a number of actual policy episodes unveil however a more complex reality. Consider for instance the remarkable turn-arounds of budgetary positions achieved by Denmark first and then by the UK in a very short time. In both cases budget cuts were followed by unexpected consequences in terms of standard analysis: more than offsetting increases in private expenditure, a strengthening of the exchange rate, and a deterioration of the current balance. We are not implying that such models are in any sense "wrong": but they fail to capture the effects on agents' behaviour and expectations which may occur when budget changes are (like those we have cited) part and parcel of a more complex policy program. The implicit mistrust of policy-makers in the possibility of deriving general rules of conduct may have some ground.

We thus conclude that externalities arising from competitive fiscal policies do not represent a very relevant problem, at least within Europe. We now turn to the issue of discipline: we shall first discuss the notion of sustainability of fiscal positions and then examine which countries exhibit this kind of problem.

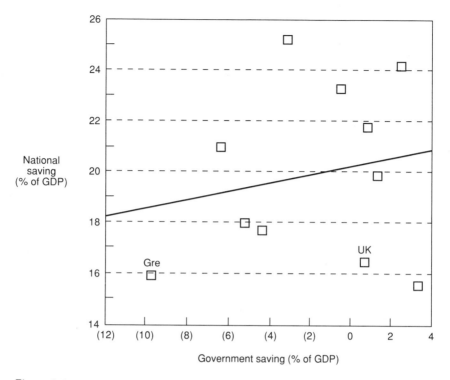

Figure 9.4
Government saving and national saving, 1985–1989, excluding Luxembourg

9.3 The Notion of Structural and Unsustainable Imbalances

9.3.1 The Notion of Sustainability

The basic theoretical construct for a discussion of sustainability is the government's intertemporal budget constraint, or solvency constraint. When the interest rate exceeds the growth rate, solvency requires that the present value of future government revenues equals the sum of the outstanding stock of debt and of the present value of the future stream of expenditures (all values expressed as ratios to GDP). A sufficient condition for the constraint to be satisfied is that, with the given fiscal policy, there exists a stationary level of the debt ratio: with a positive growth rate, this is the case if the ratio of overall deficit (inclusive interest payments) to GDP is held constant over time. The necessary condition is that debt grows at a rate lower than the ratio of the interest factor to the growth factor, so that in principle solvency can be compatible with unbounded debt growth (Mc Callum, 1984).[2]

Even leaving the latter extreme case aside, the intertemporal budget constraint is however of little help for operational policy purposes. Though it prescribes that the more debt is allowed to grow, the more taxes will have to be raised (or expenditure cut) in the future, it provides no indication as to the time path of the primary surplus and hence as to the level up to which the debt ratio can be allowed to grow. This is not surprising. Those questions have little meaning as long as we remain confined within the uninteresting environment of a (so-called) "Ricardian" world. In an economy fully described by a rational representative agent and where taxes are non-distortionary it does not matter much how high the debt ratio is allowed to go, as higher taxation will be matched by higher interest payments.

When we leave this environment and allow for distortionary taxation and for a plurality of different agents we obtain more interesting information. Increasing marginal costs of taxation, whether due to its distortionary nature or to other factors (see below), provides the rationale for positive theories of debt.[3] As cost minimization requires tax smoothening, borrowing is justified to finance temporary increases in expenditure or temporary shortfalls of revenues. An optimal policy compatible with solvency requires however that any change in permanent exhaustive expenditure be matched by a corresponding change in taxation. This positive theory is extended to the use of seigniorage as a means to finance the budget (Mankiw [1987], Grilli [1989]). With increasing marginal costs of inflation, the optimal solution is that the tax rate and the rate of seigniorage, while both a random walk, should move together and rise both with the level of outstanding debt and with the discounted stream of permanent expenditure.

The positive theory of debt, taxes and seigniorage implies that the debt ratio should not rise for prolonged periods of time and that on balance a primary surplus (net of seigniorage) should match interest payments (net of the effects of GDP growth on the debt ratio). If and when this is not the case however,[4] we cannot infer that a government is inevitably heading towards insolvency. But what we *can* say is that, as the level of the primary surplus required with solvency rises with debt, the cost of solvency rises with time.

The relevance of increasing costs becomes more obvious once we abandon the fiction of the representative agent. The direct distortionary effects on output and hence on the tax base are perhaps less important than the distributional consequences than the rise in the tax burden required to match debt service. Such consequences arise out of all inequalities which, though present in the real world are not captured, by definition, in any representative agent model. Thus inequalities in the distribution of wealth accompanied by different effective rates of taxation on labour income or profits and interest income causes debt to redistribute income not only across generations, but also across different subjects belonging to the same generation.[5] The same outcome may arise because some categories of income can be more easily ascertained, and hence taxed, than others: if the composition of the potential tax base does not reflect the actual distribution of income, any increase in the tax burden affects some categories of income more than others. These distributional effects exacerbate the political resistance to tax rises, while any attempt to find "equitable" forms of taxation meets with rising costs of collection and compliance. The need to raise the tax burden may thus meet with several obstacles: an increase in tax evasion and tax avoidance at the individual level; the birth of anti-tax movements at the political level. The possibility therefore exists that beyond a certain limit the cost of exacting more taxes may become so high as to set an effective upper limit to the tax burden: in this case, if the initial level of debt is too high, debt explosion may become inevitable (as in Blanchard [1984]) unless expenditures are cut.

9.3.2   Fiscal Imbalances in Europe

Are problems of (potential) solvency present in Europe? For reasons mentioned above this is not a question that admits of an easy or unambiguous answer.

Table 9.1 reports data on changes and levels of the debt ratio. In six countries the 1989 level of the ratio was considerably above the EEC average, and high by historical standards and in comparison to other industrialized countries. In four the ratio rose almost uninterruptedly for almost a decade; it is rapidly declining in Ireland, it appears to have stabilized in Belgium.

Table 9.2 reports data on changes and levels of general government primary balances for the six countries with higher than average debt ratios. Data differ according to sources, but the general picture is one of a general improvement in the eighties, with the exception of Greece. Greece and Italy, however, and perhaps Portugal and the Netherlands, are still running a primary deficit.

The decline in non-interest expenditure was the major factor of improvement, except in Greece and Italy (table 9.3). The latter two countries have a record increase in the overall tax burden over the whole period,

Table 9.2
General government primary balances (ratios to GDP)

	Belgium	Greece	Ireland	Italy	Netherlands	Portugal	EC
Changes 1981–5							
EC	+6.8	−0.6	+5.1	+0.7	+2.6	+2.0	+2.9
OECD	+7.1	−0.9	+5.3	+0.9	+2.5	+1.9	..
Changes 1985–9							
EC	+2.6	−2.1	+6.3	+3.2	+0.1	+4.3	+1.9
OECD	+2.1	−0.4	+5.2	+3.3	+0.7	+4.0	..
Levels 1989							
EC (a)	4.6	−10.5	5.4	−1.3	1.6	2.1	1.0
(b)	2.4	−10.1	7.7	−2.3	1.1	−3.2	1.2
OECD	3.1	−9.0	4.5	−1.9	−0.3	1.8	..

Table 9.3
General government (ratios to GDP)

	Belgium	Greece	Ireland	Italy	Netherlands	Portugal	EEC
Expenditure net of interest							
Change 1981–85	−4.6	+6.0	−1.8	+3.1	−1.6	−0.8	0.6
Change 1985–89	−4.4	−2.1	6.8	−0.2	−2.4	−2.2	−2.3
Level 1989	40.8	39.7	35.8	42.6	50.9	33.4	42.3
Taxes and social security contributions							
Change 1981–85	+2.4	+5.4	+3.2	+3.8	−0.4	+0.7	+2.3
Change 1985–89	−1.5	+1.6	−0.3	+2.9	+1.2	+1.3	+0.6
Level 1989	43.4	33.8	37.0	38.8	46.3	32.8	40.9
Taxes and social security net of transfers to household							
Change 1981–85	+3.1	+1.5	+0.5	+2.3	−0.3	+0.6[a]	
Change 1985–89	—	+2.5	+1.3	+2.0	+2.0	+2.7[a]	
Level 1989	10.6	20.2	22.2	19.8	19.8	18.3[a]	
Interests							
Change 1981–85	+2.8	+2.2	+3.0	+1.9	+1.9	+2.8	+2.0
Change 1985–89	—	+4.0	−1.3	−0.3	−0.3	+0.2	—
Level 1989	10.6	9.4	9.1	6.0	6.0	8.1	6.2

Source: ECC.
a. Total transfers.

Table 9.4
Indicators of sustainability

	Belgium (B)	Greece (Gr)	Ireland (Ir)	Italy (I)	Netherlands (N)	Portugal (P)
EC: 1989						
Debt-stabilising primary balance						
$r - g$: 1/2% for B, N, I						
0.5/111.5% for						
Gr, Ir, P	1.3/2.6	0.4/1.3	0.5/0.6	1.0/2.0	0.8/1.6	0.4/1.
Gap	−1−1/0.2	10.5/11.4	−7.2/−6.1	3.3/4.3	−0.3/0.5	3.6/4.
OECD: 1990−1						
$r - g$ (a)	1.7	−7.2	−1.3	0.7	2.2	. .
$r - g$ (b)	3.2	2.4	4.1	3.7	2.9	. .
Debt-stabilising primary surplus						
(a)	2.1	−5.7	−1.6	0.7	1.3	. .
(b)	3.9	1.9	5.1	3.5	1.7	. .
Gap (a)	−2.1	−0.1	−7.4	1.8	1.5	. .
(b)	−0.3	7.7	−0.7	4.5	1.9	. .
Our estimate: 1991						
Debt-stabilising primary surplus				1.1/1.5		
OECD						
Three-year tax gap	−1.2	+9.1	−1.7	+4.6	+1.9	. .

though a not inconsiderable part of this increase was redistributed to households through higher transfers. The share of interest payments on GDP, high in all the six countries, is still rising in only three of them.

Alternative indicators of sustainability are reported in table 9.4. The simplest and least sophisticated is the difference between the debt-stabilising primary balance at a certain date and the actual balance. Computations of this gap are however very sensitive to the specifications of the variables involved, and especially to the assumed value of the cost of debt. There is a difference between the cost of debt relevant for the dynamics of the debt ratio and the current rate of interest, as the former depends on the maturity structure of outstanding debt and on the past history of interest rates, as well as on the institutional arrangements concerning the interests paid on public debt held by the Central Bank. Setting the average cost of debt equal to the marginal interest rate, as done by

OECD (b), certainly leads to an overestimation of the gap. We computed the gap also for the polar case of a constant average cost of debt (OECD (a), on data provided in OECD [1990]). We also conducted an independent estimate for Italy, with a more accurate projection of the average cost of debt for 1991, yielding a difference with the growth rate of 1–1.4 points: our figure for the debt-stabilizing surplus is far below OECD (b) (though higher than OECD (a)), and near to the 1989 EEC range: the implicit figure for the 1991 gap is around 2%.

A more sophisticated indicator is the Blanchard-OECD gap between the actual tax burden and that required to stabilize debt over a given time horizon. Since also this measure is sensitive to the choice of the interest rate on debt, the reported figures may be somewhat exaggerated.

Though precise numbers are elusive, there are few ambiguities in the general picture, especially if the data of tables 9.1–9.3 are also considered. A sustainability problem is perhaps most acute in Greece, where it has been alleviated so far by the effects of high inflation on the average cost of debt: lower inflation would cause a very steep increase in the debt ratio. The problem is also present in Portugal and persists in Italy, though there has been an improvement in the past few years; the Netherlands represents a borderline case. The additional negative features of Italy (and Greece) are the rigidity of non interest expenditures and the steep rise of the fiscal burden which has already occurred in the eighties and which may leave little room available for further increases.

The possibility of further tax rises in these countries depends of course on a number of factors such as the level and distribution of per capita income, the width of the base on which taxes are levied, and hence the structure of the tax system and the extent of tax evasion and tax avoidance, the administrative efficiency of tax collection. In table 9.5 the figures of rows 4 and 5 provide approximate indicators of per capita non-interest expenditures and taxes relative to the EEC average and can be compared with relative per capita incomes (rows 1 and 2). On these grounds, further increase in taxation may be "justified" in the three Southern countries, but not in the Netherlands. In the former however distribution is more unequal, the tax base is narrower, evasion is more widespread, the administration is less efficient, so that it may be difficult to raise taxation to the required level.

The above analysis may help to put the European fiscal issue into a proper perspective. Problems of potential sustainability of fiscal positions do exist, but are confined to a small number of countries in the EEC. Our next question concerns the relationship between the existence of such

Table 9.5
Ratios to EC averages, 1989

	Belgium	Greece	Ireland	Italy	Netherlands	Portugal
(1) Per capita income (a)	101.8	37.4	62.8	102.4	101.8	31.1
(b)	102.4	53.6	66.0	105.1	103.5	54.5
(2) Expenditure net of interests	96.5	93.9	84.6	100.7	120.4	79.0
(3) Taxes and social security contributions	106.1	82.6	90.5	94.9	113.2	80.2
(4) (2) × (1a)	98.2	35.1	53.1	103.1	122.5	24.6
(5) (3) × (1a)	108.0	30.9	56.8	97.2	115.2	24.9

structural fiscal imbalances and EMU. There are two kinds of possible externalities here. How is monetary union going to affect potential solvency problems? Can potential solvency problems jeopardize the orderly working of a union having price stability as its explicit target?

9.4 EMU and Structural Fiscal Imbalances

9.4.1 The Effects of EMU

We now consider the effects of EMU on a country's ability to increase its revenues to the level necessary to stabilize debt growth within a finite period.

We begin with taxes. EMU is supposed to remove technical, physical and fiscal barriers to the movement of factors and goods within the European Community. While there is broad agreement on the policies to be followed on the removal of the first two kinds of barriers, there has been little progress on the fiscal issue. Fiscal barriers include, in principle, all the characteristics of national tax systems that induce distortions in the allocation of factors and the flow of goods and services within the Community. Two strategies can in principle be followed: harmonization, that is the elimination of differences in tax rules (tax rates and tax bases) affecting goods and factor movements; or a strict application of the home-country or residence principle. The Commission is about to propose a series of directives that are designed to eliminate some inconsistencies between national tax systems, but has made no attempt at pursuing either harmonization or the home-country-principle strategy. The problem is that both imply rather sweeping reforms and significant revenue redistributions; an additional difficulty is the unanimity requirement for EC directives in the area of tax policy.

Under these conditions, differences in national tax systems and the mobility of goods and factors may force countries to lower fiscal pressure on the mobile factors: this is the well-known tax-competition phenomenon. Under fairly general assumptions it can be proved that noncooperative interaction of national governments will enable them to raise less revenue from the mobile goods and factors than what is socially desirable. It is on the other hand unlikely that the actual or potential loss of revenue can be fully compensated by an increase of other taxes at the expense of less mobile factors, like labour, as this would meet, for reasons already mentioned, with social and political obstacles.

One further point can be made concerning indirect taxation on goods and services. In Southern countries, with less efficient tax systems, it is difficult to achieve an increase in the tax burden without increasing indirect taxation. At least in Italy (we do not possess comparable data for Greece and Portugal) this would be justified by the fact that the ratio of indirect taxes to GDP was almost three points below the EEC average in 1989. In all Southern countries, however, inflation, inflationary expectations and indexation are higher than in the rest of the EEC. An increase in taxes on goods and services would have undesirable inflationary consequences: there is thus a trade-off between inflation convergence and fiscal convergence.

We conclude the EMU will, if anything, reduce governments' ability to increase the tax burden and fill the tax gap.

Seigniorage is another source of revenue for the government. As both the rate and the base of seigniorage are expected to decline in the union, loss of seigniorage has often been considered as a damaging consequence of monetary union on high debt countries (Giavazzi [1989], Dornbusch [1990], Drazen [1989]). Convergence of inflation requires a lower growth of the monetary aggregates, while the proposed statutes of the European Central Bank rule out direct monetary financing of the Treasury. With the single market the coefficient of compulsory reserve requirements of commercial banks ceases to be a policy parameter. As foreign banks will have a right of establishment in all other EC countries while remaining subject to the home country rules, competition will oblige national authorities to lower reserve requirements, especially in countries like Italy, where high reserve coefficients make the seigniorage base particularly high.

The problem of seigniorage has however been overplayed. Monetary financing of the Treasury in a strict sense has lost importance in most

Table 9.6
Italy: Monetary financing of the PSBR

		Ratios to GDP	
	Share of PSBR	Treasury base	Total base
1980	26.3	13.2	16.7
1981	25.4	14.0	15.8
1982	16.4	14.1	15.4
1983	1.4	12.8	15.2
1984	13.4	12.6	15.2
1985	23.1	14.6	15.9
1986	10.0	14.5	15.4
1987	6.2	14.2	15.6
1988	2.1	13.0	15.3
1989	5.2	12.4	15.7
1990	—[e]	11.1[e]	. .

e. Estimate.

countries. Table 9.6 shows the steep decline in the share of the Italian public sector borrowing requirement financed by the central bank and in the ratio to GDP of the stock of monetary base created for the Treasury. Recent estimates of the EEC Commission (*European Economy* [1990]) show that, even allowing for inflation rates as low as 2% and for 2% compulsory reserve ratios,[6] loss of seigniorage would be small in most cases (of the order of 0.6% of GDP in Italy). We shall also argue below that the distinction between different channels of creation of monetary base loses relevance in an integrated financial market.

These observations are confirmed by a more careful analysis of Grilli, Masciandaro and Tabellini (1990), who "find no evidence that budget deficits lead to lax monetary policies" and find instead that "central bank independence may bring about monetary stability and low inflation even if there are political incentives towards lax monetary policies." They conclude that their finding "is relevant for the ... debate on the feasibility of a European Monetary Union," as it suggests the feasibility of the Union "with very different debt paths and tax systems, provided that their central bank arrangements provide the appropriate incentives for the national monetary authorities." Their results concerning the two-way independence between monetary stability and budget deficits are relevant, but we cannot fully accept their conclusion, as we shall try to argue in the next subsection.

9.4.2   The Financial Spillovers of Unsustainable Fiscal Positions

Suppose that some countries enter the union with potentially unsustainable fiscal positions and that at some stage they experience difficulties in the management of their debt. Is there a risk that such difficulties spill over the rest of the union and affect the operations of the common central bank, even if the latter's statutes forbid any direct monetary financing of the Treasury?

A debt crisis may occur because markets perceive that the (politically) *feasible* mix of revenue increases and expenditure cuts falls short of what would be necessary to stabilize the growth of the debt ratio within a finite time horizon. Growing fears that the government may sooner or later be compelled to take extraordinary measures (if not repudiation, perhaps consolidation of short-term debt, or compulsory holding of government bonds in the commercial banks' assets) are reflected by a fall in the value of government securities in the secondary market as well as by a rise in the risk premia demanded on new (gross) issues of debt.

Consider an extreme case in which there is a sudden and dramatic drop in the liquidity of government securities, so that transactions become insignificant relative to the existing stocks.

Marketable debt is held by domestic households (perhaps the largest share) and firms, by domestic banks, and by foreign investors. The households' response to a collapse in the value and liquidity of government securities depends on the nature of the services the latter provide. If (irrespective of their maturity) they are held as a long-term investment, there will be a fall in permanent income and consumption. If they are held as high-yield liquidity, there will probably be a rush for alternative sources of liquidity, with an attendant fall in the value of the securities that are still tradeable. In general, it can be expected that there will be a rise in the demand for liquidity, also because the debt crisis increases the uncertainty of returns from other assets (as would be the case if the private sector fears a capital levy).

As for banks, a fall in the value and liquidity of an important share of their assets inflicts losses and may raise fears about their solvency: in the worst scenario banks may experience a run on deposits. The increase in the fragility and the riskiness of the banking industry would dry out the interbank and the money markets.

There are three channels through which a domestic crisis may propagate to other countries. First, with an extremely large gross volume of transactions in international money and foreign exchange markets, when an individual participant fails to deliver funds when they are due, other market participants may find themselves unable to settle. Second, as a single currency and a common central bank will increase the integration of domestic interbank markets and help to develop a centralized European money market, a liquidity crisis in one country will spread more quickly and more easily: under different currencies, national central banks can intervene to limit the propagation of a crisis, while an increase of interest rates may remain confined to one country if it is matched by expectations of exchange rate depreciation. Third, if foreigners hold a significant fraction of a country's debt (a likely development after liberalization), the transmission of a crisis is direct: its mechanics depend, along the lines of the above discussion, on the nature of the holdings of debt securities.

Financial spillovers, are likely to have real effects. The increase in interest rates and uncertainty exacerbates problems of adverse selection and of credit rationing, affecting negatively lending, business investment and the level of activity.

In this scenario a proviso banning monetary financing of deficits and a no bailout clause are insufficient to immunize the common bank from the impact of debt difficulties experienced by one country. The common central bank might be forced to increase significantly its money supply, in order to limit the systemic effects on the financial industry and the real economy. In principle we would not expect the impact of this operation to be inflationary, as the increase in the supply of liquidity matches an increase in demand. As the crisis recedes, however, and more normal conditions of demand are restored, the bank will have to mop up the initial increase in liquidity to avoid future inflation. The timing of the whole operation is crucial, as the bank has to steer a difficult course between the danger of inflation and that of adversely affecting the real economy with an excess of restriction.

A debt crisis in one country may thus have external effects, which are greater in a monetary union than in a world of different currencies and national central banks. It may be objected that, though this may be true in principle, the occurrence of such financial spillovers is by no means certain, and that in any case their size is so small as not to be a cause of worry.[7]

The debt crisis of New York City in the 1970's is the precedent often invoked in this argument. The crisis did not affect monetary policy: the Federal Reserve Board officially stressed its role of lender of last resort, but no need for this function materialized after the announcement.

Table 9.7
Ratio of domestic public debt to total EUR12 public debt, 1988

Country	Percent of total
Belgium	6.9
France	12.1
Germany	19.0
Greece	0.9
Ireland	1.3
Italy	28.4
Netherlands	6.3
Portugal	1.1
Spain	5.3

Yet, it would be imprudent to generalize that experience and conclude that local financial problems are unlikely to pose threats to the system as a whole. First, relative sizes are different. At the end of 1976, the stock of NYC debt (13 billion dollars) was only 2.6% of the stock of federal government debt (506.5 billion); new issues of NYC debt in 1975 were 1% of total state and local new debt issues in the long-term market and 20.1% in the short-term market. Table 9.7, reporting the ratio of domestic public debt to total EUR12 public debt in selected countries, shows that relative sizes in Europe are larger.

Second, after 1976 a steep increase in inflation was a major factor that helped to alleviate the debt crisis of NYC, by causing a fall in the real cost of outstanding debt. This (traditional) way out of the crisis is not open to European countries for at least two reasons: in some high-debt countries a large portion of debt is short term or issued at floating rates; more importantly, the rules of the union would, by definition, be incompatible with this solution.

Two further considerations, of opposite sign, concern the banking system. On the one hand, the ratio of government debt held by banks to their capital is often quite high in high-debt countries (at the end of 1989 it was almost 2.4 for Italian banks). On the other hand, the short maturity of debt instruments minimizes the risk of capital losses to lenders, so that a crisis would be unlikely to cause significant damages to the banks' asset position.

We thus conclude that it may be imprudent to disregard the risks of potentially unsustainable fiscal positions of national economies and the problems they would pose to the management of the common monetary policy.

9.5   Incentives and Sanctions

Before drawing policy implications from the analysis of the last section, we must consider two points which are often made: a well-designed and "conservative" European Central Bank in the final stage, and adequate constraints imposed upon the freedom of national central banks in the transition, will provide a powerful incentive to fiscal discipline; market discipline will work in the same direction, and, if enhanced by prudential provisions, will insulate the system from the effects of a domestic crisis. We shall first deal with the argument that monetary and market discipline can offer an adequate set of incentives, sanctions and safeguards. As we find this argument unconvincing, we shall argue that a no-entry clause would provide a more effective solution, both for the stability of the union and for the discipline of its most unruly members.

9.5.1   Monetary and Market Discipline

It has often been argued that fixed exchange rates and freedom of capital movements will impose fiscal discipline on national authorities. The presumption is that, by tying the monetary hands, both would also tie the budgetary hands: any link between monetary policy and the Treasury's need would be severed, financing large budget deficits would become more difficult, and the fiscal authorities would be compelled to take corrective measures. An explicit ban on direct monetary financing of deficits would strengthen this constraint and make the incentive to fiscal discipline more effective. The evidence summarily reported in section 9.4.1 tells us that this has not been the case. It may be instructive to look at what has happened in the recent stage of EMS.

We have had more fixed exchange rates: since 1987 there have been no realignments in the EMS. Capital movements have been liberalized in all major countries. Neither development seems to have had a relevant impact on fiscal discipline: why? As the commitment to stick to the central parity and to avoid realignments has become credible and has lowered expectations of exchange rate changes, nominal interest rate differentials have attracted a flow of funds towards higher inflation countries. The potential contradiction between the domestic and the external targets of monetary policy has taken a somewhat unexpected form: the stance required to control domestic demand and inflation has overfulfilled the exchange rate target (see Giavazzi and Spaventa [1990] for a more complete analysis of these developments). Sterilization of capital inflows has led to a reduction of the monetary financing of the Treasury.

Why have politicians of high-debt countries sacrificed seigniorage to the exchange rate target and why have they accepted liberalization, foregoing the possibility of paying less on the debt they were incurring? The choice of low seigniorage and of a strong exchange rate is consistent with myopic political behaviour leading governments to incur high deficits without internalizing the cost which will be borne by future generations.[8] Seigniorage is after all a tax on present generations, and, after the experience of the 1970's, inflation has become no less unpopular than ordinary taxation. The central banks' objective of low inflation has thus come to be fully accepted by governments, and so has a policy of strong and credible exchange rate which is instrumental to keeping inflation under control.

The success of the central banks of weaker EMS countries in stabilizing the exchange rate and gaining credibility has on the other hand removed a potential sanction on domestic policies and an incentive to bring about the required changes. Governments have thus realized that they could enjoy a strong currency, fat foreign exchange reserves and international respectability without having to pay the political price of fiscal discipline. Faster debt growth due to lower seigniorage and higher interest rates has been the consequence: but this is a burden to be borne by future generations.

Even the effects of a reduction of monetary financing of the deficit have not been felt in the short run. If interest rates are attractive, liberalization may have a favourable stock effect, insofar as it opens an access to international portfolios which was denied to a currency in a regime of capital controls. A fraction of such portfolios will now be invested in, say, lira denominated bonds: in all probability government bonds, because of their sovereign nature and of the higher liquidity of their market. The reduction of direct monetary financing of the deficit is thus offset by foreign financing. As for monetary financing, it only changes its shape: instead of going directly to the Treasury, it consists of interventions in the foreign exchange market as a counterpart of foreign purchases of government bonds.

We have gone on at some length in describing the recent experience of the EMS to argue that we cannot expect short-run disciplinary effects from further institutional progress towards tighter monetary and exchange rate discipline in view of the final objective of monetary union. Even if national central banks are requested to comply immediately with the ban on direct monetary financing of the deficit, this will make little difference with the present situation, with one or two exceptions: not only has direct financing shrunk considerably; it is also impossible to discipline such indirect financing as inevitably occurs in an integrated market. Furthermore, as the credibility of the exchange rate commitment becomes institutionalized, the external sanctions and incentives to fiscal discipline are, if anything, likely to decrease. Which is not particularly surprising: no such incentives exist in a federal state, and the states joining EMU will, unlike those belonging to the USA or to Australia, retain sovereign power so that their debt remains sovereign debt.

We have argued that the institutional progress envisaged in the transition to monetary union cannot be expected to constrain fiscal behaviour in high-debt countries. Can the market provide this constraint in the transition phase and compel reluctant governments to eliminate structural imbalances *before* the beginning of the final stage of the union? We have already partly answered this question: liberalization of capital movements and financial market integration has provided new opportunities to the placement of sovereign debt, as long as the exchange rate is reasonably stable and there persists an interest rate differential. In a number of papers, Bishop (1989, 1990) has proposed a number of measures with the purpose of enhancing market discipline: no holding of national governments' debt on the part of the European Central Bank; statutory exposure limits towards the public sector for the country's aggregate banking sector and possibly inclusion of government bonds in the determination of prudential ratios; limits on the issue of short maturity debt.

We are not convinced that such measures are either sufficient or, in some case, desirable. Once monetary financing of deficits is forbidden, the *initial* composition of the ECB assets is not very relevant, as it does not matter much whether the claims on national governments accumulated in the past by the national central banks remain in the latter's assets or are partly conferred, together with foreign exchange reserves, to the ECB: there appears to be no other solution, as it is inconceivable that the whole stock be redeemed by the government or placed on the market. The exposure limits indicated by Bishop (no more than 60% of the country's GDP) are quite mild: for instance, they are not binding in the case of Italy. Those measures which would be effectively binding, on the other hand, may cause a crisis even if the government is making an effort to correct its fiscal imbalance. Thus, limits on the issue of short-term debt may subtract the necessary flexibility to debt management and cause an unnecessary increase in the cost of debt when the markets are still uncertain on the success of a plan of fiscal correction.

9.5.2   An Effective Sanction

We have tried to show that the relevant fiscal problems for EMU are not those of aggregate demand externalities, but those arising from the existence of structural fiscal imbalances in some countries. While full economic union will not help to correct such imbalances, membership of countries with potentially unsustainable fiscal positions may be risky for the union, in view of the size of the possible financial spillovers of a debt crisis. Empirical analysis and recent experience show that monetary and exchange rate discipline can go hand in hand with fiscal laxity, as there is no short-run trade-off between the two. Short-sighted politicians will continue to incur debt, at the expense of future generations and at the risk of a future debt crisis, while enjoying today's benefits of the central bank's credibility. Further institutional progress in the monetary and exchange rates field is unlikely to provide sanctions and incentives which have lacked so far; nor, in our view, can the market perform this job. Other means must be found to induce prospective members of the union to correct their fiscal imbalances *before* the inception of the final stage.

If our view is correct, it is necessary either to affect the politicians' preferences in the countries concerned, or to create the missing trade-off between debt and monetary stability. The recent political economy literature chooses the first possibility when it suggests that institutional and electoral reforms designed to strengthen the stability and lengthen the life of governments would provide the solution. This may well be the case. But institutional reforms are not easy to implement; nor is it obvious why politicians should be ready to accept reforms the purpose of which is to compel them do something which they have been unwilling to do so far.

We believe that there is a more readily available alternative: the plan for a monetary union can be used to increase the present cost of debt financing so as to alter the outcome of political choices. To achieve this, an effective sanction must be devised. We surmise that a threat of no entry into the Union would represent a sufficiently severe sanction, and at the same time an effective incentive not to postpone the adoption of corrective measures to an indefinite future. Being denied entry would represent a dramatic loss of prestige with the electorate, while the resulting collapse of credibility would arouse expectations of currency devaluation and of higher inflation. The threat would on the other hand offer a powerful justification to overcome political resistance to tough and unpopular measures. In brief, this would be a way to cure political myopia, by assigning a long-run cost to deficits. This choice would on the other hand be beneficial for the union, as it would remove the danger of undesirable developments after it has started.

For the threat to be effective as an incentive, the no-entry clause for countries unable to implement a timely correction of unsustainable fiscal positions should be made explicit and announced in advance. Rather than setting general rules, specific targets should be defined for each country, paying regard to the feasibility of further tax increases and to the extent to which government spending should instead be cut (and publicly owned assets privatized).

A no-entry clause would not infringe on national sovereignty. It would still leave governments free to choose, but it would also make clear that persistent debt accumulation is not a costless solution.

Notes

1. All three sets of problems are examined at length in *European Economy*, October 1990, chapter 5, which appeared after a first draft of this paper was circulated. Some of our arguments are in the same spirit as those of that report.

2. Tests on whether fiscal policies have conformed to the constraint usually refer to the sufficient condition, and in particular to the constancy of the overall deficit ratio over time. See Hamilton and Flavin [1985], Grilli [1988], Grilli, Masciandaro and Tabellini [1990].

3. The earlier formulation is in Barro [1979].

4. Grilli, Masciandaro and Tabellini (1990) find the predictions of the optimal taxation model contradicted in a number of cases and find no evidence for the theory of optimal seigniorage.

5. The point was forcibly made by Keynes (1923).

6. Compulsory reserve ratios are now near 22.5% in Italy.

7. See Buiter and Kletzer (1990).

8. There is a large literature on the political and institutional determinants of such myopic behaviour. See Roubini and Sachs (1989), Alesina and Tabellini (1990) and, with particular reference to European case, Grilli, Masciandaro and Tabellini (1990).

References

Alesina, A. and G. Tabellini. "A political theory of fiscal deficits and government debt in a democracy," *The Review of Economic Studies*, June 1990.

Barro, R. "On the determination of public debt," *Journal of Political Economy*, vol 87, 1979.

Blanchard, O. J. "Current and anticipated deficits, interest rates and economic activity," *European Economic Review*, vol 25, 1984.

Blanchard, O. J. "Suggestions for a new set of fiscal indicators," OECD, Department of Economics and Statistics Working papers, no. 79, April 1990.

Bovenberg, A. L., J. J. M. Kremers and P. R. Masson. "Economic and monetary union in Europe and constraints on national budget policies," IMF Working paper 90/60, July 1990.

Bishop, G. "Creating an EC monetary union with binding market rules," Solomon Brothers, February 1990.

Bishop, G., D. Damrau and M. Miller. "Market discipline CAN work in the EC monetary union," Solomon Brothers, November 1989.

Buiter, W. H. and K. M. Kletzer. "Reflections on the fiscal implications of a common currency," CEPR, Discussion paper no. 418, May 1990.

Commission of the European Communities, "One market, one money," European Economy, no. 44, October 1990.

Davies, G., D. Currie, N. Mac Kinnon and I. Brunskill. European Monetary Union: The issues, IPPR, Economic Study no. 4, 1990.

De Grauwe, P. "La discipline budgetaire dans les unions monetaires," in Ministere de l'Economie, des Finances et du Budget, Vers l'union economique et monetaire europeenne, Colloque du 21 juin 1990, La documentation francaise.

Dornbusch, R. "Problems of European monetary integration," mimeo. MIT, 1990.

Drazen, A. "Monetary policy, capital controls and seigniorage in an open economy," in M. De Cecco and A. Guiovannini eds., A European Central Bank?, Cambridge, 1989.

Eichengreen, B. "One money for Europe? Lessons for the US currency union," Economic Policy, no. 10, April 1990.

Giavazzi, F. "The exchange rate question in Europe," EC Economic Papers no. 74, January 1989.

Giavazzi, F. and L. Spaventa. "The 'new' EMS," CEPR discussion papers no. 369, January 1990.

Glick, R. and M. Hutchison. "Fiscal constraints and incentives with monetary coordination: implications for Europe 1992," paper written for the conference "Financial regulation and monetary arrangements after 1992," Gothenburg May 1990.

Grilli, V. "Seigniorage in Europe," in M. De Cecco and A. Giovannini eds., A European central bank?, Cambridge, 1989.

Grilli, V., D. Masciandaro and G. Tabellini. "Political and monetary institutions and public financial policies in the industrial countries," mimeo. September 1990.

Keynes, J. M. A tract on monetary reform, 1923, in vol. IV of the Collected writings of John Maynard Keynes, London 1971.

Kotlikoff, L. J. "From deficit Delusion to the fiscal balance rule: Looking for an economically meaningful way to assess fiscal policy," mimeo., Boston University, June 1990.

McCallum, B. T. "Are bond-financed deficits inflationary? A Ricardian analysis," Journal of Political Economy, vol. 92, February 1984.

Mankiw, G. "The optimal collection of seigniorage, theory and evidence," Journal of Monetary Economics, 20, 1987.

OECD, Economic Outlook, 47, June 1990.

Padoa Schioppa, T. "Fiscal prerequisites of a European monetary union," paper written for the conference "Aspects of central bank policymaking," Tel Aviv, January 1990.

Roubini, N. and J. Sachs. "Political and economic determinants of budget deficits in the industrial democracies," *Economic Policy*, April 1989.

Sachs, J. and X. Sala-i-Martin. "Federal fiscal policy and optimum currency areas," mimeo. Harvard University, 1989.

Van der Ploeg F. "Macroeconomic policy coordination during the various phases of economic and monetary integration in Europe" 1990, forthcoming in *European Economy*.

Wyplosz, C. "Monetary union and fiscal policy discipline," 1990 forthcoming in *European Economy*.

10 Money Demand and Monetary Control in an Integrated European Economy

(December 1989)

10.1 Introduction

The removal of capital controls and of barriers to competition in the banking industry wil have profound effects on monetary control within the Exchange Rate Mechanism (ERM) of the European Monetary System (EMS). Indeed, controls on international capital flows and financial intermediaries are crucial determinants of the demand for money in different countries, and as a result large swings in money demands are to be expected in the years to come.

This chapter analyzes the problems raised by these phenomena. I start with a discussion of the determinants of money demands in an economy, like the European economy, characterized by high financial integration and integration of goods markets. In section 10.2 I review the classic description of monetary instabilities in a multicurrency economy: Gresham's law and its fiat-currency present-day equivalent. Next I turn (in sections 10.3.1 and 10.3.2) to a catalogue of the determinants of the overall demand for money in Europe, and of the distribution of the currency portfolio. This discussion helps identify what kind of monetary instabilities are likely to occur in the future. In sections 10.3.3 and 10.3.4 I deal with the main problems of the transition towards a monetary union, and the desirability of introducing parallel currencies like the ECU. In section 10.4 I summarize the chapter and offer a few concluding remarks.

In the last part of the chapter I argue that monetary policy coordination in Europe should be about a concerted effort in the foreign exchange markets for the purpose of safeguarding bilateral parities, coupled with an explicit interaction of foreign exchange reserves management with domestic monetary management, to be achieved jointly by all member countries.

10.2   Gresham's Law with Fiat Currencies

The problems of central banking in an economy characterized by the coexistence of different moneys are classics in the history of monetary
theory. One of the best known propositions in monetary economics, Gresham's law, is a description of instabilities in a bimetallic standard.

According to Gresham's law, "bad money drives out good." In other
words the less valued currency substitutes for the more valuable currency
in monetary circulation. Indeed, "good" currencies are supposed to disappear from circulation. There are historical examples of phenomena resembling Gresham's law. For example, in the late 1870s countries
members of the Latin Monetary Union decided on several occasions to
close the mints to the private coinage of silver in response to the decrease
of the value of silver relative to gold in the industrial markets, and the resulting drainage of gold from monetary circulation, and of silver from the
industrial market.[1]

A question of great relevance for Europe after 1992 is whether some
version of Gresham's law could still apply, and what would be the consequence of this instability of monetary aggregates. In addition, it would
be desirable to reconcile the predictions of Gresham's law with those of
recent proposals for monetary reform in Europe, which are based on the
opposite view, that the good currency drives out the bad (see section
10.3.4).

Gresham's law is the description of the effects of arbitrage between the
monetary and nonmonetary market. In a bimetallic standard the central
bank freely exchanges at a fixed nominal price two metals (say gold and
silver) for money. Fixing the nominal value of gold and silver coins means
to fix also their relative price. Gold and silver are traded in the non-
monetary market (industrial market) as well, where also newly mined ore
is originally sold. Equilibrium occurs when the official parity equals the
relative price of the two metals in the industrial market.

Consider now what happens when some exogenous shock (say an
increase of silver ore production that tends to make silver cheaper in the
industrial market—gold more expensive) drives the relative price of the
two metals away from the official parity. Private agents would find it
profitable to buy gold from the central bank at the official parity to re-
sell it in the industrial market. This would produce a progressive disappearance of gold from monetary circulation. In other words, the "bad"
money has driven out the "good." Could anything like this occur in a

world, like Europe after the completion of the internal market, of coexisting *fiat* currencies?

Since there is no "industrial" market for the currencies we cannot think of a shock there. There could, however, be a change in their relative valuation associated with a change in their relative monetary services: transactions services and store-of-value services. Suppose, for example, private agents expect a devaluation to occur over some future horizon: in this case the store-of-value services of a currency increase relative to those of another. Agents would bring the "bad" currency to central banks in exchange for the "good" one. The "good" currency drives out the "bad" from monetary circulation. The same would occur with a change in transactions services originating, for example, when one currency gets increasingly used to make payments, and as a result it becomes more acceptable in private transactions (see section 10.3.2). Also in this case the "good" currency would drive out the "bad."

Is there an inconsistency with Gresham's law? No. In a metallic standard any increase in the *monetary* value of a currency would also bring about an increase in its monetary circulation. Suppose for example that, starting from equilibrium, agents expect the official parity of gold will increase. This makes gold more valuable as money than as a commodity. Agents would bring gold to the mint for coinage, in exchange for demonetization of silver coins. When the increase in the monetary price of gold comes about, they will be able to bring it back to the industrial market for a profit. Therefore, an increase in the monetary services of a specific currency increases its monetary circulation both under a commodity standard and under a fiat standard.

The original statement of Gresham's law could be easily misunderstood since "bad" and "good" refer to the industrial value of the currencies, not their monetary services. Rolnick and Weber (1986) also recognize the importance of the distinction between the industrial value and the monetary value of currencies. They pointed out that this distinction helps explain why in a number of historical instances Gresham's law could not be verified.

In conclusion, whenever different currencies coexist in an integrated economy, fluctuations of their relative valuation affect their circulation. As Triffin's clairvoyant book warns,[2] however, fluctuations in the use of different currencies can jeopardise, and eventually bring to its knees, a system of fixed exchange rates with free convertibility and international capital mobility. Triffin's argument was based on the observation of the dramatic increase in the international use of the dollar, in spite of an unchanged stock of monetary gold. It should be pointed out, however, that in the Bretton Woods system dollars were not convertible to gold at the mint like in the gold standard. Gold reserves were a means to maintain the public confidence, but they were not necessarily to be used to peg currency values. Hence Triffin's "dilemma" is a more general parable of the instabilities arising from large fluctuations in relative currency demands that might apply also to the present-day ERM.

In order to understand the problems for monetary management arising from these fluctuations, it is useful to discuss more in detail all the factors behind movements in money demand, with specific reference to the European reality.

10.3   Money Demand and Currency Substitution

The discussion in the previous section has left money demand unspecified, but has only alluded to transactions services and store-of-value services of different currencies. The purpose of this section is to explore more in detail the transactions and store-of-value services of different currencies coexisting in a integrated economy.

When studying the demand for different currencies coexisting in an integrated economic area one has to immediately appeal to the idea of "currency substitution," since it is possible for private agents in such an economy to hold different currencies in their portfolios. The fluctuations of equilibrium shares of different currencies in private portfolios are determined, among other things, by the degree of substitutability of these currencies, and this substitutability depends on the differences in transactions and store-of-value services that the currencies provide. It is thus useful to attempt to describe them in detail.

Traditional studies of money demand and currency substitution are, typically, empirical. The methodology of these studies is to determine whether some measures of goodness of fit of money demand equations are improved or affected at all by the introduction of foreign variables, like foreign interest rates or expectations of exchange-rate changes. This method is largely inappropriate in our case. Since Europe will undergo dramatic economic and administrative reforms in the years to come, it is quite likely that the forces affecting the demand for different currencies will also be changing dramatically. Empirical studies of money demand equations by their very nature cannot reveal directly and explicitly these determinants of money demand: therefore they have no use as a guide to understand its evolution in the years to come. By contrast, it is much more useful to attempt to bring out explicitly the reasons why money is held, and speculate how these determinants will evolve in response to the liberalization of financial markets, the removal of capital controls, and the integration in goods markets.[3]

Monetary control in Europe will be drastically affected by two classes of factors:

- factors affecting the overall demand for money;
- factors affecting the distribution of currency portfolios;

which are discussed in detail below.

10.3.1   Factors Affecting the Overall Demand for Money

In modern market economies money is held for two main reasons. The first is that it facilitates private transactions. Whenever the search for a counterparty with coincident wants is costly, or whenever a counterparty's creditworthiness (or the value of the asset used in the exchange) is costly to verify, money can provide a superior way of organizing transactions. In addition money provides a common numeraire, thus easing the calculation of prices, and it allows us to carry value across both time and space.[4] Note that these phenomena justify the presence of a common medium of exchange even in an economy with no externalities (except those created by the costs in finding partners in an exchange) and no government.

The other reason why people hold money is that they are forced to by governments. Historically, governments have seized the monopoly of the issue of the medium of exchange to gain an additional source of fiscal revenue. Currently, this monopoly is not seriously disputed (except by a small fringe of economists who believe that market failures do not justify the existence of governments), even though central banks are increasingly using it not to generate fiscal revenue but to insure stability in financial markets and more broadly in the whole economy. This monopoly is however continuously eroded by developments in transactions technologies.

In private transactions, the extent of the use of money is determined by the sophistication of the banking industry, which provides, among other services, transactions services to the public. For example, the more frequently banks are open, the less cash will individuals have to hold at any point in time to carry out their own transactions. Similarly, the easier it is to reach a bank branch (the higher is the geographical density of bank branches), the less idle balances will people hold in their pockets.

In Europe, the forthcoming liberalization of the banking industry, and in particular the ability of banks to compete over the whole territory of the EC, will increase to the maximum competitive pressures, which will also be pressures at providing better transactions services at lower costs. The competition on transactions services will very likely increase, for three reasons:

1. Since transactions services use mostly computers and networks, the cost of production of these services has dramatically fallen in the recent past.

2. The potentials for innovations are very large. They can be illustrated by considering how far can the stock of money shrink when the opportunity cost of holding cash increases dramatically. For example, in Israel at the highs of the hyperinflation (1984 and 1985) the stock of money (IFS line 34) was just 3.9 percent of GDP; by contrast, in 1985 the stock of money was equivalent to 17.2 of GDP in the F.R. of Germany. Indeed, a society where all transactions are cleared by means other than cash is nowadays technologically feasible, and economists have started considering in what ways it could work.[5]

3. The recent experience in the United States has shown that competing in transactions services can be very profitable. Money-center banks like Citibank have created their preeminence in the 1970s by exploiting to the maximum the potentials of the "consumer banking" market.

Among the areas where the banking industry in Europe has not yet fully exploited business opportunities, whose potential is demonstrated by the experience in the United States, are the use of checks, credit cards, and automatic teller machines (ATMs). Table 10.1 compares European countries with the United States in the use of a number of transactions services that are linked with consumer banking. Panel A show the availability of cash dispensers and automatic teller machines by reporting the number of inhabitants per machine. Except for the UK and, to some extent, France, all European countries in the panel are characterized by much lower availability of ATMs than the United States. Panel B reports the number of checks issued per inhabitant, and the total value of checks issued per inhabitant. The difference between the US and Europe is also quite striking: the number of checks issued per capita in the US is 10 or 20 times the same number in Belgium or Italy, 4 times that in the UK and 2 and 1/2 times that in France. The second column in the panel shows that the average denomination of checks differs markedly across countries, in-

Table 10.1A
Cash dispensers and ATMs (number of inhabitants per machine, 1988)

Country	
Belgium	11,763
France	4,862
Germany	8,213
Italy	9,958
Netherlands	14,454
United Kingdom	4,108
United States	3,024

Source: Bank for International Settlements, *Statistics on Payment Systems in Eleven Developed Countries.*

Table 10.1B
The use of cheques

Country	Number of cheques	Value in U.S. dollars
Belgium	24.6	35,937.9
France	82.4	49,813.9
Germany	10.0	34,523.0
Italy	12.9	25,990.4
Netherlands	19.0	1,229.0
United Kingdom	53.8	354,070.0
United States	214.6	234,656.0

Source: Bank for International Settlements, *Statistics on Payment Systems in Eleven Developed Countries.*

dicating that their use by households is uneven. Panel C shows the use of credit cards. Here too the difference between the US and Europe is evidently vast, and gives a strong indication of the potential for the credit card industry in the European Community.

An increased use of checks will not, of course, proportionately shrink the demand for M1, since checks are themselves part of M1. It will, however, have two effects. On one side, in front of a higher stock of circulating checks banks should decrease the ratio of (free) precautionary reserves to deposits. On the other side, the possibility of using checks instead of cash helps households and firms to rationalize their liquid-asset management, leading to lower use of money balances.

The effects of the spreading of ATMs are those already briefly sketched above. Easier access to a bank, including during holidays and weekends, will induce lower holdings of cash balances, and, to a large extent, lower

Table 10.1C
The use of credit cards

Country	Number of payments	Value per capita in U.S. dollars
Belgium	1.0	110.2
France	12.5	3,927.7
Germany	1.0	101.0
Italy	0.3	45.2
Netherlands	0.0	0.0
United Kingdom	12.2	789
United States	35.7	1,676

Source: Bank for International Settlements, *Statistics on Payment Systems in Eleven Developed Countries*. The numbers for France include "direct debt" payments, and are thus not directly comparable. The numbers for Netherlands are too small.

holdings of checkable accounts. This is facilitated if ATMs offer the widest possible array of services, including transfers across checking accounts and other accounts (like brokerage or money market accounts).[6]

Finally, credit cards provide the most obvious, and most successful to date, substitute for cash in transactions. As table 10.1C has shown, this is the area with possibly the greatest business potential in Europe.

The other reason why private agents hold currency is that they are forced to by governments. Governments can induce private agents to hold extra amount of cash either directly, by requiring the use of cash in certain transactions, and by requiring certain agents to hold cash balances in their portfolios, or indirectly, by limiting the portfolio choice available. Especially the former restrictions are clearly visible in European countries. Among the transactions in which governments prescribe the use of cash there are all transactions with governments themselves. In no country are taxes payable with credit cards, and the payments of taxes or other liabilities to the government account for a very large fraction of total payments. To illustrate this, I report in table 10.2 the annual government receipts in France, Germany and Italy as percent of the end-of-year money stock in those three countries. The table shows that the volume of government receipts accounted for as much as 160–170 percent of the end-of-year money stock in Germany and France, and 70 percent in Italy. These ratios, of course, would increase substantially if other transactions of the governments which usually require the use of cash were included, and in particular all those transactions connected with the floatation and the servicing of government securities. Finally, to obtain an estimate of

Table 10.2
Goverment receipts as percent of money stock (receipts annual, money stock end of year)

Years	France	Germany	Italy
1952–1959	64	86	52
1960–1969	63	83	45
1970–1979	112	164	36
1980–1987	158	176	69

Source: *International Financial Statistics.* Government receipts line 81; money stock line 34.

the full impact of these transactions on the demand for money it would be necessary to compute statistics of their average velocity—in other words the frequency with which money goes from the hands of the public sector to private hands in the process of tax payments is likely to be much lower than the frequency of money-financed transactions between the government and the private sector in financial markets.

A second set of legal restrictions compelling private agents to hold cash balances are those imposed on financial intermediaries to guarantee their liquidity. The most important are of course the reserve requirements of banks. Tables 10.3 and 10.4 report, respectively, the statutory reserve requirements of commercial banks, a breakdown of the monetary base, and a computation of average reserve ratios. The differences across European countries are striking: reserve requirements vary from 0 (Denmark and Belgium) to 25 percent (Italy).[7] Reserve ratios vary from 0.4 percent (United Kingdom) to 20.4 percent (Spain). These reserve requirements crucially affect bank margins: since they decrease the share of interest-yielding assets in bank portfolios, the decrease the interest banks are able to pay on their liabilities, for given returns on their productive assets.

How will the integration of goods and financial markets affect these determinants of money demand? There is no direct impact, as far as the *total* demand for money is concerned, from the government transactions. The integration of goods and financial markets is not likely to decrease them significantly, and should not exert particular pressures on governments to improve the efficiency of their own cash management systems. We should, however, expect a significant impact from changes in reserve ratios. These changes will come about from a process of competitive deregulation, forced on the governments by the integration of financial markets and the mobility of financial capital.

Competitive barriers in the banking industry will be eliminated with the implementation of the Second Banking Directive, which will be effective

Table 10.3
Reserve requirements at commercial banks (percent of demand deposits, mid-1988)

Country	Reserve requirement
Belgium	0
Denmark	0
France	5.0
Germany	6.6–12.1
Greece	7.5
Ireland	10.0
Italy	25.0
Luxembourg	0
Netherlands	15.0
Portugal	15.0
Spain	18.5
United Kingdom	0.5
United States	3.0

Source: Grilli (1989). In Greece, Italy, and Spain required reserves are remunerated to some degree. The number for Italy is applied against the increase in deposits since May 1984. In the Netherlands a small, variable, and remunerated reserve requirement was introduced in May 1988. In the United States the ratio increases to 12 percent on deposits larger than 40.5 million.

Table 10.4
Average reserve ratios, reserves and high-powered money

Country	High-powered money (% of GDP)	Reserves (% of GDP)	Reserves/ deposits
Portugal	14.8	5.8	5.8
Greece	18.3	8.4	17.3
Spain	19.8	12.3	20.5
Italy	17.5	11.8	18.7
France	6.3	2.0	5.2
Germany	9.4	3.6	6.8
United Kingdom	3.7	0.2	0.4
Belgium	8.2	0.4	1.1

Source: Giavazzi and Giovannini (1989).

starting on January 1, 1993. By that time, depositors will be able to place their funds anywhere in the Community, and banks will be able to invest anywhere they please. As a result, any bank which will want to stay in business will have to pay competitive rates on deposits and charge competitive rates on loans: in other words, deposit and loan rates will tend to be equalized in the Community, so that the Community-wide margin (difference between interest rates on the assets and those on the liabilties) will shrink towards those of the most efficient banks. Banks unable to charge the most efficient margins will be driven out of business.[8] In this scenario, governments will not be able to apply higher reserve requirements on the banks in their territory since they would have to face massive disruptions (defaults, acquisitions, shrinking of the industry), which are politically costly, and have serious side effects on the real economy. Governments will therefore have to decrease reserve requirements to the lowest acceptable levels: this will imply a very large shrinkage in the total stock of high-powered money in Europe (but also, of course, a large change in its currency composition).

To get an impressionistic estimate of the plausible shifts in the stock of high-powered money, use the data in table 10.4, and assume that a realistic Europe-wide reserve ratio will be, after the liberalization of the banking industry, 1.5 percent.[9] Applying that rate to the level of deposits in the table, one obtains a shrinkage in the stock of high-powered money ranging from 22 percent in France to 62 percent in Italy![10]

The forced convergence of reserve ratios, implying very large changes in the stock of high-powered money, will undoubtedly raise difficult problems for monetary authorities. In particular, the effect of these adjustments on money demand will depend on the policies followed by central banks. Since the impact of a decrease in reserve ratios, through the money multiplier, is a large increase in the supply of broad money, which is clearly unwanted by monetary authorities, it will have to be accompanied by a sizeable contraction. Even though in this specific case the changes in the demand for money can be predicted with both sufficient accuracy and margin for reaction, shifts in the composition of currency portfolios—that leave the total stock of money unaffected—are likely to be harder to forecast, and thus more disruptive.

10.3.2 Factors Affecting the Distribution of Currency Portfolios

A recent survey by Eurobarometer (cited by Grilli (1989)) asked whether, in a number of areas, there were more advantages than disadvantages to be expected from the creation of a single European market. Seventy-nine percent of the respondents[11] believed that the ability to make payments without complication in the Community will be an advantage, 79 percent believed that the ability to take any amount of money in any country of the Community will be an advantage, 70 percent listed as an advantage the possibility of opening a bank account in any country without hindrance. These numbers are important not only because they suggest that these innovations of the single market are strongly perceived to be desirable, but also because they signal that the public is going to actively exploit the profit and cost-saving opportunities they provide.

To organize the discussion of the factors determining the distribution of currency portfolios and the degree of currency substitution it is useful once more to make use of the distinction between transactions services and store-of-value services.

Starting from the transactions services, the first question to be tackled is what makes the transactions services of a currency different from those of another currency, that is what makes the two currencies imperfect substitutes. Most likely it is the interplay of a number of factors,[12] including the geographical distribution of transactions and the existence of government-imposed constraints.

The argument goes as follows. In Europe the single market project will multiply the number of transactions across national borders. Yet it will still be the case that for any individual or corporation, most transactions will be carried out with residents of the same country. Employers and employees are usually geographically close, and most purchases of consumptions goods and services are made locally. Because exchanging one currency for another is in general cumbersome (if anything because of the incoveniences of having to recompute prices using weird exchange rates), residents of a country will tend to use a common currency. Since the transactions involving governments and the other legal requirements described in section 10.3.1 force residents to make use of the national currency, in local markets transactions will likely be carried out using national currencies.

In summary, the combination of habit and national restrictions make currencies imperfect substitutes. Yet, it is possible to conceive of cases where the degree of imperfect substitutability due to habit and national restrictions is not enough to prevent a currency from being virtually abandoned. This will be the case when local markets are limited relative to the volume of international transactions. Since there is convenience in using widely circulating media of exchange, there is an externality at work:

the less is a currency used, the less will people want to use it, and vice versa the more a currency is used, the more it will be acceptable as a medium of exchange. This is the mechanism underlying the establishment of *vehicle currencies*.[13.] A glance at the importance of international trade in certain small European economies suggests the potential role of these effects. The sum of exports plus imports account for as much as 130 percent of GDP in Belgium, 170 percent in Luxembourg, 112 in the Netherlands and Ireland. In these countries international transactions are almost as important as local transactions,[14] and if the externality from the use of a common numeraire is sufficiently strong, there might be significant gains from the adoption of a European currency with wider circulation.

We have, however, no good description of the transition from one equilibrium to another, and no estimates of the gains from the adoption of a common numeraire in the small countries, even though there is abundant evidence, including survey evidence, suggesting that these gains are quite substantial. It is therefore difficult to determine to what extent will fluctuations in relative demands for currencies be affected by this phenomenon. By contrast, more precise characterizations of the effects of legal restrictions on currency portfolios are quite possible.

Consider government transactions. The use of national currencies in government transactions is effectively enforced by legal tender rules, which make the national currency acceptable in each country. If these rules will not be modified in the years to come, there is hardly going to be any change in the composition of money demand due to government transactions—the substitutability of different currencies in facilitating government transactions is going to be zero. On the other hand, simple changes in legal tender rules can have profound effect. For example, if the ECU was given legal tender status in Europe governments would be de facto forced to accept it in payments, and therefore the ECU would become perfectly substitutable to all national currencies in their functions as means of payments to governments. If all twelve currencies were granted legal tender status in all twelve countries of the Community, they would immediately become perfectly substitutable as means of payments to governments. This would remove a sizeable anchor that pins down the individual currencies' shares in the total demand for money in Europe.

There will also be large shifts in currency portfolios due to changes in reserve requirements. First of all, the phenomenon of regulatory competition described above will greatly affect relative demands for national currencies, since existing reserve ratios differ across countries, and thus the changes in money demand triggered by this phenomenon will differ across countries. In addition, even in the case of reserve requirements it is possible to remove the regulatory anchor of individual currency shares in total money demand. After the Second Banking Directive will be effective, banks will be able to issue checkable deposit in any currency, from any country in the Community. Thus commercial banks in, say, France will have deposit liabilities denominated in French francs, Deutsche marks, sterling and so on. The directive establishes that the main responsibility on liquidity ratios will be on host governments. So far, however, the issues of how to adapt national laws and regulations to this provision has not been brought up. Will countries require the use of specific currencies in the statutory reserve ratios? If banks will not be asked to put aside reserves (in proportion to the requirement) matching the currency composition of their liabilities, a very important determinant of the money multiplier will be eliminated. If the currency composition of banks' reserves will not be restricted (because the composition of liabilities cannot be restricted) then, as in the examples before, national currencies will become perfectly substitutable for the purpose of providing liquidity to banks: another source of stability in the demand for different currencies will be removed.

In summary, the brief discussion above has shown that the liberalization of goods and financial markets will likely give rise to very large shifts in currency composition of private portfolios. In addition, measures like the extension of legal tender rules or the application of reserve requirements without discrimination across currencies, will tend to make national moneys perfectly substitutable, leaving relative demands indeterminate, even in the presence of a more stable *overall* demand for money.

Turning to the services of money as store of value, it is important to make a distinction between a regime where exchange rates are flexible, one where they are permanently fixed and one where there is a probability that the "fixed" parities might be changed in the future. In the first case, Kareken and Wallace (1981) have shown that, in equilibrium and given exchange-rate expectations, the spot exchange rate is not pinned down by the demand for currencies as stores of value: given exchange-rate expectations currencies are perfectly substitutable as stores of value, and therefore the *composition* of the total currency portfolio is irrelevant. The exchange rate would be completely indeterminate if currencies were also perfectly substitutable in their transactions services.[15]

In Giovannini (1990) I study the determinants of currency substitutability in a regime of permanently fixed exchange rates. In that model, there is a well-defined demand for transactions services for each currency (that is currencies are not perfectly substitutable in their transactions services). I find that currencies are perfectly substitutable in their store-of-value services also under fixed exchange rates, since in that case they have an identical opportunity cost, represented by the common nominal interest rate.[16] Given the exogenous exchange rate, this perfect substitutability of currencies is reflected in an indeterminacy of the distribution of foreign exchange reserves, *within* the total demand for money as a store of value.

Finally, the maximum fluctuations in relative money demands (and hence in the distribution of foreign exchange reserves) is obtained in a regime of adjustable parities. In that case the demand for foreign exchange reserves is mostly affected by the desire of the private sector to avoid the capital losses arising from a discrete change in bilateral exchange rates. If the exchange-rate devaluations occur whenever the monetary authorities' holdings of reserves fall below a known lower bound, the private sector can forecast with some accuracy the timing of the occurrence of the exchange-rate devaluation. It will attempt to get rid of all cash balances in the depreciating currency right before the devaluation. One crucial feature of these speculative attacks is that they can be self-fulfilling. As Obstfeld (1986) shows, in fairly general settings private agents can justifiably believe that monetary authorities will ratify foreign exchange crises, by devaluing the exchange rates.

10.3.3 Threats to the Stability of Stages I and II of Economic and Monetary Union

What are the lessons for the management of the transition towards EMU? The discussion above has identified a number of important sources of fluctuations in money demand and in the composition of currency portfolios, likely to come into play in the near future. These fluctuations are unavoidable, given the planned process of European integration.[17]

The transition to EMU is therefore extremely delicate. The completion of the internal market will increase the substitutability of EC currencies. In the absence of significant reforms, this will lead to monetary instability. The threats of money-demand instabilities are especially serious because there has been no significant change in the monetary policy procedures of central banks, nor are there any to be expected during stage I of the Delors Report.

According to the Delors Report, the tasks for monetary policy during stage I are, beyond the liberalization of financial markets and the increased

EMS participation, new procedures for coordination in the Committee of Central Bank Governors and the ECOFIN Council. The new procedures are:

• a lengthening of its chairman's term from six months to three years;

• the establishment of the right of the chairman to publicize the deliberations of the Committee;

• the creation of a permanent research staff and three sub-committees.

These reforms are meant to "gradually bring about a change from *ex post* analysis to an *ex ante* approach to monetary policy coordination." (Delors Report, para. 52), by facilitating "multilateral surveillance." Understandably, however, these reforms could not extend to the replacement of current operating procedures of national central banks.

A glance at the operating procedures recently followed by some EMS members[18] can help identify where the problems will be coming from: since the most used target for monetary policy is some definition of monetary aggregate, instabilities in money demand will have to be transmitted elsewhere, to interest rate, reserves or exchange rates, and inflation. A recent timely study by the European Commission[19] warns that even the past experience has revealed a number of structural changes in the relations between various monetary aggregates and their explanatory variables. The difficulties of monetary targeting in the presence of financial innovation are probably best illustrated by the vicissitudes of the British monetary authorities, who have been forced to focus on a wide range of monetary aggregates, including M3, M4 and M0.

Similar problems affect the institutional provisions for stage II in the Delors Report. Stage II should be characterized by some form of coexistence of a European System of Central Banks and national central banks. It will "primarily constitute a training process leading to a collective decision-making, while the ultimate responsibility for policy would remain [...] with national authorities." (Delors Report, para. 55) Exchange-rate changes are permitted, even though under "exceptional circumstances" (Delors Report, para. 57). Once again, explicit references on provisions to minimize monetary instability are absent. Furthermore, ambiguities on the importance of credibly fixing exchange rates persist. These ambiguities are a necessary condition for the self-fulfilling speculative attacks mentioned above to materialize.

What are the the likely effects and the costs of the instabilities arising from currency substitution, and why are they a threat for an orderly convergence to EMU? These questions are central in the current debate on the role and the effects of monetary policy. The direct effects of fluctuations in currency demands are swings in liquidity in money markets, with ensuing swings in interest rates. Why are these swings in liquidity dangerous? If these movements are of extreme proportions, they can give rise to financial crises, which are liquidity crises accompanied by substantial increases in interest rates. These phenomena can trigger failures of financial intermediaries and increase uncertainty in the marketplace.[20] The increase in uncertainty, in turn, exacerbates two typical problems of financial intermediation: adverse selection and credit rationing. Since lenders cannot perfectly assess the riskiness of borrowers, they charge interest rates that reflect their average assessment of the quality of loan projects. This means that high-quality borrowers pay too high interest and low-quality borrowers pay too low interest (the adverse selection problem). At the same time, lenders are likely to deny arbitrarily loans to good borrowers, since they cannot tell who are the borrowers with the riskiest investment projects (the credit rationing problem). The increase in uncertainty and interest rates during a financial crisis thus dries up lending and business investment, producing the conditions for a recession. A likely side effect is also a massive deposit withdrawal in the interbank market, caused by concerns about the liquidity and the viability of the banks themselves.

The threats to an orderly convergence towards EMU are directly linked to these phenomena. Speculative attacks on individual currencies, triggered by the belief that exchange rates *can* be changed, give rise to liquidity and interest-rate crises. In order to avoid a recession, the monetary authorities thus face a tremendous pressure to increase liquidity in the money markets of the currencies under attack. This can be done in two ways:

• By actually increasing liquidity. This requires active coordination among all central banks involved in the ERM, and might give rise to resistance due to the possibly inflationary impact of liquidity injections in the currencies under pressure, the problem of establishing a precedent, and so forth.

• By devaluing the exchange rate. This is the easiest way out. It brings real interest rates back in line, and automatically increases liquidity in the markets where it is needed. Exchange-rate devaluations, however, also set the clock of EMU back to time zero, since they ratify expectations of exchange-rate changes and they give rise to inflation-rate differentials.

The choice is thus among one of three alternatives: a financial crisis and a recession; a liquidity injection (with possibly inflationary effects); and a setback of the EMU, represented by an exchange-rate realignment. The institutional reforms to support stages I and II should be designed with the explicit aim to minimize the probability of occurrence of events forcing countries to make this kind of choice.

10.3.4 The Dangers of Parallel Currencies

The second important lesson from the discussion of section 10.3 is that the introduction of parallel currencies, like the ECU, is not the way to go.

The basic idea of parallel currencies is not new. One of the first, and best known, proposals to achieve a monetary union in Europe appeared in *The Economist* and went under the name of "All Saints' Day Manifesto."[21] That proposal advocates the issuance of a new currency, "Europa," whose purchasing power would have been kept constant in terms of a basket of European goods. The stability of Europa's purchasing power would have driven private agents to progressively shift their currency portfolios towards it, in a sort of market-determined monetary reform.

A more recent, and less sophisticated, proposal for a market-determined currency reform is the one put forth by the UK Treasury.[22] In that document it is argued that a desirable transition to a common currency is one where this currency emerges as the best one in terms of efficiency of its transactions services and stability of its purchasing power. The UK document also suggests that a *private* ECU could reduce transactions costs associated with inefficient payments systems (HM Treasury (1989, para. 22)).[23]

All the problems described in sections 10.3.1 and 10.3.2 would be multiplied by the issuance of a parallel currency like the ECU. In addition the inevitable pressures for competition among central banks would contribute to enhance the general uncertainty on policy stances and the evolution of money markets which almost surely leads to financial instability.[24]

The appeal of these proposals is of course the intellectual appeal of market-driven reforms. The discussion above, however, has provided a comprehensive characterization of the reasons why these market-driven reforms are elegant only on paper, since they do not account for market imperfections, which are the very raison d'être of central banks and their operations in national money markets. Even if the probability that the counter-arguments offered above are correct was less than one, it would be inappropriate to introduce the ECU as a parallel currency, a strategy that would have a small chance to fail with so serious consequences. Our knowledge of the determinants of money demand is too imperfect to make parallel currencies a manageable option in the transition to monetary union.

10.4   The Management of Foreign Exchange Reserves during the Transition to Monetary Union

In the previous sections it has been argued that the most difficult problem of the transition towards EMU is the instability and fragility of the intermediate stages. The implication is that monetary authorities should devise institutions and operating procedures which insure the maximum credibility of the transition, as well as of the commitment to price stability. In particular, institutions and operating procedures should minimize the probability of disruptive reserve fluctuations forcing countries to react by changing bilateral parities. These accidents would be particularly damaging, since the whole spirit of the transition towards EMU is to increase the stability of currency values and the integration of markets—two objectives that are undermined by exchange-rate changes.

For these reasons, it is useful to turn the attention to the management of foreign exchange reserves, the most important tool to safeguard exchange-rate credibility. In this section I discuss the economic costs of alternative schemes for reserve management, the problems of reserve financing in the present-day EMS, and the methods to estimate the size of foreign exchange reserves necessary to insure credibility of bilateral parities.

10.4.1   Problems of Reserve Management

The techniques and costs of alternative methods of reserve management are crucial, because they give rise to different incentives to national monetary authorities, and as a result affect the credibility of a fixed rates regime. Such incentives are linked to the transfers of resources associated with balance-of-payments flows,[25] and affect the credibility of fixed exchange rates.

To illustrate the real effects of alternative fixed-exchange-rates systems it is useful to distinguish the resource costs of reserves from the international transfers of resources arising from balance-of-payments surpluses or deficits. The resource costs of reserves are the opportunity costs of the resources tied up. In a gold standard, for example, countries hold stocks of gold in their foreign exchange reserves. The opportunity cost of these gold holdings is equal to their value times the market interest rate, net of any increases in the value of gold relative to the numeraire. Similarly, countries holding reserves in a third currency (like the US dollar in the EMS) end up paying seigniorage to a foreign country: the opportunity cost of reserves denominated in the third currency is equal to the stock of reserves times the interest rate.[26]

In the case where countries hold each other's currencies in their foreign exchange reserves, they end up paying seigniorage to each other on the amount of foreign exchange reserves held. This transfer of resources advantages countries with balance-of-payments deficits, who can finance them by selling their money to the partner's central bank.[27] This problem, however, can be eliminated in a system where all reserve transactions are charged market interest rates. The condition for the absence of any resource transfer becomes the solvency condition, which in this case is equivalent to a commitment to adjust domestic monetary policy (domestic credit policy) so as to insure the ultimate consistency and viability of fixed exchange rates.

Currently, in the EMS there is a mechanism designed to provide the needed foreign exchange to central banks who are defending their bilateral parity in the markets. This mechanism is the Very Short Term Financing Facility (VSTFF). Any country whose bilateral parity reaches the margins of intervention is entitled to unlimited financing through the VSTFF. Central banks draw on VSTFF credit lines they have with the EMS partners with whom their currency is diverging. Credit lines mature 45 days after the end of the month in which the operation has taken place, and can be renewed to a maximum of three months at the request of the borrowing central bank.[28] The original rules governing the VSTFF were modified in September 1987 (the Basle-Nyborg agreement). The maturity of credit lines has been extended by one month. And the ceiling applied to the renewals has been increased. The accounting and computation of interest in these credit facilities is done in ECU.

While credit lines for margin interventions under the VSTFF are "automatic," the ones granted for interventions within the bilateral margins may be subject to approval. Indeed, the Bundesbank has required that all credits extended for interventions within bilateral margins under the VSTFF be subject to approval of its board. This is well justified. Like all financing facilities of fixed exchange-rate regimes, the VSTFF does not allocate the burden of adjustment to any specific country. Indeed, the systematic sterilization of the effects of VSTFF operations on the monetary base, by eliminating the corrective effects of reserve flows on domestic money supplies, shifts the burden of adjustment to the partner which is compelled to accommodate the policies of the sterilizing central bank (for a description of the practical working of the VSTFF, and the problems of sterilized intervention in the EMS, see Giavazzi and Giovannini (1989)). In the limiting case where both central banks fully sterilize the effects of these operations on the monetary base, the system of fixed rates can only collapse.

Notice, in addition, that the experience of EMS interventions suggests that defending parities when bilateral margins are reached is much more "costly" (in terms of volumes of reserves used) than when exchange rates are within the bands. For this reason most countries have tended to intervene before margins limits were reached, and the full automaticity of the VSTFF has thus been seldom used.

These problems of the VSTFF suggest two weaknesses of the current ERM, which make it less than perfectly credible. On one hand, it is not known how much individual countries could effectively borrow before encountering resistances from their partners, and what would be the effect of these resistances. This uncertainty, by itself, makes the VSTFF less credible, and hence less effective in absorbing foreign exchange markets fluctuations. On the other hand, there is not sufficient feedback from the VSTFF to individual countries' monetary policies. This occurs because the VSTFF is not a routine facility, but is used under exceptional circumstances, and thus it works more like a "last resort" facility. In order to achieve better coordination of monetary policies countries would have to jointly monitor, on a day-to-day basis, their operations in the foreign exchange markets in order to be able to fine-tune their domestic operations in response to international imbalances.

10.4.2   The Gains from Exchange-Rate Credibility

The discussion above suggests that one crucial element to make exchange-rate targets credible is close coordination among central banks, and in particular effective mechanisms to join the setting of domestic monetary policies to the management of foreign exchange intervention for the purpose of pegging bilateral parities. Only continuous interaction between the foreign exchange management function and the money creation function of all central banks involved can induce private markets to believe that exchange-rate targets will be held forever.

Another important ingredient to make foreign exchange-rate targets credible is the existence of enough foreign exchange reserves devoted to exchange-rate stabilization. These resources are essential to withstand temporary fluctuations in excess money demands without jeopardizing the smooth functioning of money markets and the credibility of fixed rates. Indeed the Delors Report states that during stage II "a certain amount of exchange reserves would be pooled and would be used to conduct exchange market interventions in accordance with guidelines established by the European System of Central Banks Council." (para. 57).

It is well known that the two pillars of a fixed-rates regime are foreign exchange reserves and coordination of national monetary policies. One of the implications of the discussion on money demand and financial innovation above, however, is that the management of foreign exchange reserves is proportionally more important than the coordination of monetary policies. The reason is that in order to carry out monetary policy coordination central banks have to be able to rely on stable money demand functions. Jointly setting monetary targets to support fixed exchange rates is a vacuous exercise if the demand for money shifts unpredictably. These unpredictable shifts, however, can be effectively dealt with by an efficient system of reserve management. Hence a well-working reserve-financing arrangement is an essential element in the current stage of the transition towards monetary union and is much more important than monetary policy coordination, although the latter should by no means be abandoned. A system of reserves management allows central banks to absorb unforeseeable shocks, and to slowly adapt their operating procedures to fast-evolving money markets.

How much should be devoted to exchange-rate stabilization? The discussion of the problems of the VSTFF suggests that just promising unlimited amounts in case of need is not enough to guarantee credibility, since just the promises of unlimited amounts are not credible. What would be much more realistic is a situation where, within a certain limited budget, intra-European exchange-rate stabilization is carried out in the absence of pressures from national monetary authorities, just as the Delors Report suggests. This alternative would be feasible only if the amount of foreign reserves necessary to insure credibility of bilateral rates is not "excessive."

I illustrate a method to estimate the size of the reserves pool by studying a simplified two-country world. The money-market equilibrium conditions say that the stock of money in the hands of the public should equal its demand:

$$\frac{M-R}{P} = f(\cdot)$$

$$\frac{M^* - R^*}{P^*} = f^*(\cdot)$$

where M and M^* are the stocks of money issued by national authorities, R and R^* are reserves pooled together to stabilize exchange rates (and therefore not in the hands of the public), and $f(\cdot)$ and $f^*(\cdot)$ represent two generic money-demand equations. The real exchange rate π is defined as the relative price of foreign goods, while the nominal exchange rate $\bar{E}$ is equal to the domestic-currency price of foreign currency. Hence $P^*\bar{E} = P\pi$. The nominal exchange rate is of course exogenous. Substituting the money-demand equations into the definition of the nominal and real exchange rate we have:

$$\bar{E} = \frac{P\pi}{P^*} = \frac{M-R}{M^* - R^*} \frac{f(\cdot)\pi}{f^*(\cdot)}$$

Let $\bar{R} = R + \bar{E}R^*$ represent the total stock of foreign exchange reserves. How large should it be, in order to insure that R or R^* never turn negative? Simple algebra shows that the condition for both holdings of domestic and foreign currency to be nonnegative are:

$$\bar{R} \geq \bar{E}M^* - \phi M$$

$$\bar{R} \geq M - \frac{\bar{E}M^*}{\phi}$$

where $\phi = \frac{f(\cdot)\pi}{f^*(\cdot)}$ represents relative money demand. Note that when ϕ has the maximum range, from zero to infinity, the two inequalities above imply that the total stock of foreign exchange reserves should exceed, at every time, the total stock of money in any of the two currencies. Thus when relative money demands have the maximum range the stock of foreign exchange reserves should be very large. But what do relative money demands depend on? All factors mentioned above in sections 10.3.1 and 10.3.2 come into play, especially the credibility of the exchange-rate target $\bar{E}$. To compute the equilibrium relative money demands it is thus necessary to compute the *expected future* equilibrium money demand, given assumptions about their determinants, the dynamic behavior of monetary policies and real shocks, and the nature of equilibrium in the goods and assets markets. Since equilibrium relative money demand depends on expected future equilibrium relative money demand, it is necessary to solve a *functional equation*. In Giovannini (1990) I illustrate a numerical methodology to solve this problem, and apply it to German and French data. I show that under a variety of assumptions on the behavior of relative money supplies and demands the size of total reserves holdings that is required to make bilateral targets credible (*i.e.* it is such that the holdings in any one of the currencies never turn negative) is of the order of 1/10 of the stock of money in one of the two countries.[29] These preliminary explorations seem to suggest that when fixed exchange rates are fully credible, they can be supported by a relatively limited stock of foreign exchange reserves.

10.5 Summary and Concluding Remarks

This chapter has discussed the problems of the management of the transition towards monetary union in Europe. It has argued that several factors indicate that in the near future money demand throughout the country members of the ERM will become substantially more volatile. This increase in instability makes the current ERM more vulnerable to shocks, and requires reforms aimed at making the announced plan of converging to a monetary union more credible to the public.

In the absence of credibility, shocks will more easily force countries to change bilateral parities, and will end up substantially slowing down monetary convergence, thus delaying the ultimate objective of monetary union.

The two pillars of a fixed-exchange-rates system like the ERM are the coordination of monetary policies and the management of foreign exchange reserves. The coordination of monetary policies is the joint setting of monetary targets consistently with stable exchange rates. This exercise, however, cannot be performed with a sufficient degree of accuracy whenever money demand functions become unstable. For this reason, I argued that in the near future the overriding task for monetary authorities will be to coordinate the management of foreign exchange reserves in order to provide enough of a buffer stock to withstand unforeseeable shifts in money demand, and at the same time to send a credible message to the markets that the plan of monetary convergence is strongly supported. With the help of an efficient system of reserve management, the function of monetary policy coordination will also have to be strengthened, and will have to adapt to the evolution of European money markets.

Notes

1. See De Cecco (1989).

2. Triffin (1960).

3. The alternative method I propose, however, is limited by its own infancy: the analysis sketched out below does not lend iteself to sophisticated econometric applications.

4. In this section, though, I will not deal in detail with the services of money as a store of value, since fluctuations in the *overall* demand for money due to fluctuations in expected store-of-value services (purchasing power) are not likely to be of major importance in the years to come. On the other hand, fluctuations in desired currency portfolios are likely to be affected by expectations of *relative* store-of-value services, and will be discussed below.

5. See, for example, Black (1970).

6. This observation points to a limitation in the data of table 10.1A: in countries like Italy, for example, ATMs are available only during regular office hours, are normally located just outside bank branches, and do not perform any operations beyond the withdrawal of cash, allowed only to account holders at the bank owning the machine.

7. 25 percent of the increase in deposits since 1986.

8. This argument makes use of the assumption of perfect competition in the banking industry, which is quite inappropriate in other contexts (see, for example, Baltensperger and Dermine (1989) and Vives (1990)) but can be used as an approximation here.

9. This exercise is inevitably an approximation, since differences in the definition of various aggregates, as well as differences in national regulations concerning reserve requirements, are not accounted for. The implicit assumption is that all numbers in the table are directly comparable.

10. In this calculation the stock of high-powered money ends up increasing only in the UK and in Belgium, byt 13.5 and 1.2 percent, respectively.

11. This is the overall mean obtained over the whole set of EC12 countries.

12. This view was first put forth in Giovannini (1989).

13. See, for example, Krugman (1980). General equilibrium models of money as a medium of exchange are in Kiyotaki and Wright (1989).

14. The ratio of international trade to GDP is of course a very rough estimate of the importance of transactions with non-residents, because all transactions in assets are not included (the ones in the capital account of the balance of payments, by netting out debtor and creditor positions by class of transactions, are also an approximation) and because GDP is not a good estimate of the number of local transactions.

15. Note, however, that this result is consistent with a perfectly stable *total* demand for money.

16. When the exchange rate is credibly fixed the forward rate is always equal to the spot rate.

17. Increased substitution among currencies, of course, does not necessarily imply—in equilibrium—larger fluctuations of money demand. The analysis of Woodford (1990), however,

shows how a wide array of monetary models, under a number of hypotheses on the exchage-rate regime and expectations formation, predict that increased currency substitutability is a source of monetary instability.

18. See, for example, Bank for International Settlements (1986).

19. "Monetary Policy Indicators in an Evolving Monetary Environment," *European Economy* n. 42, November 1989, pp. 123–133.

20. For an illuminating analysis of the history of financial crises in the US, and the role of monetary authorities, see Mishkin (1990), whose basic approach is adopted here.

21. *The Economist*, November 1, 1975. It was signed by G. Basevi, M. Fratianni, H. Giersch, P. Korteweg, D. O'Mahony, M. Parkin, T. Peeters, P. Salin and N. Thygesen.

22. HM Treasury (1989).

23. It is not clear, however, whether "private" means in that proposal "used by the private sector," or "privately issued."

24. This point is made by Carli (1989).

25. See Persson (1982) for a full analytical treatment of these points.

26. Net, of course, of any interest earned on foreign reserves, if they are held—at least in part—in interest-bearing assets.

27. The case of the US in the second postwar is often quoted in this respect.

28. Renewals, however, are subject to a ceiling.

29. An important condition is, of course, that the countries' monetary policies converge in the long run. This condition is imposed by allowing very substantial short-run divergences of national monetary policies.

References

Baltensperger, E. and J. Dermine. 1989. "European Banking, Prudential and Regulatory Issues," mimeo INSEAD (presented at the Salomon Brothers Center and INSEAD Conference on *European Banking After 1992*, April

Bank for International Settlements. 1986. *Changes in Money-Market Instruments and Procedures: Objectives and Implications*, Basle, March.

Black, F. 1970. "Banking and Interest Rates in a World Without Money," *Journal of Bank Research* 1 (Autumn), pp. 8–20.

Carli, G. 1989. *The Evolution Towards Economic and Monetary Union: A Response to the HM Treasury Paper*, Rome, Ministero del Tesoro, December.

de Cecco, M. 1989. "The Latin Monetary Union," mimeo, Università di Roma.

Giavazzi, F. and A. Giovannini. 1989. *Limiting Exchange-Rate Flexibility: The European Monetary System*, Cambridge, MA: MIT Press.

Giovannini, A. 1989. "Currency Substitution and Monetary Policy," in C. Wihlborg, M. Fratianni and T. D. Willet eds., *Financial Regulation and Monetary Arrangements After 1992*, Amsterdam: North Holland.

Giovannini, A. 1990. "Credibly Fixed Exchange Rates," mimeo, Columbia Business School.

Grilli, V. 1989. "Europe 1992: Issues and Prospects for the Financial Markets," *Economic Policy* 9, (October), pp. 387–422.

H. M. Treasury. 1989. *An Evolutionary Approach to Economic and Monetary Union*," London, November.

Karaken, J. and N. Wallace. 1981. "On the Indeterminacy of Equilibrium Exchange Rates," *Quarterly Journal of Economics*, pp. 207–22.

Kiyotaki, N. and R. Wright. 1989. "On Money as a Medium of Exchange," *Journal of Political Economy*.

Krugman, P. 1980. "Vehicle Currencies and the Structure of International Exchange," *Journal of Money, Credit and Banking*, 12, (August), pp. 513–26.

Mishkin, F. S. 1990. "When Do We Need A Lender of Last Resort? A Historical Perspective," mimeo, Graduate School of Business, Columbia University, February.

Obstfeld, M. 1986. "Rational and Self-Fulfilling Balance-of-Payments Crises," *American Economic Review*, 76, n. 1, pp. 72–81.

Persson, T. 1982. "Real Transfers and International Adjustment in Fixed Exchange Rates Systems," in T. Persson, *Studies of Alternative Exchange Rate Systems*, Monograph Series No. 13, Institute for International Economic Studies, University of Stockholm.

Triffin, R. 1960. *Gold and the Dollar Crisis*, New Haven: Yale University Press.

Vives, X. 1990. "Banking Competition and European Integration," mimeo, Universitat Autònoma de Barcelona. Paper presented at the Conference on *European Financial Integration*, Rome, January.

Woodford, M. 1990. "Does Competition Between Currencies Lead to Price Level and Exchange Rate Stability?" mimeo, University of Chicago. Paper presented at the Conference on *European Financial Integration*, Rome, January.

11   Is EMU Falling Apart?

(May 1991)

11.1 Introduction

Two years have passed since the Report of the Delors Committee was officially presented and subsequently endorsed by the European Council. During this period that document, and the strategy for economic and monetary union (EMU) that it set out, enjoyed very considerable success. Governments got increasingly involved in the debate of monetary union, and the efforts to create the institutions to support it were stepped up: for example, an inter-governmental conference, started in December 1990, was given the task of creating the European central bank.

The early enthusiasm for monetary union, however, seems to have waned. While in 1989 the public debate was concentrating on how to achieve the steps set out in the Delors Report, nowadays open criticism of the Delors strategy is quite common, even from government officials. What is the reason for this change in attitude? To answer this question we have to understand the basic philosophy of the Delors plan.

The Delors Report makes two main points. First, a single currency will be needed in Europe to support full goods and financial markets integration. And second, the strategy to achieve that single currency is gradualism. Gradualism is the progressive dismantling of monetary policy independence—to be replaced by tight monetary policy coordination and ultimately by a pan-European monetary authority—as well as the parallel creation of mechanisms to enhance coordination of macroeconomic policies. An important element of the gradualist strategy is the concept of economic convergence, and in particular convergence of inflation rates. The convergence of macroeconomic performances is deemed desirable because, it is argued, the final introduction of a single currency will be a less dramatic step if monetary performances have fully converged among European partners.

The experience of the last two years has shown that gradualism has very little chance of success. Now countries in the exchange-rate mechanism (ERM) of the European Monetary System are facing a very difficult choice: either to realign central parities, or to prolong relative price distortions and high interest rates. An exchange-rate realignment would be an official recognition of the failure of gradualism, not realigning means allowing the cost of gradualism to get out of hand.

11.2   Why Is Gradualism Failing?

Gradualism is failing because policymakers have very imperfect instruments to affect expectations, and because in this specific case they have made no use even of the very few instruments at their disposal.

Expectations affect the dynamics of prices, as well as interest rates. Firms set prices based on their expectations on the evolution of costs in the near future, as well as on perceptions about their competitors' pricing polices. Wages are set on the basis of expectations about their purchasing power over the length of the contract period. Interest rates are determined by expectations of inflation and of changes in exchange rates. Expectations of inflation and exchange-rate changes are in turn based on past experience as well as on guesses of the policies followed by monetary authorities.

In countries like France, Italy, Spain and the United Kingdom, the past experience is one of high inflation rates. Table 11.1 shows the average rate of increase of the consumer price index in these countries over the past twenty years, relative to the rate of inflation in Germany, as well as the rate of change of the franc, the lira, the peseta and the pound relative

Table 11.1
Relative inflation rates and exchange-rate depreciations

Country	1970–1979		1980–1989	
	Relative inflation	Exchange rate	Relative inflation	Exchange rate
U.K.	7.76	7.37	4.53	0.89
France	4.05	4.01	4.43	4.13
Italy	7.45	9.96	8.28	4.90
Spain	9.25	6.93	7.34	5.47

Source: *International Financial Statistics*. The columns labelled "Relative inflation" contain differences between the average inflation in the corresponding countries and average inflation in West Germany. The columns labelled "Exchange rate" contain average increase of the countries' currencies' price of 1 DM. All numbers are in percent per annum.

to the Deutsche mark. Both in the 1970s and—significantly—in the 1980s, the average inflation rates in all these countries were higher than West Germany's. The experience of the 1980s is significant because during this decade both France and Italy were members of the European Monetary System (EMS) and yet, on average, their inflation rates relative to West Germany were higher than in the 1970s. All countries except the UK in the 1980s have experienced sizeable average depreciations of their currencies relative to the DM (note: the pound was not part of the ERM in the 1980s!).

In summary, table 11.1 suggests that a history of high inflation should breed substantial public skepticism over the ability of these countries to reduce their domestic rate of inflation. This skepticism should be compounded by the generalized uncertainty over the stance of governments as well as over the convergence of their intentions on EMU. Among European governments there are those who would like to accelerate the process of transition as much as possible, but also those who regard a single European currency more like a theoretical concept than a matter deserving urgent policy attention. If agents are rational, not telling them when the monetary union is going to happen does not make gradualism work.

Governments have sent very few and noisy signals to the marketplace. Except for a communique on the starting date for stage two of the Delors plan, governments have shown no desire to commit themselves to specific dates and actions. Their intentions can only be gauged from what they in fact do. The rationale for this attitude of both the national governments and the EC is evident (the loss of credibility that would occur if an explicit deadline was not met is regarded as too great). Yet one cannot fail to note that in the absence of clear and unambiguous signals convergence is very unlikely to be achieved.

11.3 The Lessons from the EMS

The first ten years of the EMS should have provided a number of valuable lessons to interpret the problems Western Europe is currently facing. The EMS is often characterized by academics and policymakers as a mechanism that allows high inflation countries to defeat inflation. These academics and policymakers believe that, by pegging to the Deutsche mark, countries can import the credibility of the Bundesbank. Reality is in fact not consistent with that characterization, because the public deems exchange-rate targets not fully credible, since the cost (political and economic) of exchange-rate realignments is not especially high—and has not been in the past ten years.

Indeed, the empirical evidence indicates that, throughout the EMS years, the public expected that the exchange rate of the lira and the franc relative to the DM would go beyond the point of maximum depreciation within one year. This is documented in the figures of credibility of exchange rates which appear in chapter 8. It is thus not surprising that shifts in inflation and inflationary expectations in France and Italy have occurred not after the EMS has been instituted. In my book with Francesco Giavazzi[1] I attempted to estimate the timing and the magnitude of shifts in inflationary expectations, identified as shifts in predictions of the rate of inflation obtained from a multivariate statistical model estimated over the period preceding the EMS. Our finding was that a noticeable shift in the output-inflation tradeoff in France and Italy did not occur after these countries joined the ERM, but only after their governments decided to take drastic and very visible policy measures (in 1983 and 1985, respectively) to defeat inflation and external imbalances. These measures were justified to the public—at least in France—as required to maintain membership to the ERM.

It was not announcing the membership to the ERM that made inflationary expectations subside. Rather, it was the enactment of very unpopular policies—justified to the public as necessary to maintain membership in the ERM—that defeated inflation in France and Italy. Hence, the clear lesson for EMU is that a half-hearted endorsement of the Delors plan is not, by itself, going to bring inflation differentials with Germany down to zero in the rest of Europe. In the absence of inflation convergence, relative prices diverge, with negative effects on intra-European trade flows.

So, what has happened? How has the public interpreted the endorsement of the Delors Report in May of 1989? It is very hard to get a clear signal from the data over a short interval like this. Yet, as table 11.2 shows, interest rates in all countries except France are significantly higher than in Germany. At the same time, inflation rates, again with the exception of France, are failing to converge.

In conclusion, it does not seem that the early enthusiasm for EMU has helped to defeat inflation in Europe. The lack of convergence, however, cannot be measured accurately, since we do not know to what extent the fluctuation in relative prices could be due to real shocks. Indeed, the presence of real shocks makes the convergence of inflation rates an unreliable performance criterion.

Table 11.2
Current levels of interest rates and inflation rates

Country	Inflation rate	Interest rate
U.K.	8.9	11.94
France	3.5	9.25
Germany	2.5	9.13
Italy	6.6	11.50
Spain	5.9	12.70

Source: *The Economist*, 13–19 April 1991. All numbers in percent per annum. Inflation rates are the latest recorded annual increases in consumer prices. Interest rates are 3-month Euro-deposit rates.

11.4 The Lessons from the German Unification

Another powerful blow to EMU has been the unification of the two Germany. And this is ironic, since in December 1989 Chancellor Kohl obtained support for the German unification from his EC partners, and in particular from France, in exchange for his own support for EMU.

The currency unification of the two Germany, the replacement of the Mark with the DM, occurred very swiftly. While there have been a number of critics at home, one has the impression that the international community was somewhat taken by surprise. Clearly, not much convergence had been achieved between the two Germany. The criteria that West Germany is applying for the currency reform in the EC—gradualism and the requirement of inflation convergence—have been quickly swept under the rug in the case of its own monetary union with the East.

Why has the doctrine of gradualism and convergence—championed by the Bundesbank—not been followed in West Germany? One explanation of this puzzle is that the German government does not really believe in gradualism, and the keen support of gradualism and convergence is only a diplomatic tool, aimed at slowing down, and eventually stopping, the drive towards a single currency in the EC. Another, more complex explanation is that the conditions under which the German currency union was undertaken differ in an important respect from the conditions of a hypothetical EC currency union: the German union is the economic annexation of the East by the West, and the extension of the already existing and well-tested institutions of the West to the East. In other words, the currency union occurs in an area which has already a full political union. This important difference suggests a theory of optimum currency areas—which I would label the radical political theory of optimum currency areas—

according to which a necessary condition to have a single currency is to have a single country.

Although a rejection of this theory is implicit in the stance taken by EC partners so far, the German experience forces us to think about the degree of political cohesion that is necessary to achieve a monetary union, and the institutions that are necessary to sustain it. Two observations appear relevant in this respect. First, if much more political cohesion is necessary to have a monetary union than envisioned in the Delors Report, the strategy laid out in that document is inappropriate. To achieve a monetary unification European governments should concentrate all their efforts at building the institutions to sustain it without much worrying about the issue of economic convergence: just as the Germans did.

And second, the recent experience suggests that European governments are quite efficient at eliminating rules and regulations which, good or bad, afforded them some control of their national economies. However, their record at substituting the lost national sovereignties with pan-European institutions is mixed. In particular, in the monetary field the experience of the past years suggests that it has been much easier to destroy than to build. The liberalization of capital controls has decreased the ability of national central banks to affect interest rates, given exchange-rate parities, through open market operations. In addition, the Second Banking Directive has significantly increased the mobility of banks within the EC, without at the same time eliminating the opportunities for "regulatory arbitrage." There is still limited coordination in the supervisory and regulatory activities of individual EC countries. And finally, some very basic questions such as the domain of national governments and the domain of the European central bank on issues of financial markets' supervision and regulation have not been settled yet.

11.5   What Is to Be Done?

My position on the transition to monetary union should have emerged clearly in the discussion above. The economics of EMU calls for a sudden currency reform. At this time, however, the sudden currency reform seems to be unfeasible, both politically and administratively. It does not seem politically feasible because there is no uniform support for a sudden monetary reform among member-country governments, even assuming that they all understood and agreed with the economic arguments put forth above. It does not seem administratively feasible because the European Central Bank is not ready yet.

Hence the current dilemma can be stated as follows: how can EMU be held together despite the lack of convergence, and in the absence of the option to immediately move to a single currency? To understand the dilemma, we need to identify the available choices. They are:

- Return to floating exchange rates.
- Maintain the *status quo*. Allow exchange-rate realignments.
- Maintain the *status quo*, but do not allow exchange-rate realignments.

These strategies are discussed in detail below.

11.5.1   Floating Rates

A return to floating rates is the straightforward way out of the dilemma facing EC countries. It is of course inconsistent with the current EMU plan, but could be considered an interim regime to pursue until all the countries are ready for a currency reform. In other words, exchange rates would be allowed to fluctuate and settle to equilibrium levels until national currencies are replaced with a single European currency.

The advantage of this option is that it could eliminate the relative price distortions that have materialized as a result of countries pursuing a plan of monetary union that is not fully credible in the eyes of the public. The disadvantage of flexible rates is that, in historical experience, they never proved effective devices to stabilize relative prices. Thus, even though a return to flexible rates might in part eliminate the relative price distortions European countries are currently experiencing, such a strategy will not increase the cohesion of European economies. On the contrary, by inducing more uncertainty on relative price fluctuations, it will likely further slow down—and possibly bring to a halt—the creation of the single European market. Thus a return to flexible exchange rates should be ruled out.

11.5.2   Exchange-Rate Realignments with Status Quo

This is the strategy preferred by many, especially those who feel the negative effects of the lack of convergence, but do not want to commit to speeding up EMU (most notably, the Deutsche Bundesbank).

The possibility of making use of exchange-rate realignments during the transition to a monetary union is explicitly allowed for in the Delors Report. They are not ruled out during stage one, they are admitted, albeit under "exceptional circumstances" during stage two, but they are ruled out during stage three.

The problem of exchange-rate realignments is that they are inconsistent with convergence of inflationary expectations and inflation. Devaluing the currencies that have experienced higher inflation and higher interest rates (because the public in those countries and elsewhere did not believe the stated intentions of their governments) amounts to admitting that the public was right. Therefore, it amounts to destroying any reputation gained in the recent past. It also means turning the convergence clock back to time zero, since existing inflation-rate differentials are fully accommodated by the exchange-rate change, and thus the incentives to eliminate such differentials are also eliminated. Convergence of inflation rates and exchange-rate realignments are in sum two inconsistent concepts.

The other concern about a realignment followed by the EMS *status quo* is whether this *status quo* can actually be reestablished after the realignment. In the past three years foreign exchange markets in Europe have experienced remarkable stability, aided by the very high interest rates in most countries. The stability of exchange rates has also been helped by the perception that Italian and French authorities had changed their attitudes about modifying exchange rates: that is, they have become much more reluctant to do so. An exchange-rate realignment is a recognition that in fact French and Italian authorities are not as keen on exchange-rate stability. The result might be much more volatility in the European foreign exchange markets than what has been seen in the past.

The big difference between the present time and the early EMS experience is of course the virtual absence of controls of international capital movements, which has made central banks much more vulnerable to speculative attacks. It is not clear whether the seldom-tested automatic mechanisms of the ERM, like the Very Short Term Financing Facility, could withstand substantial market volatility.

11.5.3   Status Quo, No Realignments

This is the only strategy that in principle can achieve gradual convergence of inflation rates in a world where the latter are crucially affected by expectations of exchange-rate changes. The strategy, however, raises a fundamental problem illustrated in figure 11.1.[2]

Figure 11.1 plots the differential of inflation between two countries, and the level of relative prices when nominal exchange rates are kept fixed. The assumption in the figure is that relative prices are roughly in line when the exchange rate is fixed (at time zero). With fixed exchange rates, lack of inflation convergence means increasing divergences of relative

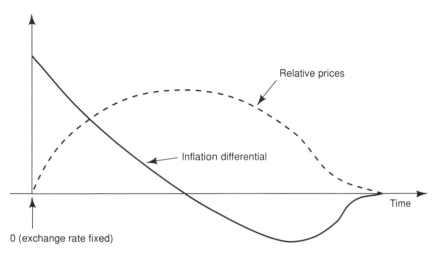

Figure 11.1
The problem of inflation convergence with fixed exchange rates

prices: this is what is plotted on the left portion of the figure. The right portion of the figure shows what has to happen to relative inflation rates for the distortions in relative prices to be eliminated in the absence of exchange-rate changes: the differential of inflation rates has to turn negative. This can be accomplished either via higher inflation in the traditionally low-inflation country, or by deflation (that is fall in prices) in the traditionally high-inflation country. Both the higher inflation in the low-inflation country or the deflation in the higher-inflation countries are transitory, and can be reconciled with a new steady state with low inflation in both countries. In other words, if the UK wanted to maintain the sterling-DM rate fixed, accomplish convergence of inflation with Germany, and at the same time eliminate any distortions in competitiveness with that country, it has to either induce higher inflation in Germany or experience price deflation.

A fall in prices of noticeable proportions is considered by most economists a phenomenon outside the normal working of modern industrial societies, to be associated with substantial political and economic disruptions. Hence the possibility of significant price deflation is routinely ruled out. Can there be higher inflation in Germany? Although the East-West reunification might prompt higher price increases than in the past, both the Bundesbank and the government are ready to fight them fiercely. Indeed their own estimates indicate no dramatic inflation surge in the foreseeable future.

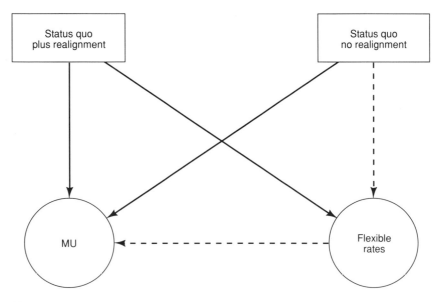

Figure 11.2
The strategic options

Hence the *status quo*-with-no-realignment strategy is also likely to prove unworkable in practice. Resistance to higher inflation in Germany does not allow both the elimination of relative price distortions and the convergence of inflation rates.

11.6   Concluding Observations

Figure 11.2 summarizes the discussion, and highlights the difficult choices that European governments are currently facing. The arrows indicate that, as the analysis above has implied, only two regimes are unambiguously stable: monetary union and flexible exchange rates. Both of these regimes, however, are currently ruled out, for very different reasons. Flexible rates are ruled out as not appropriate for the high degree of integration of European goods and financial markets, and monetary union is ruled out as an immediate option, since it is regarded, at this time, both politically and administratively unfeasible.

As I argued above, however, the *status quo* is not likely to be a stable regime. In absence of realignments (the box on the right), the frictions between the country with initially low inflation and countries with initially high inflation might lead either to a collapse (reversal to floating rates) or to an acceleration of the process of monetary union. By contrast, if realignments are resorted to, convergence of inflation rates is unlikely to occur, and volatile capital flows might break the EMS apart. This means either a return to flexible rates or monetary union.

The dashed arrows indicate the possibility that flexible rates be used as an interim regime before monetary union, or that the no-realignment *status quo* collapses to permanently flexible rates.

European governments are likely betting on the upper left corner. They hope that the instabilities I described above might be avoided, and that some convergence of inflation be achieved despite the needed periodic exchange-rate changes. They hope that the EMS could be held together until, God willing, the stage is ready for monetary union. I hope they are right.

Notes

1. Giavazzi and Giovannini (1989).

2. I am grateful to Clas Wihlborg for suggesting to me this illustration of the problem.

References

Giavazzi, F. and A. Giovannini. 1989. *Limiting Exchange Rate Flexibility: The European Monetary System*, Cambridge: MIT Press.

12

Economic and Monetary Union: What Happened? Exploring the Political Dimension of Optimum Currency Areas

(December 1992)

12.1 Introduction

The project of monetary union in Western Europe has enjoyed, in its earlier stages, tremendous success. In a rather unprecedented move, some of the largest and richest countries in the world decided to get rid of their own currencies to adopt a common medium of exchange and store of value. Never before has such a monetary reform been accomplished among large countries.

The early success of that project has given way, in the past year, to much criticism from the public, academics and political leaders. In addition, the outcome of the referendum in Denmark, which has turned down the proposed changes in the Treaty of Rome (endorsed by the Heads of State at the European Council of December 1991 held at Maastricht, the Netherlands) allowing to carry out the monetary union, has raised questions about the legal feasibility of monetary union among EC countries, at least as envisaged by the amendments to the Treaty of Rome.

This chapter is an attempt at understanding the political debate on the project of monetary union in Europe. Such debate, in individual countries, has followed very different patterns. In the United Kingdom, a country that—despite its size and political clout—has traditionally maintained some distance from EC activities, European monetary union has dominated the public debate since 1989. By contrast, the debate has been largely absent on the continent. In Italy no significant disagreement on monetary union has been recorded so far, despite the fact that the acceptance of the Maastricht convergence conditions means, in that country more than elsewhere, the adoption of extremely severe fiscal measures. In Germany and France the debate on monetary union has picked up significantly only after the Danish referendum, that is only a few months preceding these countries' own ratifications of the Maastricht Treaty.

The main question of this paper, "What happened?", can be rephrased as follows: can we make sense of the political debate on European monetary union by identifying groups that stand to gain economically from the monetary union, and groups that are likely to lose from it?

This exercise has a great tradition in international trade theory. For example, the Hecksher-Ohlin-Samuelson model predicts that a change in regime in international trade (say, the elimination of a tariff) affects different groups in the economy differently (consumers stand to gain from liberalization, producers in the import-competing industry stand to lose), and that the interaction of these groups determines a country's attitude towards trade liberalization. Can a similar methodology be applied to analyze international monetary regimes? This question is attracting growing attention in economics and political science. Work by Frieden (1991a,b, 1992) and Calomiris (1992) is aimed at analyzing the politics of monetary regimes, both in America and Europe. The main thesis of this chapter, however, is at least partly at odds with the views expressed by Frieden: this chapter concludes that stable constituencies for or against monetary union are difficult to identify.

Section 12.2 describes three popular models used to analyze the effects of monetary union, and uses them to identify constituencies for or against monetary union. Section 12.3 applies the analysis developed in section 12.2 to the European case. Section 12.4 contains a few concluding remarks.

12.2   Three Models

As mentioned in the introduction, monetary theory does not provide a consensus model of the effects of alternative monetary regimes. Despite this lack of a generally accepted benchmark, debate on monetary regimes in Europe has been extremely lively in recent years. In this debate, references have most often been made to three models, emphasizing three aspects of currency areas. The traditional optimal currency area model, emphasizing country-specific shocks and the insurance properties of alternative monetary regimes; the rules-versus-discretion model, suggesting that a monetary union in Europe would induce (through a mechanism to be discussed in detail below) lower inflation; and the transactions cost model, stressing the role of a single currency as a facilitator of transactions across European countries.

Each of these models, essentially, emphasizes a special class of either market failure or technological constraints that characterize different monetary regimes. The purpose of this section is to identify, with the help of the three models, interest groups that prefer one versus another monetary regime. I will discuss each model separately, and at the end of the section, I will compare the predictions of the models on the political support for a single currency versus adjustable exchange rates.

12.2.1 The Mundell-Fleming Model

This is a model where capital is perfectly mobile internationally, and labor is not. Prices and wages are sticky, hence unemployment can occur in equilibrium. Shocks originate from goods markets and financial markets. Because prices are sticky, monetary policy or foreign-exchange policy can offset the effects of exogenous shocks on output and employment.

The discussion of this model requires the choice of a regime that can be compared with a monetary union. For simplicity, I choose flexible exchange rates. Thus I consider the sticky-prices, perfect capital mobility model under a monetary union and under floating exchange rates.[1]

Consider a monetary union first. Output demand in the two countries depends on the union-wide rate of interest and on a country-specific shock. The union-wide rate of interest is determined in the money market, where money supply equals money demand, a function of total output in the union, and of the union-wide rate of interest.

In a monetary union, there is perfect pooling of money-market or financial risk, because of the maintained assumption of perfect financial integration. A shock in the money market affects the nominal and real interest rate, and as a result it affects demand and output, identically across the country members of the union. That is not the case with real shocks. An independent increase in demand in one country has a negative spillover to the other country. This happens because the demand increase brings about an increase in total money demand, and an increase in the rate of interest, which has contractionary effects in the other country.

Under floating exchange rates, there are different money-market equilibrium conditions in the two countries, and in each money market there is an idiosyncratic shock. Aggregate demand now depends both on the real interest rate and on the real exchange rate. Given sticky prices, the real interest rate and the real exchange rate are perfectly correlated with the nominal interest rate and exchange rate. Consider now the effects of a country-specific demand shock. On one hand, the demand shock leads to an increase in the domestic rate of interest, which is transmitted abroad through perfect international capital mobility. On the other hand, this negative spillover is offset by an appreciation of the exchange rate.

A country-specific money shock has the well-known negative spillover: an increase in, say, money at home increases home output and the domestic and foreign interest rate. Given foreign money supply, foreign output has to fall. The fall in foreign output is caused by a depreciation of the domestic currency relative to the foreign currency, which more than offsets the expansionary effect of lower world interest rates.

In summary, a monetary union brings about lower output fluctuations if shocks originate mainly in financial markets, while floating rates are stabilizing if shocks originate in goods markets. The question that we now need to address is: which groups will be keener in obtaining the insurance that floating rates provide against real shocks and a monetary union provides against monetary shocks? To answer this question we have to explore the mechanics through which exchange-rate change affect demand. Since an exchange-rate depreciation increases the relative price of foreign goods, workers that have lost their job due to a foreign shock (leading to high interest rates) go back to work—or at least some of them do—at a lower real wage. There is a tradeoff between employment and real wages. This tradeoff, however, is solved if those whose job is put at risk are a minority. In that case changes in the economy-wide real wage rate might provide an efficient risk-sharing mechanism. I thus tentatively conclude that workers prefer floating rates in a world where country-specific real shocks prevail.

This preference might even be stronger in the case of firms, especially when labor markets are rigid. A firm that cannot lay off workers would have to close down, thus incurring potentially large costs. An exchange-rate adjustment helps to avoid plant or firm closures. Hence I conclude that firms and industrialists prefer floating rates in a world where country-specific shocks prevail.

When country-specific financial shocks are prevalent, the model says that their effects on interest rates are more than offset by exchange-rate movements. The preferences of workers and industrialists should in this case again follow the model's predictions on output fluctuations. A foreign financial disturbance (a monetary expansion) appreciates the domestic currency, causing a loss of competitiveness, which lowers employment (but increases the purchasing power of wages) either through labor shedding or through firm or plant closings. Labor and industrialists should, according to this model, unite again in favor of fixed rates or, better, a monetary union.

The constituencies in favor of different monetary regimes as a function of different underlying shocks, which I have identified above, are justified—as Mundell (1968) rightly stresses—by an important assumption: the lack of mobility of labor and the lack of mobility of factories and industries. The political alliance between labor and industrialists on the exchange-rate regime would not exist if firms were able to locate production costlessly and instantaneously across the borders of the countries we are studying in response to the different shocks. Multinationals would then become efficient risk pools. Their representatives would be indifferent across alternative exchange-rate regimes.

Similarly, the financial industry is, in this model, indifferent across exchange-rate regimes. The financial industry's objective, the exploitation of arbitrage opportunities across countries, is always attained (hence rates of return are always equalized) irrespective of the exchange-rate regime.

In conclusion to the discussion of the Mundell-Fleming model, it is useful to point out two things. First, it is difficult to identify *contrasting* interests on the appropriate exchange-rate regime. I have argued that there are interest groups with coincident objectives as far as the exchange-rate regime is concerned or, at worst, groups with a preference and groups that are indifferent. But in the absence of sectoral disaggregation, contrasting interests are not there.

When considering the tradeoff between the real wage and employment discussed above, it is conceivable that it could become a source of contrasting interests across groups of workers. A change in the exchange rate affects the purchasing power of all workers, but helps the competitive position and maintains employment only of those workers that are more exposed to international competition. Thus, when real shocks prevail, sectors most exposed to international competition should be the ones where exchange-rate flexibility is welcome, against the interest of workers and employers in the nontraded sector, who would face fluctuations in their purchasing power. Similarly, in a world where financial shocks prevail, sectors most exposed to international competition should be those who welcome a monetary union. On this, they should find the support of workers and employers in the nontraded sectors, who could gain from a stabilization of their purchasing power.

The final caveat is that, in the discussion above, we have considered attitudes about *regimes*, which means that we have explored the preferences of hypothetical interest groups on *variances* of economic variables. This raises the question of the ability of various interest groups to express preferences over variances, independently from the sign of the shocks that they are experiencing.

12.2.2   The Rules-versus-Discretion Model

A second very popular model used in the discussion over the costs and benefits of a single currency in Europe is the model of rules versus discretion in monetary policy. That model postulates that the central bank is subject to pressures to generate unanticipated inflation, in order to achieve objectives on some real variables in the economy: either to induce a level of economic activity that is higher than the natural rate, or to help financing budget deficits. Such pressures originate from the presence of distortions, which could be present in labor markets, or associated with distortionary taxes.

Since monetary policy can affect economic activity only temporarily (another way of saying that unanticipated money affects output), the central bank is unable to attain its objectives consistently, because the public learns about them, and adapts to them. The equilibrium outcome is a higher rate of inflation and an unchanged level for the real economic objectives of the central bank.

A corollary of the main proposition of the rules-versus-discretion model of inflation is that, if the persons in charge of monetary policy are averse enough to inflation and are defended by appropriate institutional design against outside pressure to use the instruments of monetary policy for attaining non-monetary objectives, they will be able to pursue effective anti-inflation policies, and in equilibrium the rate of inflation will be lower.

This model is used to argue that the equilibrium rate of inflation in the European monetary union is going to be lower than the rate of inflation experienced by individual countries, because the institutional setup of the European central bank assures that it will enjoy the highest degree of independence from national political pressures—even higher than the Bundesbank's.

Without, for the moment, questioning the proposition that the European central bank can attain the lowest rate of inflation, I turn to the identification of those interest groups that favor a monetary union under this model, i.e., the groups that favor lower inflation. For this purpose, I review the economic effects of inflation following the classification proposed by Fischer and Modigliani (1978).

The first effect of inflation is the so-called inflation tax, that is the revenue that the government obtains from the fact that the economy uses a depreciating medium of exchange. A decrease in the inflation tax is a benefit to those sectors of the economy that use cash more intensely, but is also a source of additional taxation or decreased government spending.

The next set of real effects of inflation are caused by the existence of nominal government institutions, the most important of which are nominal tax rules. A decrease in inflation decreases the revenue that the government obtains from the absence of indexation of tax brackets, and affect the real rate of return on capital.

The combined effects of inflation and nominal tax systems on the real return on capital fall in four categories. First, with lower inflation effective tax rates on investment are decreased by depreciation rules based on historical cost. Second, lower inflation means lower nominal interest rates, and therefore lower deductions from corporate income, matched by lower taxes paid by corporate bondholders. The net effect of this depends on the relative magnitude of corporate and personal tax rates. Third, lower inflation affects reported income through inventory accounting and, fourth, lower inflation affects the costs of required reserves on banks and insurance companies.

The sum of these phenomena depends crucially on individual countries' institutions. King and Fullerton (1984), for example, found that lower inflation lowers the effective tax rate on capital in Sweden and Germany, but increases it in the UK.

Nominal private institutions also have real effects in the presence of inflation. These, however, tend to be discounted when contracts are signed. Hence, nominal private institutions cause redistributions of wealth with higher-than-expected or lower-than-expected inflation. As I argued above, lower inflation is normally associated with less volatile inflation, and thus the question is who gains and who loses from a decrease in inflation uncertainty.

As far as wage contracts are concerned, it appears that the largest gain from a decrease in inflation and the associated decrease in inflation uncertainty accrues to workers. Unlike firms, workers' cash flows seem to be more exposed to inflation uncertainty, since they have less opportunities to hedge, for example by taking up nominal liabilities.

As far as debt contracts are concerned, I could not think of any major asymmetry between borrowers and lenders in their ability to hedge against inflation uncertainty by taking up, for example, nominal assets and liabilities, respectively.

In summary, the economic effects of inflation are often ambiguous. We have, however, identified a potential preference for low inflation by workers, and a general-equilibrium effect arising from the decrease in seigniorage revenue. Who gains and who loses from a decline in the inflation tax? The gain goes to the economy as a whole, if money is held in equal proportions by all economic agents. If the distribution of money holdings is uneven, the distribution of economic gains from low inflation will be equally uneven: the fraction of the population that uses cash more intensely gains proportionately more from monetary union. The losses accrue to those that have to withstand the increase in taxation needed to substitute for the seigniorage revenue. The distribution of gains and losses from a fall in seigniorage across various interest groups, while in principle identifiable, are not in general predictable, since there is no firm prediction either on the distribution of cash holdings in the economy, or on the type of taxes that would substitute the inflation tax.

12.2.3 The Transaction Costs Model

This is the least developed model of the three. The savings of transactions costs is a prominent item of the cost-benefit analysis of alternative monetary regimes, emphasized by all authors. Political aspects of these transactions costs are however largely unexplored.

The European Community (1990) has carried out a thorough assessment of the magnitude of transactions costs incurred by European countries because of the presence of different currencies. Their methodology essentially amounts to multiplying estimates of the turnover in the foreign-exchange market time estimates of bid-ask spreads in the foreign-exchange market. The turnover estimates net out transactions in the interbank market, as well as transactions involving only non-member-country currencies. The result of this exercise is an estimate of ECU 6.2 billion to 10.4 billion (June 1990 US$8.5 to 14.2 billion). In addition to the wholesale foreign-exchange market, the costs incurred in the retail foreign-exchange market should be added as well as the costs of cross-border payments, of treasury management within companies, and of running separate wholesale payments systems across Europe. The total estimate of the EC (which excludes the costs of running different wholesale payments systems) ranges between 13.1 and 19.2 billion of 1990 ECUs (June 1990 US$17.8 to 26.2 billion). These estimates of transactions costs are of course conservative, since they are predicated on the assumption that the volume of cross-border transactions that would occur in the presence of a single currency is approximately the same as the volume of transactions observed with multiple currencies. If the volume of transactions were to increase significantly, the costs of multiple currencies would increase accordingly.

What is the effect of these transactions costs? The most obvious one is the distribution of resources between the non-financial sector and the financial sector. The costs mentioned above amount to 4 to 5 percent of total value added in the EC financial sector. This distribution of resources also takes on a geographical dimension: for example, since most of the foreign-exchange business in the EC goes through London, that town stands to lose more than the rest of Europe from the elimination of the EC foreign-exchange market.

Thus, the creation of a single currency represents a significant transfer of resources across two clearly identifiable interest groups: from international banks to their clients involved in cross-border transactions within Europe. This partial equilibrium model predicts that international banks would resist the adoption of a single currency, in order to avoid the costs of adjusting to a new business environment, while firms that are involved in cross-border trade within the EC should favor it. The EC figures reported above would, appropriately, represent the loss of business to international banks, but certainly underestimate the gain to firms involved in cross-border trade.[2]

12.3   What Are the Predictions of Monetary Models?

Table 12.1 summarizes the discussion of the previous section. The table reveals all the ambiguities surrounding the nature of political support on alternative monetary regimes.

Consider the Mundell-Fleming model. That model says that the preferences on monetary regimes are conditional on the variance-covariance matrix of exogenous shocks. Estimating such variance-covariance matrix is a non-trivial exercise for economists, and most likely an equally difficult problem for the public as a whole. In addition, the Mundell-Fleming model is predicated on the ability of central banks to systematically offset real disturbances through monetary policy. Much of the debate on monetary union in Europe originates from doubts about the ability of monetary policy to bring about relative price changes, especially in countries that are highly integrated with the rest of the Community. Finally, as I argued above, it is possible that preferences for adjustable rates versus a monetary union be dictated by the level that certain variables have in the economy. Thus, when the real exchange rate is overvalued (whatever the causes of overvaluation), employers in particular and possibly also workers are likely to speak against monetary union.

Table 12.1
The preferences of different groups over monetary union versus floating rates according to three popular models

	Mundell-Fleming model	Rules-vs.-discretion	Transaction costs
Workers	Prefer floating rates with real shocks (but differences within group). Prefer monetary union with financial shocks.	Prefer monetary union to hedge against purchasing power uncertainty with high inflation. Otherwise uncertain (depends on the effects of inflation tax, and on nominal government institutions).	Indifferent.
Employers	Floating rates with real shocks; monetary union with financial shocks.	Uncertain (depends on the effects of inflation on rate of return to capital, on inflation tax).	Prefer monetary union.
Financial sector	Indifferent.	Uncertain (depends on effects of inflation on the financial sector).	Prefer floating exchange rates.

The rules-versus-discretion model also delivers ambiguous predictions on the political support for a monetary union. The two main problems of that model are, first, that the connection "monetary union ⇔ low inflation" is not clear to all, and not agreed upon in low-inflation countries, like Germany and the Netherlands. Second, the gains and losses of low inflation cannot be quantified without detailed knowledge of the institutional features of individual countries. In addition, such institutions are likely to change significantly, but not predictably, if the monetary union actually occurred.

Finally, the transactions costs model (the simplest, partial-equilibrium description of the effects of a monetary union) appears to be the only one to deliver rather unambiguous predictions, although the neglect of general equilibrium effects should raise caution on its applicability.[3]

These observations lead me to the central thesis of this chapter: there are no stable or significant constituencies for or against monetary union. This proposition, of course, does not imply that there can never be political debate on such an issue. Only that such debate is conditioned by factors that are largely extraneous to the substantive economic effects of a monetary union versus a regime of adjustable rates, and are associated either with the specific condition of the countries discussing such a reform, or with the specific time in which this discussion takes place.

These "extraneous factors," explaining the political crisis in which the project of European monetary union currently finds itself are easy to identify. In the first place I would put the whole strategy of gradualism-cum-convergence, which was the hallmark of the Delors Report and is a pillar of the Maastricht Treaty. The convergence criteria imply that countries with high inflation and high debt have to undergo drastic monetary and fiscal restrictions in order to satisfy convergence criteria at the time when monetary union will be voted on by the European Council. Hence in these countries monetary union is associated with such contractions. The social costs of these contractions are identified with the social costs of monetary union.

Another, partly related, factor explaining the crisis of the movement to a single currency is the business cycle. Figure 12.1 plots an indicator of the business cycle for the 3 largest continental economies: France, Germany and Italy. The second half of the 1980s, the period when the project of integration (the Single European Market and Economic and Monetary Union) were a time of accelerating economic activity. By contrast, since the Delors Report was published (Spring 1989) economic activity has been slowing down. The case of Germany, showing high growth in 1990 and 1991, reflects the annexation of East Germany in 1990.

The experience of the German unification has been another important source of criticism and opposition to economic and monetary union. Especially in West Germany, the European monetary union was regarded to have similar effects as the German monetary union. It would have brought about an upward pressure on wages, originating from the desire of workers from less developed areas to align their standard of living with those of workers in high-productivity areas. Such a pressure for wage alignment would be the cause of unemployment in low-productivity areas, and would produce pressure for transfers from the more productive regions. Indeed, these fears were compounded by the EC initiatives to step up transfers into poorer regions, under the label "Social Europe."

These effects have to do with the monetary union only insofar as they originate from the inability of workers to use exchange rates to translate wages denominated in foreign currency. In fact, they are at work also in the absence of a single currency, but in the presence of the single European market, which gives workers the ability to move in pursuit of higher wages, and triggers the upward pressure on wages (coming from an alliance between the trade unions in the high-productivity area, who fear the inflow of foreign workers, and the trade unions in low-productivity areas, who stand to gain from an increase in wages).

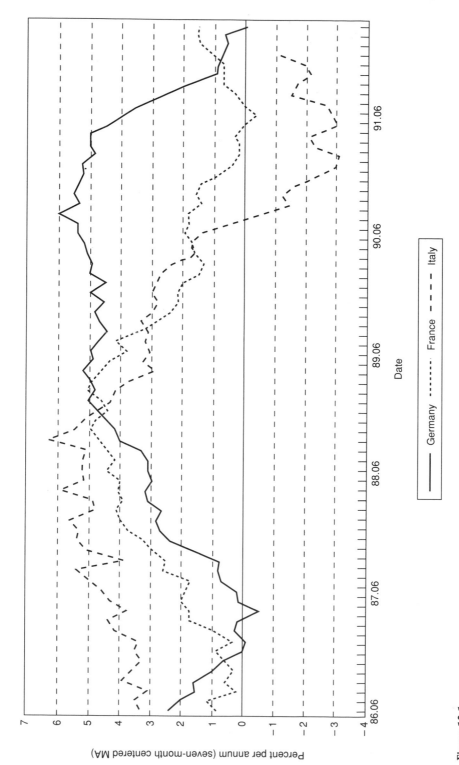

Figure 12.1
Annual growth in industrial production

A fourth set of issues which featured prominently in the recent debate on European monetary union come from the association between monetary union and political union. The connection between monetary union and political union comes from the perception that a monetary union alone could suffer from a "democratic deficit," and might create a political vacuum around the European central bank. A related issue in the debate was that monetary union was designed to remove power from European people and give it to Brussels bureaucrats. Alternatively, it has been claimed that power, instead of going to Brussels bureaucrats pursuing big government, would go to the Germans, who were building a single European currency and central bank in the image of the Deutsche mark, thus pursuing a design of economic dominance of Europe.

A fifth set of issues in the political debate on monetary union contains all the country-specific problems, arising from the fact that the Maastricht Treaty is about much more than a single currency and how to manage it. For example, Mr. Reynolds, the Irish prime minister, before his country's referendum on the Maastricht Treaty appeared on television to assure his citizens that, after the ratification the Treaty, Ireland's sons would not be drafted into a Euro-army, Irish women would not be prevented from traveling abroad for an abortion, and conversely, Irish foetuses will be safe from Godless bureaucrats in Brussels (*Financial Times*, June 16, 1992). In France a large fraction of the opposition to the Maastricht Treaty has come from farmers, who disapprove of the recent turns in Europe's agricultural policy. In France and Germany, the opposition to monetary union is a way to manifest opposition to the government, which in both countries has identified itself with the project.

The sixth and last set of issues in the political debate on European monetary union have to do with nationalism. In particular, the national currency is viewed in some countries as a symbol of national pride, which should not be given away. Giving away the national currency is a surrender of national pride. In this era of resurgent nationalism in Europe, such seemingly irrational attitudes appear surprisingly popular.

12.4 Concluding Remarks

This chapter has attempted to identify the economic interests for and against a single currency. To this end, I have taken three popular models of the economic effects of a single currency, to find out what could be their predictions on the distribution of gains and losses from alternative monetary regimes.

The result of this experiment is that the economic interests in favor of a fixed currency versus flexible exchange rates are not easily identifiable, often because the economic effects of a monetary regime depend on a number of institutional factors, which might differ significantly from country to country. Even in the case of the simple Mundell-Fleming model, preferences for alternative monetary regimes are not stable, but depend on the sources of shocks.

From this analysis, I conclude that there are no stable or significant constituencies for or against monetary union, and that debate on monetary union is conditioned by factors that are largely extraneous to the substantive economic effects of a monetary union versus a regime of adjustable rates, and are associated either with the specific condition of the countries discussing such a reform, or with the specific time in which this discussion takes place.

A survey of the arguments raised in the recent debate on monetary union highlights the importance of these extraneous factors. They include: the economic policies undertaken to achieve convergence of inflation rates and low debt-to-GDP ratios; the presence of a recession in Europe; the fears raised by the German unification, that a monetary union in Europe will require transfer of resources from the rich countries to the poor countries; the political union, the "democratic deficit" and German dominance; a number of different country-specific issues; the belief that national currencies are a symbol of national pride.

Interestingly, it is not as easy to identify factors that could justify the remarkable success enjoyed by the project of monetary union only a couple of years ago. The desirability of a single currency in Europe has been discussed at least since Scitovski (1958), and supporters of a single currency in Europe have periodically emerged. Such support has, at least until very recently, been confined in rather narrow academic and policy circles.

International monetary issues do not easily excite public opinion. When they do, they seem to do it for the wrong reasons.

Notes

1. The model I discuss, for example, in Obstfeld (1985, 1988) and Giavazzi and Giovannini (1988).

2. General equilibrium models of the effects of removal of transactions costs have been studied by Casella (1992) and Persson (1992). These models provide a serious original attempt at identifying coalitions pro or against monetary union, which however are based on very special assumptions on the effects of inflation on the welfare of international versus domestic traders.

3. For example, Persson (1992) obtains the counter-intuitive result that—when the majority of citizens are involved in cross-border trade, a monetary union would be voted down in a referendum.

References

Calomiris, C. W. 1992. "Greenback Resumption and Silver Risk: The Economics and Politics of Monetary Regime Change in the United States, 1862–1900," NBER Working Paper No. 4166, September.

Casella, A. 1992. "Voting on the Adoption of a Common Currency," in M. B. Canzoneri, V. Grilli and P. R. Masson, eds., *Establishing a Central Bank: Issues in Europe and Lessons from the US*, Cambridge, UK: Cambridge University Press.

European Community. 1990. *One Market, One Money, European Economy*, No. 44, October.

Fischer, S. and F. Modigliani. 1978. "Towards an Understanding of the Real Effects and Costs of Inflation," *Weltwirtschaftliches Archiv* 114, no. 4.

Frieden, J. A. 1991a. "Greenbacks, Gold, and Silver: The Politics of American Exchange-Rate Policy, 1870–1973," mimeo, University of California at Los Angeles, April.

Frieden, J. A. 1991b. "Exchange-Rate Politics: Contemporary Lessons from American History," mimeo, University of California at Los Angeles, October.

Frieden, J. A. 1992. "Labor and the Politics of Exchange Rates: The Case of the European Monetary System," mimeo, University of California at Los Angeles, September.

Giavazzi, F. and A. Giovannini. 1989. "Monetary Policy Interactions under Managed Exchange Rates," *Economica*, 56, pp. 199–213.

King, M. A. and D. Fullerton. 1984. *The Taxation of Income from Capital*, Chicago: Chicago University Press.

Mundell, R. A. 1968. *International Economics*, New York: Macmillan.

Obstfeld, M. 1985. "Floating Exchange Rates: Experience and Prospects," *Brookings Papers on Economic Activity*, 2, pp. 369–450.

Obstfeld, M. 1988. "Comment on Buiter," in J. A. Frenkel, ed., *International Aspects of Fiscal Policies*, Chicago: Chicago University Press for NBER.

Persson, T. 1992. "Discussion of Casella's 'Voting on the Adoption of a Common Currency'," in M. B. Canzoneri, V. Grilli and P. R. Masson, eds., *Establishing a Central Bank: Issues in Europe and Lessons from the US*, Cambridge, UK: Cambridge University Press.

Scitovski, T. 1958. *Economic Theory and Western European Integration*, London: George Allen & Unwin.

IV

Beyond Transition

13

The Currency Reform as the Last Stage of Economic and Monetary Union: Some Policy Questions

(August 1991)

13.1 Introduction

The literature on the European Community's plans for Economic and Monetary Union (EMU) has reached gigantic proportions, and yet, to my knowledge, very little has been written on the ultimate step of monetary union, the substitution of national currencies with a single currency. This chapter discusses some policy problems of a (hypothetical) currency reform among EC countries.

Perhaps the most notable effort to date to describe how the passage from a group of different currencies into a single currency would, or should, occur is represented by the proposals by the UK government. With them, the UK government offered a strategy for monetary union based on the principle of competition among currencies. According to the first UK proposal (HM Treasury, 1989), the best way to establish a single currency is to encourage currency substitution as much as possible, and let the private markets choose the national money that provides the best transactions and store-of-value services. A second document (HM Treasury, 1990) advocated the introduction of an ECU that was to be freed from its basket nature, and was to be managed in a way to ensure that it would never depreciate vis-à-vis any of the currencies participating to the arrangement.

The two UK proposals have a common feature: they object to the idea of mandating the elimination of national currencies by law, and they opt for strategy that, in a sense, allows the private sector to determine for itself whether or not to adopt a single currency in Europe. Historically, government-imposed currency reforms are, of course, the rule: see, for example, the review of the postwar reforms in Europe by Dornbusch and Wolf (1990). This observation, however, is not sufficient to conclude that monetary reforms can only succeed if mandated by the government. The economic conditions of European countries in the immediate postwar made it necessary to accompany the redefinition of national monetary units with other reforms, aimed, among other things, at eliminating the large monetary overhangs accumulated from years of monetary financing of budget deficits accompanied by price fixing. By contrast, the economic conditions of the 12 EC countries at present do not seem to require any drastic monetary adjustment.[1]

Yet, a more fundamental objection to the "laissez-faire" strategy is that it might not achieve its stated objective, the adoption of a single currency, if markets do not respond in the intended way to the incentives laid out by the government, like for example those described in the two UK proposals.[2]

In this chapter I do not plan to criticize currency reforms "from the bottom up." Instead, my more limited objective is to describe the problems of the alternative reform strategy, where national moneys are substituted with a single currency by law.[3] The rest of the chapter is organized as follows. Section 13.2 contrasts "neutral" and "nonneutral" currency reforms, and traces the effects of the choice of the conversion rates of national currencies into a single currency on relative prices. Section 13.3 discusses the policy questions, with reference to the case of the EC countries. These questions include the choice of the conversion rates and the desirability of mandating conversion rates on certain private nominal contracts outstanding at the time of the reform.[4] Section 13.4 contains a few concluding remarks.

13.2   Rates of Conversion and Rates of Exchange

For the purposes of this chapter, I define a currency reform as the replacement of several national moneys with a single one. The rate of conversion of national currencies is the rate of exchange of the national currencies vis-à-vis the new, common numeraire. Holders of cash balances can obtain from the central banks or the banking sector new banknotes by presenting the old banknotes, at a rate of exchange equal to the rate of conversion. All outstanding nominal assets and liabilities are also rewritten.

I consider first the case of a single country, under a floating exchange-rate regime, which substitutes the national currency with another currency (new or existing). Let c represent the rate of conversion of the new currency and the old currency, that is, the price of one unit of the new currency in terms of the old currency. Let P, M and E denote the domestic price level, the stock of money balances and the nominal exchange rate (price of an arbitrary foreign currency in terms of the domestic currency). I use two superscripts: the superscript o denotes those variables in terms of the old currency, while the superscript n denotes those variables in terms of the new currency.

In a single-country currency reform, authorities announce c. This is the rate at which the central bank—or commercial banks under the instruction of the central bank—will exchange old banknotes for new. Authorities could also require that all, or a subset of, outstanding nominal contracts be rewritten at the announced rate, although this additional requirement is not, strictly speaking, the monetary reform, but a form of income policy that I will discuss in more detail below.

Given our notation, the effect of the currency reform on the nominal money stock is:

$$M^n = \frac{M^o}{c} \tag{1}$$

What will be the equilibrium response of prices and the exchange rate? Suppose that, free from the enforcement of the government, the private sector adopts prices in terms of the new currency by applying the same factor as the government, and in the foreign exchange market traders exchange the new currency with foreign moneys adopting the same rule:

$$cP^n = P^o \tag{2}$$

$$cE^n = E^o \tag{3}$$

This would clearly be an equilibrium, because all real variables are the same as before the currency reform was announced:

$$\frac{M^n}{P^n} = \frac{M^o/c}{P^o/c} = \frac{M^o}{P^o} \tag{4}$$

$$\frac{P^w E^n}{P^n} = \frac{P^w E^o/c}{P^o/c} = \frac{P^w E^o}{P^o} \tag{5}$$

Where P^w stands for prices of rest-of-the-world goods, in terms of rest-of-the-world currency.

Whether this will indeed be the equilibrium chosen by the private sector depends on the nature of the equilibrium before the reform, and on whether the reform leads agents to revise of expectations. If producers had no unfulfilled desire to change prices before the reform, and if the reform does not lead to a revision of expectations, then there would be no incentive to apply a conversion rate that differs from the official one, that is, there would be no incentive to change relative prices. On the other hand, if the reform came as a surprise, leading agents to revise expectations, then changes in relative prices are to be expected. Two illustrations of this phenomenon are:

• changes in inflationary expectations in the presence of perfectly flexible wages and prices, leading to changes in the demand for real money balances;

• changes in inflationary expectations in the presence of multi-period wage contracts. If wage contracts are written at a time when the currency reform is not expected, they discount a given loss of purchasing power that does not occur as a result of the reform. Thus the reform ends up changing real wages.

In summary, if the currency reform does not lead agents to want to change relative prices, real variables are independent of the chosen rate of conversion. Hence, governments are unconstrained in their choice of the rate of conversion of the old currency with the new currency.

The choice of the rate of conversion is not unconstrained in the case where several countries join in a currency reform that replaces their national moneys with a single one. Consider now two countries, which I call the domestic and the foreign country. Prices, moneys, exchange rates and the conversion rate of the foreign country are denoted by an asterisk. When the two old currencies are substituted by a single, new currency, the following is true by definition:

$$E^n = E^{*n}, \qquad P^n = P^{*n} \tag{6}$$

Consider now the equilibrium described above, where the conversion rates announced by the governments were also used by the private sector to set the new prices and the new exchange rate. Applying that rule to exchange rates we get

$$\frac{E^{*o}}{c^*} = \frac{E^o}{c}, \tag{7}$$

that is,

$$\frac{c}{c^*} = e^o \tag{8}$$

where e^o is the (old) bilateral exchange rate, the price of the foreign currency in terms of the domestic currency before the reform. Equation (8) says that, when two countries introduce a new, single currency, the rates of conversion determine the rate of exchange between the two currencies at the time of the reform. If conversion rates do not satisfy (8) nominal exchange rates among the currencies participating in the reform are changed at the time of the reform.

The natural question at this point is about the effects of such exchange-rate changes. Consider first the case where the conversion rates apply only to the exchanges of currency. The effect of the currency reform depends on the degree of price flexibility at the time of the reform. With perfectly flexible prices, the exchange-rate change that occurs at the time of the reform will only amount to a tax on the holders of cash balances denominated in the depreciating currency. If prices were not perfectly flexible, the exchange-rate change would affect directly the relative valuation of the goods and services whose prices do not move freely at the time the reform is implemented.

The degree of price flexibility is one of the central questions in macroeconomic theory. Empirical evidence generally suggests that, especially in the second postwar period, aggregate price indices have adjusted to changes in the state of the economy apparently only to a limited extent.[5] Failure of prices and wages to adjust is ascribed to two distinct sets of phenomena: long term contracts and various kinds of adjustment costs. In the event of a currency reform, and absent government restrictions, long term contracts which specify a given payments schedule in nominal terms have to be re-written, hence this source of nominal rigidity would be absent. The once-and-for-all nature of the reform suggests that also the rigidities arising from menu costs should not be important: agents would take the opportunity of changing the unit of account to set their relative prices right. Hence my maintained assumption is that at the time of a currency reform the degree of wage and price flexibility is highest.

With flexible prices, the channels through which exchange-rate changes affect the real economy are the wealth and substitution effects of the changes in the real stock of money. In the standard two-sector model,[6] an exchange-rate change—say, a devaluation of the domestic currency—leads to a decrease in spending, a fall in output and the relative price of nontraded goods, an increase in output of traded goods and a trade-balance surplus (or a fall in the trade-balance deficit). The fall in spending arises from the decrease in the real value of wealth brought about by the nominal exchange-rate devaluation. The effect of the devaluation on the relative price of nontraded goods (the real exchange rate) equals to the change in spending on nontraded goods arising from the devaluation, divided by the absolute value of the slopes of the (general equilibrium) demand and supply functions for nontraded goods. As the discussion in the next section will argue, the crucial parameter in this expression appears to be the effect of the exchange-rate devaluation on spending in nontradeables.

In the model described above, changes in the stock of real money balances do not have any impact on marginal rates of substitution among any goods. This is of course a simplifying assumption. Models of money in the utility function[7] can be parametrized in such a way that a change in real money balances changes the marginal rate of substitution between traded and nontraded goods.

The last channel of transmission of exchange-rate changes to the real economy, typically neglected in the traditional open-economy macroeconomic models, is the financial system. Financial intermediaries are subject to reserve requirements, often in the form of cash. A currency devaluation is a tax on the reserves held by financial intermediaries. In the absence of concomitant rules adjusting reserve requirements, a currency depreciation leads to increased demand for reserves, and to a contraction of credit. See, for example, Greenwood and Williamson (1989) and Jefferson (1990).

13.3 The Policy Questions

13.3.1 The Choice of Conversion Rates

Historically, the conversion rate chosen in a currency reform is either a power of 10 or the spot exchange rate of a reference currency. The former is the case of the most recent currency reform in Argentina, the so-called Austral Plan of June 1985.[8] Currency and sight deposits were exchanged at a rate of 1000 to 1 (1000 pesos for 1 austral). The latter is the case of Nicaragua, where the new currency, the Cordoba Oro, immediately after the reform of September 1990 exchanged at par with the US dollar: the conversion rate was 9,108,715,994.4 Cordobas for 1 Cordoba Oro, not a power of 10. These choices reflect two objectives of policymakers: simplification of the operation and an attempt to bolster the credibility of the new currency and the new monetary policy. The Austral conversion rate is one that simplifies calculations of new prices. The Cordoba Oro conversion rate is meant to induce the public to think that the parity with the dollar is there to stay. In the intention of policymakers, the currency reform in Nicaragua was meant to be part of a dollarization program, which did not take place.

In the case of European countries the special nature of the currency reform, which involves the creation of a single currency out of several national currencies, does not allow using conversion rates that—for all currencies—are powers of 10. The reason is that, given the existing bilateral exchange rates of European moneys, the consistency condition in equation (8) would not be satisfied. The discussion in the previous section has shown that, if the reform did not change in a significant way expectations, the official conversion rate would be used to translate private nominal contracts and prices, but only if the exchange rate is not modified. By contrast, if the currency reform affects the exchange rate, it is in the interest of the private sector not to adopt the official conversion rate, and therefore the benefit of round numbers in terms of simplifying price calculations is lost.

Table 13.1 illustrates the size of exchange-rate changes that would be induced by the selection of a set of rounded conversion rates. The table

Table 13.1
The effect of rounding conversion rates

Country	ECU rate	Conversion rate	Implied DM rate	Actual DM rate	Percent deviation
UK	0.686789	0.6	0.333333	0.339775	−1.90
IRL	0.755968	0.7	0.388888	0.374000	3.98
GER	2.021302	1.8	1.000000	1.000000	0.00
NED	2.278833	2.0	1.111111	1.127408	−1.45
FRA	6.871380	6.0	3.333333	3.399482	−1.95
DEN	7.824769	7.0	3.888888	3.871152	0.46
BEL	41.62359	37	20.55555	20.59246	−0.18
SPA	126.6148	110	61.11111	62.64021	−2.44
POR	174.8539	160	88.88888	86.50557	2.76
GRE	222.3606	200	111.1111	110.0086	1.00
ITA	1510.901	1500	833.3333	747.4889	11.48

Note: The first column contains the name of the country (Belgium and Luxembourg under BEL). The second column contains the price of 1 ECU in terms of that country's currency (from *The Wall Street Journal*, August 3, 1991; exchange rates on August 2, 1991). The third column contains a set of conversion rates of the 11 currencies into the new single currency. The fourth column contains the implied bilateral rates for the Deutsche mark. The fifth column contains the actual bilateral rates for the Deutsche mark on August 2, 1991. The last column contains the percent difference of the fourth and the fifth column (the implied percent depreciation of each currency relative to the Deutsche mark).

reports the spot rate of the ECU on August 2, 1991, and a set of rounded conversion rates for the eleven European currencies. The implied and actual Deutsche mark rates are also shown, together with the percent implicit devaluations of national currencies relative to the mark. To understand how the table is constructed, note that if the first two sets of numbers on the left were equal (conversion rates equal to spot ECU rates), the next two columns would be equal, and the last column on the right would be a column of zeros.

The conversion rates were chosen from an arbitrary set of round numbers close to the ECU spot exchange rates. Note that the implied exchange-rate changes, except in the case of the lira and the Irish punt, are not large. Thus the table suggests that, in several countries, the public could use as a rule of thumb the official conversion rate. Note, however, that Belgium and Luxembourg's conversion rate of 37, the UK's of 0.6, Ireland's of 0.7, and Germany's of 1.8 do not appear to much facilitate price translations.

An additional important question in the choice of conversion rates is the selection of the numeraire. European parliaments could choose the ECU, as in the example of table 13.1, thus forcing all residents of the countries participating in the reform to adopt a new unit of account. Alternatively, they could choose the Deutsche mark—assuming that Germany participates in the currency reform. The choice of the Deutsche mark would save the cost of conversion at least to the residents of Germany, and could also be a psychological device, given the reputation of the German currency as a better store of value than most other European currencies. It is however highly unlikely that European parliaments will accept keeping the name "Deutsche mark" for the new European currency. Hence the adoption of the DM could be accompanied by a change of name: say, from DM to ECU. The new ECU would thus not equal the ECU currently in existence.[9] In the example of the table, by contrast, the old and the new ECU are approximately identical.

13.3.2 How to Do a "Last Realignment"

A crucial aspect of the plan of gradual monetary reform laid out in the Delors Report is the fact that it calls for convergence of inflation and at the same time allows exchange-rate realignments. If expectations are an important determinant of inflation, an exchange-rate devaluation accommodates inflation differentials and simply validates the public's expectations that the exchange-rate targets are not to be believed. Thus inflation convergence and exchange-rate devaluations are quite unlikely to go to-gether. For this reason, it has been advocated that, if at all, exchange-rate devaluations can only occur at the very last step of the gradual monetary reform, when national currencies are replaced by a single currency: from this time on the credibility of the weak currencies is no more an issue, and the expectations of wage and price setters will be formed on their percep-tion of the anti-inflationary stance of the European central bank.[10]

What would be the purpose of a last exchange-rate realignment? If price and wage setters believe that there is a positive probability that the currency will be depreciated, wages and prices increase at a rate that is not consistent with a fixed nominal exchange rate, building up misalign-ments of relative prices. Giovannini (1990b), Dornbusch (1991) and Froot and Rogoff (1991) draw attention to these misalignments. The last au-thors also provide evidence from regression analyses which they interpret as indicating that the movements of real exchange rates are due to the credibility problem described above.

Having explained what might motivate an exchange-rate realignment at the time of a currency reform, we now need to ask how such a realign-ment can induce the change in relative prices that is deemed desirable. In the previous section I have argued that at the time of a currency reform prices are likely to be highly flexible, and that an exchange-rate deprecia-tion in that case becomes a tax on nominal money balances. How much can that tax affect relative prices? As I pointed out in section 13.2 the transmission is through the wealth effect of the exchange-rate change. Table 13.2 shows that such an effect is insignificant. The table reports the percent share of high-powered money in total wealth, as in the IMF MULTIMOD model. In that model, the long-run elasticity of consump-tion with respect to financial and human wealth is unity (consumption is a constant fraction of total wealth). Thus the elasticity of spending to

Table 13.2
High-powered money as percent of total wealth (averages: 1970–1989)

Country	High-powered money: % of total wealth
France	0.32
Germany	0.49
Italy	0.68
United Kingdom	0.23

Source: International Monetary Fund, MULTIMOD model.

a change in the real value of high-powered money is just the fraction of high-powered money in total wealth. The numbers in the table imply that such elasticity is nearly insignificant.

No empirical estimates on the effects of a change in required reserves on the supply of credit and the real economy are, to my knowledge, available.[11] Reserve requirements differ widely across European countries, and interest rates paid on reserves differ as well. The effect of an exchange-rate devaluation on the real value of reserves is of course independent on whether they pay interest, since they are fixed in nominal terms. The equilibrium effects of the devaluation on credit supply, by contrast, does depend on whether the interest paid on reserves approximates a market rate, which would in part embody expectations of such devaluation, or is fixed by law.

The above discussion has indicated that, unless the public displays some form of money illusion, and wrongly applies the official conversion rates to translate outstanding nominal contracts, an exchange-rate devaluation at the time of the currency reform has little hope of significantly affecting relative prices. Perhaps for this reason all countries mandate conversion rates for a large number of nominal contracts outstanding at the time of the reform.

Mandating conversion rates is a type of incomes policy: private parties are imposed a new set of real payments in their outstanding nominal contracts. How should the conversion rates for prices and wages be chosen? If the source of misalignment that governments intend to correct is the lack of credibility of the fixed exchange rate, the answer to this question is straightforward: a conversion rate which induces exactly the same exchange-rate depreciation that was expected by wage and price setters and that gave rise to the relative-price distortion has the effect of accommodating exchange-rate expectations, thus eliminating distortions.

This clearcut policy rule, however, conceals a number of serious practical problems, familiar to observers of actual experiences of countries which enacted incomes policies:

• What exactly should be such conversion rates? A solution of this problem requires knowledge of equilibrium relative prices across countries. Widely different productivity performances across countries, the difficulty of measuring productivity in the services and government sectors, and the occurrence of structural changes in individual industries, all make the exercise of extracting the expectations component in the dynamics of prices and wages a daunting task.

• Mandatory conversion rates can be enforced easily in some sectors—consider for example public-sector employees—but can be an administrative nightmare elsewhere in the economy.

• It is not possible to avoid that those who feel hurt most by this policy will attempt to regain the lost purchasing power as soon as they are allowed to.

The question of the rate of conversion of long-term debt deserves special attention: it is particularly relevant for countries that have substantial stocks of public debt denominated in long-term fixed-rate securities. If expected inflation and interest rates decrease after the currency reform—even in the absence of exchange-rate changes—long-term lenders have a capital gain, matched by a capital loss of long-term borrowers. This wealth redistribution can be avoided with two measures, which can be shown to produce equivalent wealth transfers. The first measure is mandating a conversion rate for long-term nominal debt that decreases the real value of the principal. The second measure is allowing long-term lenders and borrowers to mark-to-market the terms of their contract. Both devices eliminate the capital gain of lenders.

In general, the proposition that surprises induce misallocation of resources can be applied to this problem as well, and suggests that fulfilling expectation of exchange-rate changes minimizes distortions. As pointed out above, however, these policies require accurate estimates of private expectations.

Both asking private parties to recontract (or mark to market) and mandating conversion rates are policies whose feasibility and social costs are determined, among other things, by legal factors. If existing contracts have clauses covering the eventuality of a change in national currency it seems that mandating conversion rates might encounter substantial resistance and litigation. If, on the other hand, such an eventuality is not covered, parties might be reluctant to recontract. In this case mandating conversion rates could meet less resistance.

13.4   Concluding Remarks

This chapter has discussed the problems of the substitution of several national currencies with a single currency. The focus has been the plan for Economic and Monetary Union of European countries. With reference to the pattern of spot exchange rates of European currencies, I have analyzed the question of the choice of the rate of conversion of each national currency to the single European currency.

A number of observers have advocated the desirability of a last exchange-rate realignment to occur at the time the single European currency
is introduced. I have shown that an exchange-rate realignment alone is
very unlikely to produce the effects that are called for by its advocates. A
significant correction of relative price distortions can only occur if authorities mandate conversion rates on a range of outstanding nominal contracts, a measure that is effectively an incomes policy.

Exchange-rate changes at the time of the currency reform might be desired by governments for two sets of reasons. On one hand, governments
might want to affect the allocation of resources by changing the exchange
rate, in pursuit of objectives that are not directly linked to monetary policy objectives. These types of exchange-rate changes have been ruled out
by the Delors Report.

Another reason why governments could pursue exchange-rate changes
is to offset the distortions created by the lack of credibility of the monetary convergence plans, discussed above in section 13.3.2. The discussion
in that section has argued that such exchange-rate changes, if chosen to
fulfill expectations, minimize the welfare costs of expectations errors. Such
a conclusion suggests an additional device to smooth out the transition
to a single currency: announcing in advance—say two years ahead of
time—the rates of conversion of the currencies participating to the reform and the new single currency. These conversion rates, which could be
a set of round numbers similar to those in table 13.1, could be declared by
the European governments—and endorsed by the European Commission—only as intentions, in order to allow for adjustments which might
be called for in case credibility problems arise, perhaps due to unforeseen
exogenous shocks. If these conversion rates are credible, economies will
have the time to adapt to them and the final reform would give rise
to minimal disruptions. If they are not, governments will have to, again,
fulfill expectations.

Notes

1. Drastic fiscal adjustments might be desirable in some EC member countries.

2. There are reasons to doubt that this strategy would lead to the adoption of a single currency. Suffices here to mention that, in the presence of "thick market" externalities that
presumably characterize money demand and currency substitution in an integrated economic area, the market coordination needed to adopt a single currency might not be easily
accomplished.

3. This exercise might help to clarify what would happen in stage three of Delors plan
(Committee for the Study of Economic and Monetary Union, 1989), which European gov-

ernments have agreed to start in 1997. According to the Delors plan, during stage three exchange rates are irrevocably fixed, monetary policy is implemented solely by the European central bank, official foreign exchange reserves are pooled, and "preparations of a technical or regulatory nature" are made for the transition to a single Community currency. These preparations are not described in any further detail in the Report.

4. I do not discuss, however, the intra EC wealth distribution arising from the reform, and the incentive that governments might have to bargain on it. For an analysis of these issues, see Chang (1991).

5. See Mussa (1986) for evidence on price stickiness in open economies, and Mankiw and Romer (1991) for a collection of theoretical essays on sticky prices.

6. See, for example, Dornbusch (1973).

7. As Feenstra (1986) shows can arise from transactions-costs models of money demand à la Baumol (1952) and Tobin (1956). See Heymann (1990) for a description and analysis of the plan.

8. The problem of finding the round conversion rates that maximize an objective function defined in terms of deviations of the implied bilateral rates from target rates can be formally setup as an integer programming problem. The numbers in the table are the result of some experiments with such a programming problem.

9. This would require that all outstanding ECU contracts be translated using the ECU/DM exchange rate.

10. See Giovannini (1990a,b) for a discussion. Froot and Rogoff (1991) argue that the anticipation of the last devaluation destabilizes exchange rates even in the early stages of the monetary reform.

11. Accounting relations imply: (Credit to nonbank sector)/(non-bank deposits) = (1 − req.res.ratio) − req.res.ratio x (inter-bank deposits)/(non-bank deposits). Given average required reserves and the size of interbank deposits in EC countries the change of credits to the nonbank sector induced by a change in required reserves is a very small number.

References

Baumol, W. J. 1953. "The Transactions Demand for Cash: An Inventory Theoretic Approach," *Quarterly Journal of Economics*, 66, pp. 545–556.

Chang, R. 1991. "Bargaining a Monetary Union," mimeo, New York University, January.

Committee for the Study of Economic and Monetary Union. 1989. *Report on Economic and Monetary Union in the European Community*, Luxembourg: Office for Official Publications of the European Communities.

Dornbusch, R. 1973. "Devaluation, Money, and Nontraded Goods," *American Economic Review*, 63, No. 5, December, pp. 871–880.

Dornbusch, R. 1991. "Problems of European Monetary Integration," in A. Giovannini and C. Mayer, *European Financial Integration*, Cambridge: Cambridge University Press.

Dornbusch, R. and H. Wolf. 1990. "Monetary Overhang and Reforms in the 1940s," mimeo, MIT, October.

Feenstra, R. C. 1986. "Functional Equivalence Between Liquidity Costs and the Utility of Money," *Journal of Monetary Economic*, 17, pp. 271–291.

Froot, K. A. and K. Rogoff. 1991. "The EMS, the EMU, and the Transition to a Common Currency," *NBER Macroeconomics Annual*.

Giovannini, A. 1990a. *The Transition to European Monetary Union*, Essays in International Finance 178, Princeton, NJ: International Finance Section, Princeton University, November, see also chapter 7 in this volume.

Giovannini, A. 1990b. "European Monetary Reform: Progress and Prospects," *Brookings Papers on Economic Activity* 2, see also chapter 8 in this volume.

Greenwood, J. and S. D. Williamson. 1989. "International Financial Intermediation and Aggregate Fluctuations Under Alternative Exchange Rate Regimes," *Journal of Monetary Economics*, 23, pp. 401–431.

Heymann, D. 1990. *Tres Ensayos Sobre Inflación y Políticas de Estabilización*, Documento de Trabajo 18, Buenos Aires: CEPAL.

HM Treasury. 1989. *An Evolutionary Approach to Economic and Monetary Union*, London: HM Treasury, November.

HM Treasury. 1990. "Economic and Monetary Union: Beyond Stage 1", Chancellor's Speech to German Industry Forum, June 20, London.

Jefferson, P. N. 1990. "Money in the Theory of Financial Intermediation," mimeo, Department of Economics, Columbia University, October.

Mankiw, N. G. and Romer, D., eds. 1991. *New Keynesian Economics I: Imperfect Competition and Sticky Prices*, Cambridge, MA: MIT Press.

Mussa, M. 1986. "Nominal Exchange Rate Regimes and the Behavior of Real Exchange Rates," in *Real Business Cycles, Real Exchange Rates, and Actual Policies*, Carnegie-Rochester Conference Series on Public Policy, 25, (eds.) K. Brunner and A. H. Meltzer. Amsterdam: North Holland.

Tobin, J. 1956. "The Interest Elasticity of Transactions Demand for Cash," *Review of Economics and Statistics*, 38, pp. 241–247.

14

Central Banking in a Monetary Union: Reflections on the Proposed Statute of the European Central Bank

(March 1992)

14.1 Introduction

The member countries of the European Community (EC) have been studying and debating the idea of forming a monetary union at least since the early 1970s. After a remarkable acceleration of events and diplomatic initiatives—which is still largely unexplained by scholars—the monetary union has become very likely, taking most observers, especially on this side of the Atlantic, by surprise.

EC governments convened, in December 1989, an Intergovernmental Conference to prepare the changes in the Treaty of Rome (the fundamental law of the EC) required to create a central bank, and the conditions for it to perform its tasks. The Conference started working in December 1990, and concluded a draft revision of the Treaty of Rome by December 1991. The new Treaty (which I will call the Maasticht Treaty, from the name of the town where the European Council met) was unanimously endorsed and signed by all Community members' heads of state in December 1991. It now needs to be ratified within individual countries.

The ratification process does not have a fixed deadline, although it is understood that member countries should not carry it much longer than the end of 1992.[1] Individual countries' ratification procedures differ: Denmark, France, and Ireland will have decided to hold a referendum. Most countries will submit the Treaty for ratification with special parliamentary sessions. Countries ratify the Treaty *in toto*, although they can express exceptions about individual articles. So far (July 1992) only three countries have completed their own ratification procedures. Ireland and Luxembourg have ratified the Treaty, while Denmark has rejected it with a national referendum.

The nonratification by Denmark has, in principle, invalidated the Maastricht Treaty. Article R of the proposed amendments states that the new

Treaty is effective only when all members of the EC have deposited their own ratification documents. Yet, the Danish referendum has not stopped the ratification process in the other EC countries. It has, however, started a very lively (and clearly very desirable) debate, both within most EC countries and internationally, on the strengths and weaknesses of Economic and Monetary Union (EMU) and on the other part of the Treaty amendments, political union. What will happen if only Denmark ends up not ratifying is not at all clear. Since most other countries are quite reluctant to reopen the negotiations on the individual articles, it is possible that the Danish government would, by its own initiative, present the Treaty for ratification to the Danish electorate one more time. On the other hand, if more countries fail to ratify, it is almost sure that EMU as currently conceived by the Maastricht Treaty will not happen.

If the amendments to the Treaty of Rome come into effect, and if governments fulfill their commitments by not repudiating the Treaty of Rome, Europe (or a subset of it) will have a new, single currency by 1999 at the latest.

A successful ratification of the Maastricht Treaty would be the conclusion of a rather exciting period, which saw governments, monetary authorities, and academics debating publicly and within conference rooms on the desirability of a monetary union in the EC, on the ways to achieve it, and on its effects on markets and institutions. Inevitably, the new Treaty reflects this debate, as well as the diplomatic efforts and bargaining power of different countries, and the experience and evolution of central banking over the years.

The purpose of this chapter is to discuss the statutes of the central bank in the Treaty of Rome from the perspective of the theory of central banking.[2] Goodfriend and King (1988) discuss central bank activities by making a distinction between monetary policy and banking policy. The former is the manipulation of the total assets of the central bank to achieve certain objectives in terms of the price level and interest rates. The latter includes changes in the composition of the assets related to loans to commercial banks or other financial institutions, together with financial regulation and banking supervision. I adopt Goodfriend and King's distinction and identify what I regard as the most important issues relating to monetary and banking policies of the European central bank.

The rest of the paper is organized as follows. Section 14.2 describes the institutional framework by providing a self-contained description of the statutes of the European Central Bank (ECB). Section 14.3 discusses the issues relating to the monetary-policy function. Section 14.4 discusses issues related to banking policy. Finally, section 14.5 contains a few concluding observations.

14.2   The Institutions

As a result of the Intergovernmental Conference, the Treaty of Rome has undergone a number of major revisions.[3] The *Title* of the Treaty of Rome on Economic Policy has been replaced by a *Title* on Economic and Monetary Policy. In addition, several protocols have been added to the Treaty, including a *Protocol on the Statute of the European System of Central Banks and of the European Central Bank* (henceforth the Protocol), a *Protocol on the Statute of the European Monetary Institute*, and a *Protocol on the Excessive-Deficits Procedure* (from now on I will use the term "statutes" when generally referring to the articles in the Treaty and in the various protocols).

One interesting feature of the proposed revisions of the Treaty is the inclusion of provisions regulating the transition to the monetary union together with provisions regulating the steady state, the monetary union and its institutions. Transitional provisions contain rules on transitional institutions, obligations for member countries and rules on convergence criteria, which have been established to determine which countries participate in the final currency reform, and when.

The transition stages covered in the Treaty are stage two and stage three. The second stage starts on January 1, 1994. By this deadline, countries have to adapt their own laws—and in particular those concerning central bank operations and relations of the central bank with government agencies—to conform with the Treaty (article 109d). During stage two there will be a European Monetary Institute (EMI) in charge of monetary policy coordination and, in particular, in charge of preparing the conditions to manage a single currency (including harmonization of macroeconomic and monetary statistics, technical preparation of banknotes, and drafting of the operating procedures of national central banks within the system of national central banks after the monetary union). In particular, the EMI has the responsibility of preparing, by the end of December 1996, the report containing the regulatory, organizational, and logistical framework necessary for the European System of Central Banks (ESCB, to be defined below) to perform its tasks in the third stage (article 109e).

The most critical set of obligations of member countries are in regard to macroeconomic performance. In particular, countries willing to join the single currency area have to achieve "a high degree of sustainable convergence" (article 109i). The criteria adopted to evaluate such convergence include price stability, sustainability of public finances, exchange-rate stability and interest-rate convergence. While price stability and interest-rate convergence are relative criteria, expressed in terms of the best performers (exchange-rate stability is a relative criterion by definition), the criterion of sustainability of public finances is defined in terms of fixed ratios of deficits and debt to GDP.[4]

Before the end of 1996 the Council of Economic and Finance Ministers has to vote, by qualified majority (whereby each country's representative casts a vote weighted by that country's size, defined appropriately), on whether each individual Member State has achieved a high degree of sustainable convergence, according to the criteria above. These criteria, therefore, are not to be regarded as binding (otherwise the Council would not have to vote). They are instead a frame of reference. In particular, in the case of the public finance ratios, a country may be regarded as fulfilling them if the deficit and debt ratios "have declined substantially and have reached a level that comes close to a reference value" (see article 104c, 2 (a) and 2 (b)). On that date, the Council also votes on whether a simple majority of Member States satisfies the convergence criteria. The outcome of these votes is passed to the Council of Heads of State, which votes (by qualified majority) on: whether a majority of member countries satisfies the convergence criteria; whether it is appropriate to move to the third stage of EMU (the irrevocable locking of exchange rates and the introduction of a single currency); and when to do so.

If the Heads of State find that a majority of countries do not satisfy the convergence criteria, or they find it not appropriate to move forward, stage three will start only in January 1999. By that time, the Heads of State only have to determine which countries are qualified to join stage three. Those countries left out of stage three have a special status: they are "Member States with a derogation." Their situation is periodically reviewed, and their membership to the monetary union is voted on by the Council every two years.

The insertion of the laws concerning monetary institutions in the Treaty of Rome raises the following question: to what extent can we regard the laws on the new central bank as "immutable?" This question does not have an easy answer, since it hinges on the interpretation of the status of the Treaty of Rome. On one hand, the Treaty of Rome has the status of any other international treaty, which countries are in a position to reject unilaterally. On the other hand, however, the Treaty of Rome is unlike other international treaties, since it sets up institutions which, as in the case of the European Central Bank, subtract some national sovereignty from member countries. In that sense, the Treaty of Rome can be regarded as constitutional law. Certainly, changes in the Treaty of Rome involve a complex coordination of all member countries' governments and parliaments, and hence are especially difficult to achieve.

The monetary authority envisaged for the European monetary union is a federal one. The European System of Central Banks is made up of a European Central Bank and of national central banks. The ECB has legal personality and governs, through its decision-making bodies, the ESCB (article 106). Monetary policy is formulated by the ECB, and is implemented, under instructions from the ECB, by the national central banks. Article 14 paragraph 2 of the Protocol states explicitly that national central banks are in a subordinate position relative to the ECB. They have to act "in accordance with the guidelines and instructions of the ECB," and the Governing Council of the ECB is responsible for ensuring that national central banks comply with these guidelines and instructions. National central banks can retain functions that are not specified in the Treaty and its protocols, to the extent that such functions do not interfere with the objectives of the ESCB. Hence these functions are not regarded as central banking functions.

The governing bodies of the ESCB are the Governing Council and the Executive Board (article 106). The former is made up of the members of the executive board and the governors of national central banks. It votes by simple majority except on financial matters relating to the capital and the income of the bank. The Executive Board is made up of the president, the vice president, and four members (article 11 paragraph 1 of the Protocol). It executes the policies formulated by the Governing Council, both directly and by instructing the national central banks. It also prepares the Governing Council meetings (article 12, Protocol).

As far as the monetary policy tasks of the ESCB are concerned, article 105 states that its primary objective is to maintain price stability, and that without prejudice to that objective the ESCB shall support the policies of the Community aimed at achieving its general objectives. These objectives are laid out in the amended article 2 of the Treaty. They are "the promotion of a harmonious and balanced development of economic activities, sustainable and non-inflationary growth respecting the environment, a high degree of convergence of economic performance, a high level of employment and of social protection, the raising of the standard and the quality of living, and economic and social cohesion and solidarity among Member States." The ECB has the exclusive right of currency issuance, it conducts foreign exchange market intervention, it manages member central banks' foreign exchange reserves, and it "defines and implement the monetary policy of the Community."

With regard to banking policy, the tasks of the ESCB are defined more ambiguously. Article 105 paragraph 5 states that the ESCB shall *contribute* to the smooth conduct of policies pursued by the competent authorities relating to prudential supervision of credit institutions and the stability of the financial system. Article 108 paragraph 4 says that, with a unanimous vote, on a proposal from the Commission, after consulting with the ECB and having received the assent of the European parliament, the Council of Ministers may confer upon the ECB specific tasks concerning policies relating to the prudential supervision of credit institutions and other financial institutions with the exception of insurance companies.

While the ECB retains control of day-to-day foreign exchange operations (article 105 paragraph 2), decisions about the foreign exchange regime are left with the Council of Ministers. According to article 109, the Council of Ministers, acting unanimously—on a recommendation from the ECB or the Commission, after consulting the ECB in order to reach consensus on the effects of such a decision on the objective of price stability, and after consulting with the European parliament—can enter formal exchange-rate arrangements involving the ECU and currencies outside the European Community.

The independence of the ESCB is codified in several articles. First, the very organization of the Treaty removes some of the ambiguities on central banks duties that surround, for example, the Federal Reserve and the Bundesbank. The stature of the ESCB is contained in a chapter of the Treaty of Rome on "Monetary Policy," separate from the chapter on "Economic Policy." The latter chapter (in article 102a) states the general principle that Member States shall conduct their economic policies with a view to contributing to the achievements of the objectives of the Community, as defined in article 2 (see above). However, the ESCB does not have to obey this general principle for two reasons. First, because its regulations are not contained in the rules on economic policies, monetary policy is regarded as partially distinct from economic policy. Second, because—as I mentioned above—its own support to the objectives of the Community is codified in article 105, where the condition of no conflict with the objective of price stability is explicitly stated.

Additional safeguards of the ESCB independence are contained in a series of articles, including article 106 (mentioning that the ECB has legal personality); article 107 (stating that neither the ECB, nor any national central bank, nor any member of their decision-making bodies can seek or accept instructions from the Community, any national or local government, and that, at the same time, the Community, national and local governments undertake to respect the principle not to influence the ECB or national central banks); article 109a (specifying that the only obligation of routine information of the ECB is the publication of an annual report, that, however, the European Parliament can request to hear the president of the ECB or another member of its Executive Board, and that the term of office of all members of the Executive Board is 8 years—a period exceeding the term of the legislature in any one Member State).

Finally, the independence of the ESCB is defended by all articles dealing with government budget deficits. Article 104 prohibits overdraft facilities or other credit facilities with the ESCB to Community institutions, state, or local governments. Article 104a prevents measures aimed at establishing privileged access of governments to any financial institution. Article 104b prevents the Community or any Member State from bailing out any other Member State, and article 104c lays out the complex "excessive deficits" procedure.

The excessive-deficits procedure is designed to force countries from running too high budget deficits and accumulating too much government debt. It is followed not only in the transition period leading to monetary union (as discussed above), but also when the monetary union is in place. Excessive deficits are identified by the Commission, which uses the two criteria involving deficits and government debt mentioned before, and takes into account other factors, including the position of the country in the business cycle. On recommendation from the Commission, the Council of Ministers decides—by qualified majority—whether excessive deficits exist. It makes recommendations to the country in question on means to correct the excessive deficits, and adopts sanctions if such recommendations are not followed.[5]

A few articles in the Protocol (Chapter on "Monetary Functions and Operations of ECB ") specify the instruments at the disposal of the European Central Bank. They include:

• Open market operations. There is no constraint in the Treaty on the securities eligible for open-market operations. In particular, there is no prohibition of the use of government securities for that purpose.

• Discount policy ("credit operations with credit institutions or other market participants, with lending being based on adequate collateral"). It is left to the ECB to state the rules under which both open market operations and discount policy will be administered.

• The setting of reserve requirements.

Article 20 of the Protocol says that the ECB is not explicitly prevented from adopting other types of monetary control. That article, however, prevents the use of instruments that are not consistent with "the principle of an open market economy with free competition," and therefore seems to rule out direct credit ceilings—which until very recently have been one of the main instruments of central bank policy in countries like France and Italy.

14.2.1 Discussion of the ECB Statutes

The most peculiar characteristic of the ECB is that it is the central bank of a monetary union which is not part of a full-fledged political union. It is, in this sense, similar to the International Monetary Fund (IMF), which was supposed to regulate an international monetary system without a political union. However, the major difference between the two institutions is their relation with national monetary authorities. One of the problems of the IMF was precisely the subsidiary role of that institution relative to national central banks. Hence, the silence of the Articles of Agreement on the causes of the "fundamental disequilibria" which justify parity realignments (and can include divergent monetary policies) and on Article VII regarding the actions to be undertaken if a currency becomes "scarce." The IMF, not being in a position to regularly affect national monetary policies in a direct way, attempts to induce a sort of monetary policy coordination indirectly, through a series of special alarm bells (including scarce currency). By contrast, the ECB is explicitly set up to substitute for national monetary authorities. It subtracts from national sovereignties even more than the gold standard, since under the gold standard countries could suspend convertibility or change gold parities.

A discussion of the laws on the ECB should start with the two main issues on the monetary policy functions of central banks. The first is the authority's accountability. It is widely suspected that central banks carry significant powers to affect the economy. How can they be prevented from using their powers to pursue policies that are not in the interest of the public? While making the central bank accountable might decrease the risk of misusing its powers, at the same time it might increase its vulnerability to external influences.

The second issue is in regard to the use of rules versus discretion. The evolution of the international monetary system has seen an increased role for central banks' discretionary policies, as countries progressively abandoned the strict gold-standard rules which prevailed until the start of

World War I. The adoption of fixed rules could resolve the accountability-independence tradeoff, since rules defend the public from the central bank authority, but at the same time they defend the central bank from external pressures. In addition, simple rules are shown to be desirable as a means to stabilize expectations. On the other hand, simple rules take away any flexibility that the monetary authority might need to face unexpected or large exogenous shocks.

Where do the ESCB statutes place an institution in the tradeoff between accountability and independence, and in the tradeoff between rules and discretion? This question is best answered with reference to other central bank statutes. The natural comparison is with the Federal Reserve System and the Bundesbank, both federal central banks, created, respectively, in 1913 and 1957.

The Federal Reserve was created with a law of Congress when the gold standard was fully in effect. Despite its original statutory obligation to follow a fixed rule, the Fed is subject to external oversight. The Chairman of the Board of Governors is regularly called by the House and Senate Committees. Furthermore, despite the gold standard rule, the Federal reserve was also supposed to "furnish an elastic currency [and] to afford means of rediscounting commercial paper." Hence, as Friedman and Schwartz (1963) note, it was subject to both the currency principle of the gold standard rule and the banking principle of the real bills doctrine—a situation of potential conflict.

The fact that the Federal Reserve Act is an ordinary law of Congress empowers Congress to change it by its own initiative, and implicitly allows Congress and the administration to exercise informal pressure to influence the Fed policies.

After the abandonment of the gold standard and the end of World War II, the objectives of the Federal Reserves have been changed. The Employment Act of 1946 stated that "it is the continuing policy and responsibility of the Federal Government to use all practicable means [...] to coordinate all its plans, functions, and resources for the purpose of coordinating and maintaining [...] conditions under which there will be afforded useful employment [...] and to promote maximum employment, production, and purchasing power." This declaration of policy implicitly called upon the Federal Reserve System to systematically use monetary policy to promote employment. The mentioning of "purchasing power" (of what?) leads one to suspect that the employment objective could not jeopardize the objective of price stability, but no further detail is furnished in the law, which is about setting up the Council of Economic Advisers and the Joint Economic Committee.

The Deutsche Bundesbank Act was, instead, drafted to empower an institution to manage a fiat currency. Article 3 of the Deutsche Bundesbank Act states that the Bundesbank regulates the quantity of money in circulation "with the aim of safeguarding the currency." Notice that—while apparently strongly worded—the article does not even specify that safeguarding the currency implies maintaining price stability.

Article 12 states that: "Without prejudice to the performance of its functions, the Deutsche Bundesbank is required to support the general economic policy of the Federal Government. In exercising the powers conferred by this Act, it is independent of instructions from the Federal Government." Yet, meetings of the Central Bank Council of the Bundesbank can be attended by members of the government, who have no right to vote, but may propose motions (article 13, paragraph 2). More importantly, the same paragraph states that decisions of the Central Bank Council can be deferred, at the request of members of the government, by up to two weeks (note that the Council is scheduled to meet every two weeks). The delay of Council decisions as stated in article 13.2 of the Bundesbank Act has never been resorted to. There is a debate on whether such a provision represents a substantial tool of control on the central bank by the government. Another subject of debate is the influence of the *Stability and Growth Law* of 1967 on the Bundesbank. By some observers, that law is regarded as a call for interventionism on all branches of government, including the central bank.[6]

A comparison of the rules mentioned above with those regulating the ESCB shows some common features of the three central banks. First, all three statutes do not explicitly specify the actions or outcomes the central bank is accountable for. The Federal Reserve Act does not contain any article stating the objectives of the central bank, perhaps due to the very limited latitude afforded by the presence of gold-standard convertibility rules. The Bundesbank Act specifies safeguarding the currency, but does not elaborate what it means. The Treaty of Rome mentions, more precisely, price stability, but does not provide procedures that are explicitly designed to assess the central bank's performance in attaining that objective.

In addition, none of the statutes explicitly specifies whom the central bank is accountable to. Is the Fed responsible to Congress for its activities? It would seem so, given the regular hearings that its chairman has to attend. Is the Bundesbank responsible to the Government? The provision regarding the power of government members to delay the Governing council decisions by up to a fortnight seems to suggest so.

Whom is the ESCB accountable to? Article 109a paragraph 3 specifies that the president of the ECB has to present an annual report of the activities of the ESCB to the Council and the European Parliament. The Parliament may hold a general debate on that basis. It may request the president or other members of the executive board to be heard by its competent committees. Finally, the president of the Council of Ministers and a member of the commission may participate, without voting, in meetings of the Governing Council of the ECB. They may also submit to that body a motion for deliberation.

In summary, the foregoing discussion of the laws governing the three federal central banks suggests that—at least from a literal interpretation of their statutes—they all enjoy substantial independence. Given the limited political importance of the European Parliament, and given its inability to affect any of the regulations concerning the ESCB, it appears that the ESCB formally enjoys more independence than the other two institutions. This impression is confirmed by the sheer number of articles that appear to be expressly devoted to guarding it from political pressures originating from national governments or any other entities.

The way in which the statutes of the Bundesbank and the ECB solve the rules-versus-discretion tradeoff is also noteworthy. Indeed, it is widely believed that in this as well as in many other aspects—including in particular the federal structure and the role of banking policy (which I discuss below)—the Treaty of Rome copied the Bundesbank Act. Rather than imposing on the bank a fixed rule, these statutes assign to it an objective (albeit vaguely worded): safeguarding of the currency and price stability. They then give it substantial independence in pursuing that single objective, and subordinate all other activities to it.

The similarity between the Bundesbank Act and the Treaty of Rome in the field of banking policy is also striking. The Bundesbank Act does not list the preservation of the stability of the financial system as a task of the central bank. Article 3 states that the central bank is only supposed to provide "for the execution by banks of domestic and external payments." In the Treaty of Rome the banking functions of the ECB are subordinate to those of national authorities. The similarity of the statutes of the ECB and the Bundesbank with regard to banking is as striking as the difference between these two institutions and the Federal Reserve System. The latter, as well as the Bank of England and most other central banks (see Goodhart, 1988) emerged to provide support to the orderly functioning of financial intermediation, and safeguards against financial panics. Such objectives are completely absent from the ECB statutes. Section 14.4 below discusses the problems raised by this structure.

The lack of prominence of rules concerning banking policy in the ESCB statutes and in the Bundesbank Act could be an indication of an important historical trend. Central banks were born, at time of commodity-backed currencies, as a device to protect the stability of the banking system. With the movement away from commodity standards, the question arises of how to preserve stable prices in the absence of commodity convertibility rules. There is a clear need to codify monetary policy, especially since the boom of macroeconomic policy in the interwar years has increased the demands on central banks as stabilizers of the business cycle. As a result, banking policy seems to have moved to the background.

14.3 Monetary Policy

As I noted in the previous section, the striking feature of the statutes of the ESCB is their similarity to the Bundesbank Act,[7] and in particular, the device of removing the central bank from direct pressures of the government and parliament, and at the same time of assigning to it the main objective of price stability. This section, devoted to the discussion of the problems of monetary policy that the ESCB is likely to face, starts with a discussion of this feature of the ESCB statutes.

The rationale and effects of central bank independence can best be discussed with reference to the so-called time-consistency problem of monetary policy. The time-consistency problem of monetary policy was first formalized by Kydland and Prescott (1977), and successively developed by Barro and Gordon (1983a,b). Their basic idea is that if the ability of monetary authorities to affect real economic activity—or more in general, to attain an objective expressed in terms of some real quantity—depends on the extent to which monetary policies surprise the private sector, these policies will be rendered ineffective by private expectations, which are best informed by knowledge of the monetary authority's objectives.

To illustrate the time-consistency problem, it is customary to consider two regimes.[8] Under the first regime, the monetary authority is committed to a fixed rule. This rule cannot be changed, but may be a function of observable shocks. The rule, for simplicity, can be represented by a functional relation between the rate of inflation and exogenous disturbances, like a supply shock. Making monetary policy a function of the supply shock may be justified if the monetary authority has an advantage over the private sector, which could be arising from the existence of contracts or other imperfections, like informational problems in the labor markets, and from the desire of the authorities to minimize inflation and fluctuations of economic activity around a given target. Asymmetric information would allow the monetary authority to respond to the supply shock more quickly than labor markets.

In this first regime, the monetary authority plays a stabilizing role, but the average rate of inflation is zero. An alternative regime is one where the monetary authority cannot commit to a rule. The absence of commitment is justified by the fact that, ex-post, the authority would always want to renege on the announced rule. As a result, in the absence of a commitment technology, the no-commitment or discretionary equilibrium is the only stable one. The discretionary equilibrium is more inflationary than the equilibrium under a rule, because the public recognizes the incentive of the monetary authority to create surprise inflation. Since the public dislikes surprises, it forces the inflation rate to a level where the marginal cost of surprises is too high. As a result, the equilibrium level of activity is the same under the rule as under discretion, but inflation is higher under discretion. Thus, asymmetric information allows the central bank to carry out its stabilizing function, but lack of credibility produces an inflationary bias.

The time-consistency problem arises from the assumption that the authority wishes to induce a level of economic activity systematically different from the natural rate. The discrepancy between the authority's objective and equilibrium is due to distortions that are typically left unexplained in the models. They include a monopoly power of trade unions (which could induce too high real wages and too low a level of economic activity); the presence of tax distortions like income taxes and unemployment insurance (which could provide disincentives to labor supply and induce too low a level of economic activity); "excessive" demands on the monetary authority (myopic politicians could believe that monetary policy could, and should, be systematically devoted to the increase of economic activity and well being, and could pressure the monetary authority to do so); the presence of a large stock of government debt, requiring a heavier use of the inflation tax or of political pressures to systematically lower real interest rates.

These incentives deprive the central bank of credibility and are at the core of the inflationary bias of the discretionary equilibrium.

A solution to the credibility problem of central banks has been proposed by Rogoff (1985). He suggests the appointment of a conservative, and independent, central banker. Remember that in the discretionary equilibrium described above the central bank can use its policy to smooth out unwanted fluctuations, but can also generate too high an equilibrium inflation rate. In the discretionary equilibrium the level of economic activity is at an optimum and inflation is significantly above the optimum. Hence, the marginal benefit of inflation reduction is larger than its marginal cost in terms of deviations from the optimum: a conservative central banker achieves just that.

Even before questioning the extent to which a central bank can be deemed independent, and questioning the evidence on the importance of independence and credibility effects in monetary performances, we should ask whether the proposed ESCB statutes could—in principle—provide the solution to the credibility problem of monetary policy along the lines proposed by Rogoff (1985). On one side the statutes fulfill Rogoff's conditions exactly: all the provisions aimed at giving the ESCB independence are the necessary condition for the conservative central banker to operate effectively. The statutes, however, cannot guarantee that the chosen central banker will display an aversion to inflation higher than the public's. The article requiring that the ECB pursue price stability as its primary objective and that, without prejudice to price stability, it sustains economic growth, is not enforceable. Members of the Executive Board or the Governors' Council cannot be removed if they do not fulfill this objective. In addition, there is no way that deviations from a vaguely worded price stability objective can be unambiguously estimated and evaluated. Thus the ESCB could only have independent, but not necessarily conservative, top management.

On one aspect, I believe, the statutes of ESCB out-perform Rogoff. As discussed above, the roots of the credibility problem lie in the incentive that the central bank has to push the level of activity above the natural rate. By making the central bank independent, limiting its objective to price stability, and, more importantly, cutting linkages between monetary policy and the financing of budgetary deficits and at the same time providing procedures to stem the buildup of large government debts, the revision of the Treaty of Rome could help eliminate the distortion at the root of the credibility problem. It could eliminate the incentives that monetary authorities have to systematically affect real economic activity beyond its natural rate.

This discussion leaves open the question of how much independence can a set of laws effectively ensure. To tackle that question, it is useful to divide it into two parts: the extent to which the law guarantees independence from external pressures (pressures originating outside the executive bodies of the central bank), and the extent to which the law guarantees independence of the appointed members of the executive bodies.

Consider the case of the Federal Reserve and the Bundesbank, which are both regarded as highly independent institutions. In the US, Federal Reserve Governors are granted a degree of autonomy second only to Supreme Court Justices. Their terms in office can be as long as 14 years (except for the chairman, whose term is 4 years). They are appointed in a staggered fashion, so that no single president can have an overwhelming influence on the Board. They enjoy budgetary independence, and hence they are subtracted from the budgetary oversight of Congress or the Office of Management and Budget. In Germany, the members of the Directorate of the Bundesbank are appointed by the government for eight years, and can be reappointed up to a maximum term of 12 years. The presidents of the Land Central Banks, members of the Bundesbank Council, are appointed by the Bundesrat, the chamber of parliament representing the Lander, for terms of eight years. The Bundesbank, too, enjoys budgetary independence. Hence, the appointment systems seem to guarantee substantial independence to both institutions. In addition, both institutions are exempted from government or parliament directives in the formulation of their policies.

Yet, especially in the US, there is a widespread view that the Federal Reserve is not at all immune from political pressure. For example, the Federal Reserve has to systematically provide information to the Congress. The famous H.R. 9710 (see Weintraub, 1978) requires the Board of Governors of the Fed to:

Consult with Congress at semiannual hearings [...] about the Board of Governors' and the Federal Open Market Committee's objectives and plans with respect to the ranges of growth or diminution of monetary and credit aggregates for the upcoming twelve months ...

These ex-ante consultations could be used to exercise substantial informal pressure on the central bank. Similarly, article 13 of the Bundesbank Act requires the central bank to provide information to the Government on request.

In the US, the institutional channels of communication between the Federal Reserve and the legislative and executive powers are numerous, and the objectives of the Federal Reserve are stated in vague language. Thus, many observers have concluded that the Federal Reserve is heavily politically influenced, and hence is not independent. For example, Milton Friedman has recently remarked (in Fischer, 1990):[9]

From revealed preference, I suspect that by far and away the two most important variables in their [the policy-makers'] loss function are avoiding accountability on the one hand and achieving public prestige on the other. A loss function that contains those two elements as its main argument will I believe come far closer to rationalizing the behavior of the Federal Reserve over the past 73 years than one such as you have used [containing inflation and deviations of economic activity from a target level].

Edward Kane (1982) makes a similar point:

Debate about the desirability of an independent Federal Reserve system proceeds from a dangerously false premise. The Fed is approximately as independent as a college student whose room and board is financed by a parentally revocable trust fund. Some conflict will be tolerated, but the limits of the benefactors' patience must always be kept in mind.

In the case of the Bundesbank, Kennedy (1991) discusses the exchanges between that institution and the government over a number of episodes, including the famous struggle between Helmut Schmidt's government and the Bundesbank over interest rates in the early eighties. She concludes that the bank's "interpretation of its own legal rights and responsibilities was effective in 1981–82 because its policy coincided with those of a decisive parliamentary actor in Bonn, the Free Democratic Party. Without a parliamentary ally of that stature, it is unlikely that the central Bank would challenge an elected government directly" (Kennedy, 1991, p. 54). As Kennedy shows, the public pronouncements that characterize the political struggles between the Bundesbank and the government are about the interpretation of the bank's rights and responsibilities, *i.e.*, of the Bundesbank Act. This supports the view that central bank statutes are too vague to automatically deliver effective political independence.

In the absence of reliable legal defense against political influence, it is not surprising that central banks exploit additional, and seemingly nonconventional, methods to defend themselves from external pressures. As Goodfriend (1986) argues, publicity of central bank policy procedures decreases the costs of becoming informed and as a result increases the intensity of the debate about monetary policy. This might make it easier for pressure groups to exert influence on the monetary authority. The Federal Reserve and the Bundesbank both have, to different degrees, confidentiality protection. The ESCB statutes specify its publicity obligations,[10] and state that the proceedings of the Governing Council meetings are to be confidential (Protocol, 10.4) and that the Council may decide to publicize only the outcome of its deliberations. While it has been shown (see for example, Cukierman and Meltzer, 1986) that central bank secrecy may enhance monetary policy effectiveness through the effects of policies on expectations, resort to confidentiality is the natural defense against too open a public debate on the central bank activity. The presence of confidentiality rules suggests that provisions about terms of appointment, budget and instructions from government agencies are not enough to defend the ECB from continuous public scrutiny—which can be easily transformed into political pressures. These observations reinforce the hypothesis that independence cannot be achieved only through laws.

Additional, statistical evidence on political influences on monetary policy comes from empirical implementations of politico-economic models of the business cycle. Alesina (1988) assumes that—in the Barro-Gordon setup—the central bank's preferences for inflation and unemployment are determined by the party currently in office, and that Democrats are less averse to inflation and more concerned about output fluctuations. One implication of this assumption is that money growth is higher under a Democratic presidency than under a Republican presidency. Alesina's regression equation, estimated with annual data over the period 1949–85, indicates that the growth rate of M1 in the US (after controlling for lagged money growth, output growth, unemployment, and deviations of unemployment from a time-varying estimate of the natural rate) is significantly negatively correlated with the presence of a Republican president in the White House. I regard this as evidence against the hypothesis that the legal independence of the Federal Reserve described above is sufficient to make it independently pursue monetary policy.

Frey and Schneider (1981) develop a political-economic model of the Bundesbank, not based on the Barro-Gordon setup exploited by Alesina, but rather on a set of ad-hoc behavioral equations. Empirical estimation of their model indicates that the relations between the central bank and the government, the presence or absence of conflicts between the two, significantly affect the stance of monetary policy. Once again, this evidence contradicts the hypothesis that the behavior of an independent central bank like the Bundesbank is invariant with respect to national political conditions. It casts doubts on the proposition that central bank independence can be achieved by designing an appropriate legal framework.

The second part of the question of the effectiveness of statutes in guaranteeing central bank independence is in regard to the extent to which the law can guarantee independence of the appointed members of the

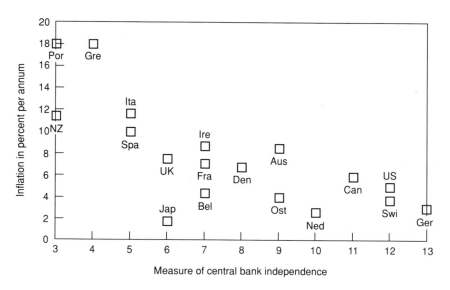

Figure 14.1
Average inflation: 1961–1969

executive bodies. In this case the experience of the Bundesbank, an institution where regional representatives sit on the board, is instructive. While Bundesbank President Pohl has argued that the regional representation on the bank's board (where Land Central Bank presidents carry each one vote, irrespective of the size of the regions they represent) is "the strongest guarantee of its independence," observers have noted an increase influence of political parties in the appointments of Land Central Bank presidents. An interesting episode revealing the tension within the Bundesbank is the recent disagreements between President Pohl and the Government on the reform of the Central Bank Council, involving a decrease in representation of Lander and an increase in weight of the Directorate. These observations suggest that a law prescribing strong regional representation in the central bank cannot at the same time avoid the regional representatives becoming channels of political influence from their own constituencies, despite their relatively long term in office.

Evidence usually brought to bear on the role of statutory independence rules in helping central-bank credibility is of the kind reported in figures 14.1, 14.2, and 14.3. The figures contain scatter plots of average inflation rates as functions of an index of statutory independence of central banks, for OECD countries. The index, constructed by Grilli, Masciandaro, and Tabellini (1991) following Bade and Parkin (1982) and using the data in

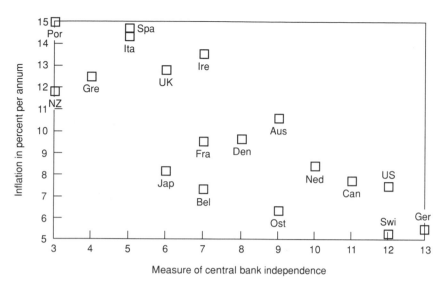

Figure 14.2
Average inflation: 1970–1979

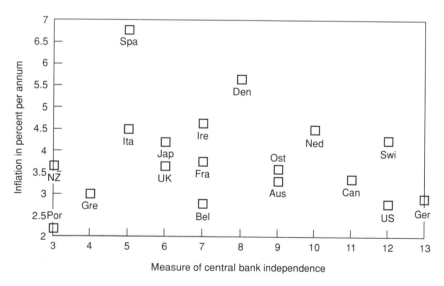

Figure 14.3
Average inflation: 1980–1989

Aufricht (1967), contains information about terms of appointment of board directors and governors, obligations of financing government deficits, and so on.[11]

Figures 14.1 to 14.3 indicate that a negative correlation between average inflation (measured by the rate of growth of the GDP deflator) and the index of statutory central bank independence is apparent during the 1970s and, less markedly, during the 1980s (the observations for Greece and Portugal are outliers that disproportionately affect the slope of the least squares line—which is not shown in the figure). No systematic relation emerges from the 1960s data.

Overall, the evidence in Figures 14.1 to 14.3 does not provide strong support for the hypothesis that central bank independence brings about a better inflation performance, for a number of reasons. First, the indices of independence, while very useful summaries of a wealth of important data, are not flowing from an explicit model, and as a result their weighting schemes are questionable. Questions should also be raised about the inter-country comparisons of rules that might imply different things within different political-institutional systems. Finally, as Swinburne and Castello-Branco (1991) stress, the observed correlations might be due to the presence of a third variable, loosely labelled "country aversion to inflation." National attitudes towards inflation could determine both the degree of independence accorded to the central bank and the inflationary performance.

In summary, the evidence in the figures is too weak to attach to it all expectations that the newly formed ECB will have instant credibility, or that it will be able to pursue stern anti-inflationary policies free of political pressures. Descriptive as well as statistical data suggest that even the more independent central banks are subject to substantial pressures from parliaments and governments, and respond to them. In the absence of substantial and consistent backing, the ECB is unlikely to fight inflation effectively. This does not imply that all the efforts of the drafters of the ESCB statutes have been a vacuous exercise, but only that statutory independence is at best just a necessary condition for the achievement of low inflation.

In conclusion to this discussion of monetary policy, it is useful to note the aspect of the ESCB statutes that most clearly reveals the difficulty of legislating full independence. Article 109 states that, if after the monetary union the ECU were to become part of a fixed-exchange rate system with other currencies, the day-to-day management of foreign exchange intervention would be left to the central bank, but decisions about changes in exchange-rate parity values would be made by the Council of Ministers. Hence, while the ESCB statutes are internally consistent under a floating exchange rate system, it becomes logically inconsistent under fixed rates. As the experience of West Germany in the postwar period has demonstrated (see, in particular, the excellent description in Emminger, 1997), the central bank is severely curtailed in its own activity when subject to exchange-rate parities that are inconsistent with its inflation objectives (the rest-of-the world inflation rate is higher than the domestic inflation objectives). Under the proposed statutes, the ESCB loses independence in a fixed-exchange-rate regime.

14.4   Banking Policy

As pointed out above, the Treaty of Rome assigns few tasks to the ECB in the field of banking policy. The ECB is supposed to contribute to the policies pursued by competent authorities relating to the prudential supervision of banking institutions and to the stability of the financial system, and it has to promote the smooth operation of the payments system. It is allowed to carry out credit operations with banks or other financial institutions, and it is free to establish general principles regulating such operations.

This structure is similar to the Bundesbank's, but very different from that of the Federal Reserve, which was established to work as a government-sponsored clearinghouse. Indeed, as Goodhart (1988) notes, during the gold standard convertibility obligations made central banks no different from commercial banks. What set them apart was instead their role as bankers' banks.

Two broad questions emerge when speculating on the functioning of the ECB as specified in the Treaty of Rome. The first is whether the subsidiary role of the central bank relative to national authorities in the field of banking could hinder its effectiveness, in particular the effectiveness of its monetary policies. The second is whether the presence of a variety of financial systems and institutions as currently observed in the EC member countries is compatible with the establishment of a single currency managed by a single central bank. In order to tackle these questions it is useful to describe the salient characteristics of banking supervision and regulation, as well as of payments systems among EC member countries.

14.4.1   Banking Supervision and Regulation

Tables 14.1 to 14.6 summarize the key features of rules affecting the banking industry in four large EC countries. Table 14.1 contains information

Table 14.1
Entry requirements

Country	Capital	Authorization from	Branches
France	4.3 mil. ECU	Comite des Establissements de Credit	Same cond. as establ.
Germany	2.9 mil. ECU	Federal Supervisory Office	Notify Sup. Office and Bundesbank
Italy	16.0 mil. ECU	Bank of Italy	BoI has to authorize
Spain	8.8 mil. ECU	Finance Ministry	Free
United Kingdom	1.4 mil. ECU	Bank of England	Free

Sources: Chiappori et al. (1991) and Associazione Bancaria Italiana, *Indagine Conoscitiva sui Sistemi Creditizi nell'Ambito della Comunitá Europea*, Rome, March 1991.

about chartering rules (capital requirements and charter authority) as well as rules on opening of branches by domestically chartered banks. The table highlights the diversity of practices across the four countries, especially regarding the chartering authority: in Spain and in Germany the authority is given to the Finance Ministry (the German Federal Supervisory Office belongs to the Finance Ministry), in Italy and the United Kingdom to the Central Bank, while in France to an independent public institution.

Table 14.2 shows rules restricting the activities of commercial banks. In Spain, the United Kingdom, Germany, and France commercial banks are not subject to significant restrictions on the range of their activities, which can include securities underwriting. The same countries' authorities allow commercial banks to hold equity stakes in industrial corporations, although in the United Kingdom equity participations are discouraged (see Chiappori *et al.*, 1991). Ownership of commercial banks by industrial groups is also subject to limitations and/or approvals by all countries in the table except Germany.

Table 14.3 lists the authorities in charge of bank supervision. Only in the United Kingdom is supervision the exclusive duty of the central bank. In Spain and Italy supervision is carried out jointly by the central bank and the Finance or Treasury Ministry. In Germany it is under the complete control of the Finance Ministry. Tables 14.4 and 14.5 report liquidity ratios and "solvency" ratios (or capital requirements). Once again, the lack of uniformity across European countries is striking. For example, while Spain and the UK do not have fixed rules, in France the *Commission Bancaire* requires 100 percent liquidity coverage, computed as the ratio of liquidity-weighted assets and liquidity-weighted liabilities.

Table 14.2
Direct restrictions

Country	Universal bank?	Equity stakes?	Ownership by industrial companies?
France	yes	up to 60% of own funds	if large transaction need authorization from Comite de Establissement de Credit
Germany	yes	yes	no specific norms
Italy	no	no	> 15% of capital subject to BoI approval
Spain	yes	up to 20% of equity in first 5 yrs. of bus.	inform c. bank; > 15% of capital need authoriz.
United Kingdom	yes	discouraged	BoE approval if 15% of capital

Sources: Associazione Bancaria Italiana, *Indagine Conoscitiva sui Sistemi Creditizi nell'Ambito della Comunitá Europea*, Rome, March 1991.

Table 14.3
Supervisory authorities

France	Commission Bancaire (chaired by the Governor of the Banque de France)
Germany	Federal Supervisory Office (Finance Ministry)
Italy	Treasury Ministry (Inter-Ministerial Committee for Credit and Savings) and Bank of Italy
Spain	Finance Ministry, Bank of Spain
United Kingdom	Bank of England

Sources: Associazione Bancaria Italiana, *Indagine Conoscitiva sui Sistemi Creditizi nell'Ambito della Comunitá Europea*, Rome, March 1991.

Table 14.4
"Solvency" ratios

France	Any risky investments cannot exceed 20 times own funds
Germany	Loans and participations cannot exceed 18 times net worth. Foreign exchange positions cannot exceed 30% own funds. Int. rate swaps cannot exceed 20% own funds. Futures contracts, 10%
Italy	Total (risk-weighted) loans cannot exceed 12.5 times own funds
Spain	Ratio of own funds to total assets: 5%
United Kingdom	Established case by case

Sources: Associazione Bancaria Italiana, *Indagine Conoscitiva sui Sistemi Creditizi nell'Ambito della Comunitá Europea*, Rome, March 1991.

Table 14.5
Liquidity ratios

France	Liquidity-weighted sum of assets has to equal liquidity-weighted sum of liabilities
Germany	Matching maturity ranges of assets and liabilities
Italy	New loans cannot exceed 22.5 of own funds
Spain	None
United Kingdom	Bank of England discretion

Sources: Associazione Bancaria Italiana, *Indagine Conoscitiva sui Sistemi Creditizi nell'Ambito della Comunitá Europea*, Rome, March 1991.

Table 14.6
Deposit insurance

France	Every category (banks, mutual credit institutions, etc.) has its own private fund
Germany	German Banking Association Manages a private fund. Members provide voluntary contributions to it
Italy	Private fund. Contributions are voluntary
Spain	Fund is owned by banks and Bank of Spain
United Kingdom	Banks have their own fund, operating with their voluntary contributions

Sources: Associazione Bancaria Italiana, *Indagine Conoscitiva sui Sistemi Creditizi nell'Ambito della Comunitá Europea*, Rome, March 1991.

Finally, table 14.6 describes the systems of deposit insurance in the four countries. Deposit insurance is a recent institution in Europe, as in the past depositors were typically bailed out by *ad hoc* bank consortia created by supervisory authorities to take over failed banks. Deposit insurance is private in all four countries (except for the participation of the Bank of Spain in the Spanish fund).

The hypothetical European central bank, when starting its operations in January 1977 or January 1999, will face a cluster of national banking systems that will also be subordinated to EC directives designed for the creation of a single market in financial services. These directives will be in effect by January 1993. The EC directives follow the general philosophy of not substituting for national regulations unless strictly necessary, and of allowing coexistence of different regulatory systems, by not permitting national regulations to prevent foreign entities to establish in the national territory of any member country (the principle of mutual recognition).

The most important of such directives, the so-called Second Banking Directive, introduces the principle of home-country supervision for branches of banks located in countries other than that of the main office. Host country's authorities are in charge of liquidity ratios. Other directives seek to harmonize some of the regulations summarized in tables 14.1 to 14.6. For example, the so-called First Banking Directive contains common chartering rules. Directive 89/299 contains common rules on own funds. Directive 89/647 provides for a common capital requirement equal to 8 percent and in line with the Basle Accord.

EC member countries are supposed to make the necessary changes in their national laws to conform to the EC directives. It is therefore plausible that, either because of the harmonized rules of the single market directives, or as a result of competitive deregulation triggered by the abolition of any hindrances to the freedom of establishment in the banking industry and the freedom to offer financial services to all residents of the Community, bank regulations will be approximately homogeneous across all member countries.[12] Yet, despite the likely homogeneity of regulations, regulatory authorities and their practices will still differ across countries. In particular, there are no proposals to create an EC-wide regulatory authority, or any mechanisms aimed at coordinating national authorities, beyond those contained in the Basle Accord.

14.4.2   Payments Systems

The payments system is the backbone of any monetary system. It is, in most countries, directly managed or regulated by the monetary authorities. Hence, the central bank is responsible for the efficiency of payments within its own jurisdiction. While cash transactions appear to take the lion's share in the total number of payments in industrial countries,[13] noncash payments have assumed progressively greater importance. Their importance, and the concern of policymakers about them, is justified by their high average value.

The development of cashless payments systems differs widely across countries. Table 14.7 reports the total value of cashless payments in terms of GNP for the BIS countries, and highlights remarkable cross-country variation. In Switzerland the value of cashless payments was equal to 185 times GNP, while in Sweden and Italy it was only 8 times GNP (these estimates are based on 1988 data). Such wide differences could be explained by the role of national financial markets. In the US, Switzerland,

Table 14.7
Total value of cashless payments as a factor of GNP

Belgium	43
Canada	30
France	10
Germany	50
Italy	8
Japan	19
Netherlands	37
Sweden	8
Switzerland	185
United Kingdom	51
United States	79

Sources: Borio et al. (1991).

the UK and Germany there are either well developed national money markets or a large number of fund transfers associated with foreign exchange trading, or both.

In the 1980s wholesale, automated payments systems were adopted by all industrial countries, led by the US, which installed Fedwire in 1982. The installation of automated wholesale systems has been occurring parallel to the "securitization" of financial markets. While in financial markets dominated by bank loans payments tend to be cleared through netting of accounts at individual banks (hence the widespread use of correspondent banking), cash or "good funds" appear to be used predominantly for payments in securities markets,[14] and in markets for derivative products like futures and options. The demand for cash in these markets also appears to be correlated with price fluctuations for two reasons. First, price fluctuations increase margin calls in futures and options markets. Second, to the extent that large price movements are associated with increases in uncertainty, they make it harder for issuers of paper to roll over their liabilities and to increase their recourse to stand-by lines of credit at commercial bank which they normally keep.

Wholesale payments systems can operate either on a continuous basis or on a discrete basis. Continuous settlement systems provide good funds with each payment order, as long as the payer bank has sufficient good funds to fulfill it. Discrete payments systems (or net settlement systems) execute payments orders only at a few specified times during the day after all positions of participating members have been netted out.

Table 14.8
Electronic payments systems in selected EC countries

Country	System	Settlement	Finality	Date of installation
Belgium	C.E.C.	Net	Yes	1986
France	SAGITTAIRE	Net	No	1984
Germany	CB Express Sys.	Gross	No	1987
Italy	BISS	Gross	Yes	1988
	ME	Net	No	1989
	SIPS	Net	Yes	1989
Netherlands	CB Curr. Acc.	Gross	No	1985
	BCH SWIFT	Net	No rule	1982
United Kingdom	CHAPS	Net	Partial	1984

Sources: Borio et al. (1991). Bank for International Settlements, *Large-Value Transfer Systems in the Group of Ten Countries*, Basel, May 1990.

Hence, banks pay only the difference between total payments and total receipts.

Payments systems may or may not provide settlement finality, that is, the guarantee that the payee receives good funds immediately, even if the payor might not have them at the moment the payment is executed. In the continuous settlement system, settlement finality can only be achieved if the institution managing the system provides daylight credit to its members. This is, for example, the case of the US Fedwire. In the net settlement system, if a member's funds are insufficient to cover its net position at the time of clearing, the clearinghouse will tap its own reserve, or will try to raise funds from its members. In the absence of payment finality, as for example in the case of the US CHIPS system, if at the end of the day a member does not have funds to cover its debit position, all the payments messages during the day are rerun by removing all messages received or initiated by the participant which fails to settle.

Table 14.8 contains information about electronic payments systems in selected EC countries. Most systems have discrete settlement, and few provide settlement finality. The issue of settlement finality is not as crucial in a net settlement system, where balances are only small fractions of the total volume of payments. Hence, the issue of finality in some countries is left to the discretion of the monetary authority. Among the countries in the table, so far no one has reported settlement failures in any of its systems.

14.4.3   Questions on ECB Banking Policy

The brief summary of the current structure of banking supervision and payments systems helps to focus on the questions currently facing European countries as they consider the operations of the European Central Bank. The most striking aspect of the relation between the monetary authority and the banking industry is the interposition of several national supervisory institutions, either Finance Ministries (or Treasury Ministries) or special independent commissions (as in the case of France). Such a peculiar structure raises the question: is there a need of coordination between the ESCB and national regulatory authorities beyond what is outlined in article 105.5?[15]

The answer to that question depends on what functions are to be expected from the European Central Bank. Following Goodfriend and King (1988), I consider banking policy to be—essentially—a sterilized discount window lending to individual banks. Banking policy does not affect the total supply of money, while monetary policy does.

What is the rationale of discount window lending? It hinges on the presence of asymmetric information between lenders and borrowers. Because information about the solvency of individual borrowers at any point in time is costly to get, the interest rate charged to any individual borrower reflects an assessment of the probability that the borrower will not repay the loan. A bank with liquidity problems has a portfolio of investments whose value would be positive under perfect information (when it is known that it will not attempt to default on its loans, and therefore is charged a lower interest rate), but is negative if computed with the going market rate. Discount window lending is therefore justified as a remedy to the market failure caused by asymmetric information, and requires supervision of all banks, in order to distinguish illiquid from insolvent borrowers. Goodfriend and King conclude that discount window lending is redundant, since it resembles private line-of-credit arrangements, which also require monitoring. In the absence of a special advantage to the central bank in the collection of information on individual banks' solvency, there is no need for the central bank to carry out that activity.

By contrast, Goodfriend and King view the lender-of-last-resort function as a monetary policy function of central banks. Since a lender-of-last-resort provides funds indiscriminately, it does not need monitoring of the borrowers, because it is simply accommodating a sudden increase in the demand for liquidity associated with a financial crisis (which might be originating either from the banking system or from securities markets). Hence, according to this reasoning, the ESCB should not advocate special regulatory and supervisory authorities, since it does not have a clearly demonstrated comparative advantage in lending to individual, liquidity constrained banks.

Without questioning the issue of redundancy of discount window lending, I want to discuss the use of lender-of-last-resort facilities. While it is certainly true that indiscriminate lending does not require information about individual borrowers, a monetary authority without access to information about the creditworthiness of individual market participants might be led to overuse of lender-of-last-resort facilities (see below for more discussion of this). The effects of such overuse are well described by Folkerts-Landau and Garber (1992):

[...] if the central bank mistakes a fundamental decline in asset prices for a temporary liquidity problem and intervenes, it will either have to (1) weaken the capital of the banking system; (2) countenance price inflation; or (3) absorb the loss itself. By erroneously adding liquidity to a market when the price of a security is higher than its ultimate level, the central bank expands reserves and pressures banks to lend against the securities. If the security price eventually falls as central bank liquidity is withdrawn, market makers will go bankrupt, leaving bad loans on the books of the banks and reducing bank capital. Depositors' confidence in banks will furthermore diminish, and banks will be less able to provide liquidity services in the future. To reduce the damage to the banks of this mistake, the central bank may decide not to contract reserves to their normal level. This leads to a permanent expansion in the money stock and to a rise in the price level.

Since the costs of misinformation can be large, and the costs of acquiring information are small in comparison, it appears that the exercise of supervisory powers might help increase the efficiency of lender-of-last-resort operations. These observations, in effect, call for an expanded lender-of-last-resort function, along the same lines as Mishkin (1991).

There are two reasons why the central bank might have a comparative advantage in supervisory activities. The first, trivial one, is that the central bank—relative to private lenders—will never have business-related conflicts of interest in the acquisition of information about individual financial market participants. This allows it to gather information with fewer formal constraints and therefore more flexibility. The second reason is that, by being formally independent from political pressures, it can make sounder decisions on which institutions should be allowed to go bankrupt. It is conceivable that national government authorities who have control of supervisory and regulatory functions might be politically motivated with respect to troubled financial firms in their own countries. If the ECB did not have any supervisory powers, a national government could exploit its own private information to pressure the ECB to provide lender-of-last-resort facilities. Once again, despite the fact that the ESCB shall not "seek or take instructions from Community institutions or bodies, from any Government of a Member State or from any other body (article 107)," the fact that it is supposed to "contribute to the smooth conduct of policies pursued by the competent [national] authorities relating to [...] the stability of the financial system," makes it vulnerable to undesirable national pressures.

What are the motivations for national regulatory authorities to pressure the ECB in its function as lender of last resort? On one hand, national authorities, especially if part of the government, have a political stake in the economic viability of domestic financial intermediaries. This political stake is larger and more evident in the case of large institutions. On the other hand, and more importantly, by inducing the central bank to lend freely to troubled domestic institutions, national governments can effectively shift the costs of insolvent financial intermediaries to the rest of the Community.

These observations represent, in my view, a compelling argument for ensuring the access of the ESCB to all supervisory activities carried out by national institutions, and for preventing any asymmetric distribution of information between the central bank and national supervisory and regulatory authorities or among national authorities.

The argument extends to national authorities. As Chiappori et al. (1991) note, to the extent that the activities of financial firms in different countries are not strictly within those countries' territories, there is a clear reason to encourage a tight coordination among national authorities. The argument—well known from the discussions on supervisory cooperation promoted by the Bank for International Settlements—stems from the observation that the distribution of the costs of financial distress among the residents of different countries depends on the distribution of financial intermediaries' depositors and borrowers. For example, if an institution relies mostly on depositors from outside its national territory (as for example is the case for most financial institutions located in Luxembourg), its own regulatory authorities would have few incentives to provide protection to its depositors.

Thus, the answer to the question raised above, whether the subsidiary role of the central bank relative to national authorities in the field of banking could hinder its effectiveness, is "yes." The statutes do not insure that the ECB have as much supervisory power as any national authority, and thereby could weaken the central bank in its pursuit of monetary policy, specifically in its lender-of-last-resort functions. An answer to the second question, whether the presence of a variety of financial systems and institutions as currently observed in the EC member countries is compatible with the establishment of a single currency managed by a single central bank, can be provided with reference to the problems of large-value payments systems.

While in the field of banking supervision there are questions about the role of the ECB, in the field of payments systems the statutes are less ambiguous. The ECB is supposed to "promote the smooth operation of payment systems" (article 105.2) which of course runs short of managing the payments systems directly. In any case, since in most European countries payments systems are owned and operated by central banks and, since central banks are an integral part of the ESCB, receive instructions from the ECB on the conduct of monetary policy and cannot interfere with the objectives and tasks of the ESCB,[16] the management or coordination of payments systems will have to be assigned to the ECB.

Even a superficial analysis of the recently installed systems suggests that they cannot be linked together in a straightforward way (see, again, table 14.8). Leaving aside legal questions and other practical, but very serious problems, like the fact that netting often occurs at different times in different countries, giving rise to inter-country settlement risks,[17] the simple linkage of national payments systems would inevitably give rise to arbitrage-induced payments routing. For example, banks will re-route payments through the systems that charge less for daylight overdrafts (See Passacantando, 1991).

Hence, the substitution of national systems with a new, EC-wide wholesale payments system managed by the ECB represents the most efficient, long-run solution to supporting an efficient single market in financial services in the European Community, despite the fact that many European countries have just made large investments to create or upgrade their own automated systems. Once again, however, this calls into question the extent to which the central bank will be allowed supervisory responsibilities. If the central bank will want to assure payments finality, as appears to be the case in the most efficient systems, it will have to be able to screen participants, to establish overdraft limits possibly tailored to individual participants, and to make informed judgments on whether or not to extend credit to a bank that fails to settle at the end of the day. All of these decisions require substantial information, to be obtained through supervisory functions. They also require the central bank to make regulations affecting banks in individual member countries.

In summary, the problems of payments systems suggest a negative answer to the question of whether the presence of a variety of financial systems and institutions as currently observed in the EC member countries is compatible with the establishment of a single currency managed by a single central bank.

In the case of payments systems, the maintenance of national institutions resembles the maintenance of national air traffic control systems (which countries justify with the need to preserve their sovereignty over their own air space), in spite of the creation of a single European market in air passenger travel. A recent study (Gellman Research Associates, 1989) has shown that the delays, excess fuel costs, and other inefficiencies arising from the coexistence of many different air traffic control systems can sum to a total cost of as much as $4.2 billion (in 1988). This number swamps the estimates of the consumer savings due to deregulation (the creation of the single European market in passenger air travel), which have been put around $3.5 billion annually. Similarly, one suspects that a half-complete monetary union, not accompanied by reforms of institutions like the payments systems and banking supervision, might give rise to efficiency costs that can easily offset the estimated benefits from the introduction of a single currency.

14.5   Concluding Remarks

This paper has described the proposed statutes of the European Central Bank, and has discussed the problems raised by them. In the field of monetary policy, I have argued that the law cannot guarantee full independence of the central bank from any political pressures, and therefore cannot deliver relatively low inflation under all possible states of the world. The extent to which the ECB will be able to make use of its statutes to pursue low-inflation policies will depend on the political support it will get.

In the field of banking policy, I have argued that national supervisory and regulatory authorities may have incentives to force the ECB to overuse lender-of-last-resort facilities, and will succeed in doing that if the central bank does not gain full powers to carry out banking supervision in all member countries.

Notes

I would like to thank Francesco Giavazzi for many discussions which shaped this chapter, George Bermann, Peter Kenen, Mario Sarcinelli and Bart Turtleboom for comments, and Reena Mithal for able research assistance.

1. The United Kingdom has already announced that it likely will complete ratification after the end of 1992.

2. Professional interest in the European Central Bank is quickly increasing. Among the many contributions that have recently appeared see, in particular, Kenen (1992) and Sarcinelli (1992).

3. In this paper I do not discuss an important set of changes in the Treaty, related to so-called political union, nor do I discuss those related to "economic and social cohesion."

4. The criteria are:

• A CPI inflation rate over the year preceding the examination that does not exceed the (average) inflation rate of the three best performers by more than 1.5 percent.

• A ratio of planned or actual government budget deficit to GDP not exceeding 3 percent.

• A ratio of government debt to GDP not exceeding 60 percent.

• Yields on long-term government bonds not exceeding by more than 2 percent the corresponding yields in the three best inflation performers.

5. The sanctions include the requirement that the member country publish additional information, that it make a non-interest-bearing deposit with the Community, and reconsideration of the country's eligibility for loans from the European Investment Bank.

6. For a discussion of these debates, see Kennedy (1991).

7. Alesina and Grilli (1992), among others, noted this as well.

8. I am here implicitly using the model in Persson and Tabellini (1990).

9. Elsewhere, he states: "[...] more frequently the person in charge is like the rooster crowing at dawn. The course of events is decided by deeper and less visible forces that determine both the character of those nominally in charge and the pressures on them." Friedman (1985).

10. The ESCB is supposed to release information about its own activity weekly (through the publication of a consolidated financial statement), quarterly (through a report on its activities) and annually (through the publication of an annual report).

11. Specifically, the index is the sum total of the following variables:

a. Whether the governor is appointed by the government (yes = 1, no = 0);

b. Whether the governor is appointed for more than 5 years (yes = 1, no = 0);

c. Whether all the board members are appointed by the government (yes = 1, no = 0);

d. Whether all board members are appointed by more than 5 years (yes = 1, no = 0);

e. Whether mandatory participation of a government representative on the board is requested (no = 1, yes = 0);

f. Whether government approval of monetary policies is required (no = 1, yes = 0);

g. Whether the statute includes monetary stability as one of the goals of the central bank (yes = 1, no = 0);

h. Whether legal provisions strengthen the central bank's position in conflicts with the government (yes = 1, no = 0);

i. Whether the government's direct credit facility with the central bank is automatic (yes = 1, no = 0);

j. Whether the interest rate charged on the direct credit facility is a market rate (yes = 1, no = 0);

k. Whether the direct credit facility is temporary (yes = 1, no = 0);

l. Whether the direct credit facility is only for a limited amount (yes = 1, no = 0);

m. Whether the central bank participates in the primary market for public debt (no = 1, yes = 0);

n. Whether the discount rate is set by the central bank (yes = 1, no = 0);

o. Whether banking supervision is entrusted to the central bank (not entrusted = 2, otherwise = 0).

p. Whether banking supervision is entrusted to the central bank alone (not entrusted = 1, otherwise = 0).

See Grilli *et al.* (1991) for a detailed explanation of the construction of the index and a discussion.

12. An important exception in regard to bank secrecy laws, which are unlikely to be harmonized, and which are more powerful in Luxembourg than elsewhere in the Community.

13. Estimates of the number of cash payments in countries are generally unavailable. Borio, Russo and Van Den Bergh (1991) cite estimates for Netherlands, according to which cash payments account for about 90 percent of the volume of all payments in that country.

14. See Folkerts-Landau and Garber (1992) for a discussion.

15. Article 105.5, mentioned above, states that "The ESCB shall contribute to the smooth conduct of monetary policies pursued by the competent authorities relating to the prudential supervision of credit institutions and the stability of the financial system."

16. Article 14.4 of the Protocol says:

"National central banks may perform functions other than those specified in this Statute unless the Governing Council finds, by a majority of two-thirds of the votes cast, that these interfere with the objectives and tasks of the ESCB. Such functions shall be performed on the responsibility and liability of national central banks and shall not be regarded as being part of the ESCB."

17. In Germany netting occurs at 1:30 pm, while in France at 5:30 pm.

References

Alesina, A. 1988. Macroeconomics and Politics. *NBER Macroeconomics Annual.*

Alesina, A. and Grilli, V. U. 1992. The European Central Bank: Reshaping Monetary Politics in Europe. *Establishing a Central Bank: Issues in Europe and Lessons from the US.* Eds. M. B. Canzoneri, V. U. Grilli and P. R. Masson. Cambridge: Cambridge University Press.

Aufricht, H., 1967. *Central Banking Legislation.* Washington, D.C.: International Monetary Fund Monograph Series.

Bade, R. and Parkin, M. 1982. Central Bank Laws and Inflation—A Comparative Analysis. (mimeo, University of Western Ontario).

Barro, R. J. and Gordon, D. B. 1983a. A Positive Theory of Monetary Policy in a Natural Rate Model, *Journal of Political Economy*, 91: 589–610.

Barro, R. J. and Gordon, D. B. 1983b. Rules, Discretion and Reputation in a Model of Monetary Policy. *Journal of Monetary Economics*, 12: 101–22.

Borio, C., Russo, D. and Van den Bergh, P. 1990. Payment System Arrangements and Related Policy Issues: A Cross-Country Comparison. *Proceedings of the Workshop on Payment System Issues in the Perspective of European Monetary Unification*. Ed. F. Passacantando. Rome: Banca d'Italia.

Chiappori, P. A., Mayer, C., Neven, D. and Vives, X. 1991. "The Microeconomics of Monetary Union." *Monitoring European Integration: The Making of Monetary Union*. London: CEPR.

Cukierman, A. and Meltzer, A. 1986. "A Theory of Ambiguity, Credibility and Inflation Under Discretion and Asymmetric Information." *Econometrica*, 53: 1099–1128.

Emminger, O. 1977. "The D-Mark in the Conflict Between Internal and External Equilibrium, 1948–75." *Essays in International Finance*, 122, International Finance Section, Princeton University.

Fischer, S. 1990. "Rules Versus Discretion in Monetary Policy." *Handbook of Monetary Economics*, B. M. Friedman and F. H. Hahn, eds., Amsterdam: North Holland.

Folkerts-Landau, D. and Garber, P. 1992. "The ECB: A Bank or a Monetary Policy Rule?" *Establishing a Central Bank: Issues in Europe and Lessons from the US*. M. B. Canzoneri, V. U. Grilli and P. R. Masson eds. Cambridge: Cambridge University Press.

Friedman, M. and Schwartz, A. J. 1963. *A Monetary History of the United States, 1867–1960*. Princeton, NJ: Princeton University Press.

Friedman, M. 1985. The Case for Overhauling the Federal Reserve. *Challenge*.

Gellman Research Associates 1989. *Towards a Single System for Air Traffic Control in Europe*. Report to the Association of European Airlines.

Goodfriend, M. 1986. "Monetary Mystique: Secrecy and Central Banking." *Journal of Monetary Economics*. 17: 63–92.

Goodfriend, M. and King, R. G 1988. "Financial Deregulation, Monetary Policy, and Central Banking." *Federal Reserve Bank of Richmond Economic Review*, 74/3: 3–22.

Goodhart, C. 1988. *The Evolution of Central Banks*. Cambridge, MA.: MIT Press.

Grilli, V. U., Masciandaro, D. and Tabellini G. 1991. "Political and Monetary Institutions and Public Financial Policies in the Industrial Countries." *Economic Policy*: 342–391.

Kane, E. J. 1982. "External Pressure and the Operations of the Fed." *Political Economy of International and Domestic Monetary Relations*, R. E. Lombra and W. E. Witte, eds. Ames, Iowa: Iowa State University Press.

Kenen, P. 1992. *EMU After Maastricht*. Washington, D.C.: Group of Thirty.

Kennedy, E. 1991. *The Bundesbank: Germany's Central Bank in the International Monetary System*. London: Royal Institute of International Affairs.

Kydland, F. and Prescott, E. C. 1977. "Rules Rather Than Discretion: The Inconsistency of Optimal Plans," *Journal of Political Economy*, 85: 473–91.

Mishkin, F. S. 1991. Anatomy of a Financial Crisis, *NBER Working Paper* No. 3934.

Passacantando, F. 1991. "The Payments System in the Context of EMU." *Proceedings of the Workshop on Payment System Issues in the Perspective of European Monetary Unification.* F. Passacantando ed. Rome: Banca d'Italia.

Persson, T. and Tabellini, G. 1990. *Macroeconomic Policy Credibility and Politics.* London: Harwood Academic Publishers.

Rogoff, K. 1985. "The Optimal Degree of Commitment to an Intermediate Monetary Target," *Quarterly Journal of Economics* 100: 1169–89.

Sarcinelli, M. 1992. La Banca Centrale Europea: Istituzione Concettualmente "Evoluta" o all'Inizio della Sua "Evoluzione"? (mimeo, EBRD).

Swinburne, M. and Castello-Branco, M. 1991. Central Bank Independence: Issues and Experience, (IMF Working Paper WP/91/58).

Weintraub, R. E. 1978. "Congressional Supervision of Monetary Policy." *Journal of Monetary Economics* 4: 341–62.

Index